THEATRE ROYAL
BATH

Theatre Royal Orchard Street, interior and exterior, 1775.

THEATRE ROYAL
BATH

A
Calendar of Performances
at the

ORCHARD STREET THEATRE

1750–1805

Compiled by

Heather Bryant, Arnold Hare, Peter Hibbard,
Margaret Jarrett, Raymond Meddick, Phyllis Parnell,
Mary Sanderson, Audrey Shaw, Denise Tett, Jean
Watson and Gordon Woodward

with additional material by

Kathleen Barker

Edited by

Arnold Hare

Kingsmead Press
Bath
1977

KINGSMEAD PRESS
ROSEWELL HOUSE
KINGSMEAD SQUARE
BATH

© ARNOLD HARE 1977

S.B.N. 901571 79 2

Printed by photolithography and bound in Great Britain at
The Pitman Press, Bath

Foreword

This work arose out of a series of University Extra-Mural courses in Bath on the literature and culture of the eighteenth century. As part of the work of the course, a group of the students agreed to embark on a research project, and after some discussion, it was decided to investigate the extent of the sources for the theatrical history of the city during that century. From this the desirability of a Calendar, as a basic research tool, emerged. For four years the work was carried on alongside the study courses. It has since occupied two additional years of more concentrated work to complete it, followed by a further period of checking and amplification.

Although our models were MacMillan's *Drury Lane Calendar 1747–1776* and the monumental volumes of *The London Stage 1660–1800,* the extent of the material and the need for economy in presentation made it impossible for us to include the ideal of reprinting full casting information throughout. We therefore adopted the system of using the plays performed as the base, and indicating every source of casting information known to us, whether newspaper, playbill or book. Coupled with the indexes of plays (with seasons of performance) and actors (indicating their years with the company) we hope that this will enable most enquiries to be located at source very quickly. That there is room for this kind of research tool is indicated by the number and kind of enquiries that have been passed on to us while the compilation was in progress. At this period the Bath theatre was undoubtedly the most significant in England outside London.

Not all the members of the original research group were able to remain to the end, but their work has been incorporated where relevant. Others joined us to assist in the later stages. We have worked as a team, and the contribution of each member has been vital to the production of the whole. We should all, however, like to record especially the work of two members, Jean Watson, who single-handed did most of the extraction from the *Bath Chronicle*, as well as other tasks; and Gordon Woodward, who, in addition to undertaking a considerable share of the compilation, was responsible for a great deal of the co-ordination and collation of the enterprise. We were delighted when Kathleen Barker, the historian of the Bristol Theatre Royal, learning of the project, offered to put at our disposal the parallel material she herself had collected for the years during which the Orchard Street company performed also in Bristol. When incorporated, this has made it possible for the first time to see the working of a unique theatrical joint operation.

An original member of the group was Miss C. M. L. Mundy, Deputy Librarian of the City of Bath, who saw to it that all our material needs were met. It was a great sorrow to all of us that her premature death prevented her from seeing the completion of a work she had so much at heart.

Throughout the project, we have had the enthusiastic backing of the former City

Librarian, Mr. Peter Pagan, and his successor, Mr. John Kite, and their staff. We are grateful to all of them for their help and forbearance. The continued support of Professor Cunliffe, Head of the Extra-Mural Department of the University, has enabled the final transcript to be produced by three secretaries in the department, Sheila Clarke, Ray Al-Karaghulli and Jean Jamison, the latter two of whom bore the brunt of the work with great cheerfulness and interest.

In a long undertaking involving more than a dozen people and a manuscript stage followed by two typescripts and a type-setting, it would be too much to hope that we have avoided all errors, omissions and inconsistencies. By a system of checking, cross-checking and sampling we have done our best to minimise these, but we shall be grateful if users of the Calendar will inform the Editor of any flaws they discover, so that Master Copies in the Bath City Library and the University of Bristol may be amended appropriately.

Arnold Hare
University of Bristol 1976

Contents

Introduction

> It is not a little to the credit of the Manager of our Theatre, that many of those whom he introduces upon it, grow so much into public esteem, and make so rapid a progress in their improvements, that they are, in the course of a few seasons, after thriving in this dramatic nursery, transplanted by the higher powers, to flourish in a RICHER soil.[1]

So wrote the *Bath Journal* in 1783, a little baroque in style, but with no ambiguity in content. And John Bernard, who was a member of the company at this time, and one who himself was later to be transplanted to a richer earth, made the same point as in old age he looked back on his apprenticeship. The Bath Theatre then, he says:

> boasted the Best company out of London—Henderson, Edwin, Dimond, Diddear, Blisset, etc. The Bath audience had long maintained the character of being the most elegant and judicious in the kingdom; and the 'School', which gradually formed under their influence and the exertions of Mr. Palmer obtained the pre-eminence in the eyes of the Dramatic Tyro and the London critic. It is well known that, for many years, the very name of Bath was a guarantee for a man's good taste in his profession; whilst, on the score of genius, it is acknowledged to have contributed more largely to the metropolitan boards, than Dublin and York put together.[2]

This then was the importance of the Bath Theatre Royal in its heyday—a splendid training ground for the young actor, with a reliable long-term body of players at its core, and an audience sophisticated enough to demand high standards and to appreciate them when they were produced.[3] The quality of the audience and the support it gave to the theatre depended a great deal on Bath's special social position (developing since the days of Queen Anne) as a fashionable place of winter resort for the middle and upper classes: for they (and their servants) were the principal frequenters of the eighteenth century theatre, demanding their entertainment even when technically, after the 1737 Licensing Act, it was outside the law. But that special relationship between audience and actors took more than half a century to build up, during which time the life of the players was often precarious in the extreme.

After the early theatre on the corner of Borough Walls and Parsonage Lane was pulled down in 1737 to make way for the Royal Mineral Water Hospital, various improvised playhouses were used, at the Lower Assembly Rooms (Simpson's), at the Globe Inn and in Kingsmead Street, but it was John Hippisley, then in control of the Jacobs Wells Theatre in Bristol who in November 1747 produced the first proposals for a purpose-built Theatre in Orchard Street. Unhappily, however, Hippisley died in the following year, and the project might have been abandoned had it not been for John Palmer, then a Brewer and Tallow Chandler, who with nine others, took it up and carried it through, so that the new Theatre

vi

in Orchard Street was opened for playing in October 1750.[4]

The early years were difficult ones, and had it not been for Palmer's vision (or stubbornness) the theatre might not have survived. Whether or not there had been some prior understanding that Simpson would abandon his theatre at the Lower Rooms when the new one was opened, he did not in fact do so, and for six years the two companies embarked on a cut-throat commercial struggle that did neither any good. A play performed one night at Orchard Street could be mounted on the following night at Simpson's; if Orchard Street gave a Benefit night for the General Hospital, so, a few evenings later did Simpson's, with the amounts of the proceeds duly publicised for comparison; and at times they even performed on the same nights. The rivalry had its unintentionally comic aspects, and it is impossible to be certain whether or not Thomas Smith, the stage carpenter and machinist at Simpson's really was made dead drunk one night in 1751 and abducted to the other house;[5] but Henry Brown, manager at Simpson's (who had complained publicly about what he believed happened to Smith) certainly transferred his allegiance to Orchard Street in 1753. There was opposition from outside the theatre, too. In March 1754 an information was laid against both houses causing a fine and a temporary closure; but there was also a public reaction in favour of the players, so they reopened, being careful, however, not to call themselves theatres, and advertising their performances as 'Concerts of Music' with the plays given 'Gratis'.

Palmer's co-proprietors seem to have taken fright, but he resolutely bought up their shares. In 1755 Richard Nash came down in favour of Orchard Street and began to use his influence on its behalf[6] and finally Palmer was able to buy out Simpson in return for an annuity (£200 per annum was hinted at as the cost),[7] and the long haul to respectability could begin.

First, however, a stable management had to be established. By 1757 Brown had had enough, and published a long self-pitiful letter describing how for six years he had been struggling against bad fortune and opposition to gain a precarious living in Bath. His programmes, he said, were chaste, and did not include such plays as *The Chances, The Double Dealer* or *The Relapse*. Nevertheless two new plays had been performed in one week to empty boxes, and receipts which covered only half the charges of the house. Moreover the accusations of extravagance made against him were unfair and untrue . . . and so on.[8] The latter charge may well have been the result of the recent raising of the box prices from 3s. to 4s. However, the letter raised no supporting voice, and at the end of the season, Brown himself departed.

The following season seems to have had an unsuccessful triumvirate (including Hull, one of the leading actors) attempting management; after that for two years Lee was more (or perhaps less) in control.[9] At the end of that time he and Palmer agreed to part company, and John Arthur, a low comedian and pantomime clown already in the company, took his place.

For the next eight years Arthur was to provide the first period of managerial continuity, though not without controversy, and ending up with a split in the company and a public campaign against him, in which he was accused among other things, of arbitrary tyranny within the company, cheese-paring in the running of the theatre, and insolence and disrespect to the audience.[10] Nevertheless, he had begun the process of building up the company and its reputation.

Perhaps the symbol of that increasing reputation, and certainly the springboard from which later progress was made, was the granting in early 1768 of a Royal Patent, the first outside the metropolis, which would free the theatre from the stigma, however notional by this time, of illegality. The man who engineered this was John Palmer the Younger, son of the original proprietor, who had come into the theatre's affairs about 1766, and was to be the power behind it for the next two decades. Having achieved the patent, he had to reorganise the company. To do this he made a tour of the best of the provincial theatres, engaging players who caught his eye (he made this a regular annual pilgrimage for some years): he also sent Arthur into retirement and brought back Lee into management again for three years; but much more fundamentally, after 1771 he appointed Keasberry his Acting Manager.

Keasberry had been continuously a member of the company since 1756, and he was to remain with it until his retirement in 1795, a record of stability that speaks much for his personality and his quality. Moreover the evidence suggests that not only was he better able than his predecessors to maintain harmonious relations within the company,[11] but that he had a shrewd eye for young talent and the understanding of how best to improve it. The steady flow of young developing talent to London—from Henderson to Elliston—bears witness to this.

The other key factor in the success of the theatre during the last two decades of the eighteenth century was the development of the dual operation between the two theatres of Orchard Street, Bath, and King Street, Bristol. Since, as we have seen, John Hippisley the then Bristol manager had made the first proposals for the construction of the Orchard Street house, and John Arthur, then manager at Bath had been involved in the building at King Street,[12] the desirability of some such combination may long have been in mind. It made considerable sense. Bristol's traditional theatre season, for many years served by *ad hoc* London companies, was in the summer, when the fashionable Hotwells filled up; Bath's flourishing period was the winter—the two could easily complement each other and provide work for the company for the bulk of the year. Moreover the distance of only twelve or thirteen miles between the two made the logistics of the operation comparatively straight forward. It was not till 1779, however, that Palmer was able to negotiate the lease of the King Street house; but from then on the dual arrangement was to continue till 1817.[13] As the *Calendar* shows, after a short period of experiment the working pattern soon became stabilised—during September and October they played three nights in Bristol, and Saturdays in Bath, with the exception of Race Week in Bath, Christmas and Easter, when a full week was played there. Then from November to May there would be three nights in Bath, with Mondays in Bristol. Benefits in Bath were taken in the spring and early summer; in Bristol, in June and July. The long coaches or 'caterpillars' as they were called—in modern terms 'mini-buses'—which Palmer had constructed, each carried twelve of the company and their luggage, a reasonably pleasant journey in summer, a tiring and occasionally dangerous one in winter.[14]

Operating permanently at the two theatres only, the company had a stability that no other contemporary touring companies could have, with their much more widespread circuits and their less predictable audiences. It is not surprising then, that a position in the Bath company became a desirable ambition, and, once attained, a professional achievement to hold on to. Many of the young members of the company had, of course, metropolitan ambitions, and a sample list of London migrations indicates their success—Dodd, Henderson, Mrs. Siddons, Miss Kemble, Mrs. Goodall to *Drury Lane,* Miss Scrace, Mr. and Mrs. Knight, Mrs. Glover, Incledon, Elliston, Murray, Cherry, Miss Wallis, Miss Smith to *Covent Garden,* John Edwin and Julia Grimani to the *Haymarket* and elsewhere. But there were also those, like William Dimond himself, who consciously chose to remain in Bath, who found greater satisfaction in a permanent position, and the regular roles that went with it, in the provinces, than in a possibly more precarious life in London. Dimond was an acting member of the company for 27 years, and in management till his death, for another 10; Floor, either as actor or prompter for 30, Blisset and Rowbotham for 25, Sherriffe for 18. Two of the ladies became even greater institutions. Mrs. Didier had joined the company in 1767, Miss Summers had come as a young girl with her mother and father two years later; both were still members when the Orchard Street theatre closed its doors for the last time in 1805.

From 1770, when the Stock Book began to be kept,[15] the core of the company was of twenty-five to thirty members, each with their recognised roles in the main plays of the repertory, to which they clung, except for occasional forays into other roles on benefit nights.[16] Other players appear occasionally, again often on benefit nights, or where a play requires a large number of small part actors. Whether they were fully salaried members of the company or given only occasional payments, or whether they combined occasional appearances with other theatre duties, we cannot say. No account books for Orchard Street appear to have survived. When the theatre opened prices were: Boxes 3s., Pit 2s., 1st Gallery 1s. 6d., Upper Gallery 1s. The latter remained constant throughout; but the Box price was raised to 4s. in 1757, then to 5s. in 1782, reduced to 4s. once more in 1786, when Dimond and Keasberry took over proprietorship from Palmer, remaining thus to the end of the theatre's record. Writing at about the turn of the century, Winston recorded that the house would hold from £140–145. £160 with the pit laid into the boxes, expenses being about £35, and the average receipts in a full season being £80–90.[17] The receipt figures for benefits recorded on a number of surviving play bills tend to confirm this.

Permanent members of the company were on salary, plus benefits at Bath and Bristol if they felt popular and secure enough to take them. Henderson in his first season was engaged at a guinea a week, increased as his skill and popularity grew; Sarah Siddons' salary during her stay was three pounds a week.[18] Benefits might be individual or shared; after the expenses of the house were paid, whatever remained went solely to or was shared by the actors involved. (If a 'clear' benefit was contracted for, the player did not have to pay the house expenses.) Often additional players or speciality 'turns' were included on benefit nights as extra inducements to the audience; these might have to be paid for, along with advertising and any special scenery or costumes needed, so that a poor benefit night of £30 or £40 could leave the player in debt. Some did not feel confident enough to risk this—and even established players had their bitter disappointments at times.[19] On the other hand a popular player with a good organisation and the 'Pit thrown into the Boxes' could make £100–140.[20] Fulsome appeals beforehand, expressions of gratitude afterwards, were expected and delivered. The newer generation of players found this expected obsequiousness somewhat degrading; though occasionally one feels it covers a genuine surprise and delight, as in the case of Stanwix in 1802, after his benefit on May 29th:

Theatre Royal, Bath

May 30th 1802

WILLIAM ROBBINS STANWIX, most powerfully, most indelibly impressed with the sincerest Gratitude, for the undeserved, unexpected, and abundant Patronage, with which he was honoured last Night, would attempt, had he the means of Expression, to return Thanks, in a Manner adequate to the Sense he entertains of such distinguished Favors; but the utmost powers of Words fall short of describing those Feelings which he experiences.

He can therefore only beg that the *Royal Patroness of his Benefit*, the *Nobility and Gentry*, who honoured it with their presence, and above all, the *Tradesmen* of this not more elegant than beauteous City, who promoted his Interest, in so warm, so unprecedented a Manner, will accept every Effusion that the overflowings of the sincerest Heart can inspire; and what He has said individually to his Friends, he now fervently addresses to the Public at large—*Thank you! and God bless you!* [21]

The principal administrators of the company (Treasurer and Box Book Keeper) at Bath and Bristol also rated Benefits, and theirs were sometimes the best supported; this may have reflected good organisation, but it must also have come of a recognition that faithful service could be given by the less glamorous members of staff. [22] In the later years performances for groups of lesser "Servants of the House" also became part of the routine. We have no record of how well they fared.

Life in the company had its professional hazards. Miss Wallis' benefit on 6th March 1792, for instance, was dogged by bad luck. The play was *Romeo and Juliet,* but Dimond was so hoarse that he could not play, Hodgkinson had to substitute for Blisset, and later when Knight was wounded in the thigh by West in the duel, for Knight also. However Miss Wallis had a large audience—part of the pit seats sold at box prices— and took £136, so doubtless she—at least—was consoled. [23] The players were skilled at such improvisation. When Murray damaged his leg in *Don Juan,* Elliston immediately substituted for him—most capably, said the report. [24] But illnesses—especially in the depth of winter when epidemics could sweep through the company—could often cause last minute changes of programme, not always to the satisfaction of the audience; though occasions when the theatre had actually to be closed because nothing could be adequately mounted were rare indeed. June 1782 was one such. Commuting between Bath and Bristol raised an additional hazard, of course. Accidents were infrequent, but there was one in April 1801 when a coach overturned, several players were badly cut and bruised, and Glassington, the new prompter, had a leg broken. [25]

If the long service we have already noted gave some of the Bath players greater security than many of their contemporaries, it should be remembered that they were the lucky ones. So long as they were fit, successful at their work, and on good terms with the management, all could be well. But there was never guarantee of re-engagement at the end of a season, and accident, or illness, or loss of public favour, or the needs of their sometimes large families could put even the most careful and prudent into severe difficulties. (And not all of them were careful and prudent.) Where there was goodwill, there was often help within the company. When Baines, former carpenter, was "in great distress" he was given a special benefit. [26] After the deaths of Paul (Treasurer) and the long-serving actor Rowbotham, their widows and families were given benefits, [27] and the others would sometimes play and organise a benefit for an actor who, because of long illness, was himself unable to appear. [28] Not till 1800 was the Theatrical Fund established to provide a capital sum from the interest of which

a permanent Relief may be given to such of the subscribers as may from AGE, INFIRMITY, or MISFORTUNE, become incapable of exercising the Duties of their Profession, and to shield them from the Chilling Blasts of Poverty, "when Service shall, in their old limbs lie lame, and Unregarded Age in Corners Thrown".

Performers paid a weekly contribution and the management gave the profits of an annual night, for which they usually tried to get some special attraction. Blisset came out of retirement for it in 1800. In 1802 George Cooke came specially down from Covent Garden to play Richard III, and would take neither fee nor expenses.[29]

In the early days of the theatre, before the joint Bath–Bristol operation kept them so heavily occupied, the players did a fair amount of touring elsewhere, helping to open up some of the towns of central southern England, and even organising the building of the Portsmouth Theatre in 1761. In one of these forays in 1758 a wagon carrying all their scenery and properties caught fire on Salisbury Plain and was completely destroyed. Stephens, the greatest sufferer, who claimed to have lost property worth several hundred pounds, was granted a special benefit in the following season.[30] But in later years there was little time for summer touring, and when they did form *ad hoc* bands for the purpose, journeys had to be shorter. Thus in early September 1796 we find a group of the players in Cheltenham; in July 1802 in Wells.[31] But these were fringe activities.

Since many of the regular players lived in Bath for long periods, they did, however, become involved in other aspects of the life of the community (a distinctive difference from the rootless travelling life of many other circuit companies at this time). Brett, for instance, was Organist and Principal Chorister at St. James' Church; Wordsworth for a number of years was Secretary of the Catch Club.[32] The musical life of the city drew them most, as one would expect, since many of them were singers performing regularly in the musical pieces. So the concerts in both Assembly Rooms, Rauzzini's regular series, and, of course, the lenten sequence of Handel Oratorios on Wednesdays in the theatre itself, found members of the company—sometimes heavily—involved. The playhouse orchestra, too, contained some of the best musicians in the city, who were also in demand for concerts—Fischer and Ashley, the oboeists, Brookes, the first violin, Herschel the cellist, the Cantelo family. The playhouse band seems to have been a more than adequate small orchestra of 12–15 players.[33] On more than one occasion performance nights were changed at the theatre to enable members of the band to appear at the Assembly Rooms.[34]

In addition to the regular company there were special attractions and visiting players from time to time, particularly in the later years, sometimes staying for a month or more. Signor Rossignol with his bird imitations in 1783 and 1800, The Little Devil and his Troupe in 1783 and 1785, Bryson's Musical Children in 1789, Richer on the tight-rope in 1795, 1800 and 1804, the Phantasmagoria making two visits in 1802 are examples of the specialities. Perhaps the most exotic of these was the Band of Bohemian Silver Miners in March 1803. The visiting players were often former members of the company who had gone on to higher things but returned periodically to acclaim and reward (Henderson, Mrs. Siddons, Murray, Incledon, Miss Wallis), but in the later years "star" visits from outsiders were welcomed (Moses Kean, the one-legged entertainer in 1789, Quick in 1797, 1798, and 1799, Signora Storace—in Vienna the first Susanna in Mozart's *Marriage of Figaro*—1797 and 1802, George Frederick Cooke in 1801 and after, John Philip Kemble in 1803, John Holman in 1804). Occasionally, too, there were special attractions with a local flavour, when gentlemen amateurs would perform leading roles "for their own diversion". Not always were they "gentlemen" in the eighteenth century sense. Just after Christmas 1777 Bellarius in *Cymbeline* was played for that occasion by Whitaker, who,

> a plain uneducated carpenter, performed with such feeling and judgment as to excite the warmest applause from the whole audience.

His "figure" was indifferent, so he was thought likely to be confined to playing old men;

nevertheless he was felt to be an acquisition to the stage, and a few years later he played Shylock to Cooke's Bassanio and Mrs. Simpson's Portia for Cooke's benefit.[35]

Young players were periodically introduced, usually anonymously "A young gentleman", "a young lady, being her first appearance on the stage". Some vanished into oblivion; for others, it was the beginning of an apprenticeship that led them to national fame. Perhaps the most notable beginning was that of the young gentleman who on 6th October 1772, appeared as Hamlet; he was successful enough to be brought out later as "Mr. Courtenay" in Benedick and Macbeth; not till December did he publicly reveal himself as John Henderson, at the start of a tragically short, but brilliant career.[36]

A detailed analysis of the repertory revealed by the Calendar, and a comparison with its London equivalents, has yet to be made; but it is clear that the managers kept in touch with London, and new plays were often mounted very quickly. Sheridan, of course had a special relationship with Bath, and The Rivals, which had its first performance at Covent Garden on 17th January 1775 was seen in Bath on 7th March, less than two months later; while The School for Scandal—Drury Lane in May 1777—followed in Bath in November. Similar speed applied to other new plays. Local authors' work was naturally exploited—Hannah More's The Inflexible Captive, Percy, and The Fatal Falsehood, Ann Yearsley, the Bristol milkwoman's tragedy of Earl Godwin, and later the plays and after-pieces of Prince Hoare and William Dimond had a special appeal in Bath and Bristol. As elsewhere local colour was often exploited in pantomimes. Brystowe, or Harlequin Mariner was written by Floor, for many years the company's prompter; and doubtless he had a lot to do with Bladud, which must have exploited some of the myths about Bath's early history. Both had considerable popularity.[37]

What of the Orchard Street playhouse itself, the heart of all this activity? Very little is known of its original form, except that if Palmer followed the Hippisley–John Wood proposals it would have been "sixty feet Long and forty feet Broad in the clear"—presumably the left hand section of the Winston engraving of 1805, with the large pedimented door as main access to the theatre. Boxes, Pit and two Galleries are provided for in the first price list. The original design was probably the work of Thomas Jelly.[38] Some improvements were made in the summer of 1755; though we do not know what they were.[39] In spite of the smallness, it was probably adequate for those early years, but with the development of John Wood's Upper Town, and the threat of proposals for a larger and more fashionable building there (and possibly also the standard set by the new Bristol theatre in King Street), Palmer decided that further improvements were necessary in 1767, and his namesake John Palmer the architect (a partner of Jelly's) submitted plans and estimates. Either these were at that time considered too costly, or they did not suit the taste of Arthur; they were rejected, no enlargement was done, but the auditorium was remodelled according to Arthur's own ideas. From October 1766–March 1767 Simpson's old theatre was used while the alterations were carried out. But soon after the reopening, a contemporary description was critical:

The Pit is altered much for the better since last season, tho' even now it is too low. Apollo and the Muses, in the Dome, are new white-washed, and some little addition has been made, we believe, to the yellow paint, gilding, etc. etc., if so, it was quite unnecessary, there having been before too much money squandered away to very little purpose. 'Tis surprising, when this Theatre was alter'd, that the person who had the management of it did not take pattern by the Bristol Theatre, as a convenient, neat, and elegant structure! far preferable to this, which is only calculated to please children and clowns, who think it's all gold that glitters, and are therefore fond of that paltry, showy daubing, that is so conspicuous here.[40]

And there were complaints of the inadequate ventilation and the intolerable heat and crowding in the Pit, especially when the curtain was down between Play and Farce

for tho' it may be necessary to let down the curtain to show us the play is done, it can by no means be requisite to continue it all the time they are changing their dresses, or waiting for more company; for it is a very improper time and place for vapour-bathing; and we are now very happily accommodated with baths for that purpose. . . ."[41]

Dresses ruined by candle-droppings because of inferior wax, and the stench of the lamps because the best spermaceti oil was not used were further cause of complaint.[42]

After Arthur's departure the situation was reconsidered, Palmer's plans were brought out again, and in 1775, in the four months between the closure at the beginning of June and the reopening at the end of September, the second reconstruction was carried out. This time the auditorium was extended at the rear, the dome (which had been bad both for sight lines and accoustics) was removed and replaced by a much more efficient ventilator, the pit was raised, the seats were given more room, the "Gothick" décor was removed and the proscenium given Ionic and Doric pillars, the stage was enlarged, and a new box lobby created. It was probably at this time that the earlier pedimented door was turned into a window and the Gallery, Pit, and Box doors at the rear were created.[43]

In that form the theatre was to operate for its remaining thirty years, and the shell, apart from some alteration to the doors, remains in that form still, though the interior has, of course been completely gutted and transformed.[44]

If the water-colour sketch by Nixon of a playhouse interior reproduced by Mowbray Green really is of the Orchard Street house (and though the original cannot now be traced, there is no reason to suppose that it is not), it must represent the interior after the 1775 remodelling.[45] Pit, Boxes and the two Galleries we should expect are clearly depicted. There is some ambiguity about the proscenium opening however—the proscenium doors cannot structurally have ended in an open stage without arch as they appear to do, so there may be a drawing error here, and the first of the classical wing pillars illustrated may have represented the Ionic and Doric proscenium. The orchestra pit is adequate for the size of the band that we know. The only aspect of the interior not shown is the curve of the boxes round the rear of the pit, but the plans in the surviving Box-Keeper's Book,[46] indicate its existence. Reading from audience left to right the boxes were labelled Henry, Richard, Edgar, Bladud (the centre and presumably ceremonial box when required) Alfred, Edward and Rufus.

The scene represented is undoubtedly Hamlet (in traditional but, of course, eighteenth century black, with Horatio and Marcellus appropriately two or three steps behind), confronting his father's Ghost, traditional armour, truncheon and all. The rear scene looks very much like one of those stock scenes we read about, with three or four basic ingredients—trees, water, hill, with some sort of building on top which, by the spectator selecting the relevant image, could do duty for many backgrounds—the Forest of Arden as well as the battlements at Elsinore! Such stock scenes must have done sterling service in both Orchard Street and King Street, though it is fair to say that one of the merits claimed for the dual operation was that it enabled the proprietor financially to mount many pieces with special scenery "equal in exhibition to the London Theatres".[47]

This was the Orchard Street house, then, during the three decades of its highest artistic achievement, popularity, and prosperity. No more major modifications were made. In 1781 a new coach road was made up to the theatre and a stand for fifty to sixty carriages, and it was this, plus the cost of enlarging the Company, Band and Servants and the extravagant price of Oil and Candles that were Palmer's justification for raising the Box price to 5s. in 1782.[48] Probably little more could be done to the interior on its restricted site. Nevertheless, visiting it in its last years, Winston found it "commodious and elegant".[49]

But by the standards then applying, it was too small and inconvenient. Though the mother-house, it must have continued to suffer by comparison with its more commodious and attractive adopted daughter in Bristol. And so with the turn of the century plans for a new larger, more elegant theatre in a more central position began to be considered, Beaufort Square was chosen, finance arranged, and in August 1804 the foundation stone was laid.

The last season in Orchard Street, 1804–5, must have been an ambivalent one, full of excitement about the new prospects, but doubtless also with much nostalgia for the old days that were coming to an end. And magnificent days (or nights) many of them had been. In all the euphoria attending the opening of the new theatre, no one could tell whether its first fifty-five years would reach the standard of those in the old house. In fact, as we can now see, they could not. Splendid as the new theatre was, it came too late, when both the Georgian provincial theatre system and the social pre-eminence of Bath had passed their peak. There were to be many notable evenings in the new building.[50] But Keasberry and Dimond, Henderson, Mrs. Siddons, Kemble, Cooke, and the host of lesser players who nevertheless were the backbone of those Georgian Companies—the Blissets, the Row-bothams, the Didiers, the Summers—were gone. And some of the glory went with them. There is a dramatic appropriateness in the record of the Orchard Street Theatre ending when it did.

Notes

1. *Bath Journal* 19 May 1783.
2. J. Bernard: *Retrospections of the Stage* (1830) Vol. I, p. 34.
3. Tate Wilkinson: *The Wandering Patentee* (York 1795) Vol. III, p. 196 confirms the superior quality of the Bath audience.
4. B. S. Penley: *The Bath Stage* (Bath 1892) reprints both Hippisley and Palmer's proposals. pp. 23–25.
5. The affidavits are in the *Bath Journal* 4, 11, 18, 25 Nov., 2 Dec. 1751.
6. His letter is in *Bath Journal* 17 Nov. 1755.
7. v. Sybil Rosenfeld: *Strolling Players and Drama in the Provinces* (1939) Chaps. VIII & IX.
8. *Bath Advertiser* 30 April 1757.
9. J. Brownsmith: *The Dangers of a Lee Shore, or an Impartial View of the Bath T***E in the year 1759* is a bitter attack by his discharged prompter.
10. v. the sequence labelled *The Theatrical Review* in the *Bath Chronicle* 8 Oct. 1767–3 Mar. 1768.
11. There were occasional explosions of ill-feeling, of course, e.g. Mrs. Esten's accusations of unfairness over her Benefits in 1786–7, but these were rare. And Mrs. Esten seems to have been a particularly difficult creature. v. John Genest: *Some Account of the English Stage* (Bath 1832) Vol. VI, p. 462. Tate Wilkinson: *op cit* Vol. III, p. 109–124.
12. Kathleen Barker: *The Theatre Royal Bristol 1776–1966* (1974) is the standard work; pp. 3–66 deal admirably with the Bristol story during the years covered by the *Orchard Street Calendar*.
13. *ibid:* pp. 45–6.
14. v. *Bath Journal* 11 Oct. 1779. J. Winston: *The Theatrical Tourist* (1805) p. 5.
15. The *Stock Book* is preserved in the Strong Room of the Bath Reference Library. It was originally given to Bellamy, Manager of the Beaufort Square Theatre in 1829 by General Palmer, descendent of John Palmer, and still "Proprietor and Patentee".
16. This proprietorial attitude to parts could be a great frustration to the young aspiring player. v., e.g. W. Van Lennep (ed): *The Reminiscences of Sarah Kemble Siddons* (Harvard 1942) p. 7–8.

17. Winston: *op. cit.* p. 5.
18. Davies: *Life of Henderson.* p. 6. Siddons: *ibid.*
19. v. Brett's outburst on 19 June 1782. Genest: *op. cit.* Vol. VI.
20. e.g. Knight 24 Mar. 1795, £131.12 Mrs. Keasberry 21 May 1791, £124. Evidence of the Harvard Bills.
21. *Bath Journal* 31 May 1802. The Royal Patroness was the Duchess of York.
22. e.g. Paul and Bartley took £142.8.6 on 17 Mar. 1796.
23. M S notes on the Harvard Play Bill.
24. *Bath Chronicle* 29 Jan. 1795.
25. *Bath Chronicle* 27 Apr. 1801.
26. *PB.* 5 June 1761.
27. *Bath Journal* 31 Mar. 1800. 12 Dec. 1800, 17 June 1801.
28. e.g. Sherriffe's long illness. *Bath Chronicle* 10 Feb. 1774.
29. *Bath Journal* 7, 14 June 1802. Sat. 12 July 1800.
30. *Bath Journal* 13 Mar. 1759. Some of these touring activities of the Bath Company are recorded in Chapter III of A. Hare: *The Georgian Theatre in Wessex* (1958).
31. *Bath Chronicle* 3 Sept. 1796. 29 July 1802.
32. *Bath Journal* 13 May 1782. *Bath Chronicle* 13 Mar. 1794.
33. The Stock Book lists their names for 1770–77.
34. e.g. 20–21 Dec. 1780.
35. *Bath Chronicle* 26 Dec. 1777. *Bath Journal* 23 June 1783. Whether this was the young George Frederick Cooke trying to find a niche in the Bath Company is not certain. It is not impossible, since this is one of the blank years in his biography.
36. J. Ireland: *Letters and Poems of John Henderson* (1786) pp. 66–90 has an account of that first performance.
37. *Bath Chronicle* 11 Feb. 1790. Seasons 1777–81 and 1788–94.
38. Walter Ison: *The Georgian Buildings of Bath* (1948) pp. 101–2.
39. *Bath Journal* 22 Sept. 1755.
40. *Bath Chronicle* 8 Oct. 1767.
41. *Bath Chronicle* 5 Nov. 1767.
42. *Bath Chronicle* 10 Dec. 1767. 18/25 Feb. 1768.
43. v. Penley: *op. cit.* pp. 34–5.
44. A thread of the theatrical ran through its later transformations. It became first a Roman Catholic chapel, later (and still) a Masonic Temple.
45. Mowbray Green: *The Eighteenth Century Architecture of Bath* (1904).
46. Bath Reference Library.
47. *Bath Journal* 21 Jan. 1782.
48. *Bath Journal* 4 Sept. 1781, 21 Jan. 1782.
49. Winston: *op. cit.* p. 6.
50. Penley: *op. cit.* Chaps. 16–25 record the story of the new theatre during the nineteenth century.

Editorial Method

The main sources for the *Calendar* have been the *Bath Journal* (1750–1805, with a few gaps), *Bath Chronicle* (1760–1805, 1755–60 as the *Bath Advertiser*), and Felix Farley's *Bristol Journal* (1779–1805); supplemented from time to time by the other newspapers, and by playbills, where they have survived. In the newspapers, often only a brief mention of titles in the social columns is all that remains, and in the early years there are many gaps. Occasionally the only source is an advance note at the bottom of an earlier playbill. We have printed all positive information known to us, but have not recorded likely playing dates for which there is no certain information. Where a brief announcement refers to "entertainments as will be expressed in the bills of the day" or some such phrase, we have omitted this; it may be taken for granted that the standard Georgian pattern of afterpieces and/or entertainments normally applies. The one exception we have made is to indicate where the unnamed afterpiece is specifically mentioned as a pantomime. Except where special visiting performers like Richer or The Little Devil were involved, we have made no attempt to list other miscellaneous entertainments provided—especially on benefit nights. Where, as happens from time to time, there is a conflict between two newspaper announcements (and possibly also a playbill) we have taken the playbill or the later newspaper to represent the final choice for that night, and have not recorded the alternatives. It is, of course impossible to guarantee that every performance took place precisely as announced—the occasional cancellation notice that has survived, usually because of the illness of a principal player, reminds us of this hazard to the historian. Where only titles are known, it would have made an unnecessarily complex typographical problem to have listed every source individually; but where any casting information exists, even if for one player only, all known sources have been recorded. Thus:

PB/H,Ba, C/BJ,BC

means a playbill in the Harvard University Theatre Collection, another in the Bath Reference Library, and casting information in the *Bath Journal* and *Chronicle*. In locating these at source, it should be borne in mind that sometimes a playbill-type announcement in the press may be placed a week or more before the date of performance—this is especially true for benefit nights—or a mention in the social columns may be either in advance or retrospective. Secondary sources like Genest and William Tyte occasionally contain information for which the primary source has disappeared. In such cases they have been used, though it should be added that where they contain material for which primary sources survive, there are occasional conflicts of evidence.

Though titles of plays are sometimes spelled differently in the sources, we have in general tried to standardise to the spelling in the *Alphabetical Catalogue of Plays,* Vol VI of

Nicoll's *History of English Drama 1660–1900*. To save space we have not printed alternative titles even though they appear in the source. Occasionally the sources use the alternative title rather than the more common, e.g. *Flora* is most often called *Hob in the Well*. Here we have not tried to standardise but have used the title in the source. A cross reference in the Play Index should make the matter clear. Indications are rarely given as to which version of a rewritten or adapted play is being used. Often from the date it may be possible to deduce this, but we have not tried to do so. The *Calendar* is a factual record; deductions must be left to the user.

Actor's names sometimes provide a problem. Apart from the notorious Mrs. Belfille (Belville, Bellefield, Bellfield), Blisset is sometimes Blissett, Claget can be Claggett, Rossignol Rossignole. Where there is no ambiguity we have tried to standardise, but in some cases there are clearly two people of similar name (Brown, Browne). There are problems, too, with the children. Sorting out the various Masters and Misses Keasberry, for instance, is a work of divination. We have recorded such initials as appear in the source, but there may be some duplication. In the Company lists, for reference purposes, we have tried to include every actor whose name appears during a particular season, apart from obvious short term visitors. But it should be remembered that a few of these may appear only occasionally (e.g. at benefits, or when large casts are involved) and may not have been full members of the company. Visitors names are recorded separately, in brackets, for each known performance.

No attempt has been made to record the patrons of particular evenings or benefits. Interesting as they are socially, and as an indication of the quality of support, this would have additionally complicated the layout, and it is of marginal interest theatrically.

Sources and Abbreviations

Newspapers

BJ	Bath Journal
BC	Bath Chronicle
BA	Bath Advertiser
BH	Bath Herald
BR	Bath Register
FF	Felix Farley's Bristol Journal
SF	Sarah Farley's Bristol Journal
BMn	Bonnor and Middleton's Bristol Journal
BG	Bristol Gazette and Public Advertiser
My	Bristol Mercury
BWI	Bristol Weekly Intelligencer.

C/BJ means some casting information in the named source. b: Indicates Benefit performance of the actor named. An actor's name in brackets indicates a guest appearance. From 1779 onwards, Bristol entries are in *Italics*.

Playbills

PB/A	Assembly Rooms, Bath
PB/BM	British Library Collection
PB/Ba	Bath Reference Library Collection
PB/F	Folger Shakespeare Library, Washington
PB/H	Harvard University Theatre Collection
PB/HU	Henry E. Huntington Library, San Marino, California
PB/P	Bills in various private collections
PB/R	Central Reference Library, Bristol
PB/TC	Bristol City Archives (Collection of Trustees of Theatre Royal)
PB/U	University of Bristol Drama Department
PB/Y	York Minster Library

Other Sources

BKB	Box-Keepers Book, Bath
BP	Box-booking Plans, Bristol
ME	Michael Edkins' Account Book

T	William Tyte: Bath in the 18th Century (MS. Notebooks in Reference Library)
A	Typescript in Bath City Archives
G	Genest: Some Account of the English Stage (Bath 1832)

Season 1750/51

Company

Mr: Brookes, Cox, Dancer, Kennedy, Morgan, Malone.

Mrs: Bishop, Brookes, Kennedy.

Miss: Kennedy.

1750

SAT. 27 OCT.
Henry IV (1)   Opening Performance

MON. 29 OCT.
The Fair Penitent

MON. 5 NOV.
The Spanish Fryar

THURS. 8 NOV.
The Conscious Lovers   b: Bath General Hospital

MON. 3 DEC.
The Merry Wives of Windsor
Lethe

MON. 10 DEC.
Measure for Measure
The Honest Yorkshireman   b: Mr. & Mrs. Brookes

THURS. 27 DEC.
Hamlet
The Cobbler of Preston   b: Morgan & Malone

MON. 31 DEC.
Venice Preserv'd
Miss in her Teens   b: Mrs. Bishop & Miss Kennedy

1751

MON. 7 JAN.
Hamlet   b: Dancer & Cox
Damon and Phillida

MON. 8 APRIL
The Suspicious Husband   C/BJ
Miss in her Teens

MON. 15 APRIL
Measure for Measure
The Mock Doctor

MON. 22 APRIL
Love Makes a Man
The Virgin Unmask'd

MON. 29 APRIL
The Way of the World
Miss in her Teens

MON. 6 MAY
Macbeth

MON. 13 MAY
Edward the Black Prince   C/BJ
The Virgin Unmask'd   b: Morgan & Malone

MON. 20 MAY
The Fair Penitent   C/BJ b: Mrs. Bishop
The Anatomist   & Miss Kennedy

MON. 27 MAY
The Distrest Mother   C/BJ b: Mr. &
The Honest Yorkshireman   Mrs. Kennedy

MON. 3 JUNE
Cato   C/BJ b: Mr. &
Lethe   Mrs. Brookes

MON. 10 JUNE
Richard III

MON. 17 JUNE
Hamlet   C/BJ

End of Season

(Prices during season – Boxes 3s, Pit 2s,
First Gallery 1s. 6d, Upper Gallery 1s.)

Season 1751/52

Company

Mr: Blakey, Bland, Brookes, Carthy, Castle, Cox, Dancer, Elrington, Furnival, Green, Kennedy, Lacey, Morgan, Otway, Stephens.

Mrs: Bishop, Clayton, Kennedy, Elrington, Green, Hippisley, Lindley.

Miss: Kennedy.

Master: Claggett.

1751

MON. 23 SEPT.
Hamlet   C/BJ
The Lying Valet

MON. 30 SEPT.
Henry IV   C/BJ

MON. 7 OCT.
Richard III   C/BJ
The Virgin Unmask'd

THURS. 10 OCT.
The Conscious Lovers   b: Bath General
Lethe   Hospital

MON. 14 OCT.
Othello   C/BJ
Phoebe

MON. 21 OCT.
Romeo and Juliet   C/BJ

MON. 28 OCT.
Macbeth   C/BJ

MON. 4 NOV.
The Tempest   C/BJ

MON. 11 NOV.
The Confederacy   C/BJ
The Lottery

MON. 18 NOV.
Jane Shore   C/BJ
Miss in her Teens

MON. 25 NOV.
The Confederacy   C/BJ
The Lottery

MON. 2 DEC.
A Bold Stroke For a Wife   C/BJ
Queen Mab

MON. 9 DEC.
The Stratagem   C/BJ
Queen Mab

MON. 16 DEC.
The Pilgrim   C/BJ
Queen Mab

THURS. 26 DEC.
George Barnwell   C/BJ
Queen Mab

MON. 30 DEC.
She Wou'd And She Wou'd   C/BJ
  Not
Queen Mab

1752

MON. 6 JAN.
The Tempest   C/BJ
Lethe

MON. 13 JAN.
The Tender Husband   C/BJ
Phoebe   b: Miss Kennedy

MON. 20 JAN.
The Royal Merchant   C/BJ b: Blakey
Queen Mab

TUES. 28 JAN.
The Country Lasses   C/BJ b: Castle
Queen Mab

WED. 5 FEB.
The Wonder   C/BJ b: Kennedy
Miss in her Teens

THURS. 13 FEB.
Love Makes a Man   C/BJ b: Brookes
Queen Mab

MON. 17 FEB.
The Gamester   C/BJ
Queen Mab

TUES. 25 FEB.
Othello   C/BJ b: Bland
The Mock Doctor

MON. 2 MAR.		**THURS. 7 MAY**	
The Mourning Bride	C/BJ	Aesop	C/BJ
Queen Mab		The Lottery	
MON. 9 MAR.		**WED. 13 MAY**	
The Pilgrim	C/BJ b: Mrs. Kennedy	Aesop	C/BJ
The Intriguing Chambermaid		Phoebe	
MON. 16 MAR.		**TUES. 19 MAY**	
The Orphan	C/BJ b: Mrs. Clayton	Love Makes a Man	C/BJ b: Dancer
Miss in her Teens		A Dish of Mr. Foote's Tea	& Mrs. Bishop
MON. 30 MAR.		**MON. 25 MAY**	
The Recruiting Officer	C/BJ, BWI,	The Provok'd Wife	C/BJ b: Mr. &
The Schoolboy	b: Morgan	Lethe	Mrs. Kennedy
WED. 8 APRIL		**TUES. 2 JUNE**	
Othello	C/BJ b: Elrington	Jane Shore	C/BJ b: Miss Kennedy
Phoebe		The Lottery	& Cox
MON. 13 APRIL		**MON. 8 JUNE**	
The Confederacy	C/BJ b: Furnival	Hamlet	C/BJ
Lethe		Miss in her Teens	b: Blakey & Carthy
MON. 20 APRIL		**MON. 15 JUNE**	
She Wou'd And She Wou'd		The Fair Quaker of Deal	C/BJ b: Morgan
Not	C/BJ	Damon and Phillida	& Otway
The Lying Valet			
MON. 27 APRIL		**WED. 17 JUNE**	
The Country Lasses	C/BJ	No information available	b: Stephens &
Queen Mab			Furnival

End of Season

Season 1752/53

Company

Mr: Blakey, Brookes, Cartwright, Castle, Cox, Dancer, Furnival, Hibbert, Kennedy, Mason, Morgan, Richardson, Stephens.

Mrs: Bishop, Brookes, Cartwright, Kennedy, Pye, Richardson.

Miss: Ibbott, Kennedy, Roche.

1752		**SAT. 18 NOV.**	
MON. 9 OCT.		The Foundling	
Jane Shore	C/BJ	Miss in her Teens	
The Lottery			
MON. 16 OCT.		**MON. 20 NOV.**	
Hamlet		Love Makes a Man	
The Honest Yorkshireman	C/BJ	Queen Mab	
MON. 13 NOV.		**THURS. 23 NOV.**	
The Mourning Bride		The Country Lasses	
Queen Mab			
THURS. 16 NOV.		**SAT. 25 NOV.**	
The Beaux Stratagem	b: Bath General	The Wonder	
The Lying Valet	Hospital	The Mock Doctor	

MON. 27 NOV.
The Recruiting Officer
Queen Mab

THURS. 30 NOV.
King Lear
Lethe

SAT. 2 DEC.
The Tender Husband
The Lottery

MON. 4 DEC.   C/BJ
Jane Shore
A Dish of Mr. Foote's Tea

MON. 11 DEC.
The Provok'd Husband   C/BJ b: Miss Kennedy
A Dash of Mr. Foote's Tea

MON. 18 DEC.
Richard III   C/BJ b: Dancer
The Schoolboy

THURS. 28 DEC.
The Confederacy   C/BJ b: Castle
Queen Mab

1753

MON. 1 JAN.
The Suspicious Husband   C/BJ b: Miss Roche
Queen Mab

MON. 8 JAN.
The Busybody   C/BJ b: Mason
The Lying Valet

MON. 15 JAN.
Love for Love   C/BJ b: Mrs. Bishop
The Lover's Opera

MON. 22 JAN.
The Merry Wives of Windsor   C/BJ b: Stephens
The Devil To Pay

MON. 29 JAN.
The Way of the World   C/BJ b: Mrs. Kennedy
The King and the Miller of
  Mansfield

MON. 5 FEB.
Hamlet   C/BJ
Lethe   b: Dancer &
                                     Mrs. Richardson

MON. 12 FEB.
Love Makes a Man   C/BJ b: Morgan
Hob In The Well

MON. 19 FEB.
The Foundling   C/BJ
Harlequin Ranger

MON. 26 FEB.
Aesop   C/BJ
Harlequin Ranger

THURS. 1 MAR.
The Gamester

MON. 5 MAR.
The Gamester
Harlequin Ranger

TUES. 13 MAR.
The Earl of Essex   C/BJ
Harlequin Ranger

TUES. 20 MAR.
The Earl of Essex   C/BJ
Harlequin Ranger

TUES. 27 MAR.
Romeo and Juliet   C/BJ

TUES. 3 APRIL
The Brothers   C/BJ
The Lottery

TUES. 10 APRIL
The Gamester   C/BJ
Phoebe

SAT. 14 APRIL
Every Man In His Humour

MON. 23 APRIL
Every Man In His Humour   C/BJ
Queen Mab

MON. 30 APRIL
The Conscious Lovers   C/BJ
Queen Mab

THURS. 3 MAY
The Suspicious Husband   C/BJ b: Miss Kennedy

MON. 7 MAY
The Earl of Essex   C/BJ b: Miss Ibbot
The Lovers' Opera

MON. 14 MAY
Hamlet   C/BJ b: Dancer
A Dish of Mr. Foote's Tea

TUES. 22 MAY
Macbeth   C/BJ b: Furnival
Lethe

TUES. 29 MAY
The Pilgrim   C/BJ b: Mr. &
Phoebe   Mrs. Kennedy

TUES. 5 JUNE			TUES. 19 JUNE	
The London Merchant	C/BJ b: Castle		The Suspicious Husband	C/BJ b: Blakey &
Queen Mab			The Mock Doctor	Mason
			(Ross & Mrs. Bland)	

TUES. 12 JUNE
Richard III   C/BJ b: Blakey
Miss in her Teens   *End of Season*

Season 1753/54

Company

Mr: Bishop, Blakey, Brookes, Brown, Cartwright, Castle, Costollo, Cox, Furnival, Kennedy, Maclelan, Moody, Pitt, Richardson, Sanders, Stephens, Williamson.

Mrs: Bishop, Campbell, Kennedy, Richardson, Sanders.

Miss: Kennedy, Lowe, Morrison, Roche.

1753

THURS. 4 OCT.
The Beaux Stratagem
The Lottery

MON. 8 OCT.
The Miser   C/BJ
The Virgin Unmask'd

MON. 15 OCT.
The Recruiting Officer   C/BJ
Miss in her Teens

MON. 22 OCT.
The Roman Revenge   C/BJ
                          b: The daughters of
                          Aaron Hill

MON. 29 OCT.
The Gamester   C/BJ
Queen Mab

MON. 5 NOV.
The Beggar's Opera   C/BJ b: Brown
Lethe

MON. 12 NOV.
The Merry Wives of Windsor   C/BJ
Queen Mab

MON. 19 NOV.
Love Makes a Man   C/BJ
Harlequin Ranger   b: Mrs. Richardson

MON. 26 NOV.
The Merry Wives of Windsor C/BJ b: Mrs. Sanders
Queen Mab

MON. 3 DEC.
King Lear   C/BJ b: Richardson
Damon and Phillida

MON. 10 DEC.
The Beggar's Opera   C/BJ b: Miss Lowe
The Mock Doctor

MON. 17 DEC.
The Merchant of Venice   C/BJ b: Cox
The Lottery

TUES. 27 DEC.
The Provok'd Wife   C/BJ b: Brown

MON. 31 DEC.
The Merchant of Venice   C/BJ b: Mrs. Bishop
Miss in her Teens

1754

MON. 7 JAN.
The Committee   C/BJ b: Mrs. Kennedy
Queen Mab

MON. 14 JAN.
The Gamester   C/BJ b: Stephens
Hob in the Well

MON. 21 JAN.
Measure for Measure   C/BJ
Queen Mab

MON. 28 JAN.
The City Wives' Confederacy C/BJ
The Virgin Unmask'd

MON. 4 FEB.
Jane Shore   C/BJ
Miss in her Teens

MON. 11 FEB.
Eurydice   C/BJ

MON. 18 FEB.
The Confederacy   C/BJ
Hob in the Well

MON. 25 FEB.	
Jane Shore	C/BJ
Hob in the Well	

MON. 4 MAR.	
Hamlet	C/BJ

MON. 11 MAR.	
Measure for Measure	C/BJ

TUES. 19 MAR.	
The Roman Father	C/BJ

TUES. 26 MAR.	
Richard III	C/BJ

Following this performance, information was laid against the Company, they had to appear at Guildhall, and were fined. For a short while the House was closed. (v.FF, 30/3/54).
The performance of Comus advertised for 30 March almost certainly did not take place. From 15 April all performances are advertised as "Concerts of Music".

SAT. 30 MAR.	
Comus	

MON. 15 APRIL	
Comus	b: Brown

MON. 22 APRIL	
The Roman Father	b: Miss Lowe
The Chaplet	

MON. 29 APRIL	
Macbeth	b: Castle
Queen Mab	

WED. 1 MAY	
Eurydice	b: Cox

MON. 6 MAY	
Zara	b: Moody & Brookes
Queen Mab	

WED. 8 MAY	
Romeo and Juliet	b: Pitt
Queen Mab	

MON. 13 MAY	
The Merchant of Venice	b: Miss Morrison
The Mock Doctor	

MON. 20 MAY	
The Beggar's Opera	b: Blakey & Pitt
Queen Mab	

WED. 22 MAY	
Edward The Black Prince	b: Furnival

End of Season

Season 1754/55

Company

Mr: Brookes, Brown, Cox, Fawkes, Hull, Martin, Richardson, Stephens.

Mrs: Martin, Richardson.

Miss: Lowe, Morrison.

Box Keeper: Knowles.

All performances throughout the season are announced as "Concerts of Music".

1754

SAT. 2 NOV.
The Beggar's Opera

MON. 4 NOV.
The Beggar's Opera

THURS. 14 NOV.
The Roman Father

MON. 18 NOV.
Richard II
The Mock Doctor

THURS. 21 NOV.
Comus

MON. 25 NOV.
Measure for Measure
Queen Mab

THURS. 28 NOV.
The Fair Penitent

MON. 2 DEC.
Comus

SAT. 7 DEC.
Macbeth   b: Brown
The Anatomist

MON. 16 DEC.
The Beaux Stratagem
Queen Mab

SAT. 21 DEC.
Rule a Wife and Have a Wife   C/BJ

MON. 23 DEC.
Rule a Wife and Have a Wife
Miss in her Teens

MON. 30 DEC.
Phaedra and Hippolitus
The King and the Miller of   b: Hull
  Mansfield

1755

MON. 6 JAN.
The Beggar's Opera   b: Cox
Lethe

MON. 13 JAN.
Rule a Wife and Have a Wife   C/BJ b: Miss Lowe
Lethe

MON. 20 JAN.
The Merry Wives of Windsor   b: Martin
The What D'ye Call It

MON. 27 JAN.
Hamlet   C/BJ b: Brown
The Devil To Pay

MON. 3 FEB.
The Mourning Bride   b: Mr. &
Flora   Mrs. Richardson

MON. 10 FEB.
The Busybody   C/BJ b: Brookes
Chrononhotonthologos

TUES. 18 FEB.
The Beaux Stratagem   C/BJ b: Fawkes
Queen Mab

THURS. 27 FEB.
Othello   b: Stephens
The Honest Yorkshireman

TUES. 4 MAR.
The Rehearsal   C/BJ

MON. 10 MAR.
Measure for Measure
The Mock Doctor

MON. 17 MAR.
The Beggar's Opera   b: Knowles

MON. 31 MAR.
George Barnwell
The Mock Doctor

MON. 7 APRIL
The Recruiting Officer
The King and the Miller of
  Mansfield

MON. 14 APRIL
Richard III
Queen Mab

MON. 21 APRIL
The Rehearsal   C/BJ
Queen Mab

MON. 28 APRIL
Much Ado About Nothing   b: Miss Morrison
The Devil To Pay

MON. 5 MAY
The Beggar's Opera   b: Mr. &
The Lying Valet   Mrs. Richardson

MON. 12 MAY
The Mourning Bride   b: Hull
Love At A Venture

MON. 19 MAY
The Gamester   b: Mr. & Mrs. Martin
The Cheats of Scapin

MON. 26 MAY
The Rehearsal   C/BJ b: Brown

MON. 2 JUNE
The Foundling   C/BJ b: Hull
The Oracle

End of Season

Season 1755/56

Company

Mr: Brookes, Brown, Castle, Fawkes, Furnival, Hacket, Hull, Martin, Stephens, Waker.

Mrs: Green, Martin, Price, Richardson, Rowley.

Miss: Lowe, Morrison, Manwaring, Wilkinson.

1755

Many performances this season are announced as "Concerts of Music"

MON. 29 SEPT.
Concert, plus   C/BJ
The Miser

MON. 6 OCT.
Richard III   C/BJ
The Virgin Unmask'd

MON. 13 OCT.
The Beggar's Opera   C/BJ
The Lottery

THURS. 16 OCT.
The Merchant of Venice
The Virgin Unmask'd

MON. 20 OCT.
Much Ado About Nothing   C/BJ
The Lottery

MON. 27 OCT.
Measure for Measure   C/BJ

SAT. 1 NOV.
A Bold Stroke for a Wife

MON. 3 NOV.
Richard III   C/BJ

WED. 5 NOV.
Tamerlane

THURS. 6 NOV.
Comus

SAT. 8 NOV.
The Conscious Lovers

MON. 10 NOV.
Much Ado About Nothing   C/BJ
The Intriguing Chambermaid

WED. 12 NOV.
Zara
Queen Mab

THURS. 13 NOV.
The Constant Couple

MON. 17 NOV.
The Beaux Stratagem   C/BJ
The Virgin Unmask'd

MON. 24 NOV.
The Conscious Lovers   C/BJ b: Miss Morrison
The Oracle

?   ?
The Pilgrim   C/BJ

MON. 1 DEC.
The Lady's Last Stake   C/BJ b: Mrs. Green
Lethe

MON. 8 DEC.
The Beaux Stratagem   C/BJ
               b: Miss Wilkinson

?   ?
The Chaplet   C/BJ

MON. 15 DEC.
Richard III   C/BJ

THURS. 18 DEC.
The Provok'd Husband   C/BJ b: Brown

MON. 22 DEC.
The Country Lasses   C/BJ
The Old Fairy of the Wood

MON. 29 DEC.
The Provok'd Husband   C/BJ b: Mrs. Price
The Devil To Pay

1756

SAT. 24 JAN.
King Lear
The Old Fairy of the Wood

MON. 26 JAN.
Much Ado About Nothing
The Schoolboy

WED. 28 JAN.
The Tender Husband
The Chaplet

THURS. 29 JAN.
Comus   b: Bath General
The Virgin Unmask'd   Hospital

MON. 9 FEB.
The Provok'd Wife
The Oracle

WED. 11 FEB.
Don Quixote
Catherine and Petruchio

THURS. 12 FEB.
The Merchant of Venice
The Devil To Pay

SAT. 14 FEB.
The Tender Husband
Catherine and Petruchio

MON. 16 FEB.
Much Ado About Nothing
Catherine and Petruchio

WED. 18 FEB.
Hamlet
Miss in her Teens

THURS. 19 FEB.
Comus
Catherine and Petruchio

SAT. 21 FEB.
Every Man in his Humour

TUES. 24 FEB.
Every Man in his Humour

WED. 25 FEB.
The Gamester
Miss in her Teens

THURS. 26 FEB.
The Tender Husband
Miss in her Teens

SAT. 28 FEB.
Every Man in his Humour
The Intriguing Chambermaid

MON. 1 MARCH
The Merry Wives of Windsor
The Oracle

THURS. 4 MARCH
Love for Love
Catherine and Petruchio

SAT. 6 MARCH
The Busybody
The Chaplet

TUES. 9 MAR.
The Rehearsal
Miss in her Teens

THURS. 11 MAR.
Every Man in his Humour
Catherine and Petruchio

SAT. 13 MAR.
Zara
The Virgin Unmask'd

MON. 15 MAR.
The Wife's Resentment
Catherine and Petruchio

THURS. 18 MAR.
The Confederacy
The Old Fairy of the Wood

SAT. 20 MAR.
Athelstan

MON. 22 MAR.
Athelstan
The What-d'ye-Call-It

TUES. 23 MAR.
Comus
The Old Fairy of the Wood

THURS. 25 MAR.
Athelstan
The Old Fairy of the Wood

SAT. 27 MAR.
The Constant Couple
The What-d'ye-Call-It

TUES. 30 MAR.
The Tender Husband
The Old Fairy of the Wood

THURS. 1 APRIL
The Way of the World
The Old Fairy of the Wood

SAT. 3 APRIL
Romeo and Juliet

MON. 5 APRIL
Don Quixote
The Old Fairy of the Wood

TUES. 6 APRIL
The Conscious Lovers   C/BA
The Schoolboy   b: Mrs. Green

THURS. 8 APRIL
Measure for Measure
The Old Fairy of the Wood

MON. 19 APRIL
The Rehearsal
The Old Fairy of the Wood

WED. 21 APRIL
The Journey to London
The Apprentice

THURS. 22 APRIL
The Way of the World
The Oracle

SAT. 24 APRIL
Every Man in his Humour
The Old Fairy of the Wood

MON. 26 APRIL
Don Quixote
Catherine and Petruchio

WED. 28 APRIL
The Busybody
The Mock Doctor

THURS. 29 APRIL
The Rehearsal
The Apprentice

SAT. 1 MAY
The Provok'd Husband
The Lottery

MON. 3 MAY
The Fop's Fortune
The What-d'ye-Call-It

WED. 5 MAY
Romeo and Juliet
The Apprentice

THURS. 6 MAY
The Careless Husband
The New Rais'd Recruits

SAT. 8 MAY
The Lady's Last Stake
The Apprentice

MON. 10 MAY
Every Man in his Humour
Lethe

WED. 12 MAY
The Beggar's Opera
The Lying Valet

THURS. 13 MAY
The Confederacy
The Honest Yorkshireman

SAT. 15 MAY
The Fair Penitent
Catherine and Petruchio

MON. 17 MAY
The Conscious Lovers   C/BA
The Lottery   b: Miss Manwaring

THURS. 20 MAY
Rule a Wife and Have a Wife
Damon and Philida

SAT. 22 MAY
Hamlet
The Miller of Mansfield

TUES. 25 MAY
The Merry Wives of Windsor
The Honest Yorkshireman

THURS. 27 MAY
The Miser
Lethe

FRI. 28 MAY
Much Ado About Nothing
The Oracle

End of Season

Season 1756/57

Company

Mr: Beckham, Brookes, Brown, Castle, Daly, Fawkes, Furnival, Griffith, Harper, Hull, Keasberry, Martin, Richardson, Stephens, Sullivan, Waker.

Mrs: Bishop, Daly, Fawkes, Keasberry, Richardson, Waker.

Miss: Ibbott, Lowe, Morrison, Plym.

Treasurer: Knowles.   *Box Keeper:* Palmer.   *Musician:* Resek.

1756

THURS. 28 OCT.
Comus   C/BA

SAT. 30 OCT.
Romeo and Juliet   C/BA

SAT. 6 NOV.
Macbeth   C/BA
The Intriguing Chambermaid

THURS. 11 NOV.
Othello

SAT. 13 NOV.
Comus   C/BA

MON. 15 NOV.
The Rehearsal

SAT. 20 NOV.
Macbeth   C/BA
The Lottery

THURS. 25 NOV.
Othello   C/BA b: Brown

SAT. 27 NOV.
The Suspicious Husband   C/BA
Queen Mab

MON. 29 NOV.
The Rehearsal

SAT. 4 DEC.
Much Ado About Nothing   C/BA
The Lying Valet

MON. 6 DEC.
Every Man in his Humour

WED. 8 DEC.
Comus   C/BA b: Sullivan
The Intriguing Chambermaid

THURS. 9 DEC.
The Wonder

SAT. 11 DEC.
Hamlet   C/BA
The Devil To Pay

MON. 13 DEC.
The Wonder

WED. 15 DEC.
The Earl of Essex   C/BA

MON. 27 DEC.
Henry IV   C/BA
The Old Fairy of the Wood

1757

SAT. 1 JAN.
The Wonder   C/BA
The Old Fairy of the Wood

SAT. 8 JAN.
Rule a Wife and Have a Wife   C/BA
The Old Fairy of the Wood

MON. 10 JAN.
The Provok'd Husband   C/BA
Damon and Phillida   b: Miss Morrison

WED. 12 JAN.
Merope   C/BA b: Miss Ibbott

THURS. 13 JAN.
The Merry Wives of Windsor   C/BA b: Griffith
The Lottery

SAT. 15 JAN.
The Wonder   C/BA b: Miss Lowe
Catherine and Petruchio

MON. 17 JAN.
The Mistake   C/BA b: Castle
The Old Fairy of the Wood

THURS. 20 JAN.
The Merchant of Venice   C/BA b: Brookes
The Contrivances

SAT. 22 JAN.
Comus   C/BA b: Furnival
Lethe

MON. 24 JAN.
The Provok'd Wife   C/BA
The Brave Irishman   b: Mr. & Mrs. Daly

WED. 26 JAN.
Much Ado About Nothing   C/BA b: Waker
The Apprentice   Richardson

THURS. 27 JAN.
King Henry IV   C/BA b: Martin

SAT. 29 JAN.
The Provok'd Husband   C/BA b: Mr. &
The Old Fairy of the Wood   Mrs. Fawkes

WED. 2 FEB.
Romeo and Juliet   C/BA
                            b: Knowles & Palmer

SAT. 5 FEB.
Henry IV   C/BA
Damon and Phillida

SAT. 12 FEB.
Henry VIII   C/BA b: Brown

?
Tancred and Sigismunda
Duke and No Duke

SAT. 19 FEB.
A Bold Stroke For A Wife   C/BA
The What-d'ye-Call-It

SAT. 26 FEB.
Macbeth   C/BA
Queen Mab

SAT. 5 MAR.
Merope   C/BA
The Contrivances

SAT. 12 MAR.
The Rehearsal   C/BA
Queen Mab

SAT. 19 MAR.
Comus   C/BA
Queen Mab

SAT. 26 MAR.
The Suspicious Husband   C/BA
Catherine and Petruchio

SAT. 2 APRIL
Hamlet   C/BA

   Price of boxes to be increased by 1/-
   Future prices to be: — Boxes 4/- Pit 2/-,
   First Gallery 1/6, Upper Gallery 1/-.

MON. 11 APRIL
Henry VIII   C/BA

SAT. 16 APRIL
The Alchemist   C/BA

SAT. 23 APRIL
The Alchemist   C/BA
Damon and Phillida

SAT. 30 APRIL
The Beaux Stratagem   C/BA
Harlequin's Revels

WED. 4 MAY
The Wonder   C/BA b: Resek

SAT. 7 MAY
Henry VIII   C/BA
The What-d'ye-Call-It

SAT. 14 MAY
Richard III   C/BA
The Old Fairy of the Wood

MON. 16 MAY
The Rehearsal   C/BA

THURS. 19 MAY
Douglas   b: Miss Ibbott

SAT. 21 MAY
The Provok'd Husband   C/BA b: Griffith
The Lottery

MON. 23 MAY
Rule a Wife and Have a Wife C/BA b: Miss Lowe
Lethe

WED. 25 MAY
The Mistake   C/BA b: Keasberry
The Apprentice

THURS. 26 MAY
The Drummer   C/BA
                            b: Brookes &
                            Mrs. Bishop

SAT. 28 MAY
The Suspicious Husband   C/BA b: Waker & Daly
The Old Fairy of the Wood

MON. 30 MAY
The Provok'd Husband   C/BA b: Harper &
Queen Mab   Mrs. Fawkes

TUES. 31 MAY
The Provok'd Wife   C/BA b: Stephens

MON. 13 JUNE
Othello   C/BA b: Stephens &
The Beggar's Wedding   Beckham

End of Season

Season 1757/58

Company

Mr: Barry, Brookes, Claget, Daly, Fawkes, Fisher, Furnival, Giffard, Griffith, Harper, Hull, Keasberry, Martin, Smyth, Stephens, Sullivan, Waker, Wilkinson.

Mrs: Bishop, Carmichael, Daly, Fawkes, Keasberry, Richardson, Smyth, Waker.

Miss: Ibbott, Morrison.

Master: Fisher.

Dancer: Robert Lewkenor.

Box Keeper: Knowles.   *Musicians:* Samuel Eve, Resek.

1757

SAT. 1 OCT.
Hamlet   C/BA

SAT. 8 OCT.
A Bold Stroke for a Wife   C/BA
The Honest Yorkshireman

SAT. 15 OCT.
The Provok'd Husband   C/BA
The Virgin Unmask'd

SAT. 22 OCT.
The Suspicious Husband   C/BA
The Honest Yorkshireman

SAT. 29 OCT.
The Mistake
The Mock Doctor

SAT. 5 NOV.
Hamlet   C/BA
Miss in her Teens

MON. 7 NOV.
The Suspicious Husband

SAT. 12 NOV.
Amphitryon
Lethe

SAT. 19 NOV.
The Wonder
The Mock Doctor

MON. 21 NOV.
Douglas   C/BA
The King and the Miller of
  Mansfield

WED. 23 NOV.
Comus   C/BA b: Sullivan
Catherine and Petruchio

SAT. 26 NOV.
The Conscious Lovers
Lethe

SAT. 3 DEC.
The Wonder   b: The Marine
                                Society

MON. 5 DEC.
Rule a Wife and Have a Wife C/BA
Catherine and Petruchio

SAT. 10 DEC.
The Suspicious Husband   C/BA
The Reprisal

SAT. 17 DEC.
The Busybody   C/BA
The Author

MON. 26 DEC.
Henry VIII
The Mock Doctor

TUES. 27 DEC.
George Barnwell

1758

MON. 2 JAN.
The Wonder   C/BA
The Virgin Unmask'd

THURS. 5 JAN.
Twelfth Night

SAT. 7 JAN.
The Provok'd Wife   C/BA
The Author

MON. 9 JAN.
Twelfth Night   C/BA
The Author   b: Miss Morrison

WED. 11 JAN.
The Careless Husband   C/BA b: Griffith
The Reprisal

THURS. 12 JAN.
Much Ado About Nothing   C/BA b: Hull
Catherine and Petruchio

SAT. 14 JAN.
Douglas   C/BA b: Miss Ibbott
The Author

MON. 16 JAN.
Rule a Wife and Have a Wife C/BA b: Keasberry
The Reprisal

WED. 17 JAN.
The Wonder   C/BA b: Furnival
The Contrivances

SAT. 21 JAN.
The Careless Husband   C/BA b: Mrs. Bishop
Catherine and Petruchio

MON. 23 JAN.
The Rehearsal   C/BA
The Author   b: Mr. & Mrs. Waker

WED. 25 JAN.
The Provok'd Husband   C/BA b: Brookes
The Apprentice

THURS. 26 JAN.
Love Makes a Man   C/BA b: Martin

SAT. 28 JAN.
King Lear and his Three   C/BA b: Smyth
  Daughters
Lethe

WED. 1 FEB.
The Committee   C/BA b: Harper
The Oracle

THURS. 2 FEB.
The Inconstant   C/BA
The Author   b: Mrs. Richardson

SAT. 4 FEB.
The Confederacy   C/BA b: Knowles
The Author

TUES. 7 FEB.
The Beggar's Opera   C/BA
The Apprentice   b: Robert Lewkenor

SAT. 11 FEB.
The Committee   C/BA
The Author

SAT. 18 FEB.
Twelfth Night   C/BA
The Devil To Pay

SAT. 25 FEB.
The Careless Husband   C/BA
Duke and no Duke

SAT. 4 MAR.
The Careless Husband   C/BA
Duke and no Duke

SAT. 11 MAR.
The Fair Quaker of Deal   C/BA
The Reprisal

TUES. 14 MAR.
The Busybody

THURS. 16 MAR.
Rule a Wife and Have a Wife C/BA
                            b: Samuel Eve, Resek
                            (Band of Music)

SAT. 18 MAR.
Romeo and Juliet   C/BA

MON. 27 MAR.
The Stratagem   C/BA
Harlequin's Revel

SAT. 1 APRIL
The Conscious Lovers   C/BA
Harlequin's Revel

SAT. 8 APRIL
The Provok'd Husband   b: General Hospital
The Honest Yorkshireman

MON. 1 MAY
The Suspicious Husband   C/BA b: Griffith
Harlequin's Revel

MON. 8 MAY
Othello   C/BA
The Apprentice   b: Miss Morrison

WED. 10 MAY
Comus   C/BA b: Hull

SAT. 13 MAY
The Earl of Essex
The Author   C/BA b: Miss Ibbott

MON. 15 MAY
The Mistake   C/BA b: Waker,
Lethe   Smyth, Mrs.Richardson

TUES. 16 MAY
Rule a Wife and Have a Wife C/BA/BJ
Tom Thumb   b: Fire victims

WED. 17 MAY		THURS. 18 MAY	
Love Makes a Man	b: Martin, Brookes, Harper	The Provok'd Husband	C/BA b: Furnival, Mr. & Mrs. Daly, Mrs. Carmichael

End of Season

Season 1758/59

Company

Mr: Brookes, Castle, Furnival, Griffith, Harper, Keasberry, Lee, Martin, Stephens, Waker.

Mrs: Bishop, Keasberry, Lee, Richardson, Waker.

Miss: Ibbott, Morrison, Rosco.

1758

No announcements can be found for the first part of this season.

1759

SAT. 20 JAN.	
King Lear	C/BJ b: Lee

MON. 22 JAN.	
The Rehearsal	C/BJ b: Furnival
Duke and no Duke	

TUES. 20 FEB.	
The Provok'd Husband	C/BJ
The Old Fairy In The Wood	

After this, announcements of "concerts of music" end.

TUES. 27 FEB.	
The Foundling	C/BJ
The Author	

THURS. 1 MAR.	
Douglas	C/BJ

SAT. 3 MAR.	
Tancred and Sigismunda	C/BJ b: Mrs. Lee

TUES. 6 MAR.	
The Rehearsal	C/BJ
The Old Fairy In The Wood	

TUES. 13 MAR.	
King Lear	C/BJ

(for the benefit of Mr. Stephens, who was the principal sufferer from the fire on Salisbury Plain last summer)

SAT. 17 MAR.	
Cleone	C/BJ

MON. 19 MAR.	
Cleone	C/BJ
The Oracle	

TUES. 20 MAR.	
Tancred and Sigismunda	C/BJ

MON. 26 MAR.	
Rule a Wife and have a Wife	C/BJ
Queen Mab	

TUES. 27 MAR.	
The Conscious Lovers	C/BJ
The Author	

TUES. 3 APRIL	
The Suspicious Husband	C/BJ

MON. 16 APRIL	
Richard III	C/BJ
Damon and Phillida	

TUES. 17 APRIL	
George Barnwell	
Queen Mab	

WED. 18 APRIL	
The Provok'd Husband	C/BJ
The Old Fairy In The Wood	

MON. 23 APRIL	
The Constant Couple	C/BJ
The Mock Doctor	

WED. 25 APRIL	
Drummer	
Lethe	

MON. 30 APRIL	
The Provok'd Wife	C/BJ
The Lottery	

SAT. 5 MAY
The Inconstant   C/BA b: Lee
The Guardian

MON. 7 MAY
Love Makes a Man   C/BA b: Miss Morrison
Catherine and Petruchio

WED. 9 MAY
The Merchant of Venice   C/BJ, BA
Damon and Phillida   b: Keasberry

THURS. 10 MAY
Tancred and Sigismunda   C/BJ, BA b: Miss Ibbott

SAT. 12 MAY
The Suspicious Husband   C/BA b: Castle and
Queen Mab   Mrs. Richardson

SAT. 19 MAY
The Rehearsal   C/BA
The Mock Doctor

MON. 21 MAY
Romeo and Juliet   C/BJ b: Mrs. Lee

WED. 23 MAY
The Conscious Lovers   C/BA b: Martin
Hob in the Well

THURS. 24 MAY
The Recruiting Officer   C/BA

SAT. 26 MAY
The Inconstant   C/BA, BJ b: Brookes
The Guardian   & Mrs. Bishop

MON. 28 MAY
Macbeth   C/BJ, BA
The Apprentice   b: Mrs. Keasberry

WED. 30 MAY
The Foundling   C/BA b: Mr. &
The Lying Valet   Mrs. Waker

WED. 6 JUNE
Romeo and Juliet   C/BJ, BA

End of Season

Season 1759/60

Company

Mr: Adams, Arthur, Atkins, Brookes, Brownsmith, Collins, Freeman, Furnival, Griffith, Harper, Keasberry, Lee, Martin, Price, Sherriffe, Stephens, Sullivan, Watts, White, Williams.

Mrs: Bishop, Farran, Lee, Keasberry, O'Hara, Richardson, Williams.

Miss: Ambrose, Caroline, Ibbott, Reynolds, Scudder.

Singer: Mrs Adams.

Treasurer: Samuel Palmer.   *Painter:* Woolley.

1759

SAT. 29 SEPT.
Hamlet   C/BA

MON. 1 OCT.
The Beaux Stratagem
Damon and Phillida

SAT. 6 OCT.
The Suspicious Husband   C/BA
The Lottery

SAT. 13 OCT.
The Recruiting Officer   C/BA
The Author

SAT. 20 OCT.
The Conscious Lovers   C/BA
Flora

SAT. 27 OCT.
The Provok'd Husband   C/BA
The Contrivances

SAT. 3 NOV.
The Foundling   C/BA
Lethe

MON. 5 NOV.
Richard III   C/BJ
Damon and Phillida

SAT. 10 NOV.
The Drummer
Flora

MON. 12 NOV.
The Beaux Stratagem   C/BJ, BA
The Upholsterer

SAT. 17 NOV.
The Inconstant   C/BA
The Upholsterer

SAT. 24 NOV.
Macbeth   C/BA
The Honest Yorkshireman

MON. 26 NOV.
The Beggar's Opera   C/BJ
The Guardian

SAT. 1 DEC.
The Provok'd Husband   C/BA
The Lottery

MON. 3 DEC.
Romeo and Juliet   C/BJ

SAT. 8 DEC.
The Foundling   C/BA
The Upholsterer

SAT. 15 DEC.
Tancred and Sigismunda   C/BA
The Guardian

SAT. 22 DEC.
King Lear   C/BA
The King and the Miller
 of Mansfield

MON. 24 DEC.
Much Ado About Nothing   C/T, BA

WED. 26 DEC.
The Suspicious Husband   C/BJ
High Life Below Stairs

SAT. 29 DEC.
The Provok'd Wife   C/BA
High Life Below Stairs

MON. 31 DEC.
The Beaux Stratagem   C/BJ
High Life Below Stairs

1760

WED. 2 JAN.
The Busybody
The Guardian

THURS. 3 JAN
Douglas
The Virgin Unmask'd

SAT. 5 JAN.
The Rehearsal   C/BA
High Life Below Stairs

MON. 7 JAN.
Much Ado About Nothing   C/BJ, BA
High Life Below Stairs   b: Keasberry

THURS. 10 JAN.
Comus   C/BJ, BA
High Life Below Stairs   b: Griffith

SAT. 12 JAN
Othello   C/BA, BJ b: Mrs. Lee
The Guardian

MON. 14 JAN.
The Suspicious Husband   C/BJ
High Life Below Stairs

WED. 16 JAN.
Love Makes a Man   C/BJ, BA b: Brookes
The Reprisal

THURS. 17 JAN.
The Merry Wives of Windsor   C/BA

SAT. 19 JAN.
The Provok'd Husband   C/BA b: Martin
High Life Below Stairs

MON. 21 JAN.
The Country Lasses   C/BA b: Miss Ambrose

WED. 23 JAN.
The Suspicious Husband   C/BJ, BA b: Collins
The Apprentice

SAT. 26 JAN.
The Foundling   C/BA b: Harper
Damon and Phillida

MON. 28 JAN.
The Provok'd Wife   C/BA b: Samuel
Duke and No Duke   Palmer (Treasurer)

THURS. 31 JAN.
Romeo and Juliet   C/BA

SAT. 2 FEB.
The Wonder   C/BA, BJ
A Dish of Mr. Foote's Tea   b: Lee
Rumour

MON. 4 FEB.
The Country Lasses   C/BJ
The Apprentice

SAT. 9 FEB.
Rule a Wife and Have a Wife C/BA
The Lottery

MON. 11 FEB.
The Only Two Left   C/BA
The Dignity of the Stage

SAT. 16 FEB.
Much Ado About Nothing   C/BA

SAT. 23 FEB.
The Suspicious Husband   C/BA
Lethe

TUES. 26 FEB.
The Provok'd Husband   C/BJ
The Contrivances

SAT. 1 MAR.
The Merry Wives of Windsor   C/BA b: Price
High Life Below Stairs

TUES. 4 MAR.
The Pilgrim   C/BC b: Price and
The Devil to Pay   Watts

SAT. 8 MAR.
The Wonder   C/BA
The Apprentice

MON. 10 MAR.
The Conscious Lovers   C/BA b: Sullivan
The Reprisal

SAT. 15 MAR.
The Inconstant   C/BA
Duke or No Duke

TUES. 18 MAR.
The Provok'd Husband   C/BJ

SAT. 22 MAR.
Tancred and Sigismunda   C/BA
High Life Below Stairs

MON. 24 MAR.
The Busybody
The Contrivances

TUES. 25 MAR.
The Foundling
The Guardian

SAT. 29 MAR.
The Suspicious Husband   C/BA
High Life Below Stairs

MON. 7 APR.
Much Ado About Nothing   C/BJ, BA

SAT. 12 APR.
The Provok'd Husband   C/BA
The Spirit of Contradiction

SAT. 19 APR.
The Wonder   C/BA
Lethe

THURS. 24 APR.
The Suspicious Husband   C/BA b: Woolley
Hob in the Well   (Painter)

SAT. 26 APR.
Much Ado About Nothing   C/BA
The Contrivances

MON. 28 APR.
The Squire of Alsatia

SAT. 3 MAY
The Busybody   C/BA
The Spirit of Contradiction

MON. 5 MAY
The Squire of Alsatia   C/BJ
The King and the Miller
  of Mansfield

WED. 7 MAY
The Way to Keep Him

SAT. 10 MAY
The Way to Keep Him   C/BJ, BA b: Lee
Florizel and Perdita

MON. 12 MAY
The Fair Quaker of Deal   C/BJ, BA
The Guardian   b: Keasberry

WED. 14 MAY
The Squire of Alsatia   C/BJ, BA
The Reprisal   b: Griffith

SAT. 17 MAY
The Rehearsal   C/BA, BJ B. Mrs. Lee
The Englishman in Paris

MON. 19 MAY
The Foundling   C/BA b: Furnival

WED. 21 MAY
Hamlet   C/BJ, BA b: Keasberry
The Bashful Virgin

THURS. 22 MAY
The Way to Keep Him   C/BA b: Martin

SAT. 24 MAY
The Provok'd Husband   C/BA b: Arthur
Wit at a Pinch

MON. 26 MAY
Henry IV (1)   C/BA b: Harper
Florizel and Perdita

THURS. 29 MAY
Macbeth   C/BA b: Collins
The Walking Statue

SAT. 31 MAY
The Conscious Lovers   C/BJ, BA b: Miss Caroline
Florizel and Perdita   Ambrose & Watts

MON. 2 JUNE
The Suspicious Husband   C/BA b: Samuel Palmer
The Spirit of Contradiction   (treasurer) & Mr. Jesson
                                 (a person in distress)

End of Season

Season 1760/61

Company

Mr: Arthur, Atkins, Brookes, Furnival, Harper, Hartry, Keasberry, Martin, Price, Sherriffe, Stephens, Watts, White, Wilkinson.

Mrs: Baker, Bishop, Farran, Keasberry, Lee, Sherriffe.

Miss: Ambrose, Reynolds, Scudder

Master: Atkins.

Staff: Fisher, Knowles, Palmer, Wesley, Woolley.

1760

SAT. 25 OCT.
The Recruiting Officer   C/BC
The King and the Miller
  of Mansfield

In early November the theatre closed because of the death of George II. It was to re-open on 17 Nov.

1761

THURS. 22 JAN.
The Minor   C/BJ b: Hartry
Damon and Phillida

TUES. 24 FEB.
Romeo and Juliet   C/BC b: Harper

TUES. 3 MAR.
The Pilgrim   C/BJ b: Price
The Devil To Pay

MON. 27 APR.
The Confederacy   b: Wilkinson
The Guardian
Scene from Love a la Mode
A Dish of Tea

WED. 13 MAY
Romeo and Juliet   C/BJ, FF b: White
The Spirit of Contradiction

MON. 18 MAY
The Provok'd Husband   C/BJ b: Brookes
The Devil To Pay

WED. 20 MAY
The Merchant of Venice   C/BJ
The Author   b: Mrs. Keasberry

THURS. 21 MAY
The Rival Queens   C/BJ
The Virgin Unmask'd   b: Miss Reynolds

THURS. 28 MAY
Comus   C/BC b: Harper
The Spirit of Contradiction

MON. 1 JUNE
The Beggar's Opera   C/BJ b: Palmer,
Polly Honeycombe   Knowles, Fisher (staff)

FRI. 5 JUNE
Hamlet   PB/H b: Wm. Baines
                                 (late carpenter) "in
                                 great distress"

MON. 8 JUNE
Richard III
Hob in the Well   C/BJ b: Woolley
                                 (painter)

End of Season

Season 1761/62

Company

Mr: Arthur, Brookes, Cresswick, Doyle, Keasberry, Martin, Rothery, Sherriffe, White.

Mrs: Baker, Bishop, Brookes, Hartley, Keasberry, Lee, Sherriffe.

Miss: Reynolds.

Box Keepers: Fisher, Knowles.   *Treasurer:* Palmer

1761

MON. 7 DEC.

Romeo and Juliet

MON. 14 DEC.
C/BJ

The Confederacy
The Upholsterer

1762

WED. 20 JAN.
C/BJ b: Mrs. Lee

The Refusal
The Old Maid

WED. 10 FEB.
C/BJ b: Mrs. Brookes

Henry VIII
The Guardian

THURS. 25 FEB.

The Conscious Lovers   b: Palmer, Knowles
The Lying Valet

SAT. 27 FEB.

The Merchant of Venice   C/BJ b: Fisher
The Male Coquette

MON. 24 MAY

She Wou'd And she   C/BJ b: Palmer,
  Wou'd not   Knowles, Fisher
The Devil to Pay

End of Season

Season 1762/63

Company

Mr: Arthur, Booth, Brookes, Collins, Creswick, Dibbens, Doyle, Furnival, Harper, Hartley, Holland, Keasberry, Martin, Rothery, Sherriffe, Sullivan, Watts.

Mrs: Hamilton, Hartley, Keasberry, Lee, Sherriffe, Workman.

Miss: Reynolds.

Master: Elrington

Treasurer: Palmer   *Box Keepers:* Fisher, Knowles

1762

SAT. 18 DEC.

The Wonder

MON. 20 DEC.

Richard III
Damon and Phillida

WED. 22 DEC.

The Provok'd Husband
High Life Below Stairs

THURS. 23 DEC.

The Double Gallant
Lethe

MON. 27 DEC.

Romeo and Juliet
The Virgin Unmask'd

TUES. 28 DEC.

Henry VIII
The Honest Yorkshireman

WED. 29 DEC.
The Royal Merchant
The Contrivances

THURS. 30 DEC.
Hamlet
The Mock Doctor

1763

SAT. 1 JAN.
The School For Lovers
Lethe

MON. 3 JAN.
The Conscious Lovers
Florizel and Perdita

WED. 5 JAN.
As You Like It
The Spirit Of Contradiction

THURS. 6 JAN.
The Fop's Fortune
The Englishman In Paris

SAT. 8 JAN.
The Double Gallant   C/BC
The Honest Yorkshireman   b: Mrs. Hamilton

MON. 10 JAN.
The Jealous Wife
The Male Coquette

THURS. 13 JAN.
Love For Love
The Anatomist

SAT. 15 JAN.
All in the Wrong
The Beggar's Wedding

MON. 17 JAN.
The Refusal
The Guardian

WED. 19 JAN.
The Inconstant
The Chaplet

SAT. 22 JAN.
The Way to Keep Him   C/BJ, BC b: Mrs. Lee
The Author

MON. 24 JAN.
Oroonoco
Thomas and Sally

THURS. 27 JAN.
Henry IV   C/BJ b: Brookes
The Author

SAT. 29 JAN.
She Wou'd And she
  Wou'd not
The Intriguing Chambermaid

WED. 2 FEB.
The Miser
The Guardian

SAT. 5 FEB.
The Twin Rivals   C/BJ b: Mrs. Sherriffe
Thomas and Sally

MON. 7 FEB.
Cato
The What d'ye-Call-It

THURS. 10 FEB.
The Man's Bewitched
Florizel and Perdita

SAT. 12 FEB.
Rule a Wife and have a Wife
The Devil To Pay

TUES. 15 FEB.
The Jealous Wife
High Life Below Stairs

SAT. 19 FEB.
The Wife's Relief   C/BC b: Harper
Who'd Have Though It

TUES. 22 FEB.
The Jealous Wife   C/BJ b: Fisher
The Beggar's Wedding

SAT. 26 FEB.
The Beggar's Opera   C/BJ
The School Boy   b: Palmer, Knowles

TUES. 1 MAR.
Comus   C/BJ b: Sullivan
The Lying Valet

SAT. 5 MAR.
The Conscious Lovers
The Citizen

TUES. 8 MAR.
The Busybody
The Citizen

SAT. 12 MAR.
The Fop's Fortune
The Author

THURS. 28 APRIL
Macbeth   C/BC
The Honest Yorkshireman   b: Mrs. Hamilton

SAT. 7 MAY
The Pilgrim   C/BC b: Arthur
The Auricula Feast

THURS. 12 MAY
Much Ado About Nothing   C/BJ b: Mrs. Lee
Out Of The Frying Pan

WED. 18 MAY
The Refusal   C/BC
Polly Honeycombe   b: Miss Reynolds

THURS. 19 MAY
The Merry Wives of Windsor   C/BJ b: Brookes
Metamorphoses of Harlequin

THURS. 26 MAY
The Provok'd Husband   C/BJ b: Furnival
The Old Maid

SAT. 29 MAY
The Kind Imposter   C/BC b: Harper
Florizel and Perdita

WED. 15 JUNE
Measure for Measure   C/BJ b: Palmer,
Florizel and Perdita   Knowles, Fisher.

End of Season

Season 1763/64

Company

Mr: Arthur, Bannister, Bates, Brookes, Bryan, Death, Furnival, Keasberry, Martin, Sherriffe, Turner, Watts.

Mrs: Goodwin, Keasberry, Lee, Martin, Quelch, Sherriffe.

Miss: Read.

Prompter: Bryan

1763

SAT. 8 OCT.
The Busybody   C/BC
The Devil To Pay

SAT. 5 NOV.
Love at First Sight

1764

SAT. 14 JAN.
The Jealous Wife   C/BC b: Arthur
The Devil To Pay

MON. 16 JAN.
The Foundling   C/BC b: Mrs. Lee
The Deuce is in him

SAT. 4 FEB.
Love Makes a Man   b: Mrs. Goodwin
The Honest Yorkshireman

MON. 6 FEB.
All In The Wrong   b: Bannister
Entertainments

MON. 13 FEB.
The Provok'd Wife   C/BC b: Brookes
High Life Below Stairs

SAT. 18 FEB.
The Refusal   b: Watts
Thomas and Sally

MON. 20 FEB.
The Distrest Mother   b: Bates, Bryan
Catherine and Petruchio

MON. 23 APRIL
George Barnwell
Harlequin Florist

TUES. 24 APRIL
The Fair Penitent

WED. 25 APRIL
Romeo and Juliet

THURS. 26 APRIL
The Distrest Mother
Harlequin Florist

SAT. 5 MAY
The Committee   C/BC b: Mrs. Lee
Thomas and Sally

MON. 21 MAY
She Wou'd And she   C/BC b: Furnival
  Wou'd not
Thomas and Sally

THURS. 24 MAY
The Refusal   C/BC b: Brookes
The Old Maid

End of Season

Season 1764/65

Company

Mr: Arthur, Bannister, Bates, Brookes, Dodd, Furnival, Haughton, Keasberry, Martin, Rothery, Sherriffe, Watts.

Mrs: Dodd, Keasberry, Lee, Martin, Quelch, Sherriffe.

Miss: Read, Reynolds.

Master: Bates.

Box Keepers: Fisher and Knowles.   *Prompter:* Bryan.

1764

WED. 26 SEPT.
The Beaux' Stratagem
Thomas and Sally

SAT. 29 SEPT.
The Suspicious Husband
The Deuce is in Him

— No further theatre information in 1764 —

1765

SAT. 12 JAN.
As You Like It   C/BC b: Arthur
The Auricula Feast

MON. 14 JAN.
Richard III   C/BC b: Sherriffe
The Citizen

SAT. 19 JAN.
The School For Lovers   C/BC b: Keasberry
Love at First Sight

MON. 21 JAN.
The Jealous Wife   C/BC b: Mrs. Lee
What we Must All Come To

SAT. 26 JAN.
The Double Gallant   C/BC b: Miss Reynolds
The Citizen

MON. 28 JAN.
The Constant Couple   C/BC b: Dodd
Polly Honeycombe

MON. 11 FEB.
Othello   C/BC
Thomas and Sally   b: Mrs. Keasberry

WED. 13 FEB.
The Earl of Essex   C/BC
The Mayor of Garret   b: Mrs. Sherriffe

SAT. 16 FEB.
The Beggar's Opera   C/BC b: Mrs. Dodd
Catherine and Petruchio

TUES. 19 FEB.
The Conscious Lovers   C/BC
The Chaplet   b: Bryan, Knowles

SAT. 23 FEB.
As You Like It   C/BC b: Watts
The Male Coquette

TUES. 26 FEB.
The Beggar's Opera   C/BC b: Bates
High Life Below Stairs

TUES. 5 MAR.
Love's Last Shift   b: Fisher
Thomas and Sally   (Box Book Keeper)

MON. 8 APRIL
Love's Last Shift   C/BC
The Auricula Feast

TUES. 9 APRIL
The Earl of Essex
The Florist Feast

WED. 10 APRIL
The Beggar's Opera
The Mayor of Garret

FRI. 12 APRIL
Much Ado About Nothing
The Florist Feast

SAT. 27 APRIL
The Provok'd Husband   C/BC b: Arthur
The Chaplet

MON. 29 APRIL
The Beggar's Opera   C/BC b: Mrs. Dodd
What We Must All Come To

WED. 1 MAY
She Wou'd and she Wou'd   b: Mrs. Sherriffe
Not
The Citizen

SAT. 4 MAY

The Lady's Last Stake   C/BC b: Miss Reynolds
The Devil to Pay

MON. 6 MAY

The Suspicious Husband   C/BC b: Mrs. Lee
Thomas and Sally

SAT. 11 MAY

As You Like It   C/BC b: Miss Read
Thomas and Sally

MON. 13 MAY

The Double Gallant   C/BC
The Guardian   b: Mrs. Keasberry

SAT. 18 MAY

The Funeral   C/BC b: Furnival
The Deuce Is In Him

MON. 20 MAY

Love's Last Shift   C/BC
The Chaplet   b: Watts, Mrs. Quelch

SAT. 25 MAY

The Wonder   C/BC
Florizel and Perdita   b: Bannister, Bates

MON. 27 MAY

The Constant Couple   C/BC b: Dodd
Thomas and Sally

SAT. 1 JUNE

The Beggar's Opera   C/BC b: Keasberry
The Citizen

MON. 3 JUNE

The Refusal   C/BC b: Bryan
Catherine and Petruchio   (prompter) & Knowles
                                       (Box Book Keeper)

End of Season

Season 1765/66

Company

Mr: Arthur, Bannister, Brookes, Cecil, Dibbens, Fox, Furnival, Harper, Haughton, Keasberry, Martin, Preston, Rothery, Sherriffe, Turner, Watts.

Mrs: Keasberry, Lee, Lessingham, Martin, Quelch, Sherriffe.

Miss: Read, Reynolds.

Treasurer: Palmer.   *Box Keepers:* Fisher, Knowles.   *Prompter:* Hartley

1765

WED. 25 SEPT.

The Conscious Lovers
The Old Maid

MON. 23 DEC.

The Refusal
The Citizen

THURS. 26 DEC.

Jane Shore
The Metamorphoses of Harlequin

FRI. 27 DEC.

Hamlet
The Auricula Feast

SAT. 28 DEC.

The Country Lasses

1766

SAT. 11 JAN.

The Country Lasses   C/BC b: Arthur
The Female Fortune Teller

MON. 13 JAN.

The Jealous Wife   C/BC b: Fox
Thomas and Sally

SAT. 18 JAN.

She Wou'd And she   C/BC
  Wou'd Not   b: Mrs. Lessingham
The Englishman in Paris

MON. 20 JAN.

Hamlet   C/BC, BJ
The Citizen   b: Sherriffe

WED. 22 JAN.

The Beggar's Opera   C/BC, BJ
The Deuce Is In Him   b: Miss Read

SAT. 25 JAN.

All In The Wrong   C/BC, BJ b: Mrs. Lee
The Mayor of Garret

MON. 27 JAN.

The Funeral   C/BC b: Miss Reynolds
Farce

SAT. 1 FEB.

Love's Last Shift   C/BC b: Keasberry
Catherine and Petruchio

MON. 3 FEB.

The Double Gallant   C/BC,BJ b: Preston
The Lying Valet

WED. 5 FEB.

As You Like It   C/BC, BJ
The Author   b: Brookes

SAT. 8 FEB.

Love Makes a Man   C/BC b: Haughton
The Chaplet

SAT. 15 FEB.

The Lady's Last Stake   C/BC b: Bannister
Florizel and Perdita

TUE. 18 FEB.

The Merchant of Venice   C/BC b: Dibbens

TUE. 25 FEB.

Othello   C/BC, BJ b: Furnival
The Author

SAT. 1 MAR.

The Constant Couple   C/BC
The Devil to Pay   b: Mrs. Keasberry

TUE. 4 MAR.

Richard III   C/BC, BJ
The Englishman In Paris   b: Sherriffe

SAT. 8 MAR.

The Lady's Last Stake   C/BC, BJ
Thomas and Sally   b: Hartley, Knowles

SAT. 15 MAR.

The Jealous Wife   C/BC, BJ b: Watts
The Lying Valet

TUE. 18 MAR.

The Beggar's Opera   C/BC, BJ b: Fisher
Catherine and Petruchio

SAT. 22 MAR.

The Foundling   C/BC, BJ b: Palmer
Thomas and Sally

Being the last night of performing till the holidays.

MON. 31 MAR.

The Merchant of Venice
The Auricula Feast

TUES. 1 APRIL

Romeo and Juliet
The Metamorphoses of Harlequin

WED. 2 APRIL

Love in a Village

SAT. 3 MAY

The Double Gallant   C/BC b: Arthur
The Auricula Feast

MON. 5 MAY

Jane Shore   C/BC
The Guardian   b: Mrs. Lessingham

THURS. 8 MAY

The Foundling   C/BJ b: Miss Read
Thomas and Sally

SAT. 10 MAY

Love's Last Shift   C/BC, BJ b: Sherriffe
The Author

MON. 12 MAY

The Beggar's Opera   C/BC, BJ b: Keasberry
The Mayor of Garret

THURS. 15 MAY

The Country Lasses   C/BC b: Bannister
The Citizen

SAT. 17 MAY

The Constant Couple   C/BC, BJ b: Mrs. Lee
The Old Maid

MON. 19 MAY

The Refusal   C/BC b: Miss Reynolds
Miss in her Teens

THUR. 22 MAY

The Committee   C/BC, BJ b: Fox, Brookes
The Guardian

SAT. 24 MAY

She Wou'd And She Wou'd   C/BC, BJ b: Preston
   Not
Damon and Phillida

MON. 26 MAY

The Double Mistake   C/BC, BJ
Thomas and Sally   b: Mrs. Sherriffe
                   Mrs. Keasberry

WED. 28 MAY

The Distrest Mother   C/BJ
The Devil To Pay   b: Haughton, Watts

SAT. 31 MAY		**TUE. 3 JUNE**	
The Provok'd Husband	C/BC	A Bold Stroke For a Wife	C/BC, BJ
The Citizen	b: Furnival, Martin	The Mock Doctor	b: Fisher, Palmer

End of Season

Season 1766/67

Company

Mr: Adcock, Arthur, Bannister, Brookes, Furnival, Gaudry, Harper, Haughton, Keasberry, Nepecker, Reddish, Sherriffe, Watts.

Mrs: Adcock, Gordon, Keasberry, Martin, Nepecker, Quelch, Reddish, Sherriffe.

Miss: Adcock, P. Adcock, Read.

Prompter: Hartley.

No announcements have been found for the first part of this season. Simpson's Theatre was used from October — March while alterations were carried out in Orchard Street.

1767

MON. 15 JAN.
The Merchant of Venice   C/BC b: Arthur
The Virgin Unmask'd

THURS. 22 JAN.
The Country Lasses   C/BC b: Keasberry
Thomas and Sally

SAT. 24 JAN.
The Jealous Wife   C/BC b: Bannister
Polly Honeycombe

MON. 26 JAN.
Macbeth   C/BC b: Adcock

SAT. 31 JAN.
The Clandestine Marriage   C/BC b: Sherriffe
The Devil To Pay

MON. 2 FEB.
The Merry Wives of Windsor   C/BC b: Brookes
The Virgin Unmask'd

THURS. 5 FEB.
Venice Preserv'd   C/BC
The Chaplet   b: Mrs. Keasberry

SAT. 7 FEB.
The Suspicious Husband   C/BC b: Furnival
High Life Below Stairs

MON. 9 FEB.
The Orphan   C/BC b: Mrs Sherriffe
Florizel and Perdita

SAT. 14 FEB.
The Beggar's Opera   C/BC b: Mr. &
The Old Maid   Mrs. Nepecker

MON. 16 FEB.
King Richard III   C/BC b: Mrs. Adcock
The Deuce is in him

SAT. 21 FEB.
The Merchant of Venice   C/BC b: Hartley
The Citizen   (Prompter) & Gaudry

MON. 23 FEB.
The Pilgrim   C/BC b: Harper
Florizel and Perdita

SAT. 28 MARCH
The Orchard Street Theatre reopened after alterations. A Prologue for the occasion spoken by Arthur.

MON. 20 APRIL
All in the Wrong   C/BC
The Metamorphoses of Harlequin

TUES. 21 APRIL
Jane Shore   C/BC
The Metamorphoses of Harlequin

WED. 22 APRIL
The Maid of the Mill   C/BC
Miss in her Teens

THURS. 23 APRIL
Romeo and Juliet   C/BC

SAT. 2 MAY
Love in a Village   C/BC b: Arthur
The What-d-ye-Call It

MON. 4 MAY
Venice Preserv'd   C/BC b; Reddish
Miss in her Teens

SAT. 9 MAY
The Funeral   C/BC b: Mrs. Sherriffe
Thomas and Sally

MON. 12 MAY
The English Merchant   C/BC b: Miss Read
The Deuce is in Him

SAT. 16 MAY
The Conscious Lovers   C/BC b: Miss Adcock
Miss in her Teens

MON. 18 MAY
The Foundling   C/BC b: Mrs Reddish
The Old Maid

SAT. 23 MAY
The Clandestine Marriage C/BC b: Mrs. Keasberry
The Citizen   & Mr. Sherriffe

THURS. 28 MAY
As You Like It   C/BC b: Furnival &
The Mayor of Garret   Haughton

SAT. 30 MAY
The English Merchant   C/BC b: Watts &
Polly Honeycombe   Mrs. Martin

End of Season

Season 1767/68

Company

Mr: Arthur, Baker, Brooks, Collins, Didier, Furnival, Gaudry, Harper, Haughton, Keasberry, Salisbury, Sherriffe, Watts, Wayte, Wood.

Mrs: Didier, Keasberry, Kirby, Martin, Phillips, Sherriffe, Wood, Wortley.

Miss: Read, Wood.

Treasurer: Palmer   *Box Book Keeper:* Fisher   *Prompter:* Hartley

1767

SAT. 26 SEPT.
The Clandestine Marriage   C/BC
Lethe

MON. 28 SEPT.
Beggars Opera   C/BC
Lethe

WED. 7 OCT.
The Conscious Lovers   C/BC
The Devil to Pay

SAT. 10 OCT.
The English Merchant   C/BC
The Honest Yorkshireman

MON. 12 OCT.
The Busybody   C/BC
The Anatomist

THURS. 15 OCT.
As You Like It   C/BC
Catherine and Petruchio

SAT. 17 OCT.
The Clandestine Marriage
The Contrivances

MON. 19 OCT.
Love Makes a Man, or the
Fop's Fortune   C/BC
The Old Maid

THURS. 22 OCT.
The Jealous Wife   C/BC
High Life Below Stairs

SAT. 24 OCT.
The Miser
The Lottery

MON. 26 OCT.
The Earl of Warwick
The Lottery

THURS. 29 OCT.
As You Like It
The Mayor of Garret

SAT. 31 OCT.

The Kind Imposter   C/BC
The Mayor of Garret

THURS. 5 NOV.

The Beaux Stratagem
The Citizen

SAT. 7 NOV.

The Refusal
The Contrivances

MON. 9 NOV.

The Earl of Warwick   C/BC
The Lying Valet

WED. 11 NOV.

The English Merchant   C/BC
Florizel and Perdita

SAT. 14 NOV.

Maid of the Mill   C/BC
Miss in her Teens

MON. 16 NOV.

The Mayor of Garret
The Devil to Pay

THURS. 19 NOV.

Love in a Village   C/BC
The King and the Miller of
Mansfield

SAT. 21 NOV.

The Conscious Lovers   C/BC
The Chaplet

MON. 23 NOV.

Hamlet   C/BC
The Honest Yorkshireman

WED. 25 NOV.

The Clandestine Marriage   C/BC
Thomas and Sally

SAT. 28 NOV.

The Foundling   C/BC
The Deuce is in Him

MON. 30 NOV.

King Lear   C/BC
The Lottery

THURS. 3 DEC.

Maid of the Mill   C/BC
The Anatomist

SAT. 5 DEC.

The Double Gallant   C/BC
Thomas and Sally

MON. 7 DEC.

As You Like It
The Chaplet

WED. 9 DEC.

Love in a Village
Lethe

SAT. 12 DEC.

The Provok'd Husband   C/BC
The Contrivances

MON. 14 DEC.

The Clandestine Marriage   C/BC
Florizel and Perdita

THURS. 17 DEC.

The Rehearsal   C/BC
The Honest Yorkshireman

SAT. 19 DEC.

The Jealous Wife   C/BC
The Citizen

MON. 21 DEC.

The Rehearsal   C/BC
Damon and Phillida

WED. 23 DEC.

The Kind Imposter   C/BC
Thomas and Sally

SAT. 26 DEC.

The English Merchant   C/BC
Midas

1768

THURS. 4 FEB.

The Maid of the Mill   C/BJ b: Keasberry
Lethe

SAT. 6 FEB.

Love in a Village   C/BJ b: Miss Read
Farce

MON. 8 FEB.

The Clandestine Marriage   C/BJ b: Mrs Sherriffe
The Metamorphoses of
Harlequin

THURS. 11 FEB.

The Suspicious Husband   C/BC b: Mr. &
Polly Honeycombe   Mrs. Didier

In 1768 the Orchard Street Theatre received its
Royal Patent. This is referred to in BJ, 1 Feb.
1768, in an extract from the **London Gazette**,
as having been given the Royal Assent at Westminster
on 29 Jan. 1768. The first notice of the "Theatre
Royal", and referring to the company as "His
Majesty's Servants", occurs on 28 April 1768.

THURS. 28 APRIL

She Wou'd and She Wou'd   C/BJ b: Furnival
  Not
The Deuce is in Him

SAT. 30 APRIL

Love in a Village   C/BJ b: Mrs. Keasberry

MON. 2 MAY

False Delicacy   C/BJ b: Mr. &
The Citizen   Mrs. Sherriffe

SAT. 7 MAY

The Jealous Wife   C/BC b: Mr. &
Lethe   Mrs. Didier

MON. 9 MAY

The Clandestine Marriage   C/BC b: Brookes
Thomas and Sally

THURS. 12 MAY

The Beggar's Opera   C/BC b: Mrs. Phillips
The Old Maid

SAT. 14 MAY

Love in a Village   C/BC b: Mr. Mrs.
The What d'Ye Call It   & Miss Wood

MON. 16 MAY

The Provok'd Husband   C/BC b: Harper

WED. 18 MAY

Hamlet   C/BJ
The Metamorphoses of   b: Hartley (Prompter)
  Harlequin   & Wayte

MON. 30 MAY

Hamlet   C/BJ
The Lyar

WED. 1 JUNE

Love in a Village   C/BC b: Watts
The Lyar

SAT. 4 JUNE

False Delicacy   C/BJ
The Metamorphoses of   b: Palmer (Treasurer)
  Harlequin   & Fisher (Box Book
                                Keeper)

End of Season

Season 1768/69

Company

Mr: Brookes, Didier, Edwin, Floor, Furnival, Gaudrey, Guion, Harper, Haughton, Keasberry, Lee, Moor, Richards, Sherriffe, Watts, Wood.

Mrs: Didier, Glover, Keasberry, Kirby, Lee, Mahon, Martin, Sherriffe, Sherwood, Wood.

Miss: Willoughby, Wood.

Treasurer: Palmer   *Box Book Keeper:* Fisher

1768

SAT. 24 SEPT.

The Rehearsal
The Honest Yorkshireman

MON. 26 SEPT.

King Richard II
The King and The Miller of
Mansfield

SAT. 1 OCT.

The Rehearsal
The Honest Yorkshireman

MON. 3 OCT.

A Bold Stroke for a Wife
The Virgin Unmask'd

MON. 10 OCT.

The Recruiting Officer
The Old Maid

MON. 17 OCT.

The Busy-Body
The Intriguing Chamber-Maid

MON. 24 OCT.

The Foundling
The Devil to Pay

MON. 31 OCT.

Love in a Village
The King and The Miller of
Mansfield

MON. 7 NOV.
The Maid of the Mill
The Old Maid

MON. 14 NOV.
Oroonoko
Miss in her Teens

MON. 21 NOV.
The Beggar's Opera
Lethe

MON. 28 NOV.
Love in a Village
The Mock Doctor

MON. 5 DEC.
The Maid of the Mill
Polly Honeycombe

MON. 12 DEC.
The Rehearsal
The Deuce is in Him

MON. 19 DEC.
The Conscious Lovers
The Musical Lady

MON. 26 DEC.
George Barnwell
The Honest Yorkshireman

1769

MON. 2 JAN.
All in the Wrong
The Intriguing Chamber-Maid

MON. 9 JAN.
The Suspicious Husband
The Apprentice

MON. 16 JAN.
Macbeth
The Virgin Unmask'd

MON. 23 JAN.
Macbeth   C/BJ, BC b: Mrs Lee
Flora, or Hob in the Well

THURS. 26 JAN.
The Clandestine Marriage   C/BC b: Gaudrey
Thomas and Sally

SAT. 28 JAN.
The Provok'd Husband   C/BC, BJ, G
Phoebe   b: Keasberry

WED. 1 FEB.
Much Ado About Nothing   C/BC, BJ
The Upholsterer   b: Sherriffe

SAT. 4 FEB.
Love in a Village   C/BC, BJ
The Citizen   b: Mrs Didier

TUES. 7 FEB.
The Inconstant   C/BJ, BC
Florizel and Perdita   b: Palmer & Fisher

TUES. 21 FEB.
The Way to Keep Him
Phoebe

TUES. 28 FEB.
The Maid of the Mill
The Virgin Unmask'd

TUES. 7 MAR.
Love in a Village
Polly Honeycombe

TUES. 14 MAR.
Hamlet
High Life Below Stairs

MON. 27 MAR.
King Richard III
Daphne and Amintor

MON. 3 APR.
The Clandestine Marriage
Daphne and Amintor

MON. 10 APRIL
The Inconstant
Thomas and Sally

MON. 17 APRIL
The Beggar's Opera
Flora

MON. 24 APRIL
Macbeth
The Padlock

SAT. 29 APRIL
The School for Lovers   C/BC b: Lee
High Life Below Stairs

MON. 1 MAY
The Lady's Last Stake   C/BC
Daphne and Amintor   b: Mrs Keasberry

THURS. 4 MAY
The Maid of the Mill   C/BC, BJ
The Intriguing Chamber-Maid   b: Mrs. Sherriffe

SAT. 6 MAY
Love in a Village   C/BJ b: Mrs Mahon
The Intriguing Chamber-Maid

MON. 8 MAY
Merry Wives of Windsor   C/BC b: Didier
Thomas and Sally

WED. 10 MAY
The Suspicious Husband   C/BJ b: Furnival
Daphne and Amintor

SAT. 13 MAY
The Clandestine Marriage   C/BC, BJ
The Chaplet   b: Mrs Glover,
                                            Mrs Martin

MON. 15 MAY
The Miser   C/BJ, BC b: Edwin
The Musical Lady

THURS. 18 MAY
The Fair Quaker of Deal   C/BJ, BC
Daphne and Amintor   b: Haughton

SAT. 20 MAY
Love Makes a Man   C/BJ, BC
Thomas and Sally   b: Guion & Moor

MON. 22 MAY
Love in a Village   C/BJ, BC b: Brookes
The Lying Valet

SAT. 27 MAY
Macbeth   C/BC b: Watts
The Guardian

MON. 29 MAY
The Beggar's Opera   C/BC
The Citizen   b: Mr. & Mrs. Wood

WED. 31 MAY
The Constant Couple   C/BJ
The Intriguing Chamber-Maid b: Palmer & Fisher

End of Season

Season 1769/70

Company

Mr: Brookes, Cooke, Didier, Edwin, Floor, Furnival, Gaudry, Giles, Guion, Harper, Haughton, Keasberry, Lee, Moor, Pyne, Sherriffe, Summers, Watts.

Mrs: Didier, Farran, Keasberry, Kirby, Lee, Martin, Pyne, Read, Sherriffe, Summers.

Miss: Farran, Summers.

Treasurer: Palmer   *Box Book Keeper:* Fisher   *Prompter:* Floor

1769

SAT. 23 SEPT.
The Busybody   C/BC
Entertainments

MON. 25 SEPT.
Love Makes a Man   C/BJ
The Chaplet

THURS. 28 SEPT.
Hamlet   C/BC
Polly Honeycombe

MON. 2 OCT.
The Suspicious Husband   C/BJ
Florizel and Perdita

SAT. 7 OCT.
The Inconstant   C/BC
High Life Below Stairs

MON. 9 OCT.
The Constant Couple
The Devil to Pay   C/BJ

THURS. 12 OCT.
Macbeth   C/BC
The Virgin Unmask'd

MON. 16 OCT.
The Recruiting Officer   C/BJ
Catherine and Petruchio

THURS. 19 OCT.
The Clandestine Marriage   C/BC
The Lying Valet

MON. 23 OCT.
The Beggar's Opera   C/BJ
The Intriguing Chamber-Maid

SAT. 28 OCT.
The Rehearsal   C/BC
The Contrivances

MON. 30 OCT.
Hamlet   C/BJ
Phoebe

SAT. 4 NOV.
The Foundling   C/BC
The Padlock

MON. 6 NOV.
The Provok'd Wife   C/BJ
The Padlock

THURS. 9 NOV.
Much Ado About Nothing   C/BC
The Padlock

MON. 13 NOV.
Love in a Village   C/BJ
The Deuce is in Him

SAT. 18 NOV.
The School for Lovers   C/BC
The Padlock

MON. 20 NOV.
The Merry Wives of Windsor C/BJ
The Intriguing Chambermaid

SAT. 25 NOV.
The Way to Keep Him   C/BC
Thomas and Sally

MON. 27 NOV.
The Beggar's Opera   C/BC
The Lyar

SAT. 2 DEC.
The Wonder   C/BC
Daphne and Amintor

MON. 4 DEC.
The Funeral   C/BJ
Daphne and Amintor

THURS. 7 DEC.
The Good Natur'd Man   C/BC
The Citizen

MON. 11 DEC.
The Good Natur'd Man   C/BJ
The Padlock

SAT. 16 DEC.
The Clandestine Marriage   C/BC
The Author

MON. 18 DEC.
A Bold Stroke for a Wife   C/BJ
The Padlock

THURS. 21 DEC.
The Good Natur'd Man   C/BC
Trick upon Trick

TUES. 26 DEC.
The London Merchant   C/BJ
Trick upon Trick

THURS. 28 DEC.
Lionel and Clarissa   C/BC
Trick upon Trick

1770

MON. 1 JAN.
Love in a Village   C/BJ
Trick upon Trick

SAT. 6 JAN.
The Inconstant   C/BC
Catherine and Petruchio

MON. 8 JAN.
The Brothers   C/BJ
The Citizen

THURS. 11 JAN.
The Brothers   C/BC
The Author

MON. 15 JAN.
Douglas   C/BJ
Trick upon Trick

SAT. 20 JAN.
The Way to Keep Him   C/BC
The Lyar

MON. 22 JAN.
Hamlet
Duke and No Duke

MON. 29 JAN.
The Way to Keep Him   C/BJ b: Lee
The Absent Man

THURS. 1 FEB.
The Widow'd Wife   C/BJ, BC b: Didier
The Musical Lady

SAT. 3 FEB.
The Good Natur'd Man   C/BJ, BC b: Keasberry
Daphne and Amintor

MON. 5 FEB.
Douglas   C/BJ, BC b: Guion
The Absent Man

WED. 7 FEB.
The Clandestine Marriage   C/BJ, BC b: Furnival
The Deuce is in Him

SAT. 10 FEB.
The School for Lovers   C/BJ, BC
Florizel and Perdita   b: Mr. & Mrs. Pyne

MON. 12 FEB.
Douglas   C/BJ, BC b: Guion
The Absent Man

THURS. 15 FEB.
The Way to Keep Him   C/BJ, BC
Daphne and Amintor   b: Mrs. Didier

SAT. 17 FEB.
The English Merchant   C/BJ, BC
The Lyar   b: Sherriffe

MON. 19 FEB.
Maid of the Mill   C/BC b: Gaudry
The Lying Valet

WED. 21 FEB.
The Brothers   C/BJ, BC b: Palmer
The Intriguing Chamber-Maid   (Treasurer), Fisher
                (Box Book Keeper)

SAT. 24 FEB.
The Jealous Wife
The Padlock

MON. 26 FEB.
Henry IV (1)
Duke and No Duke

TUES. 6 MAR.
Macbeth
The Author

TUES. 13 MAR.
Douglas
Midas

TUES. 20 MAR.
King Lear
Lethe

TUES. 27 MAR.
King Lear
The Lyar

MON. 2 APRIL
The Merry Wives of Windsor
Trick upon Trick

MON. 16 APRIL
Douglas
Trick upon Trick

MON. 23 APRIL
Maid of the Mill
The Citizen

MON. 30 APRIL
The Constant Couple
Shakespeare's Jubilee

MON. 7 MAY
Hamlet   C/BJ, BC b: Mrs. Lee
A Trip to Scotland

WED. 9 MAY
The Clandestine Marriage   C/BJ, BC
The Padlock   b: Mrs. Sherriffe

SAT. 12 MAY
The Good Natur'd Man   C/BC b: Edwin
The Mayor of Garrat

TUES. 15 MAY
The Suspicious Husband   b: Cooke, Mrs. Martin
The Trip to Scotland

THURS. 17 MAY
Henry IV (1)   C/BC b: Brookes
The Padlock

SAT. 19 MAY
Love in a Village   b: Floor & Moor
The Lyar

MON. 21 MAY
The Twin Rivals   C/FF b: Harper
Daphne and Amintor

WED. 23 MAY
The Orphan of China   b: Mrs. Keasberry
A Trip to Scotland

SAT. 26 MAY
Love for Love   b: Haughton
The Padlock

MON. 28 MAY
The Jealous Wife   b: Watt & Summers
Daphne and Amintor

WED. 30 MAY
The Funeral   b: Palmer & Fisher
A Trip to Scotland

End of Season

Season 1770/71

Company

Mr: Barrett, Brookes, Brunsdon, Death, Didier, Edwin, Floor, Furnival, Guion, Haughton, Keasberry, Knight, Lee, McGeorge, Moor, Sherriffe, Summers, Watts.

Mrs: Brunsdon, Didier, Farran, Keasberry, Lee, McGeorge, Martin, Saunders, Sherriffe, Summers.

Miss: Farran, Glassington, Summers, Townsend.

Treasurer: Palmer.   *Box Book Keeper:* Fisher.

1770

SAT. 6 OCT.
The Busybody

MON. 8 OCT.
The Merry Wives of Windsor
The Mock Doctor

MON. 15 OCT.
Hamlet
Florizel and Perdita

MON. 22 OCT.
The Conscious Lovers
The Apprentice

TUES. 30 OCT.
King Lear
The Chaplet

MON. 5 NOV.
The Inconstant Lover
Midas

MON. 12 NOV.
Douglas
Midas

MON. 19 NOV.
Macbeth
The Mock Doctor

TUES. 27 NOV.
Henry IV (I)
Thomas and Sally

MON. 3 DEC.
The Way to Keep Him
Trick Upon Trick

MON. 10 DEC.
The Beggar's Opera
The Intriguing Chambermaid

MON. 17 DEC.
Douglas
The Padlock

WED. 26 DEC.
The London Merchant
Trick Upon Trick

MON. 31 DEC.
The Clandestine Marriage
The Intriguing Chambermaid

1771

MON. 28 JAN.
King Lear   C/BC b: Lee

THURS. 31 JAN.
The Earl of Warwick   C/BC b: Guion
A Trip to Scotland

SAT. 2 FEB.
The Provok'd Husband   C/BC b: Keasberry
The Author

MON. 4 FEB.
The Jealous Wife   C/BC
                             b: Floor/Mrs Martin
Midas

MON. 6 MAY
The Countess of Salisbury   b: Mrs McGeorge

THURS. 9 MAY
The West Indian   C/BC b: Edwin
The Lyar

SAT. 11 MAY
Rule a Wife and Have a Wife   C/G b: Mrs Saunders
The Author

MON. 13 MAY
The School for Rakes   C/BC b: Furnival

THURS. 16 MAY
The West Indian
Midas   b: Moor/Brunsdon

SAT. 18 MAY
The Way to Keep Him
The Guardian   b: Keasberry

THURS. 20 MAY

The Merchant of Venice   b: Death/Barrett
Chrononhotonthologos

SAT. 25 MAY

The West Indian   b: Summers/McGeorge
The Padlock

MON. 27 MAY

The County Lasses   b: Haughton
The Lying Valet

End of Season

Season 1771/72

Company

Mr: Arthur, Barrett, Brookes, Brunsdon, Didier, Edwin, Floor, Furnival, Haughton, Keasberry, Moor, Penn, Robson, Sherriffe, Stow, Summers, Watts.

Mrs: Arthur, Didier, Keasberry, Martin, Saunders, Sherriffe, Summers.

Miss: Curtis, Summers, Townshend.

Master: Deneuville.

Treasurer: Palmer   *Box Book Keeper:* Fisher.

1771

THURS. 3 OCT.

The Busybody
The Lyar

SAT. 5 OCT.

As You Like It   PB/Ba
The Old Maid

THURS. 10 OCT.

The Merchant of Venice   PB/Ba
The Lyar

SAT. 12 OCT.

The English Merchant   PB/Ba
Midas

THURS. 17 OCT.

The Suspicious Husband
Midas

SAT. 19 OCT.

The Maid of the Mill
The Deuce is in Him
Allemande

THURS. 24 OCT.

Lionel and Clarissa
The Apprentice

SAT. 26 OCT.

The School for Lovers
The Chaplet
Allemande

MON. 28 OCT.

The Conscious Lovers
Daphne and Amintor

THURS. 31 OCT.

The Provok'd Husband
The Padlock

SAT. 2 NOV.

Rule a Wife and Have a Wife

THURS. 7 NOV.

Oroonoko
The Musical Lady

SAT. 9 NOV.

The West Indian
The Ghost

THURS. 14 NOV.

Oronooko
The Commissary

SAT. 16 NOV.

False Delicacy

TUES. 19 NOV.

The Maid of the Mill

THURS. 21 NOV.

The Jealous Wife
The Capricious Lovers

SAT. 23 NOV.

The Foundling

THURS. 28 NOV.
Love in a Village
The Commissary

SAT. 30 NOV.
The Clandestine Marriage
The Capricious Lovers

THURS. 5 DEC.
Romeo and Juliet
The Ghost

SAT. 7 DEC.
Lionel and Clarissa
The Lyar

TUES. 10 DEC.
The Good Natured Man
The Capricious Lovers

THURS. 12 DEC.
The Wonder
The Padlock

SAT. 14 DEC.
All in the Wrong

TUES. 17 DEC.
As You Like It
The Capricious Lovers

THURS. 19 DEC.
Rule a Wife and Have a Wife
The Old Maid
Allemande

SAT. 21 DEC.
The English Merchant
The Capricious Lovers

THURS. 26 DEC.
The Maid of the Mill
Trick upon Trick

FRI. 27 DEC.
George Barnwell
Trick upon Trick

SAT. 28 DEC.
The Way to Keep Him

MON. 30 DEC.
Romeo and Juliet

1772

THURS. 2 JAN.
The Merchant of Venice
The Ladies' Frolick

SAT. 4 JAN.
The Jealous Wife

TUES. 7 JAN.
The West Indian
Trick upon Trick

THURS. 9 JAN.
Much Ado About Nothing
The Ladies' Frolick

SAT. 11 JAN.
The Beggar's Opera
Neck or Nothing

TUES. 14 JAN.
Cyrus
Trick upon Trick

THURS. 16 JAN.
Much Ado about Nothing
The Ladies' Frolick

SAT. 18 JAN.
Love in a Village

MON. 20 JAN.
Oroonoko
The Recruiting Sergeant
Like Master, Like Man

TUES. 21 JAN.
Rule a Wife and Have a Wife
The Ladies' Frolick

THURS. 23 JAN.
Maid of the Mill
Neck or Nothing

SAT. 25 JAN.
The West Indian
The Capricious Lovers

TUES. 28 JAN.
Love in a Village   C/BJ b: Mrs. Arthur
The Guardian

WED. 29 JAN.
Douglas   b: Keasberry
Like Master, Like Man

SAT. 1 FEB.
False Delicacy   C/BC, BJ
Midas   b: Keasberry

TUES. 4 FEB.
The Funeral   C/BJ b: Edwin
The Capricious Lovers

THURS. 6 FEB.
Jane Shore   C/BJ, BC
The Padlock   b: Mrs. Saunders

SAT. 8 FEB.

The Way to Keep Him   C/BJ, BC
The Commissary   b: Mrs. Didier

TUES. 11 FEB.

The Conscious Lovers   C/BJ
The Capricious Lovers   b: Miss Townshend

THURS. 13 FEB.

Cyrus   C/BJ, BC
The Ladies' Frolick   b: Sherriffe

SAT. 15 FEB.

The Provok'd Husband   C/BJ, BC
The Devil to Pay   b: Robson

TUES. 18 FEB.

The Conscious Lovers   C/BJ, BC
The Capricious Lovers   b: Miss Townshend

THURS. 20 FEB.

Cyrus   C/BJ b: Sherriffe
The Ladies' Frolick

SAT. 22 FEB.

The Maid of the Mill   C/BJ, BC b: Robson
The Lyar

TUES. 25 FEB.

The West Indian   C/BJ
                 b: Master Deneuville
                   & Miss Curtis
The Capricious Lovers

THURS. 27 FEB.

As You Like It   C/BJ, BC
The Ladies' Frolick   b: Palmer & Fisher

SAT. 29 FEB.

The Provok'd Husband

TUES. 3 MAR.

Cymbeline
The Mock Doctor

THURS. 5 MAR.

Cymbeline
Harlequin's Metamorphoses

SAT. 7 MAR.

Lionel and Clarissa
The Old Maid

TUES. 10 MAR.

Much Ado About Nothing
The Capricious Lovers

SAT. 14 MAR.

Love in a Village
Trick Upon Trick

MON. 16 MAR.

Cymbeline
The Recruiting Sergeant
Like Master, Like Man

TUES. 17 MAR.

The Fashionable Lover
The Old Maid

SAT. 21 MAR.

The Clandestine Marriage
Harlequin's Metamorphoses

TUES. 24 MAR.

The Fashionable Lover
The Musical Lady

THURS. 26 MAR.

Jane Shore
Harlequin's Metamorphosis

SAT. 28 MAR.

The West Indian

TUES. 31 MAR.

The Fashionable Lover
The Capricious Lovers

THURS. 2 APRIL

Cymbeline
Harlequin at Stockwell

SAT. 4 APRIL

The Jealous Wife
The Shepherds' Lottery

TUES. 7 APRIL

The Fashionable Lover
The Shepherds' Lottery

THURS. 9 APRIL

The Grecian Daughter
High Life Below Stairs

SAT. 11 APRIL

The Way to Keep Him
Harlequin at Stockwell

MON. 20 APRIL

Cymbeline
Harlequin at Stockwell

TUES. 21 APRIL

The Fashionable Lover
The Shepherds' Lottery

WED. 22 APRIL

The Grecian Daughter
Harlequin at Stockwell

THURS. 23 APRIL

The Maid of the Mill
The Commissary

SAT. 25 APRIL

The English Merchant
The Padlock

TUES. 28 APRIL

Love in a Village
The Old Maid

WED. 29 APRIL

The Grecian Daughter
The Shepherds' Lottery

THURS. 30 APRIL

A Word to the Wise
Harlequin at Stockwell

SAT. 2 MAY

The Fashionable Lover
The Capricious Lovers

TUES. 5 MAY

A Word to the Wise
Harlequin at Stockwell

THURS. 7 MAY

The Fair Penitent   C/BJ, BC
Daphne and Amintor   b: Mrs. Arthur

SAT. 9 MAY

The Grecian Daughter   C/BJ, BC
The Shepherd's Lottery   b: Mrs. Keasberry

TUES. 12 MAY

A Word to the Wise   C/BJ b: Didier
The Capricious Lovers

THURS. 14 MAY

The Fashionable Lover   C/BJ b: Furnival
Thomas and Sally

SAT. 16 MAY

The West Indian   C/BJ b: Mrs Sherriffe
Midas

TUES. 19 MAY

A Word to the Wise   C/BJ b: Brunsdon &
The Devil to Pay   Barrett

THURS. 21 MAY

Love in a Village   C/BJ, BC
The Lying Valet   b: Brookes

SAT. 23 MAY

The Fashionable Lover   C/BC, b: Floor &
The Capricious Lovers   Mrs. Martin

TUES. 26 MAY

A Word to the Wise   C/BJ b: Moor
Midas   and Summers

THURS. 28 MAY

The Beggar's Opera   C/BJ b: Stow
The Ghost

SAT. 30 MAY

As You Like It   C/BJ b: Haughton
The Capricious Lovers

MON. 1 JUNE

Romeo and Juliet   C/BJ b: Penn & Watts
The Ladies' Frolick

WED. 3 JUNE

The Wonder . .   C/BJ
The Ghost   b: Palmer & Fisher

SAT. 6 JUNE

Cymbeline
Harlequin at Stockwell

End of Season

Season 1772/73

Company

Mr: Barrett, Brookes, Didier, Edwin, Egan, Floor, Furnival, Haughton, Henderson (Courtenay), Jackson, Keasberry, Moor, Robson, Sherriffe, Summers, Watts.

Mrs: Arthur, Didier, Keasberry, Martin, Sherriffe, Summers, Taylor, Ward.

Miss: Curtis, Summers, Townshend.

Master: Deneuville, Summers.

Treasurer: Palmer. *Box Book Keeper:* Fisher.

1772

MON. 21 SEPT.
The Maid of the Mill
The Old Maid

TUES. 22 SEPT.
As You Like It
Harlequin at Stockwell

WED. 23 SEPT.
A Word to the Wise
The Capricious Lovers

THURS. 24 SEPT.
The Fashionable Lover
Harlequin at Stockwell

SAT. 26 SEPT.
The Way to Keep Him

TUES. 29 SEPT.
Cymbeline
The Ghost

THURS. 1 OCT.
A Word to the Wise
The Old Maid

SAT. 3 OCT.
The Fashionable Lover
The Capricious Lovers

TUES. 6 OCT.
Hamlet   C/G Henderson's first
The Ladies' Frolick   appearance as "a
       young gentleman"

THURS. 8 OCT.
The West Indian
The Padlock

SAT. 10 OCT.
Love in a Village
The Lyar

TUES. 13 OCT.
Hamlet   C/G
The Mock Doctor

THURS. 15 OCT.
The Busy Body
Shakespeare's Jubilee

SAT. 17 OCT.
The Clandestine Marriage

TUES. 20 OCT.
Richard III   C/G
The Citizen

THURS. 22 OCT.
A Word to the Wise
The Capricious Lovers

SAT. 24 OCT.
Twelfth Night
The Shepherds' Lottery

TUES. 27 OCT.
Much Ado About Nothing C/BJ
High Life Below Stairs

THURS. 29 OCT.
Twelfth Night   C/G, BC
Shakespeare's Jubilee

SAT. 31 OCT.
The Beggar's Opera C/BJ
The Author

TUES. 3 NOV.
Richard III   C/G, BC
The Shepherds' Lottery

THURS. 5 NOV.
Much Ado About Nothing C/G
The Commissary

SAT. 7 NOV.
The Wonder

TUES. 10 NOV.
A Word to the Wise
The Padlock

THURS. 12 NOV.
Macbeth   C/G, BC, BJ
The Old Maid

SAT. 14 NOV.
The Fashionable Lover
The Recruiting Sergeant
The Ghost

TUES. 17 NOV.
Macbeth   C/G
High Life Below Stairs

THURS. 19 NOV.
The Maid of the Mill
The Commissary

SAT. 21 NOV.
Every Man in His Humour   C/G
The Capricious Lovers

TUES. 24 NOV.
Hamlet   C/G
Harlequin at Stockwell

THURS. 26 NOV.
A Word to the Wise
Harlequin at Stockwell

SAT. 28 NOV.
The Rehearsal   C/G, BC, BJ
The Citizen

TUES. 1 DEC.
Every Man in His Humour or
Macbeth   C/G
The Irish Widow

THURS. 3 DEC.
The Grecian Daughter
The Irish Widow

SAT. 5 DEC.
Rule a Wife and Have a Wife

TUES. 8 DEC.
The Rehearsal   C/G
The Irish Widow

WED. 9 DEC.
The West Indian
The Jubilee

THURS. 10 DEC.
Cymbeline
The Irish Widow

SAT. 12 DEC.
The Wonder   C/G
The Capricious Lovers

TUES. 15 DEC.
Every Man in His Humour   C/G
The Commissary

WED. 16 DEC.
A Word to the Wise
Harlequin at Stockwell

THURS. 17 DEC.
The Earl of Essex   C/G
The Irish Widow

SAT. 19 DEC.
Much Ado About Nothing   C/G
The Ghost
The Recruiting Sergeant

TUES. 22 DEC.
Hamlet   C/G, BJ
The Irish Widow

WED. 23 DEC.
She Wou'd and She Wou'd Not
Midas

SAT. 26 DEC.
Henry IV   C/G, BC "Courtenay"
Cross Purposes   first announced
                               as Henderson.

MON. 28 DEC.
George Barnwell
Harlequin at Stockwell

TUES. 29 DEC.
The Earl of Essex   C/G
Cross Purposes

WED. 30 DEC.
The Fashionable Lover   C/G
Shakespeare's Jubilee

THURS. 31 DEC.
The Clandestine Marriage
Cross Purposes

1773

SAT. 2 JAN.
The Rehearsal   C/G
Midas

TUES. 5 JAN.
Macbeth   C/G
Harlequin at Stockwell

THURS. 7 JAN.
Every Man in His Humour   C/G
Cross Purposes

SAT. 9 JAN.
She Wou'd and She Wou'd Not
Miss in Her Teens   C/G

TUES. 12 JAN.
Richard III   C/G
The Irish Widow

WED. 13 JAN.
A Word to the Wise
The Old Maid

THURS. 14 JAN.
The Earl of Essex   C/G
Harlequin at Stockwell

SAT. 16 JAN.
Henry IV   C/G
Cross Purposes

TUES. 19 JAN.
Hamlet   C/G
The Unequal Match

THURS. 21 JAN.
The Rehearsal   C/G
Cross Purposes

SAT. 23 JAN.
Much Ado About Nothing   C/G

TUES. 26 JAN.
Macbeth   C/BJ, G b: Keasberry
The Irish Widow

THURS. 28 JAN.
Hamlet   C/BJ, BC, G
The Lyar   b: Brookes

TUES. 2 FEB.
Richard III   C/BJ, BC b: Henderson
Cross Purposes

THURS. 4 FEB.
A Word to the Wise   C/BC
The Commissary   b: Floor &
                Mrs Martin

FRI. 5 FEB.
The Way to Keep him
Cross Purposes

SAT. 6 FEB.
The Grecian Daughter   C/BJ, C/BC
The Capricious Lovers   b: Robson

TUES. 9 FEB.
The Jealous Wife   C/BJ b: Mrs Didier
The Irish Widow

THURS. 11 FEB.
The Rehearsal   C/BJ, G, BC
                b: Master Deneuville
                   & Miss Curtis
Cross Purposes

SAT. 13 FEB.
Hamlet   C/BJ, BC
The Padlock   b: Mrs Sherriffe

TUES. 16 FEB.
The Earl of Warwick   C/BJ, G
                b: Miss Townshend

THURS. 18 FEB.
Much Ado About Nothing   C/BJ, G, BC
                b: Palmer & Fisher

SAT. 20 FEB.
King Lear   C/G, BC
The Lying Valet

TUES. 23 FEB.
Macbeth   C/G
The Contrivances

THURS. 25 FEB.
Rule a Wife and Have a Wife
The Musical Lady

SAT. 27 FEB.
The Discovery
(Sgr. Ferci — Tight Rope — appears throughout March)

TUES. 2 MAR.
The Rehearsal   C/G
Cross Purposes

THURS. 4 MAR.
King Lear   C/G
The Ghost

SAT. 6 MAR.
Every Man in His Humour   C/G
The Irish Widow

TUES. 9 MAR.
Henry IV   C/G
Cross Purposes

THURS. 11 MAR.
Richard III   C/G
Like Master, Like Man

SAT. 13 MAR.
The West Indian
Harlequin at Stockwell

TUES. 16 MAR.
Jane Shore   C/G
Cross Purposes

THURS. 18 MAR.
The English Merchant
The Citizen

SAT. 20 MAR.
The Earl of Essex
The Irish Widow

TUES. 23 MAR.
The Discovery
Cross Purposes

THURS. 25 MAR.
Love in a Village   C/BJ, G, BC
The Irish Widow

SAT. 27 MAR.
Much Ado About Nothing   C/G
The Wedding Ring

TUES. 30 MAR.
King Lear   C/G
The Wedding Ring

THURS. 1 APRIL
Alonzo   C/G
Harlequin at Stockwell

SAT. 3 APRIL
Alonzo   C/G
The Wedding Ring

MON. 12 APRIL
Alonzo
Harlequin at Stockwell

TUES. 13 APRIL
Love in a Village
The Irish Widow

WED. 14 APRIL
Macbeth   C/G
The Wedding Ring

THURS. 15 APRIL
She Stoops to Conquer   C/G
The Padlock

FRI. 16 APRIL
She Stoops to Conquer
Shakespeare's Jubilee

SAT. 17 APRIL
The Maid of the Mill

TUES. 20 APRIL
Alzuma   C/G
The Wedding Ring

WED. 21 APRIL
Hamlet
Cross Purposes

THURS. 22 APRIL
She Stoops to Conquer
The Capricious Lovers

SAT. 24 APRIL
Alzuma
The Irish Widow

TUES. 27 APRIL
She Stoops to Conquer
The Shepherds' Lottery

WED. 28 APRIL
King Lear
Cross Purposes

THURS. 29 APRIL
The Rehearsal   C/G
The Recruiting Sergeant
The Ghost

SAT. 1 MAY
The West Indian

TUES. 4 MAY
Hamlet
Harlequin at Stockwell

THURS. 6 MAY
She Stoops to Conquer

SAT. 8 MAY
The Fashionable Lover   b: Mrs Keasberry
The Ladies' Frolick

TUES. 11 MAY
Alzuma   C/G b: Mrs Arthur
The Capricious Lovers

THURS. 13 MAY
She Stoops to Conquer   b: Sherriffe
The Wedding Ring

SAT. 15 MAY
The Stratagem   b: Edwin
The Devil to Pay

TUES. 18 MAY
Richard III   C/G b: Didier
Cross Purposes

THURS. 20 MAY
Much Ado About Nothing   C/G
The Padlock   b: Barrett &
                                 Summers

SAT. 22 MAY
Jane Shore   b: Jackson
The Recruiting Sergeant

SAT. 29 MAY
The Beggar's Opera   C/BJ b: Watts
Entertainments

TUES. 25 MAY
Hamlet   C/G, BJ b: Haughton
The Lottery

TUES. 1 JUNE
King Lear   C/G, BC, BJ
The Irish Widow   b: Palmer (Treasurer)
                                   & Fisher (Box
                                   Book Keeper)

THURS. 27 MAY
The Clandestine Marriage   C/BJ b: Egan & Moor
The Mayor of Garrett

End of Season

Season 1773/74

Company

Mr: Blisset, Brett, Brookes, Chalmers, Didier, Edwin, Egan, Floor, Haughton, Henderson, Jackson, Keasberry, Moor, Penn, Rowswell, Sherriffe, Summers, Watts.

Mrs: Delane, Didier, Keasberry, Martin, Sherriffe, Summers, Ward.

Miss: Curtis, Mansell, Summers, Wheeler.

Master: Deneuville.

1773

TUES. 14 SEPT.
Hamlet

WED. 15 SEPT.
The Rehearsal   C/G
Cross Purposes

THURS. 16 SEPT.
Richard III   C/G
The Irish Widow

FRI. 17 SEPT.
She Stoops to Conquer
The Padlock

SAT. 18 SEPT.
Much Ado About Nothing   C/G
The Commissary

WED. 22 SEPT.
The Beggar's Opera
Cross Purposes

SAT. 25 SEPT.
King Lear   C/G
Miss in her Teens

SAT. 2 OCT.
Love in a Village

TUES. 5 OCT.
Venice Preserved   C/G
Miss in her Teens

THURS. 7 OCT.
The West Indian
Cross Purposes

SAT. 9 OCT.
Macbeth   C/G
The Irish Widow

TUES. 12 OCT.
Maid of the Mill
The Musical Lady

THURS. 14 OCT.
Venice Preserved   C/G
The Recruiting Sergeant
The Ghost

SAT. 16 OCT.
Richard III   C/G
The Shepherd's Lottery

TUES. 19 OCT.
Henry IV
The Chaplet

THURS. 21 OCT.
The Maid of the Mill
Cross Purposes

SAT. 23 OCT.
The Chances   C/G

TUES. 26 OCT.
Hamlet   C/G
Daphne and Amintor

THURS. 28 OCT.
The Chances   C/G
The Lyar

SAT. 30 OCT.
The Jealous Wife
Shakespeare's Jubilee

TUES. 2 NOV.
Much Ado About Nothing C/G
The Recruiting Sergeant
The Ghost

THURS. 4 NOV.
King Lear
Daphne and Amintor

SAT. 6 NOV.
The Rehearsal   C/G

TUES. 9 NOV.
Comus   C/G
The Old Maid

THURS. 11 NOV.
Comus
High Life Below Stairs

SAT. 13 NOV.
Othello   PB/F C/G
The Irish Widow

TUES. 16 NOV.
Comus   C/G
Miss in her Teens

THURS. 18 NOV.
The Miser
The Capricious Lovers

SAT. 20 NOV.
The Fashionable Lover
The Wedding Ring

TUES. 23 NOV.
The Chances   PB/F C/G
The Irish Widow

THURS. 25 NOV.
Every Man in His Humour C/G
The Padlock

SAT. 27 NOV.
Comus   C/G
Cross Purposes

TUES. 30 NOV.
The Stratagem   C/G
The Irish Widow

WED. 1 DEC.
The West Indian
The Padlock

THURS. 2 DEC.
Oroonoko
Daphne and Amintor

SAT. 4 DEC.
Lionel and Clarissa

TUES. 7 DEC.
The Stratagem   C/G
The Capricious Lovers

THURS. 9 DEC.
Richard III   C/G
Like Master, Like Man

SAT. 11 DEC.
The Hypocrite
Thomas and Sally

TUES. 14 DEC.
The Suspicious Husband C/G
The Mock Doctor

WED. 15 DEC.
Hamlet
The Irish Widow

THURS. 16 DEC.
The Hypocrite
Daphne and Amintor

SAT. 18 DEC.
Much Ado About Nothing
The Old Maid

TUES. 21 DEC.
The Chances   C/G
Cross Purposes

WED. 22 DEC.
She Stoops to Conquer
Harlequin at Stockwell

THURS. 23 DEC.
Macbeth   C/G
The Deuce is in Him

MON. 27 DEC.
George Barnwell
Harlequin at Stockwell

TUES. 28 DEC.
Maid of the Mill   C/G
Pantomime

WED. 29 DEC.
Henry IV
The Devil to Pay

THURS. 30 DEC.
Comus   C/G
Harlequin's Metamorphoses

FRI. 31 DEC.

The Rehearsal   C/G
The Capricious Lovers

1774

SAT. 1 JAN.

The Provok'd Wife   C/G
The Citizen

FRI. 7 JAN.

Love in a Village
The Commissary

SAT. 8 JAN.

Comus   C/G
The Irish Widow

TUES. 11 JAN.

Othello
The Golden Pippin

WED. 12 JAN.

The Suspicious Husband   C/G
Pantomime

THURS. 13 JAN.

Romeo and Juliet   C/G
The Golden Pippin

SAT. 15 JAN.

The Chances
The Golden Pippin

WED. 19 JAN.

Venice Preserv'd   C/G

THURS. 20 JAN.

Comus   C/G
Pantomime

SAT. 22 JAN.

The Fashionable Lover
The Golden Pippin

TUES. 25 JAN.

The Grecian Daughter   C/BC b: Keasberry
The Capricious Lovers

SAT. 29 JAN.

Hamlet   C/BC, G
Lethe   b: Henderson

TUES. 1 FEB.

As You Like It   C/BC b: Mrs Didier
The Ladies' Frolick

THURS. 3 FEB.

Macbeth   C/G
Cross Purposes
           b: Mrs Martin &
               Mrs Delane

SAT. 5 FEB.

Lionel and Clarissa   b: Mrs Ward
Catherine and Petruchio

TUES. 8 FEB.

The Jealous Wife   b: Brett
The Wedding Ring

SAT. 12 FEB.

Richard III   C/G b: Sherriffe
The Lyar

THURS. 17 FEB.

The School for Wives   C/G
Daphne and Amintor

SAT. 19 FEB.

The Chances
The Golden Pippin

TUES. 22 FEB.

The School for Wives   C/G

THURS. 24 FEB.

King Lear
The Golden Pippin

SAT. 26 FEB.

The Stratagem
The Padlock

TUES. 29 FEB.

The School for Wives

THURS. 3 MAR.

Romeo and Juliet
The Note of Hand

SAT. 5 MAR.

She Stoops to Conquer

WED. 9 MAR.

Henry II   C/G

THURS. 10 MAR.

Comus   C/G
The Note of Hand

SAT. 12 MAR.

The Clandestine Marriage
The Portrait

THURS. 17 MAR.

The School for Wives   C/G
The Portrait

SAT. 19 MAR.

The Hypocrite   C/G
The Golden Pippin

THURS. 24 MAR.

Henry II
The Golden Pippin

SAT. 26 MAR.
The School for Wives

MON. 4 APRIL
George Barnwell
The Puppet Show

TUES. 5 APRIL
Henry II
The Portrait

WED. 6 APRIL
The Man of Business   C/G
Pantomime

THURS. 7 APRIL
Jane Shore
The Devil to Pay

FRI. 8 APRIL
The Rehearsal
The Golden Pippin

SAT. 9 APRIL
Hamlet
A Trip to Newmarket

TUES. 12 APRIL
The Man of Business   C/G

THURS. 14 APRIL
Macbeth   C/G
The Portrait

SAT. 16 APRIL
The Chances

THURS. 21 APRIL
Comus   C/G
Oxonian in Town

SAT. 23 APRIL
Much Ado About Nothing
Cross Purposes

TUES. 26 APRIL
The School for Wives   C/G

THURS. 28 APRIL
Richard III
A Trip to Newmarket

SAT. 30 APRIL
The Fashionable Lover
Shakespeare's Jubilee

TUES. 3 MAY
Every Man in his Humour   C/BC b: Edwin
The Portrait

SAT. 7 MAY
The Provok'd Wife   C/BC b: Mrs Keasberry
A Trip to Scotland

TUES. 10 MAY
The Grecian Daughter   C/BC b: Miss Mansell
The Author

SAT. 14 MAY
The Maid of the Mill   C/BC b: Didier
The Apprentice

SAT. 21 MAY
The Suspicious Husband   C/BC b: Jackson
The Irish Widow

THURS. 26 MAY
Othello   C/BC b: Haughton
The Ghost

SAT. 28 MAY
The Chances   C/BC, G
A Trip to Scotland   b: Mrs Sherriffe

TUES. 31 MAY
Much Ado About Nothing   C/BC, G b: Moor

FRI. 3 JUNE
The Revenge   C/G
The Portrait

TUES. 7 JUNE
Comus
Harlequin and Columbine

THURS. 9 JUNE
As You Like It
The Golden Pippin

SAT. 11 JUNE
The Revenge
Midas

End of Season

During this season there are frequent dancing appearances by "Master and Miss West of Covent Garden"

Season 1774/75

Company

Mr: Blisset, Brett, Brookes, Brunsdon, Didier, Dimond, Edwin, Egan, Floor, Haughton, Henderson, Jackson, Keasberry, Moor, Rowswell, Summers, G. Summers, Watts.

Mrs: Brett, Didier, Keasberry, Martin, Sherriffe, Summers, Ward, Wheeler.

Miss: Curtis, Mansell, Summers, Wheeler.

Master: Deneuville, Lewis Deneuville, Summers.

Treasurer: Palmer   *Box Book Keeper:* Fisher

1774

MON. 26 SEPT.
Macbeth
The Irish Widow

TUES. 27 SEPT.
Much Ado About Nothing
The Golden Pippin

WED. 28 SEPT.
The School for Wives   C/G
The Trip to Newmarket

THURS. 29 SEPT.
The Chances   C/G

FRI. 30 SEPT.
The Rehearsal
The Portrait

SAT. 1 OCT.
Lionel and Clarissa
The Lyar

THURS. 6 OCT.
The Suspicious Husband
The Sheperd's Lottery

SAT. 8 OCT.
The Provok'd Husband
The Padlock

THURS. 13 OCT.
The Maid of the Mill
The Citizen

SAT. 15 OCT.
The Chances   C/G
The Hob in the Well

TUES. 18 OCT.
The Wonder
Lethe

THURS. 20 OCT.
Richard III   C/G
The Register Office

SAT. 22 OCT.
The Merchant of Venice
Miss in her Teens

TUES. 25 OCT.
The Merry Wives of Windsor   C/G

THURS. 27 OCT.
Romeo and Juliet
The Waterman

SAT. 29 OCT.
The Provok'd Wife   C/G
A Trip to Scotland

THURS. 3 NOV.
The Revenge
The Golden Pippin

SAT. 5 NOV.
The Conscious Lovers
The Capricious Lovers

TUES. 8 NOV.
Henry II

THURS. 10 NOV.
She Stoops to Conquer
Hob in the Well

SAT. 12 NOV.
The Revenge
The Waterman

TUES. 15 NOV.
Macbeth
The Englishman in Paris

THURS. 17 NOV.
The Constant Couple   C/BC
A Trip to Newmarket

SAT. 19 NOV.
Much Ado About Nothing
The Register Office

(Sgt. Rossignol - until 31 Dec.)

TUES. 22 NOV.
Cymon   C/G

THURS. 24 NOV.
Cymbeline   C/BC, G
The Irish Widow

SAT. 26 NOV.
The Rehearsal   C/G
The Portrait

TUES. 29 NOV.
Cymon

THURS. 1 DEC.
Hamlet   C/G
The Waterman

SAT. 3 DEC.
The Fashionable Lover
The Ghost

TUES. 6 DEC.
Cymbeline   C/G
Miss in her Teens

THURS. 8 DEC.
The Spanish Friar
Cross Purposes

SAT. 10 DEC.
The Chances   C/G
The Golden Pippin

TUES. 13 DEC.
Cymon

THURS. 15 DEC.
The Spanish Friar
The Waterman

SAT. 17 DEC.
The West Indian
A Trip to Scotland

TUES. 20 DEC.
Hamlet   C/G

WED. 21 DEC.
The Merchant of Venice   C/G

FRI. 23 DEC.
The Constant Couple
The Deserter

MON. 26 DEC.
The Merchant of Venice   BKB
Pantomime

TUES. 27 DEC.
Comus   C/G
Pantomime

WED. 28 DEC.
Henry II   BKB
The Deserter

THURS. 29 DEC.
Lionel and Clarissa   C/G
The Commissary

SAT. 31 DEC.
The Clandestine Marriage

1775

TUES. 3 JAN.
The Spanish Friar   C/G
The Waterman

THURS. 5 JAN.
Richard III   C/G, BKB
Romance of an Hour

SAT. 7 JAN.
The West Indian   BKB
The Romance of an Hour

TUES. 10 JAN.
The Merchant of Venice   C/G
The Country Wife

THURS. 12 JAN.
The Careless Husband   C/G, BKB
The Romance of an Hour

SAT. 14 JAN.
The Chances   BKB
The Deserter

TUES. 17 JAN.
The Spanish Friar   BKB
Harlequin's Metamorphoses

THURS. 19 JAN.
King Lear
The Irish Widow

SAT. 21 JAN.
The Careless Husband
The Golden Pippin

TUES. 24 JAN.
The Fair Penitent   C/BJ, G b: Keasberry
The Waterman

THURS. 26 JAN.
The Stratagem   C/BC b: Blisset
Hob in the Well

SAT. 28 JAN.
She Wou'd and She Wou'd   C/BC b: Edwin
Not
The Deserter

TUES. 31 JAN.
The Merchant of Venice   C/BC, BJ b: Henderson
The Wedding Ring

THURS. 2 FEB.
The Spanish Friar   C/BC, BJ b: Brookes
The Portrait

SAT. 4 FEB.
The Recruiting Officer   C/BC, BJ
The Waterman   b: Mrs Didier

TUES. 7 FEB.
The Grecian Daughter   C/BC, BJ b: Mrs Brett
The Devil to Pay

THURS. 9 FEB.
King Henry II   C/BC, BJ, G
The Deserter   b: Palmer & Fisher

SAT. 11 FEB.
Cymon   BKB
The Irish Widow

TUES. 14 FEB.
The Choleric Man   C/G, BKB
The Chaplet

THURS. 16 FEB.
Hamlet   BKB
Cross Purposes

SAT. 18 FEB.
The Careless Husband
The Capricous Lovers

TUES. 21 FEB.
The Choleric Man   BKB
The Waterman

THURS. 23 FEB.
Matilda   C/G, BKB
The Deserter

SAT. 25 FEB.
Comus
The Register Office

TUES. 28 FEB.
Macbeth
The Irish Widow

THURS. 2 MAR.
The Choleric Man
Daphne and Amintor

SAT. 4 MAR.
Matilda   BKB
The Trip to Scotland

TUES. 7 MAR.
The Rivals   C/G
The Citizen

THURS. 9 MAR.
Lionel and Clarissa   BKB
The Commissary

SAT. 11 MAR.
The Rivals
The Padlock

TUES. 14 MAR.
Matilda
The Waterman

THURS. 16 MAR.
The Rivals
The Romance of an Hour

SAT. 18 MAR.
The Choleric Man
The Deserter

TUES. 21 MAR.
Braganza
The Trip to Newmarket

THURS. 23 MAR.
The Merchant of Venice
The Two Misers

SAT. 25 MAR.
Braganza
Harlequin's Metamorphoses

TUES. 28 MAR.
The Rivals
The Two Misers

THURS. 30 MAR.
Braganza
The Deserter

SAT. 1 APRIL
The Chances
The Two Misers

TUES. 4 APRIL
Hamlet
The Waterman

THURS. 6 APRIL
The Rehearsal
The Rival Candidates

SAT. 8 APRIL
Matilda

MON. 17 APRIL
Henry II   (Signor Rossignol)
Harlequin's Metamorphoses

TUES. 18 APRIL

The Inflexible Captive
The Irish Widow

WED. 19 APRIL

The Rivals   (Signor Rossignol)
The Misers

THURS. 20 APRIL

Braganza   (Signor Rossignol)
The Rival Candidates

FRI. 21 APRIL

The Inflexible Captive

SAT. 22 APRIL

The Clandestine Marriage   (Signor Rossignol)
The Misers

TUES. 25 APRIL

Much Ado About Nothing
The Portrait

THURS. 27 APRIL

The Merchant of Venice
Cross Purposes

SAT. 29 APRIL

Much Ado About Nothing
The Rival Candidates

TUES. 2 MAY

The Grecian Daughter   b: Miss Mansell
The Two Misers

THURS. 4 MAY

Othello   C/BC b: Egan & Floor
The Deserter

SAT. 6 MAY

The Inflexible Captive   C/BC
                b: Mrs. Keasberry
The Recruiting Sergeant
Polly Honeycomb

TUES. 9 MAY

Venice Preserv'd   C/BJ, G, BC
The Rival Candidates   b: Dimond

THURS. 11 MAY

The Conscious Lovers   C/BC, BJ
The Capricious Lovers   b: Bro. Jackson

SAT. 13 MAY

The Careless Husband   C/BC, BJ b: Didier
Polly Honeycomb

TUES. 16 MAY

Love in a Village   C/BJ b: Mrs Ward
The Citizen

THURS. 18 MAY

Braganza   C/BJ, BC
The Waterman   b: Rowswell &
                 Mrs Martin

SAT. 20 MAY

The Beggar's Opera   C/BC
Lethe   b: Mrs Wheeler &
                 Miss Wheeler

TUES. 23 MAY

The Suspicious Husband   C/BC, BJ b: Brunsdon
The Portrait

THURS. 25 MAY

As You Like It   C/BJ
The Two Misers   b: Mr & Miss
                 Summers

SAT. 27 MAY

The Maid of the Mill   C/BC b: Brett
High Life Below Stairs

TUES. 30 MAY

Richard III   C/BJ
The Waterman   b: Master Deneuville
                 & Miss Curtis

THURS. 1 JUNE

Cymbeline   C/BC, BJ b: Haughton
The Padlock

SAT. 3 JUNE

Matilda   C/BC, BJ
Hob in the Well   b: Palmer & Fisher

End of Season

Season 1775/76

Company

Mr: Blisset, Brett, Brookes, Brunsdon, Didier, Dimond, Edwin, Egan, Floor, Haughton, Henderson, Jackson, Keasberry, Rowswell, Summers, West.

Mrs: Brett, Didier, Keasberry, Martin, Sherriffe, Summers, Ward.

Miss: Mansell, Scrace, Summers, Wheeler.

Master: Sherriffe.

Treasurer: Palmer.   *Box Book Keeper:* Fisher.

1775

SAT. 23 SEPT.
Hamlet

MON. 25 SEPT.
The Merchant of Venice
The Trip to Newmarket

TUES. 26 SEPT.
The Rivals
The Deserter

WED. 27 SEPT.
Comus
The Irish Widow

THURS. 28 SEPT.
Much Ado About Nothing
The Waterman

SAT. 30 SEPT.
The Clandestine Marriage

TUES. 3 OCT.
Love in a Village
Cross Purposes

THURS. 5 OCT.
Jane Shore
The Portrait

SAT. 7 OCT.
The Merry Wives of Windsor
The Trip to Scotland

TUES. 10 OCT.
The West Indian
The Deserter

THURS. 12 OCT.
Braganza
Polly Honeycomb

SAT. 14 OCT.
The Careless Husband
The Golden Pippin

TUES. 17 OCT.
The Chances   C/G
The Register Office

THURS. 19 OCT.
Matilda
The Waterman

SAT. 21 OCT.
The Hypocrite   C/G

TUES. 24 OCT.
The Revenge
The Recruiting Sergeant

THURS. 26 OCT.
The Spanish Friar
The Dragon of Wantley

SAT. 28 OCT.
The School for Wives
The Capricious Lovers

TUES. 31 OCT.
Henry II
The Dragon of Wantley

THURS. 2 NOV.
As You Like It
St. Patrick's Day

SAT. 4 NOV.
Henry IV
The Dragon of Wantley

TUES. 7 NOV.
Lionel and Clarissa
St. Patrick's Day

THURS. 9 NOV.
She Wou'd and She Wou'd Not
The Two Misers

SAT. 11 NOV.
The Rehearsal
St. Patrick's Day

TUES. 14 NOV.
Macbeth
The Commissary

THURS. 16 NOV.
The Fashionable Lover
The Dragon of Wantley

SAT. 18 NOV.
The Provok'd Wife
The Rival Candidates

TUES. 21 NOV.
Love for Love
The Dragon of Wantley

THURS. 23 NOV.
Richard III
The Deserter

SAT. 25 NOV.
Rule a Wife and Have a Wife
The Waterman

TUES. 28 NOV.
Rule a Wife and Have a Wife
The Waterman

THURS. 30 NOV.
Douglas
The Misers

SAT. 2 DEC.
The English Merchant   C/G
The Dragon of Wantley

TUES. 5 DEC.
The Chances
Midas

THURS. 7 DEC.
Venice Preserved
The Rival Candidates

SAT. 9 DEC.
The Careless Husband
The Register Office

TUES. 12 DEC.
The West Indian
The Waterman

THURS. 14 DEC.
Edward & Eleanora   C/G
The Golden Pippin

SAT. 16 DEC.
The Provok'd Husband
St. Patrick's Day

TUES. 19 DEC.
The Spanish Friar
Bon Ton

THURS. 21 DEC.
Maid of the Mill
Bon Ton

SAT. 23 DEC.
The Clandestine Marriage
Midas

TUES. 26 DEC.
Edward & Eleanora
Bon Ton

WED. 27 DEC.
Romeo and Juliet
The Scheming Lieutenant

THURS. 28 DEC.
The Man's the Master
The Deserter

FRI. 29 DEC.
George Barnwell
The Dragon of Wantley

SAT. 30 DEC.
The Rivals
The Waterman

1776

THURS. 4 JAN.
The Orphan
The Lyar

SAT. 6 JAN.
The Man's The Master
Cross Purposes

TUES. 9 JAN.
Hamlet
The Irish Widow

THURS. 11 JAN.
Henry IV
Pantomime "The Medley"

SAT. 13 JAN.
Rule a Wife and Have a Wife

TUES. 16 JAN.
The Way to Keep Him

SAT. 20 JAN.
The Spanish Friar
Bon Ton

TUES. 23 JAN.
The Good Natur'd Man

THURS. 25 JAN.
Douglas
Pantomime "The Medley"

SAT. 27 JAN.
Every Man in his Humour
The Dragon of Wantley

WED. 31 JAN.
The Man's the Master   C/BC b: Mrs Brett
The Padlock

THURS. 1 FEB.
King Lear   C/BC b: Brookes
Bon Ton

SAT. 3 FEB.
Cymon   C/BC b: Keasberry
The Scheming Lieutenant

TUES. 6 FEB.
Oroonoko   C/BC b: Henderson
Lethe

THURS. 8 FEB.
The Orphan   C/BC b: Floor & Egan
Midas

SAT. 10 FEB.
The Jealous Wife   C/BC b: Mrs. Didier
The Recruiting Sergeant
The Ghost

TUES. 13 FEB.
Braganza   C/BC b: Miss Mansell
The Ladies' Frolick

THURS. 15 FEB.
The Maid of the Mill   C/BC b: Haughton
A Trip to Scotland

SAT. 17 FEB.
Love Makes a Man   C/BC b: Dimond
The Waterman

TUES. 20 FEB.
Venice Preserved   b: Miss Wheeler
The Padlock

THURS. 22 FEB.
The Fair Penitent   PB/F b: Palmer
The Two Misers   & Fisher

SAT. 24 FEB.
The School for Wives
The Deserter

TUES. 27 FEB.
The Drummer
Pantomime "The Medley"

THURS. 29 FEB.
The Mourning Bride
The Chaplet

SAT. 2 MAR.
Merchant of Venice
Pantomime "The Medley"

THURS. 7 MAR.
Cymbeline
St. Patrick's Day

SAT. 9 MAR.
Much Ado About Nothing
Bon Ton

TUES. 12 MAR.
The Provok'd Husband
Daphne and Amintor

THURS. 14 MAR.
The Revenge
Pantomime "The Medley"

SAT. 16 MAR.
The Runaway
A Trip to Scotland

TUES. 19 MAR.
The Merry Wives of Windsor
Daphne and Amintor

THURS. 21 MAR.
The Merry Wives of Windsor
Daphne and Amintor

SAT. 23 MAR.
Twelfth Night
The Capricious Lovers

THURS. 28 MAR.
The Runaway
Pantomime "The Medley"

SAT. 30 MAR.
The Chances
The Dragon of Wantley

MON. 8 APRIL
Jane Shore
The Medley

TUES. 9 APRIL
The Runaway
The Waterman

WED. 10 APRIL
Comus
Pantomime

THURS. 11 APRIL
The Mourning Bride
The Devil to Pay

SAT. 13 APRIL

The Spanish Friar

THURS. 18 APRIL

King John
The Spleen

SAT. 20 APRIL

The Way to Keep Him
Midas

TUES. 23 APRIL

The Runaway

THURS. 25 APRIL

King John
The Deserter

SAT. 27 APRIL

The West Indian
The Spleen

TUES. 30 APRIL

The Runaway
The What d-ye Call It

THURS. 2 MAY

Richard III
Pantomime "The Medley"

SAT. 4 MAY

The Drummer
Bon Ton

SAT. 11 MAY

The Rivals   C/BC b: Mrs Sherriffe
The Old Maid

TUES. 14 MAY

Rule a Wife and Have a Wife   C/BC b: Didier
The Honest Yorkshireman

THURS. 16 MAY

Matilda   C/BC b: Miss Scrace
High Life Below Stairs

SAT. 18 MAY

The Runaway   C/BC b: Blissett
The Two Misers

TUES. 21 MAY

The Stratagem   C/BC b: Edwin
The Ghost

THURS. 23 MAY

Edward and Eleanora   C/BC b: Rowswell
Midas   & Mrs. Martin

SAT. 25 MAY

The Conscious Lovers   C/BC b: Brunsdon
The Rival Candidates

TUES. 28 MAY

The Provok'd Husband   C/BC b: Mrs Ward
The Devil to Pay

THURS. 30 MAY

Cymon   C/BC b: Brett
The Waterman

SAT. 1 JUNE

The Spanish Friar   C/BC
The Lyar   b: Summers & West

TUES. 4 JUNE

Douglas   C/BC
                             b: Palmer & Fisher

End of Season

Season 1776/77

Company

Mr: Blisset, Brett, Brookes, Brunsdon, Didier, Dimond, Edwin, Floor, Haughton, Henderson, Hitchcock, Jackson, Keasberry, Payne, Rowbotham, Summers, G. Summers.

Mrs: Brett, Didier, Hitchcock, Keasberry, Martin, Robinson, Sherriffe, Summers, Ward, Wheeler.

Miss: Cantelo, Egan, Hitchcock, H. Keasberry, Mansell, Mitchell, Summers, Wheeler.

Master: Edwin, Hitchcock, Keasberry, Payne, Sherriffe, Summers.

Treasurer: Palmer.   *Box Book Keeper:* Fisher.

1776

MON. 16 SEPT.
The Fair Penitent   PB/Ba
Polly Honeycombe

TUES. 17 SEPT.
The Spanish Friar
The Medley

WED. 18 SEPT.
Comus
Bon Ton

THURS. 19 SEPT.
Henry IV
The Waterman

FRI. 20 SEPT.
The Runaway
The Medley

SAT. 21 SEPT.
Love in a Village   PB/Ba
The Scheming Lieutenant

THURS. 26 SEPT.
The Beggar's Opera
Lethe

SAT. 28 SEPT.
The Chances
The Capricious Lovers

THURS. 3 OCT.
Macbeth   C/G
The Commissary

SAT. 5 OCT.
The Distrest Mother   C/G
High Life Below Stairs

TUES. 8 OCT.
Much Ado About Nothing   C/G
The Man of Quality

THURS. 10 OCT.
The Distrest Mother
The Man of Quality

SAT. 12 OCT.
The Fashionable Lover
The Dragon of Wantley

THURS. 17 OCT.
Venice Preserv'd
The Waterman

SAT. 19 OCT.
Amphitrion   C/G
The Man of Quality

THURS. 24 OCT.
The Runaway   C/G
The Deserter

SAT. 26 OCT.
The Way to Keep Him
Bon Ton

TUES. 29 OCT.
Amphitrion

THURS. 31 OCT.
Hamlet   C/G
The Two Misers

SAT. 2 NOV.
The Careless Husband   C/G
The What d-ye Call It

TUES. 5 NOV.
The Man's the Master
The Rival Candidate

THURS. 7 NOV.
Braganza
The Cooper

SAT. 9 NOV.
The Merry Wives of Windsor

TUES. 12 NOV.
The Plain Dealer   C/G

THURS. 14 NOV.
King John   C/G
The Cooper

SAT. 16 NOV.
The Careless Husband
The Padlock

TUES. 19 NOV.
The Plain Dealer
Chrononhotonthologos

THURS. 21 NOV.
Amphitrion
The Scheming Lieutenant

SAT. 23 NOV.
The Maid of the Mill   PB/H
The Ghost

TUES. 26 NOV.
The Grecian Daughter   C/G
Lethe

THURS. 28 NOV.
The Clandestine Marriage
Lilliput

SAT. 30 NOV.
The Runaway
Bon Ton

TUES. 3 DEC.
The Chances

THURS. 5 DEC.
Merope
Lilliput

SAT. 7 DEC.
The Man's the Master   C/G
The Waterman

TUES. 10 DEC.
The Rehearsal

THURS. 12 DEC.
The Plain Dealer
Lilliput

SAT. 14 DEC.
The Spanish Friar   C/G
The Hotel

TUES. 17 DEC.
The Rehearsal   C/G

THURS. 19 DEC.
Merope
The Hotel

SAT. 21 DEC.
The Foundling   C/G
The Deserter
The Merry Wives of Windsor

MON. 23 DEC.
Richard III
Midas

THURS. 26 DEC.
Henry II
The Cooper

FRI. 27 DEC.
Comus
Lilliput

SAT. 28 DEC.
The Way to Keep Him
The Man of Quality

MON. 30 DEC.
George Barnwell
The Dragon of Wantley

1777

THURS. 2 JAN.
Macbeth
The Rival Candidates

SAT. 4 JAN.
The Merchant of Venice
Bon Ton

THURS. 9 JAN.
Macbeth
Lilliput

SAT. 11 JAN.
The Plain Dealer
The Deserter

TUES. 14 JAN.
Semiramis

THURS. 16 JAN.
Semiramis   C/G
The Rival Candidates

SAT. 18 JAN.
Amphitrion
The Portrait

TUES. 21 JAN.
She Wou'd and She Wou'd Not
Hob in the Well   C/G

THURS. 23 JAN.
The Stratagem   C/G
The Rival Candidates

SAT. 25 JAN.
The Jealous Wife
The Golden Pippin

TUES. 28 JAN.
Semiramis
Lilliput

WED. 29 JAN.
Lionel and Clarissa PB/H b: Mrs Brett
The Hotel

SAT. 1 FEB.
Love for Love C/FF, BC, G
The Citizen   b: Mrs. Didier

TUES. 4 FEB.
Rule a Wife and Have a Wife C/B, BC
The Deuce is in Him b: Henderson

THURS. 6 FEB.
Semiramis   PB/H b: Summers &
Midas   Hitchcock

SAT. 8 FEB.
The Rivals   PB/H b: Keasberry
The Recruiting Sergeant
Lilliput

TUES. 11 FEB.
Love Makes a Man PB/H, C/G, BC
The Portrait   b: Edwin

THURS. 13 FEB.
Hamlet   PB/F, C/BC
The Waterman   b: Miss Wheeler

SAT. 15 FEB.
Cymon   C/G, BC
The Author   b: Miss Mansel

TUES. 18 FEB.
Merope   C/G, BC
The Cooper   b: Dimond

THURS. 20 FEB.
The School for Wives C/BC b: Floor &
The Capricious Lovers Mrs. Martin

SAT. 22 FEB.
King John   PB/H, C/BC
The Deserter   b: Palmer & Fisher

THURS. 27 FEB.
The Runaway
Bladud

SAT. 1 MAR.
Love in a Village
Bladud

TUES. 4 MAR.
Sir Thomas Overbury C/G
The Padlock

THURS. 6 MAR.
Henry IV   C/G
Bladud

SAT. 8 MAR.
The Wonder   C/G
Bladud

TUES. 11 MAR.
Sir Thomas Overbury
The Spanish Lady

THURS. 13 MAR.
The Suspicious Husband C/G
Bladud

SAT. 15 MAR.
The Rivals
The Spanish Lady

TUES. 18 MAR.
Sir Thomas Overbury PB/P
Bladud

THURS. 20 MAR.
A Trip to Scarborough C/G
The Golden Pippin

SAT. 22 MAR.
The Foundling
Lilliput

MON. 31 MAR.
Romeo and Juliet C/G
Bladud

TUES. 1 APRIL
A Trip to Scarborough
Midas

WED. 2 APRIL
Semiramis   PB/P, C/G
Selima and Azor

THURS. 3 APRIL
Jane Shore   PB/H, C/G
Bladud

SAT. 5 APRIL
The Way to Keep Him
The Waterman

THURS. 10 APRIL
Sir Thomas Overbury
Bladud

SAT. 12 APRIL
A Trip to Scarborough
The Two Misers

TUES. 15 APRIL
The Merry Wives of Windsor
Selima and Azor

THURS. 17 APRIL
Henry V   C/G
Lilliput

SAT, 19 APRIL
The Provok'd Husband   PB/H
Bladud

TUES. 22 APRIL
Selima and Azor

THURS. 24 APRIL
Braganza   C/G
The Dragon of Wantley

SAT. 26 APRIL
The Runaway
Bon Ton

TUES. 29 APRIL
Amphytrion
Bladud

THURS. 1 MAY
The Contess of Salisbury   C/G
Selima and Azor

SAT. 3 MAY
The Spanish Friar   C/G
All the World's a Stage

TUES. 6 MAY
Henry V   PB/F
All the World's a Stage

THURS. 8 MAY
The Countess of Salisbury   PB/H, C/BC
Midas   b: Haughton

SAT. 10 MAY
The School for Wives   C/BC b: Mrs. Hitchock
The Irish Widow

TUES. 11 MAY
Merope   PB/H, P, C/BC, G
All the World's a Stage   b: Mrs. Keasberry

THURS. 15 MAY
The Jealous Wife   PB/H, C/BC
The Cooper   b: Rowbotham & Payne

SAT. 17 MAY
The Busybody   PB/H, C/BC, G
The Recruiting Sergeant   b: Didier
The Mayor of Garrett

TUES. 20 MAY
The Beggar's Opera   PB/H, C/BC
All the World's a Stage   b: Brett

THURS. 22 MAY
The Fair Penitent   PB/H, C/BC,
The Deserter   b: Brookes

SAT. 24 MAY
Amphitrion   PB/H b: Blissett
The Two Misers

TUES. 27 MAY
The Countess of Salisbury   PB/H, C/BC
The Devil to Pay   b: Mrs. Sherriffe

THURS. 29 MAY
The Way to Keep Him   PB/H, C/BC, G
The Capricious Lovers   b: Palmer (Treasurer)
                                  Fisher (Box Book-
                                  Keeper)

SAT. 31 MAY
The Fashionable Lover   C/G
Selima and Azor

End of Season

Season 1777/78

Company

Mr: Barnett, Blisset, Bonnor, Brett, Brookes, Browne, Didier, Dimond, Edwin, Egan, Floor, Griffin, Grist, Houghton, Keasberry, Payne, Rowbotham, Summers, G. Summers.

Mrs: Barnett, Brett, Didier, Edwin, Keasberry, Martin, Montague, Sherriffe, Summers, Ward.

Miss: Cantelo, Egan, H. & J. Keasberry, Summers, Wheeler.

Master: Edwin, H. & J. Keasberry, Payne.

Treasurer: Palmer.   *Box-Book-Keeper:* Fisher.

1777

TUES. 16 SEPT.

The Fair Penitent   C/BC, G

WED. 17 SEPT.

The Merchant of Venice   C/BC (Henderson)
The Waterman

THURS. 18 SEPT.

The Merry Wives of Windsor   C/BC (Henderson)
Selima and Azor

FRI. 19 SEPT.

Hamlet   PB/F C/BC
Midas   (Henderson)

SAT. 20 SEPT.

Henry IV   PB/F (Henderson)
Bladud

THURS. 25 SEPT.

The Chances
Selima and Azor

SAT. 27 SEPT.

Hamlet   PB/F
The Ghost

TUES. 30 SEPT.

Lionel and Clarissa

THURS. 2 OCT.

She Wou'd and She Wou'd Not   PB/H
Bladud

SAT. 4 OCT.

The West Indian   PB/H, C/BC, G
The Deserter

TUES. 7 OCT.

Othello   PB/F, C/BC, G
All the World's a Stage

THURS. 9 OCT.

The West Indian
Selima and Azor

SAT. 11 OCT.

The Fashionable Lover   PB/H C/G
Cross Purposes

TUES. 14 OCT.

She Stoops to Conquer   C/G

THURS. 16 OCT.

The Orphan
Bladud

SAT. 18 OCT.

The Suspicious Husband   C/G, BC
Midas

TUES. 21 OCT.

The Beggars Opera

THURS. 23 OCT.

Polly   C/G
Bon Ton

SAT. 25 OCT.

The Rivals   PB/H
The Citizen

THURS. 30 OCT.

Venice Preserv'd   PB/H
Bladud

SAT. 1 NOV.

The West Indian   PB/H, C/BC
Selima and Azor

TUES. 4 NOV.

The School for Scandal   C/G

THURS. 6 NOV.

The School for Scandal
The Irish Widow

SAT. 8 NOV.

The Provok'd Husband
The Waterman

TUES. 11 NOV.

The School for Scandal
The Cooper

THURS. 13 NOV.
Philaster
Selima and Azor

SAT. 15 NOV.
The Clandestine Marriage   PB/H
The Scheming Lieutenant

TUES. 18 NOV.
The School for Scandal
The Waterman

THURS. 20 NOV.
The School for Scandal
The Deserter

SAT. 22 NOV.
The Spanish Friar   PB/H
The Portrait

TUES. 25 NOV.
Philaster   PB/H, C/G
The Quaker

THURS. 27 NOV.
The School for Scandal
All the World's a Stage

SAT. 29 NOV.
The Way to Keep Him
The Quaker

TUES. 2 DEC.
Cymbeline

THURS. 4 DEC.
The School for Scandal
Lilliput

SAT. 6 DEC.
The Runaway
The Cooper

TUES. 9 DEC.
The Miser   C/G

THURS. 11 DEC.
The School for Scandal
The Quaker

SAT. 13 DEC.
The Way to Keep Him

TUES. 16 DEC.
The School for Scandal

THURS. 18 DEC.
The School for Scandal   C/G
April Day

SAT. 20 DEC.
The Jealous Wife
Bladud

TUES. 23 DEC.
The School for Scandal   PB/H
The Two Misers

FRI. 26 DEC.
Know your Own Mind
The Waterman

SAT. 27 DEC.
The Spanish Friar
The Quaker

MON. 29 DEC.
Cymbeline
Bladud

TUES. 30 DEC.
Know your Own Mind
Lilliput

WED. 31 DEC.
Jane Shore   C/G
The Quaker

1778

THURS. 1 JAN.
Comus   PB/H
Lilliput

FRI. 2 JAN.
Comus
Lilliput

SAT. 3 JAN.
The School for Scandal   PB/F
The Milesian

TUES. 6 JAN.
The Merchant of Venice   C/BC (Henderson
engaged for a fortnight)

WED. 7 JAN.
The Chances
Bladud

THURS. 8 JAN.
The Countess of Salisbury   PB/F
The Two Misers

SAT. 10 JAN.
Hamlet   PB/F
The Capricious Lovers

TUES. 13 JAN.
Macbeth   PB/F
The Milesian

WED. 14 JAN.
Henry IV
The Quaker

THURS. 15 JAN.
Henry V
The Waterman

SAT. 17 JAN.
Every Man in His Humour   C/G
The Deserter

TUES. 20 JAN.
Know your Own Mind   PB/H
The Quaker

THURS. 22 JAN.
The School for Scandal
Bladud

SAT. 24 JAN.
The Funeral   PB/H, C/G
The Milesian

TUES. 27 JAN.
The School for Scandal

THURS. 29 JAN.
Cymbeline   C/BC
The Milesian

SAT. 31 JAN.
Know your Own Mind   PB/H
Selima and Azor

TUES. 3 FEB.
Henry II   PB/H, C/BC
The Quaker   b: Keasberry

THURS. 5 FEB.
The Maid of the Mill   PB/H, C/BC
The Devil to Pay   b: Mrs. Brett

SAT. 7 FEB.
As You Like It   PB/H, C/BC
The Mayor of Garrett   b: Edwin

TUES. 10 FEB.
A Word to the Wise   PB/H, C/BC, G
The Author   b: Mrs. Didier

THURS. 12 FEB.
Love Makes a Man   PB/H, C/BC
The Milesian   b: Egan & Payne

SAT. 14 FEB.
The Earl of Warwick   C/BC, G b: Dimond
The Ladies' Frolick

TUES. 17 FEB.
The Way to Keep Him   PB/H, C/BC
Midas   b: Blisset

THURS. 19 FEB.
The Busybody   PB/H, C/BC
The Padlock   b: Brookes

SAT. 21 FEB.
The Suspicious Husband   PB/H, C/BC
The Lying Valet   b: Mrs. Barnett

TUES. 24 FEB.
The Funeral   PB/H,
The Rival Candidates   b: Miss Wheeler

THURS. 26 FEB.
The Rivals   C/BC b: Palmer
The Milesian   (Treasurer) Fisher
                            (Box Book-keeper)

SAT. 28 FEB.
Percy
All the World's a Stage

TUES. 3 MAR.
The School for Scandal   PB/H
The Capricious Lovers

THURS. 5 MAR.
Percy
Bladud

SAT. 7 MAR.
Know Your Own Mind   PB/H
Selima and Azor

TUES. 10 MAR.
The School for Scandal   PB/H
Bladud

THURS. 12 MAR.
Semiramis   PB/H
The Deserter

SAT. 14 MAR.
The Way to Keep Him   PB/H
The Two Misers

TUES. 17 MAR.
Percy
The Scheming Lieutenant

THURS. 19 MAR.
Know your Own Mind   PB/H
The Portrait

SAT. 21 MAR.
The School for Scandal
Bon Ton

TUES. 24 MAR.
The Devil upon Two Sticks   C/G

THURS. 26 MAR.
The Mourning Bride   PB/H
Bladud

SAT. 28 MAR.
The Devil Upon Two Sticks   PB/H, C/G
The Lyar

TUES. 31 MAR.
The Cozeners   C/BC, G
The Golden Pippin

THURS. 2 APRIL
Love in a Village   PB/H, C/BC
The Devil Upon Two Sticks

SAT. 4 APRIL
Know your Own Mind   PB/H
The Cozeners

TUES. 7 APRIL
Lionel and Clarissa   PB/H
The Devil Upon Two Sticks

THURS. 9 APRIL
Love in a Village   PB/H, C/G
The Nabob

SAT. 11 APRIL
The School for Scandal   PB/H
The Dragon of Wantley

MON. 20 APRIL
George Barnwell   C/G
Bladud

TUES. 21 APRIL
The Battle of Hastings   PB/H
The Cozeners

WED. 22 APRIL
Know your Own Mind   PB/H
Lilliput

THURS. 23 APRIL
The Maid of the Mill   PB/H
The Devil Upon Two Sticks

SAT. 25 APRIL
A Word to the Wise   PB/H
The Quaker

TUES. 28 APRIL
The Battle of Hastings   PB/H
Belphegor

WED. 29 APRIL
Philaster
Bladud

THURS. 30 APRIL
The Maid of the Mill   PB/H
The Cozeners

SAT. 2 MAY
Know your Own Mind   PB/H
Belphegor

TUES. 5 MAY
The School for Scandal
Belphegor

THURS. 7 MAY
The Battle of Hastings   PB/H, C/BC, G
The Apprentice   b: Mrs. Montague

SAT. 9 MAY
Rule a Wife and Have a Wife PB/H, C/BC
Edgar and Emmeline   b: Mrs. Keasberry

TUES. 12 MAY
King Richard III   PB/H, C/BC b: Grist
Bon Ton

THURS. 14 MAY
Cymon   PB/H, C/BC
High Life Below Stairs   b: Rowbotham &
                                Barnett

SAT. 16 MAY
The Provok'd Husband   PB/H, C/BC
Edgar and Emmeline   b: Mrs. Didier

TUES. 19 MAY
The School for Wives   C/BC b: Brett
The Honest Yorkshireman

THURS. 21 MAY
The Funeral   PB/H, C/BC
Midas   b: Mrs. Martin

SAT. 23 MAY
The Hypocrite   PB/H, C/BC
The Cozeners   b: Mrs. Sherriffe

TUES. 26 MAY
Hamlet   PB/H, C/BC
The Devil Upon Two Sticks

WED. 27 MAY
She Wou'd and She Wou'd   PB/H, C/BC
  Not   b: Palmer (Treasurer
Edgar and Emmeline   Fisher (Box Book keeper)

SAT. 30 MAY
The School for Scandal
The Golden Pippin

End of Season

Season 1778/79

Company

Mr: Du Bellamy, Blisset, Bonnor, Brett, Brookes, Brown, Browne, Didier, Dimond, Edwin, Floor, Haughton, Griffin, Grist, Jackson Keasberry, Matthews, Payne, Rowbotham, Siddons, Summers, G. Summers.

Mrs: Bellfield, Brett, Didier, Edwin, Grist, Keasberry, Lovemore, Martin, Siddons, Summers, Ward.

Miss: Byrne, Keasberry, Scrace, Summers, Wheeler.

Master: Byrne, Edwin, Keasberry, Payne.

Treasurer: Palmer.   *Box Book Keeper:* Fisher.

1778

SAT. 24 OCT.
The Provok'd Husband   C/BC, G. Mrs. Siddons
The Quaker   first appearance in Bath.

TUES. 26 OCT.
The School for Scandal   C/G
The Ghost

THURS. 29 OCT.
The Wonder
Bladud

SAT. 31 OCT.
The Way to Keep Him   C/G
Selimà and Azor

TUES. 3 NOV.
Percy
The Flitch of Bacon   C/ G

THURS. 5 NOV.
As You Like It
The Flitch of Bacon

SAT. 7 NOV.
Know Your Own Mind   C/G

TUES. 10 NOV.
The School for Scandal

THURS. 12 NOV.
Venice Preserv'd   C/G
Bladud

SAT. 14 NOV.
The Funeral   C/G
Selima and Azor

TUES 17 NOV.
Hamlet (Henderson)   C/G

WED. 18 NOV.
The Chances (Henderson)   C/BC, G

THURS. 19 NOV.
The Merchant of Venice   C/BC, G
(Henderson)

SAT. 21 NOV.
Henry IV (Henderson)   C/BC, G

TUES. 24 NOV.
Much Ado About Nothing   C/BC, G
(Henderson)

WED. 25 NOV.
The Countess of Salisbury   C/BC, G
(Henderson)

THURS. 26 NOV.
The Merry Wives of Windsor   C/BC, G
(Henderson)
The Flitch of Bacon

SAT. 28 NOV.
The Wonder   C/BC, G
Midas   (b: Henderson)

TUES. 1 DEC.
The Duenna   C/G

THURS. 3 DEC.
The Duenna
The Lying Valet

SAT. 5 DEC.
The School for Scandal
The Flitch of Bacon

TUES. 8 DEC.
The Duenna

THURS. 10 DEC.
The Grecian Daughter   C/G
The Quaker

SAT. 12 DEC.
The Spanish Barber   C/G
The Devil upon Two Sticks

TUES. 15 DEC.
The Duenna

THURS. 17 DEC.
The Spanish Barber
The Liar

SAT. 19 DEC.
The Merchant of Venice
Bladud

WED. 23 DEC.
The School for Scandal
The Invasion

SAT. 26 DEC.
The Duenna
The Invasion

MON. 28 DEC.
George Barnwell   C/G
Bladud

TUES. 29 DEC.
The Duenna
The Scheming Lieutenant

WED. 30 DEC.
The Countess of Salisbury
Bladud

THURS. 31 DEC.
The Spanish Barber
The Recruiting Sergeant
The Invasion

1779

SAT. 2 JAN.
The School for Scandal
The Milesian

TUES. 5 JAN.
The Camp   C/G

THURS. 7 JAN.
Henry II   C/G
The Camp

SAT. 9 JAN.
Know your Own Mind

TUES. 12 JAN.
The Duenna

THURS. 14 JAN.
The School for Scandal
The Camp

SAT. 16 JAN.
The Fathers   C/G
The Camp

TUES. 19 JAN.
The Spanish Friar   C/G
The Camp

THURS. 21 JAN.
The Fathers
The Camp

SAT. 23 JAN.
The Duenna
The Scheming Lieutenant

TUES. 26 JAN.
The School for Scandal
The Camp

WED. 27 JAN.
The Duenna
Bladud

FRI. 29 JAN.
The Spanish Barber
Lilliput
The Camp

TUES. 2 FEB.
The Runaway
The Golden Pippin   C/BC b:Keasberry

THURS. 4 FEB.
Know Your Own Mind   C/BC b: Mrs. Brett
The Milesian

SAT. 6 FEB.
The Rivals   C/BC b: Edwin
The Flitch of Bacon

TUES. 9 FEB.
The Constant Couple   C/BC, G b: Dimond
The Golden Pippin
Like Master, Like Man

THURS. 11 FEB.
The West Indian   C/BC b: Siddons and
The Padlock   Rowbotham

SAT. 13 FEB.
She Stoops to Conquer   C/BC b' Mrs. Didier
The Devil to Pay

TUES. 16 FEB.
Cymon   PB/Ba, C/BC
The Reprisal   b: Miss Wheeler

THURS. 18 FEB.
The Fashionable Lover   C/BC b: Floor and
Thomas and Sally   Mrs. Martin

SAT. 20 FEB.
Douglas   C/BC, G b: Mrs. Grist
The Devil to Pay

TUES. 23 FEB.	**MON. 22 MAR.**
The Jealous Wife C/BC b: Blisset	*The Duenna* C/FF
The Padlock	*Selima and Azor*
THURS. 25 FEB.	**TUES. 23 MAR.**
The Maid of the Mill C/BC b: Palmer and	Venice Preserv'd C/BC (b: Melmoth)
Cross Purposes Fisher	A Plot Discovered
SAT. 27 FEB.	**THURS. 25 MAR.**
The Duenna	The Law of Lombardy C/G
The Register Office	The Bristol Prize
TUES. 2 MAR.	**SAT. 27 MAR.**
Romeo and Juliet C/G	The School for Scandal
The Camp	The Camp
THURS. 4 MAR.	**MON. 5 APR.**
The School for Scandal	Romeo and Juliet
The Milesian	The Camp
SAT. 6 MAR.	**TUES. 6 APR.**
Hamlet (Melmoth) C/BC	The Duenna
	The Bristol Prize
TUES. 9 MAR.	
Know Your Own Mind	**THURS. 8 APR.**
The Camp	The Law of Lombardy
	The Camp
WED. 10 MAR.	
?	**SAT. 10 APR.**
The Camp	Know Your Own Mind
	The Touchstone C/G
THURS. 11 MAR.	
Oroonoko C/G	**TUES. 13 APR.**
	The School for Scandal
FRI. 12 MAR.	The Touchstone
?	
The Camp	**THURS. 15 APR.**
	Cymbeline C/G
SAT. 13 MAR.	The Touchstone
The Lady of the Manor C/G	
	SAT. 17 APR.
MON. 15 MAR.	Lionel and Clarissa
The Countess of Salisbury C/FF	The Touchstone
The Camp	
	MON. 19 APR.
TUES. 16 MAR.	*Lionel and Clarissa* C/FF
Philaster (Melmoth) C/BC,C/G	*St. Patrick's Day*
The Flitch of Bacon	
	THURS. 22 APR.
WED. 17 MAR.	The Runaway
The Duenna G/FF	The Waterman
Selima and Azor	
	SAT. 24 APR.
THURS. 18 MAR.	The Fashionable Lover C/G
The Rivals	The Camp
The Liverpool Prize	
	MON. 26 APR.
SAT. 20 MAR.	*The Merchant of Venice* C/FF
Rule a Wife and Have a Wife C/BC	*The Camp*
(Melmoth)	
Edgar and Emmeline	

TUES. 27 APRIL
The Law of Lombardy
The Touchstone

THURS. 29 APR.   C/G
Richard III
The Two Millers

SAT. 1 MAY
The School for Scandal   C/G
The Touchstone

MON. 3 MAY
The School for Scandal   C/FF
The Touchstone

TUES. 4 MAY
The Conscious Lovers   C/G, BJ b: Brett
The Waterman

THURS. 6 MAY
The Law of Lombardy   C/BC, BJ b: Haughton
The Flitch of Bacon

SAT. 8 MAY
The Grecian Daughter   C/G, C/BC, BJ
Edgar and Emmeline   b: Mrs Siddons

MON. 10 MAY
The Law of Lombardy   C/FF b: Clarke
The Flitch of Bacon

TUES. 11 MAY
The Maid of the Mill   C/BC b: Didier
The Register Office

THURS. 13 MAY
The Provok'd Husband   C/BC b:Brookes
Selima and Azor

SAT. 15 MAY
Tancred and Sigismunda   C/G, C/BC
Midas   b: Mrs. Keasberry

MON. 17 MAY
The Provok'd Husband   C/FF
The Touchstone

TUES. 18 MAY
The Beaux Stratagem   C/BC b: Bonnor
The Golden Pippin

THURS. 20 MAY
Douglas   C/BC, G, BJ b: Summers
The Rival Candidates   & Miss Summers

SAT. 22 MAY
The Merchant of Venice   C/BC, BJ b: Mrs Ward
The Quaker

MON. 24 MAY
The Grecian Daughter   C/FF
The Touchstone

TUES. 25 MAY
The Law of Lombardy   C/BC, BJ b: Payne &
The Citizen   Griffin

THURS. 27 MAY
The Funeral   C/BC, BJ b: Palmer (Treas)
The Flitch of Bacon   & Fisher (BBK)

SAT. 29 MAY
Jane Shore   C/BC, BJ, G
The Touchstone

MON. 31 MAY
The Fatal Falsehood   C/FF
Who's The Dupe?

TUES. 1 JUNE
The Fatal Falsehood   C/BC, G
Who's The Dupe?

End of Season

Season 1779/80

Company

Mr: Blisset, Bonnor, Brookes, Browne, Didier, Dimond, du Bellamy, Floor, Griffin, Haughton, Jackson, Keasberry, Lloyd, Lee, Payne, Rowbotham, Siddons, Summers, G. Summers.

Mrs: Didier, Keasberry, Martin, Siddons, Summers, Younger, Ward

Miss: Summers, H. & J. Keasberry, Wheeler.

Master: Gowen, Jennings, Keasberry, J. Keasberry, Payne.

Dancers: Master and Miss Byrne.

Treasurer: Palmer.   *Box Book Keepers:* Fisher (Bath), Walker (Bristol).   *Prompter:* Floor.

1779

MON. 27 SEPT.
The Law of Lombardy   C/BC, G
Edgar & Emmeline

TUES. 28 SEPT.
The School for Scandal
The Touchstone

WED. 29 SEPT.
Richard III   C/BC, G, BJ
Who's the Dupe?

THURS. 30 SEPT.
The Beaux Stratagem   C/BC, G, BJ
The Camp

SAT. 2 OCT.
Douglas   C/G, BJ
The Touchstone

MON. 4 OCT.
The Merchant of Venice   C/FF
The Devil Upon Two Sticks

WED. 6 OCT.
Love in a Village
Who's The Dupe?

FRI. 8 OCT.
As You Like It   C/BG
The Touchstone

SAT. 9 OCT.
Venice Preserv'd
The Camp

MON. 11 OCT.
Venice Preserv'd   C/FF
The Touchstone

WED. 13 OCT.
?
The Camp

FRI. 15 OCT.
?
The Camp

SAT. 16 OCT.
The Duenna
Who's the Dupe?

MON. 18 OCT.
The Way to Keep Him   C/FF
The Touchstone

FRI. 22 OCT.
Douglas   C/BG
Bladud

SAT. 23 OCT.
The Way to Keep Him   C/G
The Devil upon Two Sticks

MON. 25 OCT.
The School for Scandal   C/FF
Bladud

FRI. 29 OCT.
Jane Shore   C/BG
Bladud

SAT. 30 OCT.
Jane Shore   C/BC, G
Harlequin's Invasion

MON. 1 NOV.
Percy   C/FF
The Rival Candidates

WED. 3 NOV.
The Duenna   C/FF
Bladud

FRI. 5 NOV.
Comus   C/BG
Who's The Dupe?

SAT. 6 NOV.
Know your Own Mind   C/BC, BJ
The Rival Candidates

MON. 8 NOV.
Know Your Own Mind   C/FF
The Touchstone

TUES. 9 NOV .
The Duenna
Harlequin's Invasion

THURS. 11 NOV.
As You Like It   C/BC, G
Harlequin's Invasion

SAT. 13 NOV.
Much Ado About Nothing   C/G

MON. 15 NOV.
Comus   C/FF
Bladud

TUES. 16 NOV.
The School for Scandal   C/G
The Padlock

THURS. 18 NOV.
Macbeth   C/G
The Waterman

SAT. 20 NOV.
Comus   C/G
Bon Ton

MON. 22 NOV.
Tancred and Sigismunda   C/FF
The Waterman

TUES. 23 NOV.
The Jealous Wife
Harlequin's Invasion

THURS. 25 NOV.
Percy   C/G
The Flitch of Bacon

SAT. 27 NOV.
The Bondman   C/G
The Quaker

MON. 29 NOV.
The Bondman   C/FF
The Touchstone

TUES. 30 NOV.
The Fashionable Lover   C/G
The Camp

THURS. 2 DEC.
The Bondman
The Touchstone

SAT. 4 DEC.
The Provok'd Husband   C/G
Plymouth in an Uproar

MON. 6 DEC.
The School for Scandal
Plymouth in an Uproar   C/FF

TUES. 7 DEC.
Love in a Village
The Guardian

THURS. 9 DEC.
The Bondman
Plymouth in an Uproar

SAT. 11 DEC.
Measure for Measure   C/G

MON. 13 DEC.
Measure for Measure   C/FF
The Flitch of Bacon

TUES. 14 DEC.
The School for Scandal
Thomas and Sally

THURS. 16 DEC.
Venice Preserv'd   C/G
The Chaplet

SAT. 18 DEC.
The Duenna
Edgar and Emmeline   C/G

MON. 20 DEC.
The Spanish Friar   C/FF
The Camp

TUES. 21 DEC.
Comus
Cross Purposes

THURS. 23 DEC.
The Fatal Falsehood   C/G
Plymouth in an Uproar

MON. 27 DEC.
The Duenna   C/FF
Bladud

MON. 27 DEC.
Douglas
The Register Office
     (Evidence for both - possibly experiment in
     mounting two performances on same night)

TUES. 28 DEC.
Much Ado about Nothing   C/BC, G, BJ
Harlequin Touchstone

THURS. 30 DEC.
The Bondman
The Camp

FRI. 31 DEC.
The Rivals

1780

SAT. 1 JAN.
The Way to Keep Him
The Waterman

MON. 3 JAN.
Measure for Measure   C/FF
Selima and Azor

TUES. 4 JAN.
Measure for Measure
Harlequin Touchstone

THURS. 6 JAN.
The Rivals   C/G
Selima and Azor

SAT. 8 JAN.
The School for Scandal
The Camp

MON. 10 JAN.
The Law of Lombardy   C/FF
The Quaker

TUES. 11 JAN.
Douglas
Who's the Dupe?

WED. 12 JAN.
The Bondman   C/G
The Critic

SAT. 15 JAN.
The Rivals
The Waterman

MON. 17 JAN.
Henry VIII   C/FF
The Chaplet

TUES. 18 JAN.
The Merchant of Venice   C/G
The Critic

WED. 19 JAN.
Henry VIII   C/G
The Flitch of Bacon

SAT. 22 JAN.
Measure for Measure
The Critic

MON. 24 JAN.
As you Like it   C/FF
The Rival Candidates

TUES. 25 JAN.
The Maid of the Mill
The Critic

WED. 26 JAN.
Othello   C/G, BC, BJ
The Rival Candidates

SAT. 29 JAN.
The Duenna
The Critic

TUES. 1 FEB.
The Times   C/G
Plymouth in an Uproar

WED. 2 FEB.
The Law of Lombardy
The Critic

THURS. 3 FEB.
The Fatal Falsehood   C/FF
The Flitch of Bacon

SAT. 5 FEB.
The School for Scandal

MON. 7 FEB.
Much Ado about Nothing   C/FF
The Critic

TUES. 8 FEB.
Braganza   C/BC, G, BJ
The Touchstone   b: Keasberry

THURS. 10 FEB.
Measure for Measure   C/BC, BJ
Who's the Dupe?   b: Rowbotham, Summers

SAT. 12 FEB.
Edward and Eleonora   C/BC, BJ b: Mrs Siddons
Lethe

MON. 14 FEB.
Comus   C/FF
The Critic

TUES. 15 FEB.
The Conscious Lovers   C/BC, G, BJ
The Contrivances   b: du Bellamy

THURS. 17 FEB.
The Countess of Salisbury   C/BC, G, BJ b: Haughton
The Devil to Pay

SAT. 19 FEB.
The Careless Husband   C/BC, G, BJ b: Dimond
Edgar and Emmeline

MON. 21 FEB.
The Fatal Falsehood   C/FF
The Touchstone

TUES. 22 FEB.
Henry VIII   C/BC, BJ
The Capricious Lovers   b: Miss Wheeler

THURS. 24 FEB.
The Suspicious Husband　　C/BC, G, BJ b: Griffin
The Quaker

SAT. 26 FEB.
The Inconstant　　　　　　C/BC, BJ, G
Like Master Like Man　　　　b: Mrs Didier

MON. 28 FEB.
The Times　　　　　　　　C/FF
The Critic

TUES. 29 FEB.
The Way to Keep Him　　　C/BJ
The Ghost　　　　　　　b: Master & Miss Byrne

THURS. 2 MARCH.
Macbeth　　　　　　　　C/FF
The Camp

SAT. 4 MAR.
The Provok'd Wife　　　　C/BC, BJ, G
The Flitch of Bacon　　　　b: Bonnor

MON. 6 MAR.
The Careless Husband　　C/FF
The Critic

TUES. 7 MAR.
Cymbeline　　　　　　　　C/BJ, G
The Deserter　　　　b: Floor & Mrs Martin

THURS. 9 MAR.
Tancred and Sigismunda　　C/BC, G, BJ
The Waterman　　　　b: Palmer & Fisher

SAT. 11 MAR.
The Times
The Deaf Lover

MON. 13 MAR.
Edward and Eleonora　　C/FF
The Deaf Lover

TUES. 14 MAR.
Know Your Own Mind
The Critic

WED. 15 MAR.
Concert — Alexander's Feast etc. PB/Ba, C/BC, BJ

THURS. 16 MAR.
The Bondman
The Deaf Lover

SAT. 18 MAR.
The Double Falsehood　　C/G
The Irish Widow

MON. 27 MAR.
The Double Falsehood　　C/FF
The Golden Pippin

TUES. 28 MAR.
The Double Falsehood
Harlequin Touchstone

WED. 29 MAR.
The Duenna
The Critic

THURS. 30 MAR.
The Countess of Salisbury
The Camp

SAT. 1 APRIL
The Chances

MON. 3 APRIL
Cymbeline　　　　　　　C/FF
Selima and Azor

TUES. 4 APRIL
The School for Scandal
The Critic

THURS. 6 APRIL
Braganza
The Two Misers

SAT. 8 APRIL
Measure for Measure
The Quaker

MON. 10 APRIL
The Times　　　　　　　C/FF
Selima and Azor

TUES. 11 APRIL
The Times
Who's the Dupe?

THURS. 13 APRIL
The Hypocrite
The Golden Pippin

SAT. 15 APRIL
The Provok'd Husband

MON. 17 APRIL
The School for Scandal　　C/FF
The Critic

TUES. 18 APRIL
The Inconstant
The Capricious Lovers

WED. 19 APRIL
Venice Preserv'd
The Touchstone

SAT. 22 APRIL
The Belle's Stratagem　　C/G
The Waterman

MON. 24 APRIL
The Belle's Stratagem   C/FF
The Waterman

TUES. 25 APRIL
The Grecian Daughter
The Camp

THURS. 26 APRIL
The Belle's Stratagem
The Deserter

SAT. 29 APRIL
The Careless Husband
The Golden Pippin

MON. 1 MAY
The Belle's Stratagem   C/FF
The Devil Upon Two Sticks

TUES. 2 MAY
The Belle's Stratagem
Who's the Dupe?

WED. 3 MAY
Comus
The Critic

FRI. 5 MAY
Zoraida
The Touchstone

SAT. 6 MAY
Zoraida   C/G
The Touchstone

MON. 8 MAY
Zoraida   C/FF
The Two Misers

TUES. 9 MAY
Measure for Measure   C/BC
The Casino

WED. 10 MAY
The Fair Penitent   C/G b: Mrs Siddons

SAT. 13 MAY
The Countess of Salisbury   C/BC
Damon and Phyllida   b: Mrs Keasberry

MON. 15 MAY
The Duenna   C/FF
The Touchstone

TUES. 16 MAY
The School for Wives   C/BC, G, BJ b: Didier
Neck or Nothing

WED. 17 MAY
The Times   C/BC b: Mrs Ward
The Flitch of Bacon

SAT. 20 MAY
Richard III   C/BC, BJ b: Blisset
The King and the Miller of Mansfield

MON. 22 MAY
The School for Scandal   C/FF
Damon and Phyllida
The Capricious Lovers

TUES. 23 MAY
The Orphan   C/BJ, G b: Browne
Florizel and Perdita

WED. 24 MAY
The Merchant of Venice   C/BJ b: Mrs Younger
Damon and Phyllida
Lethe

SAT. 27 MAY
The Conscious Lovers   C/BC, BJ b: Jackson
The Mayor of Garret

MON. 29 MAY
The Belle's Stratagem   C/FF
The Critic

TUES. 30 MAY
The Fashionable Lovers   C/BJ b: Brookes
The Recruiting Sergeant
The Irish Widow

WED. 31 MAY
Percy   C/BJ b: Lloyd
High Life Below Stairs

SAT. 3 JUNE
Douglas   C/BC
The Capricious Lovers   b: Palmer & Fisher

TUES. 6 JUNE
Braganza   C/FF b: Keasberry
Damon and Phyllida
Neck or Nothing

WED. 7 JUNE
Measure for Measure   C/FF b: Lee
The Casino

FRI. 9 JUNE
Love in a Village   C/BG
The Toy Shop   b: Summers &
High Life Below Stairs   Rowbotham

SAT. 10 JUNE
The Belle's Stratagem   C/BJ, BJ
The Quaker

MON. 12 JUNE
The Inconstant   C/FF b: Mrs Didier
The Recruiting Sergeant
The Devil to Pay

WED. 14 JUNE
The London Merchant   C/FF, G b: Bonnor
Florizel and Perdita

FRI. 16 JUNE
The Provok'd Wife   C/FF b: Winstone

MON. 19 JUNE
The Conscious Lovers   C/FF b: Miss Wheeler
Selima and Azor

WED. 21 JUNE
The Orphan   C/FF b: Griffin
The Toy Shop
The Milesian

FRI. 23 JUNE
Cymbeline   C/BG
Female Curiosity   b: Floor (prompter)
The Padlock

SAT. 24 JUNE
Isabella   C/G, BC, BJ
The Touchstone

MON. 26 JUNE
Isabella   C/FF b: Mrs Siddons
Britons Strike Home
Edgar and Emmeline

WED. 28 JUNE
Braganza   C/FF b: Mrs Ward
Buxom Joan
The Two Misers

FRI. 30 JUNE
The Countess of Salisbury   C/BG
The Quaker   b: Payne & Walker

MON. 3 JULY
The Grecian Daughter   C/FF, G b: Dimond
The Press Gang
The Guardian

WED. 5 JULY
Much Ado About Nothing   C/FF b; Browne
Like Master Like Man

FRI. 7 JULY
Venice Preserv'd   C/BG
The Golden Pippin

MON. 10 JULY
Henry VIII   C/FF b: Clarke
The Toy Shop
The Irish Widow

WED. 12 JULY
The Busy Body   C/FF, G b: Didier
The Recruiting Sergeant
The Contrivances

FRI. 14 JULY
Macbeth   C/FF b: Jackson
Buxom Joan
The Capricious Lovers

MON. 17 MAY
The Belle's Stratagem   C/FF
The Critic

End of Season

Season 1780/81

Company

Mr: Blisset, Bonnor, Brett, Brookes, Browne, Brunton, Didier, Dimond, Floor, Griffin, Haughton, Jackson, Keasberry, Payne, Rowbotham, Siddons, Summers, G. Summers.

Mrs: Brett, Didier, Griffin, Hedges, Keasberry, Martin, Siddons, Summers.

Miss: Brett, Jones, H & J Keasberry, Kemble, Palmer, Scrace, Storer, Summers, Wheeler.

Master: Brett, Broderick, Gowen, Griffin, Keasberry, J. Keasberry, Payne, Siddons.

Treasurer: Lloyd   *Prompter:* Floor   *Box Book Keeper:* Fisher

1780

FRI. 1 SEPT.
Love in a Village   C/FF
The Touchstone

MON. 4 SEPT.
Hamlet   C/FF
The Capricious Lovers

FRI. 8 SEPT.
The Provok'd Husband   C/BG
The Register Office

MON. 11 SEPT.
Jane Shore   C/FF
The Capricious Lovers

FRI. 15 SEPT.
Douglas   C/BG
The Padlock

MON. 18 SEPT.
The Spanish Friar   C/FF
The Waterman

TUES. 19 SEPT.
Jane Shore   C/G
Harlequin Touchstone

WED. 20 SEPT.
The Belle's Stratagem   C/G
The Camp

THURS. 21 SEPT.
The Countess of Salisbury   C/G
The Waterman

FRI. 22 SEPT.
The Spanish Barber
The Critic

SAT. 23 SEPT.
The Maid of the Mill
Who's The Dupe?

MON. 25 SEPT.
The School for Scandal   C/FF
Selima and Azor

FRI. 29 SEPT.
Percy   C/BG
The Camp

SAT. 30 SEPT.
The Times   C/G
The Flitch of Bacon

MON. 2 OCT.
The Spanish Friar   C/FF
The Rival Candidates

WED. 4 OCT.
Lionel and Clarissa
Who's the Dupe?

FRI. 6 OCT.
Henry II   C/BG
The Devil upon two sticks

SAT. 7 OCT.
Henry II   C/G
Who's The Dupe?

MON. 9 OCT.
The Chapter of Accidents   C/FF
The Quaker

WED. 11 OCT.
Lionel and Clarissa
Like Master Like Man

FRI. 13 OCT.
The Chapter of Accidents   C/BG

SAT. 14 OCT.
The Chapter of Accidents   C/G
The Quaker

MON. 16 OCT.
The Distress'd Mother   C/FF
The Deserter

TUES. 17 OCT.
The Distress'd Mother   C/G
The Deserter

SAT. 21 OCT.
The Way to Keep Him   C/G
The Two Misers

MON. 23 OCT.
The Chapter of Accidents   C/FF
The Devil to Pay

TUES. 24 OCT.
The Chapter of Accidents
The Two Misers

SAT. 28 OCT.
The Law of Lombardy   C/G
The Camp

MON. 30 OCT.
The Lady of the Manor   C/FF
The Man's the Master

TUES. 31 OCT.
The Belle's Stratagem
The Man's the Master

SAT. 4 NOV.
The Chapter of Accidents

MON. 6 NOV.
Timanthes   C/FF
The Critic

TUES. 7 NOV.
Timanthes   C/G
The Devil Upon Two Sticks

SAT. 11 NOV.
The Rivals   C/G
The Critic

TUES. 14 NOV.
The School for Scandal   C/G
The Scheming Lieutenant

WED. 15 NOV.
The Chapter of Accidents   C/FF
The Two Misers

SAT. 18 NOV.
The Times
Tony Lumpkin in Town

MON. 20 NOV.
The Rivals   C/FF
Tony Lumpkin in Town

TUES. 21 NOV.
Elfrida   C/G
Who's the Dupe?

THURS. 23 NOV.
Timanthes
Tony Lumpkin in Town

SAT. 25 NOV.
The Careless Husband   C/G
The Capricious Lovers

MON. 27 NOV.
Elfrida   C/FF
Who's The Dupe?

TUES. 28 NOV.
The Chapter of Accidents
Selima and Azor

WED. 29 NOV.
The Duenna
Cross Purposes

SAT. 2 DEC.
Elfrida
The Scheming Lieutenant

MON. 4 DEC.
The Duenna   C/FF
The Cozeners

TUES. 5 DEC.
The Fashionable Lover   C/G
The Cozeners

WED. 6 DEC.
Timanthes
The Critic

SAT. 9 DEC.
The School for Scandal
Selima and Azor

MON. 11 DEC.
Timanthes   C/FF, PB/P
The Shepherd's Lottery

TUES. 12 DEC.
Elfrida
Bon Ton

WED. 13 DEC.
The Belle's Stratagem
The Shepherd's Lottery

SAT. 16 DEC.
All in the Wrong   C/G

MON. 18 DEC.
Elfrida   C/FF
Bon Ton

TUES. 19 DEC.
The Chapter of Accidents
The Deserter

THURS. 21 DEC.
Douglas   C/G
The Touchstone

SAT. 23 DEC.
Know Your Own Mind
The Camp

TUES. 26 DEC.
Elfrida
The Critic

WED. 27 DEC.
Henry V
The Touchstone

THURS. 28 DEC.
The Chapter of Accidents   C/FF
The Camp

SAT. 30 DEC.
The Chapter of Accidents
The Shepherd's Lottery

1781

MON. 1 JAN.
All in the Wrong   C/FF
The Critic

TUES. 2 JAN.
The West Indian
The Devil Upon Two Sticks

WED. 3 JAN.
All in the Wrong
Bladud

SAT. 6 JAN.
The Times
The Critic

MON. 8 JAN.
The Generous Imposter   C/FF
The Touchstone

TUES. 9 JAN.
The Generous Imposter
The Shepherd's Lottery

WED. 10 JAN.
The Countess of Salisbury
Bladud

SAT. 13 JAN.
The Provok'd Husband   C/G
The Golden Pippin

MON. 15 JAN.
Percy   C/FF
The Ephesian Matron
Who's The Dupe?

TUES. 16 JAN.
Elfrida
The Critic

WED. 17 JAN.
The Chapter of Accidents

SAT. 20 JAN.
The Belle's Stratagem
The Flitch of Bacon

MON. 22 JAN.
Lionel and Clarissa   C/FF
The Mayor of Garratt

TUES. 23 JAN.
Henry II
Bladud

WED. 24 JAN.
All in the Wrong
The Critic

SAT. 27 JAN.
The Duenna
Bladud

MON. 29 JAN.
The School for Scandal   C/FF
Selima and Azor

WED. 31 JAN.
The Gamester   C/BJ, G
The Humours of an Election

THURS. 1 FEB.
Lionel and Clarissa
Bladud

SAT. 3 FEB.
Elfreda

MON. 5 FEB.
The Gamester   C/FF
The Flitch of Bacon

TUES. 6 FEB.
Isabella   C/BJ, BC, G
Three Weeks after Marriage   b: Dimond

WED. 7 FEB.
The Gamester   C/BJ,b: Jackson
The Flitch of Bacon

SAT. 10 FEB.
The School for Wives   C/BJ, BC b: Keasberry
Damon and Phillida
Hob in the Well

MON. 12 FEB.
The Orphan   C/FF
The Two Misers

TUES. 13 FEB.
The Belle's Stratagem   C/BJ, BC b: Browne
Daphne and Amintor

WED. 14 FEB.
The Beggar's Opera   C/BJ, b: Mrs Brett
Midas

SAT. 17 FEB.
Jane Shore   C/BJ, BC, G
All The World's A Stage   b: Mrs Siddons

MON. 19 FEB.
The Duenna   C/FF
All The World's a Stage

TUES. 20 FEB.
The Rivals   C/BJ, BC,
The Toyshop   b: Miss Wheeler
The Contrivances

THURS. 22 FEB.
The Funeral   C/BJ, BC, G b: Floor
Bucks Have at Ye All
Midas

SAT. 24 FEB.
She Stoops to Conquer   C/BJ, G, b: Mrs. Didier
Linco's Travels
A Trip to Scotland

MON. 26 FEB.
The Beggar's Opera   C/FF
A Trip to Scotland

TUES. 27 FEB.
The Conscious Lovers   C/BJ, BC, G,
The Waterman   b: Griffin

THURS. 1 MAR.
The Bondman   C/BJ, G,
The Death of Harlequin   b: Mr. & Mrs.Summers

MON. 5 MAR.
The West Indian   C/FF
The Waterman

TUES. 6 MAR.
The Inconstant   C/BJ, G, b: Bonnor
Buxom Joan
High Life Below Stairs

THURS. 8 MAR.
The Gamester   C/BJ,
The Padlock   b: Lloyd & Fisher

SAT. 10 MAR.
The Chapter of Accidents
The Camp

MON. 12 MAR.
Know Your Own Mind   C/FF
The Humours of an Election

TUES. 13 MAR.
The Times
Midas

THURS. 15 MAR.
The School for Scandal   PB/Ba
Bladud

SAT. 17 MAR.
The Careless Husband
Midas

MON. 19 MAR.
The Lord of the Manor   C/FF
Who's The Dupe?

TUES. 20 MAR.
The Times
The Critic

THURS. 22 MAR.
The Lord of the Manor
Who's The Dupe?

SAT. 24 MAR.
Much Ado About Nothing   C/BJ
The Rival Candidates

MON. 26 MAR.
Rule a Wife and Have a Wife C/FF
The Humours of an Election

TUES. 27 MAR.
The Lord of the Manor
Bladud

THURS. 29 MAR.
Henry V   C/G
Selima and Azor

SAT. 31 MAR.
Rule a Wife and Have a Wife   C/G
The Flitch of Bacon

MON. 2 APR.
Henry V   C/FF
The Flitch of Bacon

TUES. 3 APR.
The Duenna
The Scheming Lieutenant

THURS. 5 APR.
The Provok'd Husband
Bladud

SAT. 7 APR.
The Lord of the Manor
The Camp

MON. 16 APR.
The Beggar's Opera   C/FF
The Devil Upon Two Sticks

TUES. 17 APR.
The Beggar's Opera   C/G, BJ
The Lying Valet

WED. 18 APR.
Rule a Wife and Have a Wife
Robinson Crusoe

THURS. 19 APR.
Richard III   C/G
Robinson Crusoe

SAT. 21 APR.
The Belle's Stratagem
Daphne and Amintor

MON. 23 APR.
The Chapter of Accidents   C/FF
The Conquest of St. Eustatia
The Capricious Lovers

TUES. 24 APR.
The Chapter of Accidents
Robinson Crusoe

WED. 25 APR.
The Lord of the Manor
Robinson Crusoe

SAT. 28 APR.
Dissipation   C/G, BC
The Quaker

MON. 30 APR.
Dissipation   C/FF
The Conquest of St. Eustatia
Cross Purposes

TUES. 1 MAY
The School for Scandal
Robinson Crusoe

WED. 2 MAY
Dissipation   C/BJ
Robinson Crusoe

SAT. 5 MAY
Elfreda
Cross Purposes

MON. 7 MAY
Elfrida   C/FF
All the World's a Stage

TUES. 8 MAY
The Duenna
Robinson Crusoe

WED. 9 MAY
The Gamester
Robinson Crusoe

SAT. 12 MAY
The Royal Suppliants   C/G

MON. 14 MAY
The Gamester   C/FF
Robinson Crusoe

TUES. 15 MAY
Cymon   C/BJ, G, b: Brett
The Guardian

WED. 16 MAY
The Grecian Daughter   C/BJ, G, b: Siddons &
Britons Strike Home   Rowbotham
The Rival Candidates

SAT. 19 MAY
The Double Falsehood   C/BJ, BC, G,
The Rose Wreath   b: Mrs. Keasberry
The Ghost

MON. 21 MAY
(Performance cancelled — accident to Miss Kemble)

SAT. 26 MAY
The Beaux Stratagem   C/BC, G, b: Mrs.Hedges

MON. 28 MAY
The Royal Suppliants   C/FF
Robinson Crusoe

TUES. 29 MAY
The Clandestine Marriage   C/BJ, BC, G,b: Didier
The Rose Wreath   (who is leaving stage)
All the World's a Stage

WED. 30 MAY
Law of Lombardy   C/BJ, b: Brookes
Thomas and Sally

SAT. 2 JUNE
The Fair Penitent   C/BJ, G, BC b: Brunton
The Golden Pippin
The Rose Wreath

TUES. 5 JUNE
All in the Wrong   C/FF
Robinson Crusoe

WED. 6 JUNE
The Countess of Salisbury   C/BJ, b:Mrs. Martin
Damon and Phyllida   & Payne
The Quaker

THURS. 7 JUNE
Braganza   C/BJ, BC, G,
Harlequin Skeleton   b:Haughton
Selima and Azor

SAT. 9 JUNE
Jane Shore   C/BJ, BC, G, b:Lloyd
The Toy Shop   & Fisher
The Flitch of Bacon

MON. 11 JUNE
The Fair Penitent   C/FF, G, b:Dimond
Death of Harlequin
The Contrivances

WED. 13 JUNE
The Careless Husband   C/FF, b: Mrs.Didier
Linco's Travels
The Padlock

SAT. 16 JUNE
Isabella   C/BJ b: Child
The Rose Wreath   Performers
The Death of Harlequin

MON. 18 JUNE
The Lord of the Manor   C/FF b:Brett
True Blue
The Devil to Pay

WED. 20 JUNE
The Merchant of Venice   C/FF b:Jackson
Hob in the Well

FRI. 22 JUNE
The Gamester   C/FF b:Winstone
The Recruiting Sergeant
The Capricious Lovers

SAT. 23 JUNE
The Siege of Sinope   C/BJ, BC
Robinson Crusoe

MON. 25 JUNE
Jane Shore   C/FF b:Miss Wheeler
The Golden Pippin

WED. 27 JUNE
Hamlet   C/FF, G b:Miss Kemble
The Sheep Shearing   & Siddons
The Sheep Shearing

MON. 2 JULY
Cymbeline   C/FF b:Browne
The Waterman

WED. 4 JULY
The Inconstant   PB/Ba C/FF, G
The Irish Widow   b: Bonnor

SAT. 7 JULY
The Siege of Sinope   C/G, BC, BJ
Robinson Crusoe

MON. 9 JULY
The Funeral   C/FF, G b:Mrs.Siddons
The Citizen

WED. 11 JULY
Othello   C/G b:Houghton &
The Toy Shop   Payne
? The Fortune Teller

FRI. 13 JULY
The Gamester   C/FF b:Miles, Guy,
                               Hopkins "and Co."
The Two Misers

MON. 16 JULY
Isabella   C/FF b:Keasberry
The Rose Wreath
The Ghost

WED. 18 JULY
Percy   C/FF b:Miss Storer
                               & Brunton
The Toy Shop
The Flitch of Bacon

FRI. 20 JULY
The Fatal Falsehood   C/FF, G
The Fortune Teller

MON. 23 JULY
The West Indian   C/FF b:Browne
The Toy Shop
The King and the Miller of
   Mansfield

WED. 25 JULY
The Maid of the Mill   PB/Ba C/FF
Damon and Phyllida   b: Mrs. Brett
The Fortune Teller

FRI. 27 JULY
She Stoops to Conquer   C/FF,G b:Didier
The Rehearsal
Lethe

End of Season

Season 1781/82

Company

Mr: Blanchard, Blisset, Brett, Bonnor, Brookes, Browne, Brunsdon, Brunton, Creswick, Dimond, Haughton, Jackson, Keasberry, Payne, Powell, Rowbotham, Siddons, Summers, G. Summers.

Mrs: Brett, Didier, Keasberry, Powell, Siddons, Summers.

Miss: Brett, Scrace, Summers, Twist, Wewitzer, Wheeler

Masters: Brett, Gavin, George, Hendy, Johnson, J. Keasberry, H. Keasberry, Williams.

Junior Miss: H. & J. Keasberry, Jacobs, Jones, Palmer, Selwyn

Treasurer: Lloyd   *Box Book-Keeper:* Fisher

1781

MON. 3 SEPT.
The Beggar's Opera (Vernon) C/FF
The Citizen

TUES. 4 SEPT.
The Merchant of Venice   C/FF
Robinson Crusoe

MON. 10 SEPT.
Lionel and Clarissa (Vernon) C/FF
The Devil Upon Two Sticks

TUES. 11 SEPT.
Percy   C/BJ, G
Robinson Crusoe

WED. 12 SEPT.
The Beggar's Opera (Vermon) C/BJ
The Critic

THURS. 13 SEPT.
Chapter of Accidents   C/G
Midas

FRI. 14 SEPT.
The Merchant of Venice   C/BJ, G
Robinson Crusoe

SAT. 15 SEPT.
Lionel and Clarissa (Vernon) C/G, BJ
The Times
The Lying Valet

MON. 17 SEPT.
The Busy Body   C/FF b:Vernon
The Quaker

FRI. 21 SEPT.
Venice Preserv'd
Robinson Crusoe

SAT. 22 SEPT.
Douglas   C/G
Selima and Azor

MON. 24 SEPT.
The Siege of Sinope   C/FF
Robinson Crusoe

WED. 26 SEPT.
As You Like It   C/FF
The Flitch of Bacon

FRI. 28 SEPT.
Jane Shore

SAT. 29 SEPT.
As You Like It   C/G
Harlequin Touchstone

MON. 1 OCT.
As You Like It   C/FF
Robinson Crusoe

SAT. 6 OCT.
The Mourning Bride   C/G
The Portrait

MON. 8 OCT.
The Times   C/FF
Tom Thumb the Great

SAT. 13 OCT.
Jane Shore   C/BC, BJ, G
Tom Thumb the Great

MON. 15 OCT.
The Grecian Daughter   C/FF
Tom Thumb the Great

SAT. 20 OCT.
Rule a Wife and Have a   C/BC, BJ, G
   Wife
Tom Thumb the Great

MON. 22 OCT.
The Countess of Salisbury   C/FF
Tom Thumb the Great

TUES. 23 OCT.
The Countess of Salisbury   C/BJ, G
The Flitch of Bacon

WED. 24 OCT.
Know Your Own Mind
Robinson Crusoe

SAT. 27 OCT.
The Rivals   C/BJ, G
Midas

MON. 29 OCT.
The Times   C/FF
Tom Thumb the Great

TUES. 30 OCT.
The Mourning Bride
Tom Thumb the Great

WED. 31 OCT.
The Clandestine Marriage   C/BJ
Lovewell and Fanny
The Son-in-Law

SAT. 3 NOV.
Isabella   C/G, PB/A
The Son-in-Law

MON. 5 NOV.
Elfrida   C/FF
The Son -in-Law

TUES. 6 NOV.
The Grecian Daughter   PB/Ba C/BJ, G
Robinson Crusoe

WED. 7 NOV.
Merchant of Venice
The Son-in-Law

SAT. 10 NOV.
The Clandestine Marriage
The Quaker

MON. 12 NOV.
Caractacus   C/FF
The Son-in-Law

TUES. 13 NOV.
As You Like It   C/BJ
Tom Thumb the Great

WED. 14 NOV.
The Gamester
Robinson Crusoe

SAT. 17 NOV.
Caractacus   C/G
Who's the Dupe?

MON. 19 NOV.
Caractacus   C/FF
Who's the Dupe?

TUES. 20 NOV.
Percy   PB/A, C/BJ
Midas

WED. 21 NOV.
The Clandestine Marriage   PB/A
The Son-in-Law

SAT. 24 NOV.
School for Scandal   C/G

MON. 26 NOV.
The Fatal Falsehood   C/FF
Tom Thumb the Great

TUES. 27 NOV.
Jane Shore   C/BJ
The Portrait

WED. 28 NOV.
Caractacus

SAT. 1 DEC.
The Chapter of Accidents

MON. 3 DEC.
The Duenna   C/FF
Catherine and Petruchio

TUES. 4 DEC.
The Mourning Bride   C/BJ
Robinson Crusoe

WED. 5 DEC.
The Rivals
The Flitch of Bacon

SAT. 8 DEC.
The West Indian

MON. 10 DEC.
All in the Wrong   C/FF
Tom Thumb the Great

TUES. 11 DEC.
The Grecian Daughter

WED. 12 DEC.
The Duenna   PB/A
The Touchstone

SAT. 15 DEC.
Elfrida
The Son-in-Law

MON. 17 DEC.
Zara   C/FF
Robinson Crusoe

TUES. 18 DEC.
Zara   C/BJ, G

THURS. 20 DEC.
The Belle's Stratagem
Touchstone

SAT. 22 DEC.
The Merchant of Venice   PB/Ba
Who's the Dupe?

THURS. 27 DEC.
Caractacus   C/FF
The Touchstone

FRI. 28 DEC.
Caractacus
Damon and Phillida
Tom Thumb

SAT. 29 DEC.
Duplicity   C/BC, G
The Flitch of Bacon

MON. 31 DEC.
Duplicity   C/FF
Tom Thumb

1782
TUES. 1 JAN.
Douglas
Robinson Crusoe

THURS. 3 JAN.
Venice Preserv'd   C/BC, G

SAT. 5 JAN.
The Way to Keep Him   C/G
Interlude from Damon and
Phillida
The Son-in-Law

MON. 7 JAN.
The Gamester   C/FF
The Gentle Shepherd

TUES. 8 JAN.
Duplicity   PB/A, C/BJ, BC
The Gentle Shepherd

THURS. 10 JAN.
Zara   PB/H C/BC
Robinson Crusoe

SAT. 12 JAN.
The Grecian Daughter   PB/H
Who's the Dupe?

MON. 14 JAN.
Duplicity   C/FF
The Gentle Shepherd

TUES. 15 JAN.
All in the Wrong   PB/H, A, C/BJ, G
The Gentle Shepherd

THURS. 17 JAN.
Elfrida   PB/H, A
The Gentle Shepherd

SAT. 19 JAN.
The Chapter of Accidents PB/H
Robinson Crusoe

MON. 21 JAN.
The Chapter of Accidents C/FF
The Gentle Shepherd

TUES. 22 JAN.
The Fair Circassian   PB/H C/BJ, BC, G
The Ghost

Box Price raised to 5s from 22 Jan.

THURS. 24 JAN.
The Provok'd Husband
The Gentle Shepherd

SAT. 26 JAN.
The School for Scandal   PB/H
The Critic

MON. 28 JAN.
The Fair Circassian   C/FF
The Ghost

TUES. 29 JAN.
The Fair Circassian   C/BJ, BC
The Gentle Shepherd

THURS. 31 JAN.
The Fair Circassian
Robinson Crusoe

SAT. 2 FEB.
The Fair Circassian   PB/H
The Gentle Shepherd

MON. 4 FEB.
The Fair Circassian   C/FF
The Son-in-Law

TUES. 5 FEB.
Caractacus   C/BJ, BC
The Dragon of Wantley   b: Mrs Brett
The King and the Miller of
Mansfield

WED. 6 FEB.

The Provok'd Husband   C/BJ, G b: Dimond
Catherine and Petruchio

SAT. 9 FEB.

The Mourning Bride   PB/F C/BJ, BC, G
The Devil to Pay   b: Mrs Siddons

MON. 11 FEB.

The Provok'd Husband   C/FF
Robinson Crusoe

TUES. 12 FEB.

Jane Shore   PB/H C/BJ, BC,
Midas   b: Miss Wewitzer,
A Grand Fete   Miss Twist

THURS. 14 FEB.

The Conscious Lovers   PB/H C/BJ, BC,G
Selima and Azor   b: Payne &
                                  Brunsdon

SAT. 16 FEB.

The Law of Lombardy   PB/H C/BJ, BC,G
The Rose Wreath   b: Keasberry
The Cozeners

MON. 18 FEB.

The Fair Circassian   C/FF
The Dragon of Wantley
Catherine and Petruchio

TUES. 19 FEB.

Venice Preserv'd   PB/H, C/BJ, BC
Damon and Phillida   b: Browne
Bon Ton

THURS. 21 FEB.

The Inconstant   PB/HU, C/BJ, BC, G
True Blue   b: Jackson
Catherine and Petruchio

SAT. 23 FEB.

The Jealous Wife   PB/H, C/BJ, BC/G
The Rehearsal   b: Mrs Didier
The Irish Widow

TUES. 25 FEB.

Measure for Measure   C/FF, PB/H
Robinson Crusoe

TUES. 26 FEB.

Tancred and Sigismunda   PB/H, C/BJ, G
The Rehearsal   b: Brunton
The Scheming Lieutenant

THURS. 28 FEB.

The Chapter of Accidents   PB/H, C/BJ, BC
The Birth and Adventures of b: G. Summers &
Harlequin   Miss Summers

FRI. 1 MAR.

Hamlet   PB/H
Robinson Crusoe

SAT. 2 MAR.

The Law of Lombardy   PB/H (incomplete)

MON. 4 MAR.

The Countess of Salisbury   C/FF
Selima and Azor

TUES. 5 MAR.

The Gamester   C/BJ, BC, G b: Powell
The Birth and Adventures of Harlequin
Hobby Horses and other Entertainments

THURS. 7 MAR.

Much Ado About Nothing   C/BJ, G
The Scheming Lieutenant   b: Lloyd & Fisher

SAT. 9 MAR.

Measure for Measure   PB/H C/G
Tom Thumb the Great

MON. 11 MAR.

The Fair Circassian   C/FF
Midas

TUES. 12 MAR.

The Fair Circassian   PB/H, C/BJ
The Son-in-Law

THURS. 14 MAR.

Duplicity   PB/H
The Cozeners

SAT. 16 MAR.

All in the Wrong   PB/H
The Touchstone

MON. 18 MAR.

Caractacus   C/FF
Tom Thumb the Great

TUES. 19 MAR.

The Mourning Bride   C/BJ
The Gentle Shepherd

THURS. 21 MAR.

The Count of Narbonne   PB/F C/G
Who's the Dupe?

SAT. 23 MAR.

The Times
Robinson Crusoe

MON. 1 APRIL

The Count of Narbonne   C/FF
The Scheming Lieutenant

TUES. 2 APRIL

The Count of Narbonne   PB/H, C/BJ
The Scheming Lieutenant

WED. 3 APRIL

The Spanish Barber
Robinson Crusoe

THURS. 4 APRIL

The Provok'd Husband   PB/F C/G
The Son-in-Law

SAT. 6 APRIL

Venice Preserv'd   PB/F
The Gentle Shepherd

MON. 8 APRIL

The Count of Narbonne   C/FF
The Gentle Shepherd

TUES. 9 APRIL

The Grecian Daughter   PB/F C/BJ
Tom Thumb the Great

THURS. 11 APRIL

The Belle's Stratagem   PB/H
Robinson Crusoe

SAT. 13 APRIL

The Way to Keep Him   PB/F
The Son-in-Law

MON. 15 APRIL

The Count of Narbonne   C/FF
The Son-in-Law

TUES. 16 APRIL

The Count of Narbonne   PB/F C/BJ
The Maid of the Oaks

WED. 17 APRIL

The Maid of the Oaks

THURS. 18 APRIL

King John   PB/F, C/G, BJ
The Gentle Shepherd

SAT. 20 APRIL

The School for Scandal   PB/F
The Maid of the Oaks

MON. 22 APRIL

King John   C/FF
The Maid of the Oaks

TUES. 23 APRIL

King John   PB/F C/BJ
Tom Thumb the Great

THURS. 25 APRIL

Know Your Own Mind
The Maid of the Oaks

SAT. 27 APRIL

Elfrida   PB/F C/G
The Gentle Shepherd

MON. 29 APRIL

The Fair Circassian   C/FF
Tom Thumb the Great

TUES. 30 APRIL

The Count of Narbonne   PB/F C/BJ
The Maid of the Oaks

THURS. 2 MAY

All in the Wrong   PB/F
Robinson Crusoe

SAT. 4 MAY

The Fair Circassian
The Positive Man

MON. 6 MAY

The Duenna   C/FF
The Positive Man

TUES. 7 MAY

Jane Shore   PB/F C/BJ
The Positive Man

WED. 8 MAY

Measure for Measure   PB/F
The Maid of the Oaks

SAT. 11 MAY

Variety   PB/F C/BJ, G
The Gentle Shepherd

MON. 13 MAY

Variety   C/FF
The Maid of the Oaks

TUES. 14 MAY

The Count of Narbonne   PB/F C/BJ, BC
The Rose Wreath   b: Mrs Keasberry
Tom Thumb the Great

WED. 15 MAY

The School for Wives   PB/F C/BJ, G
The Toy Shop   b: Rowbotham &
The Positive Man   Brookes

SAT. 18 MAY

The Mourning Bride   PB/F, C/BJ, BC
The Recruiting Sergeant   b: Brett
The Deserter

MON. 20 MAY

The Count of Narbonne   C/FF
True Blue
The Gentle Shepherd

TUES. 21 MAY

The Distress'd Mother   PB/F, Ba, C/BJ, G, BC
The Devil to Pay   b: Mrs. Siddons

WED. 22 MAY
The Merchant of Venice   PB/F, C/BJ, BC
The Deuce is in Him   b: Haughton

SAT. 25 MAY
The Rivals   PB/F, C/BJ, BC
The Harmonic Meeting   b: Bonnor
Love at First Sight

MON. 27 MAY
Variety   C/FF
The Positive Man

TUES. 28 MAY
Edward and Eleanora   PB/F, C/BJ, G
The Nosegay   b: Miss Scrace
The Devil Upon Two Sticks

WED. 29 MAY
King John   PB/F, C/BJ b: Lloyd
True Blue
Barnaby Brittle

SAT. 1 JUNE
The Chapter of Accidents PB/F, Ba, C/BJ, G
The Maid of the Oaks

MON. 3 JUNE
The Law of Lombardy   C/FF b: Keasberry
The Rose Wreath
Barnaby Brittle

WED. 5 JUNE
Zara   C/FF b: Brunton
True Blue
Flora

FRI. 7 JUNE, MON. 10 JUNE, WED. 12 JUNE
Closed owing to illness

SAT. 8 JUNE
Venice Preserv'd   C/BJ, BC
St. Patrick's Day

FRI. 14 JUNE
? Bristol   b: Winstone

SAT. 15 JUNE
Venice Preserv'd   C/BJ
Retaliation

MON. 17 JUNE
Tancred and Sigismunda C/FF, G
The Devil to Pay   b: Mrs. Siddons

WED. 19 JUNE
The School for Wives   C/FF, G b: Mrs. Brett
The Deserter

SAT. 22 JUNE
The School for Scandal   PB/H, C/BJ, BC
Tom Thumb the Great

MON. 24 JUNE
Much Ado About Nothing C/FF, b: Dimond
The Rehearsal
The Deuce is in Him

WED. 26 JUNE
The Chances   C/FF, G b: Miss Scrace
Chit Chat
The Cozeners

FRI. 28 JUNE
The Spanish Friar   PB/H, C/FF
Robinson Crusoe   b: The Band

MON. 1 JULY
The Suspicious Husband C/FF b: Bonnor
Harvest Home
Love at First Sight

WED. 3 JULY
The Belle's Stratagem   C/FF b: Payne &
Robinson Crusoe   Houghton

SAT. 6 JULY
The Spanish Friar   PB/H, C/BJ
Retaliation   b: The Band

MON. 8 JULY
The Hypocrite   C/FF, G
Bon Ton   b: Mrs. Didier & Miss
                          Wewitzer

WED. 10 JULY
The Jealous Wife   C/FF b: Blissett
The Citizen   & Rowbotham

FRI. 12 JULY
The London Merchant   C/FF b: G. Summers
The Birth and Adventures of & Miss Summers
  Harlequin

SAT. 13 JULY
Duplicity   PB/H, C/BJ b: The
The Quaker   Servants of the House

MON. 15 JULY
The Beaux Stratagem   C/FF b: Browne
The Quaker

WED. 17 JULY
The Count of Narbonne   C/FF b: Mrs. &
Miss in Her Teens   Master Keasberry
The Birth and Adventures & Jackson
  of Harlequin

FRI. 19 JULY
School for Wives   C/G b: Mrs. Brett
The Deserter

End of Season

Season 1782/83

Company

Mr: Blanchard, T. Blanchard, Blisset, Bonnor, Brookes, J. Brown, Browne, Brunton, Church, Cooke, Dimond, Dutton, Hasker, Jackson, Keasberry, Mathews, Mills, Payne, Rowbotham, Simpson, Stanfield, Summers, G. Summers.

Mrs: Baker, J. Brown, Didier, Hasker, Keasberry, Simpson, Summers.

Miss: E. & H. Brunton, Catchpole, Jackson, H. & J. Keasberry, Ross, F. Ross, Scrace, Summers, Twist, Wewitzer

Master: J. Brunton, Cooke, George, Hendy, H. & J. Keasberry, Thompson.

Treasurer: Lloyd   *Box Book-Keeper:* Fisher (Bath), Walker (Bristol)

1782

TUES. 17 SEPT.

Love in a Village   PB/H, C/BC, BJ, G
Robinson Crusoe

WED. 18 SEPT.

Tancred and Sigismunda   PB/H, C/BJ, G
The Gentle Shepherd

THURS. 19 SEPT.

The Rivals   PB/H, C/BC
The Maid of the Oaks

FRI. 20 SEPT.

Percy   PB/H, C/BC
Robinson Crusoe

SAT. 21 SEPT.

The Beggar's Opera   PB/H, C/G, C/BC
The Virgin Unmask'd

MON. 23 SEPT.

Tancred and Sigismunda   C/FF
The Gentle Shepherd

WED. 25 SEPT.

Love in a Village   PB/H
The Virgin Unmask'd

FRI. 27 SEPT.

The Chapter of Accidents   PB/H
Tom Thumb the Great

SAT. 28 SEPT.

The Chapter of Accidents   PB/H, C/BJ, G
The Gentle Shepherd

MON. 30 SEPT.

The Rivals   C/FF
The Maid of The Oaks

WED. 2 OCT.

The Times   PB/H
The Gentle Shepherd

FRI. 4 OCT.

The Clandestine Marriage   PB/H
The Virgin Unmask'd

SAT. 5 OCT.

The Clandestine Marriage   PB/H, C/BJ, BC
The Virgin Unmask'd

MON. 7 OCT.

The Duenna   C/FF
Retaliation

WED. 9 OCT.

The Count of Narbonne   PB/H, Ba
The Gentle Shepherd

FRI. 11 OCT.

Love for Love   PB/H
Retaliation

SAT. 12 OCT.

Love for Love   PB/H, C/BJ
Retaliation

MON. 14 OCT.

The Maid of the Mill   C/FF
Who's The Dupe?

WED. 16 OCT.

The Chapter of Accidents   PB/H
The Maid of the Oaks

FRI. 18 OCT.

Percy   PB/H
The Necromancer

SAT. 19 OCT.

The Maid of the Mill   PB/H, C/BJ
Miss in Her Teens

MON. 21 OCT.

Love for Love   C/FF
The Necromancer

FRI. 25 OCT.
The London Merchant   PB/H
The Necromancer

SAT. 26 OCT.
The English Merchant   PB/H, C/BJ, BC
The Devil to Pay

MON. 28 OCT.
The Rivals   (Mrs.Belfille) C/FF
The Devil to Pay

WED. 30 OCT.
The Spanish Friar   PB/H
The Necromancer

FRI. 1 NOV.
Cleone   PB/H
The Virgin Unmask'd

SAT. 2 NOV.
The Provok'd Husband   PB/H, C/BJ
Tom Thumb the Great

MON. 4 NOV.
The English Merchant   C/FF
The Quaker

TUES. 5 NOV.
Jane Shore (Mrs. Belfille)   C/BJ
The Gentle Shepherd

WED. 6 NOV..
The Provok'd Husband   PB/H
The Necromancer

SAT. 9 NOV.
The Way to Keep Him
Midas

MON. 11 NOV.
The Way to Keep Him   C/FF
The Necromancer

TUES. 12 NOV.
Love in a Village   C/BJ
The Devil upon Two Sticks

THURS. 14 NOV.
Love for Love   PB/H
The Positive Man

SAT. 16 NOV.
The School for Scandal
The Maid of the Oaks

MON. 18 NOV.
The School for Scandal   C/FF
The Son-In-Law

TUES. 19 NOV.
The Foundling   PB/H, C/BJ, G
The Son-in-Law

THURS. 21 NOV.
Cleone   PB/H, C/G
The Flitch of Bacon

SAT. 23 NOV.
The Chapter of Accidents   PB/H
The Gentle Shepherd

MON. 25 NOV.
The Foundling   C/FF
The Positive Man

TUES. 26 NOV.
The Rivals   C/BJ
The Necromancer

THURS. 28 NOV.
The Hypocrite   C/BJ
Thomas and Sally

SAT. 30 NOV.
The Foundling   C/BC, BJ
The Son-in-Law

MON. 2 DEC.
Othello   C/FF
Thomas and Sally

TUES. 3 DEC.
Venice Preserv'd   C/BJ
The Necromancer

THURS. 5 DEC.
The Spanish Friar
The Quaker

SAT. 7 DEC.
Much Ado About Nothing   PB/H, Ba
Tom Thumb

MON. 9 DEC.
Henry II   C/FF
The Maid of The Oaks

TUES. 10 DEC.
The Clandestine Marriage   C/BJ
The Necromancer

THURS. 12 DEC.
Othello   PB/H
Selima and Azor

SAT. 14 DEC.
The English Merchant   PB/H
The Gentle Shepherd

MON. 16 DEC.
The Way to Keep Him   C/FF, PB/H
The Gentle Shepherd

TUES. 17 DEC.
The School for Scandal   PB/H, C/BJ
The Necromancer

THURS. 19 DEC.
Henry II   PB/H
The Padlock

SAT. 21 DEC.
A Word to the Wise   PB/H
The Agreeable Surprise

MON. 23 DEC.
A Word to the Wise   C/FF
The Agreeable Surprise

THURS. 26 DEC.
The Maid of the Mill   PB/H, C/BJ
The Necromancer

FRI. 27 DEC.
Romeo and Juliet   PB/H
The Agreeable Surprise

SAT. 28 DEC.
The West Indian   PB/H, C/BJ
The Virgin Unmask'd

MON. 30 DEC.
Romeo and Juliet   C/FF
Robinson Crusoe

TUES. 31 DEC.
The Chapter of Accidents   PB/H, C/BJ
The Agreeable Surprise

1783

THURS. 2 JAN.
The Beggar's Opera   PB/H
The Necromancer

SAT. 4 JAN.
Which is the Man?   PB/H, C/G
Maid of the Oaks

MON. 6 JAN.
The Beggar's Opera   C/FF
The Agreeable Surprise

TUES. 7 JAN.
Which is the Man?   PB/H, C/BJ
The Agreeable Surprise

THURS. 9 JAN.
Love for Love   PB/H
The Gentle Shepherd

SAT. 11 JAN.
The Provok'd Husband   PB/H
The Necromancer

MON. 13 JAN.
Which is the Man?   C/FF
Robinson Crusoe

TUES. 14 JAN.
Which is the Man?   PB/H, C/BJ
The Necromancer

THURS. 16 JAN.
George Barnwell   PB/H
The Agreeable Surprise

SAT. 18 JAN.
She Stoops to Conquer   PB/H
The Gentle Shepherd

MON. 20 JAN.
King Lear   C/FF
The Agreeable Surprise

TUES. 21 JAN.
King Lear and His Three   PB/H, C/BJ
  Daughters
Poor Vulcan

WED. 22 JAN.
The Maid of the Mill   PB/H Mathews "first
The Necromancer   appearance on any
                           stage" C/BJ

SAT. 25 JAN.
The Jealous Wife   PB/H
Poor Vulcan

MON. 27 JAN.
Which is the Man?   C/FF
The Agreeable Surprise

TUES. 28 JAN.
Which is the Man?   PB/H, C/BJ
The Agreeable Surprise

WED. 29 JAN.
The Maid of the Mill   PB/H, Ba, C/BJ
The Virgin Unmask'd   Late change — illness

SAT. 1 FEB.
The School for Scandal   PB/H
The Critic

MON. 3 FEB.
She Stoops to Conquer   C/FF
Robinson Crusoe

TUES. 4 FEB.
Which is the Man?   PB/H, C/BJ
Poor Vulcan

WED. 5 FEB.
The Maid of the Mill   PB/H, C/BJ
The Necromancer

SAT. 8 FEB.
The Pilgrim   PB/H, C/G, BC
The Agreeable Surprise

MON. 10 FEB.
The Gamester   C/FF
Poor Vulcan

TUES. 11 FEB.
Cymbeline   C/BJ, G, BC b: Dimond
Linco's Travels
A Trip to Scotland

WED. 12 FEB.
The Gamester   PB/H, C/BJ
The Recruiting Sergeant   b: Mrs. Hasker
The Waterman

SAT. 15 FEB.
The Recruiting Officer   PB/H, C/BJ, G, BC
Edgar and Emmeline   b: Keasberry

MON. 17 FEB.
The Maid of the Mill   C/FF
Who's the Dupe?

WED. 19 FEB.
The Fashionable Lover   PB/H, C/BJ, G
The Oracle   b: Mrs. J. Brown
The Man of Quality

SAT. 22 FEB.
Know Your Own Mind   PB/H, C/BJ b: Browne
Shadows of Shakespeare
Florizel and Perdita

MON. 24 FEB.
Cymbeline   C/FF
The Agreeable Surprise

TUES. 25 FEB.
The Belle's Stratagem   PB/H, C/BJ
The Register Office   b: Mrs. Didier
The Quaker

WED. 26 FEB.
The Conscious Lovers   C/BJ, G
The Harmonic Meeting   b: T. Blanchard
The Deserter

SAT. 1 MAR.
The Busybody   PB/H, C/BJ, G
The Gentle Laird   b: Bonnor
The Miller of Mansfield

MON. 3 MAR.
Henry II   C/FF
Poor Vulcan

TUES. 4 MAR.
The Wonder   PB/H, C/BJ
Harvest Home   b: Miss Wewitzer
The Rival Candidates

THURS. 6 MAR.
The Gamester   PB/F, C/BJ b: Payne
The Toy Shop   & Simpson
The Citizen

SAT. 8 MAR.
King Lear   PB/H, C/BJ, BC
Thomas and Sally   b: Brunton

MON. 10 MAR.
The Pilgrim   C/FF
The Rival Candidates

TUES. 11 MAR.
The Rivals   PB/H, C/BJ b: Jackson
Physic
The Capricious Lovers

THURS. 13 MAR.
Lionel and Clarissa   PB/H, C/BJ, BC
The Recruiting Sergeant   b: Lloyd & Fisher
The Lying Valet

SAT. 15 MAR.
The Foundling   PB/H
Poor Vulcan

MON. 17 MAR.
The Count of Narbonne   C/FF
The Agreeable Surprise

TUES. 18 MAR.
The Count of Narbonne   PB/H, C/BJ
The Necromancer

THURS. 20 MAR.
The Jealous Wife   PB/H
The Agreeable Surprise

SAT. 22 MAR.
All in the Wrong   PB/H
Selima and Azor

MON. 24 MAR.
Lionel and Clarissa   C/FF
The Scheming Lieutenant

TUES. 25 MAR.
The Chapter of Accidents   PB/H, C/BJ
Poor Vulcan

THURS. 27 MAR.
Which is the Man?   PB/H
The Necromancer

SAT. 29 MAR.
The Mysterious Husband   PB/H, C/G
The Flitch of Bacon

MON. 31 MAR.
The Mysterious Husband   C/FF
Poor Vulcan

TUES. 1 APR.
As You Like It   C/BJ
Rosina

THURS. 3 APR.
The Mysterious Husband   PB/H
Rosina

SAT. 5 APR.
The Spanish Barber   PB/H
The Agreeable Surprise

MON. 7 APR.
The Mysterious Husband   C/FF
Rosina

TUES. 8 APRIL
The Mysterious Husband   C/BJ
Rosina

THURS. 10 APR.
The School for Scandal   PB/H
The Critic

SAT. 12 APR.
The Pilgrim   PB/H
The Necromancer

MON. 21 APR.
King Lear   C/FF
The Necromancer

TUES. 22 APR.
The Belle's Stratagem   C/BJ
Robinson Crusoe

WED. 23 APR.
King Lear   PB/H
Poor Vulcan

THURS. 24 APR.
George Barnwell   PB/H
The Agreeable Surprise

SAT. 26 APR.
Which is the Man?   PB/H
The Rival Candidates

MON. 28 APR.
Which is the Man?   C/FF
The Agreeable Surprise

TUES. 29 APR.
The Mysterious Husband   PB/H, C/BJ
Robinson Crusoe

WED. 30 APR.
The Provok'd Husband   PB/H
Rosina

SAT. 3 MAY
The Pilgrim   PB/H
Rosina

MON. 5 MAY
The Provok'd Husband   C/FF
Rosina

TUES. 6 MAY
The Mysterious Husband   PB/H, C/BJ
Poor Vulcan

WED. 7 MAY
Which is the Man?
Rosina

SAT. 10 MAY
The Clandestine Marriage
The Agreeable Surprise

MON. 12 MAY
The Duenna   C/FF
The Necromancer

TUES. 13 MAY
Cymbeline   (S. Rossignol)   PB/H, C/BJ, BC
The Gentle Laird   b: Mrs. Simpson
The Citizen

WED. 14 MAY
As You Like It   PB/H, C/BJ b: Brookes
The Order of the Garter   & Hasker
The Deaf Lover

SAT. 17 MAY
False Delicacy   PB/H, C/BJ, BC
Miss in Her Teens   b: Mrs. Keasberry
The Gentle Shepherd

MON. 19 MAY
The Mysterious Husband (S. Rossignol)   C/FF
Rosina

TUES. 20 MAY
The Fair Penitent   PB/F, C/BJ
Three Old Women Weatherwise b: Miss Scrace
The Maid of the Oaks

WED. 21 MAY

Hamlet	PB/F, C/BJ
Linco's Travels	b: Rowbotham
The Brave Irishman	

SAT. 24 MAY

The Beaux Stratagem	PB/H, C/BJ
The Pigmies	b: J. Brown
The Register Office	

MON. 26 MAY

Rosina (S. Rossignol)	C/FF
The Spanish Barber	
The Agreeable Surprise	

TUES. 27 MAY

Cymon	PB/H, C/BJ, BC
The Recruiting Sergeant	b: Miss Twist
The Deuce is in Him	

WED. 28 MAY

A Word to the Wise (S. Rossignol)	PB/H, C/BJ
The Capricious Lovers	b: G. Summers & Miss Summers

SAT. 31 MAY

She Stoops to Conquer	PB/H, C/BJ, BC
True Blue	b: Catchpole
The Deserter	

MON. 2 JUNE

False Delicacy (S. Rossignol)	C/FF
Miss In Her Teens	b: Keasberry
The Deaf Lover	

TUES. 3 JUNE

The Fashionable Lover	PB/H, C/BJ b: Lloyd
Three Old Women Weatherwise	& Fisher
Hob in the Well	

FRI. 6 JUNE

A Word to the Wise	C/FF b: Winstone
The Maid of the Oaks	

SAT. 7 JUNE

Rosina (S. Rossingol)	PB/H, C/BJ
The Spanish Barber	
The Agreeable Surprice	

MON. 9 JUNE

Cymbeline	C/FF b: Mr. &
The Man of Quality	Mrs. J. Brown

WED. 11 JUNE

Percy	C/FF b: Mrs. Hasker
True Blue	
Hob in the Well	

FRI. 13 JUNE

The English Merchant	C/FF
The Recruiting Sergeant	b: Door-keepers &
Selima and Azor	Servants of House

SAT. 14 JUNE

Love in a Village	PB/H, C/BJ
The Toy Shop	b: Mathews
The Critic	

MON. 16 JUNE

Hamlet	C/FF, BC b: Dimond
Linco's Travel	
A Trip to Scotland	

WED. 18 JUNE

The Rivals	C/FF b: Jackson
What News?	
The Padlock	

FRI. 20 JUNE

The West Indian	C/FF
	b: G. Summers & Miss Summers

MON. 23 JUNE

Jane Shore	C/FF
Linco's Travels	b: Mrs. Simpson
The Citizen	

WED. 25 JUNE

The Provok'd Husband	C/FF
The True-born Scotchman	b: Mills &
The Flitch of Bacon	Miss Twist

FRI. 27 JUNE

The Fashionable Lover	C/FF b: Lloyd (treas) & Walker (Box-book Keeper)

SAT. 28 JUNE

The Merchant of Venice	PB/H, C/BJ
Linco's Travel	b: Cooke
Hob in the Well	

MON. 30 JUNE

The Conscious Lovers	C/FF
True Blue	b: Mrs Didier &
The Country Wife	Miss Wewitzer

WED. 2 JULY

Richard III	C/FF
The Honest Welchman	b: Rowbotham &
The Sultan	Miss Scrace

FRI. 4 JULY

The Mysterious Husband	C/FF
The Waterman	b: S. Rossignol

MON. 7 JULY
Romeo and Juliet   C/FF, G b: Bonnor
The Gentle Laird
The Critic

WED. 9 JULY
Venice Preserv'd   C/FF b: Browne
One Rake in a Thousand

FRI. 11 JULY
She Stoops to Conquer   C/FF b: The Band
The Gentle Shepherd

SAT. 12 JULY
The Mysterious Husband   PB/H, C/BJ
The Recruiting Sergeant   b: Servants of the
The Flitch of Bacon   Theatre

MON. 14 JULY
The Count of Narbonne   C/FF, PB/F
The Harmonic Meeting   b: T. Blanchard
Bon Ton

WED. 16 JULY
King Lear   C/FF b: Brunton
Charles I
One Rake in a Thousand

FRI. 18 JULY
Love in a Village   C/FF b: Mathews
The Deuce is in Him

MON. 21 JULY
Rosina   C/FF
The Agreeable Surprise
The Necromancer

End of Season

Season 1783/84

Company

Mr: Blanchard, T. Blanchard, Blisset, Bonner, J. Brown, Browne, Brunton, Cooke, Dimond, Floor, Hasker, Head, Jackson, Johnson, Keasberry, Mathews, Mills, Pollett, Rowbotham, Simpson, Summers, G. Summers, Williamson.

Mrs: Bernard, J. Brown, Browne, Didier, Farren, Keasberry, Simpson, Summers.

Miss: French, Jackson, Jones, H. & J. Keasberry, Stanton, Summers, Twist, Wood, Wewitzer, Wright.

Master: Cooke, Hendy, H. Keasberry, J. Keasberry, Thomas.

Treasurer: Lloyd   *Box Book Keeper:* Fisher (Bath), Walker (Bristol)   *Prompter:* Floor.

1783

TUES. 16 SEPT.
Venice Preserv'd   C/BJ, G
Robinson Crusoe

WED. 17 SEPT.
The Merchant of Venice   C/G
Rosina

THURS. 18 SEPT.
She Stoops to Conquer
The Agreeable Surprise

FRI. 19 SEPT.
Much Ado About Nothing
Poor Vulcan

SAT. 20 SEPT.
The Grecian Daughter   C/G

TUES. 23 SEPT.
The Grecian Daughter   C/FF
Rosina

SAT. 27 SEPT.
Chapter of Accidents   C/BJ
The Gentle Shepherd

MON. 29 SEPT.
Jane Shore   C/FF
The Gentle Shepherd

SAT. 4 OCT.
The Mysterious Husband   C/BJ
The Maid of the Oaks

MON. 6 OCT.
The Merchant of Venice   C/FF
Linco's Travels
Thomas and Sally

SAT. 11 OCT.
Jane Shore   C/BJ, G
Rosina

MON. 13 OCT.
The Gamester   PB/Ba, C/FF
Tom Thumb the Great

WED. 15 OCT.
The Maid of the Mill

FRI. 17 OCT.
Macbeth

SAT. 18 OCT.
The School for Scandal   C/BJ, G
Tom Thumb

MON. 20 OCT.
The Spanish Barber   C/FF
Hob in the Well

(Dancing on the Tightrope and Tumbling by
Monsieur Duprée, M. Merimée and The Little
Devil. They appear at both theatres until
17 January).

FRI. 24 OCT.
The Countess of Salisbury

SAT. 25 OCT.
The Pilgrims
Hob in the Well

MON. 27 OCT.
The West Indian   C/FF
Miss in her Teens

WED. 29 OCT.
Mahomet

FRI. 31 OCT.
Love in a Village   PB/R
The Agreeable Surprise

SAT. 1 NOV.
Which is the Man?   C/BJ
The Virgin Unmask'd

MON. 3 NOV.
Mahomet   C/FF
The Enchanted Wood

THURS. 4 NOV.
Mahomet   C/BJ, G
Miss in her Teens

SAT. 8 NOV.
The Lord of the Manor   C/BC, C/BJ
The Agreeable Surprise

MON. 10 NOV.
The Pilgrim   C/FF
The Enchanted Wood   b: Little Devil
                              Dupuis, Meunie

TUES. 11 NOV.
Mahomet   C/BJ
Rosina

WED. 12 NOV.
Mahomet
Poor Vulcan

SAT. 15 NOV.
The Provok'd Husband
Poor Vulcan

MON. 17 NOV.
The Duenna   C/FF
The Lying Valet

TUES. 18 NOV.
The Duenna   C/BJ, G
The Enchanted Wood

THURS. 20 NOV.
The Count of Narbonne   C/G
The Enchanted Wood

SAT. 22 NOV.
The West Indian

MON. 24 NOV.
King Lear   C/FF
The Rival Candidates

TUES. 25 NOV.
The Merchant of Venice   C/BJ
The Enchanted Wood   b: The Little
                              Devil, Duprée,
                              Merimée

THURS. 27 NOV.
Macbeth   C/G
The Enchanted Wood

SAT. 29 NOV.
The Spanish Barber

MON. 1 DEC.
The Receipt-Tax   C/FF
Midas
The Mayor of Garratt

TUES. 2 DEC.
A Bold Stroke for a Husband C/BJ, G
Poor Vulcan

THURS. 4 DEC.
Mahomet
The Receipt-Tax

SAT. 6 DEC.
A Bold Stroke for a Husband
Rosina

MON. 8 DEC.
A Bold Stroke for a Husband C/FF
Rosina   (Signora Leonelli)

TUES. 9 DEC.
The Pilgrim   C/BJ
Thomas and Sally

THURS. 11 DEC.
King Lear
The Virgin Unmask'd

SAT. 13 DEC.
A Bold Stroke for a Husband
The Enchanted Wood

MON. 15 DEC.
Mahomet   C/FF
The Gentle Shepherd

TUES. 16 DEC.
The Chapter of Accidents   C/BJ
The Capricious Lover

THURS. 18 DEC.
The Maid of the Mill
The Enchanted Wood

SAT. 20 DEC.
The Rivals   C/G
The Gentle Shepherd

MON. 22 DEC.
A Bold Stroke for a Husband C/FF
The Enchanted Wood

TUES. 23 DEC.
The Earl of Essex   C/BJ, G
The Enchanted Wood

FRI. 26 DEC.
Jane Shore
The Enchanted Wood

SAT. 27 DEC.
She Stoops to Conquer
The Lying Valet

MON. 29 DEC.
The Earl of Essex   C/FF
The Devil to Pay

TUES. 30 DEC.
Which is the Man?   C/BJ
The Enchanted Wood

1784

THURS. 1 JAN.
The Earl of Essex
The Enchanted Wood

SAT. 3 JAN.
A Bold Stroke for a Husband

MON. 5 JAN.
A Bold Stroke for a Husband C/FF
Who's the Dupe?

WED. 7 JAN.
The Gamester
Fancy's Bower

SAT. 10 JAN.
The Clandestine Marriage   C/G
Entertainments

MON. 12 JAN.
Mahomet   C/FF
Rosina

FRI. 16 JAN.
George Barnwell   b: Little Devil,
The Enchanted Wood   Monsieur Duprée,
                            Meriurée

SAT. 17 JAN.
The Spanish Barber
Fancy's Bower

TUES. 20 JAN.
The Castle of Andalusia   C/G
Who's the Dupe?

THURS. 22 JAN.
The Pilgrim   C/FF
The Agreeable Surprise

SAT. 24 JAN.
The School for Scandal
Rosina

MON. 26 JAN.
The Distress'd Mother   C/FF
Rosina

TUES. 27 JAN.
A Bold Stroke for a Husband
Poor Vulcan

WED. 28 JAN.
The Distress'd Mother   C/G
The Castle of Andalusia

SAT. 31 JAN.
The Way to Keep Him   C/G
The Gentle Shepherd

MON. 2 FEB.
The Castle of Andalusia   C/FF
St. Patrick's Day

TUES. 3 FEB.
St. Patrick's Day   C/G

WED. 4 FEB.
The Son-in-Law   C/G
Entertainments

SAT. 7 FEB.
The Chapter of Accidents
The Citizen

MON. 9 FEB.
The Castle of Andalusia   C/FF
The Ghost

TUES. 10 FEB.
Hamlet   C/BC, G
Three Weeks after Marriage   b: Dimond

SAT. 14 FEB.
The Runaway   C/BC b: Keasberry
Selima and Azor

MON. 16 FEB.
A Bold Stroke for a Husband C/FF
The Deserter

TUES. 17 FEB.
The Belle's Stratagem   C/BC, G
The Deserter   b: T. Blanchard

SAT. 21 FEB.
As You Like It   PB/Ba C/Bc, G
A Trip to Scotland   b: Mrs Simpson

MON. 23 FEB.
The Castle of Andalusia   C/FF
All the World's a Stage

TUES. 24 FEB.
Richard III   C/BC b: Browne
One Rake in a Thousand

THURS. 26 FEB.
King Lear   C/BC
Hob in the Well   b: Mr & Mrs
                                Summers

MON. 1 MAR.
A Bold Stroke for a Husband C/FF
The Agreeable Surprise

TUES. 2 MAR.
The Funeral   C/BC, G
The Upholsterer   b: Mrs Didier

THURS. 4 MAR.
Cymbeline   C/G b: Mrs Browne
All the World's a Stage

SAT. 6 MAR.
The Conscious Lovers   C/BC
Midas   b: Miss Wewitzer

MON. 8 MAR.
The School for Scandal   C/FF
The Poor Soldier

TUES. 9 MAR.
The Fashionable Lover   PB/Ba, b: Brunton
One Rake in a Thousand

THURS. 11 MAR.
Know Your Own Mind   C/BC
The Capricious Lovers   b: Lloyd & Fisher

SAT. 13 MAR.
The Poor Soldier   C/G

MON. 15 MAR.
The Chapter of Accidents   C/FF
The Poor Soldier

SAT. 20 MAR.
She Wou'd and She Wou'd Not   C/G
Rosina

MON. 22 MAR.
Venice Preserv'd   C/FF
Rosina

SAT. 27 MAR.
The Clandestine Marriage
The Agreeable Surprise

MON. 29 MAR.
All Castle of Andalusia   C/FF
All The World's a Stage

SAT. 3 APRIL
The Castle of Andalusia
Robinson Crusoe

MON. 12 APRIL
She Wou'd and She Wou'd Not   C/FF
The Poor Soldier

TUES. 13 APRIL
The Times
Robinson Crusoe

WED. 14 APRIL
A Bold Stroke for a Husband
The Poor Soldier

THURS. 15 APRIL
The Gamester
Robinson Crusoe

SAT. 17 APRIL
As You Like It
The Agreeable Surprise

MON. 19 APRIL
The School for Scandal   C/FF
The Agreeable Surprise

SAT. 24 APRIL
The School for Scandal
Rosina

MON. 26 APRIL
The Reparation   C/FF
Poor Vulcan

TUES. 27 APRIL
The Reparation   C/G

SAT. 1 MAY
The Merchant of Venice
Poor Vulcan

MON. 3 MAY
As You Like It   C/FF
The Poor Soldier

TUES. 4 MAY
The Duenna

SAT. 8 MAY
The Castle of Andalusia

MON. 10 MAY
The Reparation   C/FF
Rosina

MON. 17 MAY
The Castle of Andalusia   C/FF
The Scheming Lieutenant

TUES. 18 MAY
The Suspicious Husband   C/BC
     b: Miss Wright

WED. 19 MAY
Lionel and Clarissa   C/G
     b: Mr & Mrs
         Brown
The Man of Quality

SAT. 22 MAY
The Double Falsehood   C/BC
The Two Misers   b: Mrs Keasberry

MON. 24 MAY
The Belle's Stratagem   C/FF
The Poor Soldier

TUES. 25 MAY
The West Indian   C/BC b: Miss Stanton
The Irish Widow

SAT. 29 MAY
All in the Wrong   C/G

MON. 31 MAY
All in the Wrong   C/FF
The Two Misers

TUES. 1 JUNE
The School for Wives   C/BC b: Floor
Midas

THURS. 3 JUNE
She Wou'd and She Wou'd Not   C/BC
The Two Misers   b: Lloyd & Fisher

SAT. 5 JUNE
The Poor Soldier
The Agreeable Surprise

MON. 7 JUNE
She Wou'd and She Wou'd Not   C/FF, G
The Irish Widow   b: Blissett

WED. 9 JUNE
The Suspicious Husband
The Padlock.

FRI. 11 JUNE
A Bold Stroke for a Husband   C/FF b: Winstone
The Son-in-Law

SAT. 12 JUNE
The Beggar's Opera   C/BC
The Quaker

MON. 14 JUNE
The Revenge   C/FF, G
Three Weeks after Marriage   b: Dimond

WED. 16 JUNE
The School for Wives   C/FF
The Deaf Lover   b: Rowbotham &
         Johnson

FRI. 18 JUNE
Mahomet   C/FF
The Author

SAT. 19 JUNE
The Revenge   C/BC b: Cooke
Selima and Azor

MON. 21 JUNE
Tancred and Sigismunda   C/FF b: Mrs Simpson
A Trip to Scotland

WED. 23 JUNE

The Beaux' Stratagem   C/FF b: Jackson
The Mayor of Garratt

FRI. 25 JUNE

The Mysterious Husband   C/FF
Selima and Azor   b: Servants &
                 Doorkeepers

SAT. 26 JUNE

As You Like It
The Son-in-Law

MON. 28 JUNE

The Runaway   C/FF b: Keasberry
Thomas and Sally

WED. 30 JUNE

The Revenge   C/FF b: Brunton
The Two Misers

FRI. 2 JULY

The School for Scandal   C/FF
            b: Mr & Miss
                 Summers

MON. 5 JULY

Richard III   C/FF b: Browne
One Rake in a Thousand

WED. 7 JULY

The Rivals   C/FF b: Lloyd
The Deserter   (Treas) & Floor
                 (Prompter)

FRI. 9 JULY

The Fair Penitent   b: Part of Band
The Gentle Shepherd

SAT. 10 JULY

The Rivals   (Miss Wheeler)   C/BC
Rosina

MON. 12 JULY

Cymbeline   C/FF b:
The Lying Valet   b: T. Blanchard

WED. 14 JULY

Cymon   C/FF
Midas   b: Miss Wewitzer
                 & Miss Twist

FRI. 16 JULY

The Beggar's Opera   C/FF b: Mathews
The Quaker

SAT. 17 JULY

Richard III   (Meyler)   C/G, CB b: Whitaker
The Deserter   Charitable Benefit

MON. 19 JULY

Hamlet   PB/R, C/FF, G,
Rosina   b: Mrs Keasberry

MON. 26 JULY

"Attic Evening's   C/FF b: Bonnor
Entertainment"

End of Season

Season 1784/85

Company

Mr: Bernard, Blanchard, T. Blanchard, Blisset, Brunton, Dimond, Floor, Incledon, Jackson, Johnson, Keasberry, Owens, Payne, Powell, Rowbotham, Summers, G. Summers, Williamson, Wordsworth.

Mrs: Bernard, Didier, Keasberry, Powell, Summers.

Miss: Brunton, Cleland, Evans, Harvey, Jackson, Stanton, Summers, Twist, Wood, Wright.

Master: Keasberry, J. Keasberry.

Treasurer: Lloyd.   *Box Book Keepers:* Phillips (Bath), Walker (Bristol)   *Prompter:* Floor.

1784

WED. 16 SEPT.

She Wou'd and She Wou'd Not
The Agreeable Surprise

THURS. 17 SEPT.

As You Like It
The Poor Soldier

SAT. 19 SEPT.

She Stoops to Conquer
The Quaker

MON. 20 SEPT.

Hamlet   C/FF
The Quaker

MON. 27 SEPT.

As You Like It   C/FF
Robinson Crusoe

SAT. 2 OCT.

Which is the Man?   C/G, BC
The Irish Widow

MON. 4 OCT.

She Stoops to Conquer   C/FF
The Padlock

SAT. 9 OCT.

Hamlet   C/G, BC
The Citizen

MON. 11 OCT.

The Merchant of Venice   C/FF
The Rival Candidates

SAT. 16 OCT.

The Maid of the Mill   C/BC
All the World's a Stage

MON. 18 OCT.

The Maid of the Mill   C/FF
Who's The Dupe?

FRI. 22 OCT.

More Ways Than One   FF

SAT. 23 OCT.

More Ways Than One   C/G, BC
The Poor Soldier

MON. 25 OCT.

George Barnwell   PB/TC
Robinson Crusoe

WED. 27 OCT.

Othello   (Amateur
The Upholsterer   Performance)

FRI. 29 OCT.

More Ways Than One

SAT. 30 OCT.

The Castle of Andalusia   C/BC
Bon Ton

MON. 1 NOV.

The Provok'd Husband   C/FF
Midas

SAT. 6 NOV.

Rule a Wife and Have a Wife   C/BC
The Waterman

MON. 8 NOV.

The Fair Penitent   (Amateur
High Life Below Stairs   Performance)

MON. 15 NOV.

Rule a Wife and Have a Wife C/FF
The Waterman

THURS. 18 NOV.

Macbeth
The Ghost

SAT. 20 NOV.

The Suspicious Husband

MON. 22 NOV.

Hamlet   C/FF
The Ghost   b: The Infirmary

THURS. 25 NOV.

Love in a Village
Bon Ton

SAT. 27 NOV.

The Pilgrim
The Devil to Pay

MON. 29 NOV.

The Pilgrim   C/FF
The Deserter

WED. 1 DEC.

The Beggar's Opera
All the World's a Stage

SAT. 4 DEC.

King Lear
Rosina

MON. 6 DEC.

The Foundling   C/FF
Tom Thumb the Great

WED. 8 DEC.

King Lear
The Two Misers

SAT. 11 DEC.

More Ways than One

MON. 13 DEC.

The Castle of Andalusia   C/FF
The Deaf Lover

TUES. 14 DEC.

A New Way to Pay Old Debts

WED. 15 DEC.

Romeo and Juliet
Thomas and Sally

SAT. 18 DEC.

The Foundling   C/G
Old Robin Gray

MON. 20 DEC.

A New Way to Pay Old Debts C/FF
Old Robin Gray

TUES. 21 DEC.
The Miser   C/G

WED. 22 DEC.
A New Way to Pay Old Debts
Old Robin Gray

MON. 27 DEC.
The Duenna   C/FF
Robinson Crusoe

WED. 29 DEC.
Venice Preserv'd
The Necromancer

THURS. 30 DEC.
The Revenge   C/G
The Necromancer

1785

SAT. 1 JAN.
The Jealous Wife
Old Robin Gray

MON. 3 JAN.
More Ways Than One   C/FF
Old Robin Gray

WED. 5 JAN.
The Fair Penitent
Rosina

SAT. 8 JAN.
The Chapter of Accidents
The Necromancer   C/G, BC

MON. 10 JAN.
The Suspicious Husband   C/FF
The Poor Soldier

THURS. 13 JAN.
George Barnwell
The Necromancer

SAT. 15 JAN.
The Agreeable Surprise
Old Robin Gray
The Spanish Barber

MON. 17 JAN.
Douglas   C/FF
Rosina

WED. 19 JAN.
The Follies of a Day
The Necromancer

SAT. 22 JAN.
The Pilgrim

MON. 24 JAN.
The Follies of a Day   C/FF
Old Robin Gray

WED. 26 JAN.
George Barnwell
Old Robin Gray
The Necromancer

SAT. 29 JAN.
The Castle of Andalusia
The Agreeable Surprise

MON. 31 JAN.
The Follies of a Day   C/FF
The Gentle Shepherd

TUES. 1 FEB.
The Follies of a Day

WED. 2 FEB.
Merope
The Necromancer

SAT. 5 FEB.
The Miser
The Gentle Shepherd

MON. 7 FEB.
Merope   C/FF
The Agreeable Surprise

TUES. 8 FEB.
The Follies of a Day

THURS. 10 FEB.
The School for Scandal
Rosina

SAT. 12 FEB.
The Follies of a Day

MON. 14 FEB.
The Follies of a Day   C/FF
Poor Vulcan

TUES. 15 FEB.
A New Way to Pay Old   C/G b: Keasberry
  Debts
The Intriguing Chambermaid

THURS. 17 FEB.
The Grecian Daughter   C/G, BC b: Brunton
The Padlock

SAT. 19 FEB.
Henry IV   C/G, BC b: Williamson
The Quaker

MON. 21 FEB.
Percy   C/FF
Robinson Crusoe

TUES. 22 FEB.

Much Ado About Nothing   C/G, BC b: Dimond
Bon Ton

THURS. 24 FEB.

The School for Scandal   C/BC
The Citizen   b: Miss Stanton

SAT. 26 FEB.

The Belle's Stratagem   C/BC b: Floor
Selima and Azor

MON. 28 FEB.

Fontainbleau   C/FF
The Deaf Lover

TUES. 1 MAR.

Know Your Own Mind   C/BC b: Mrs. Bernard
The Critic

THURS. 3 MAR.

The West Indian   C/BC b: Jackson
Midas

MON. 7 MAR.

The Miser   C/FF
The Poor Soldier

TUES. 8 MAR.

The Wonder   C/BC b: T. Blanchard

SAT. 12 MAR.

Lionel and Clarissa   C/G, BC b: Miss Wright
Three Weeks After Marriage

MON. 14 MAR.

The Follies of a Day   C/FF
Old Robin Gray

TUES. 15 MAR.

Rule a Wife and Have a Wife   b: Lloyd & Fisher

SAT. 19 MAR.

The Follies of a Day

MON. 28 MAR.

Fontainbleau   C/FF
The Deuce is in Him

TUES. 29 MAR.

Fontainbleau   C/G
The Deuce is in Him

WED. 30 MAR.

The Grecian Daughter   C/G, BC
Rosina

THURS. 31 MAR.

The Pilgrim
Robinson Crusoe

SAT. 2 APR.

A Bold Stroke for a Husband

MON. 4 APR.

The Wonder   C/FF
The Necromancer

WED. 6 APR.

The Follies of a Day
Poor Vulcan

SAT. 9 APR.

The Conscious Lovers   C/G
The Gentle Shepherd

MON. 11 APR.

The Conscious Lovers   C/FF
The Author

TUES. 12 APR.

She Wou'd and She Wou'd Not

WED. 13 APR.

The Duenna
The Son-in-Law

SAT. 16 APR.

The Rivals

MON. 18 APR.

The School for Scandal   C/FF
The Necromancer

TUES. 19 APR.

The Castle of Andalusia

WED. 20 APR.

The School for Scandal   C/G b: Miss Stanton
The Poor Soldier

SAT. 23 APR.

The Grecian Daughter

MON. 25 APR.

The Grecian Daughter   C/FF
The Waterman

TUES. 26 APR.

Robin Hood   C/G

WED. 27 APR.

The Follies of a Day
The Agreeable Surprise

SAT. 30 APR.

Robin Hood
Who's the Dupe?

MON. 2 MAY

Robin Hood   C/FF
Cross Purposes

TUES. 3 MAY
The Roman Father   C/G

WED. 4 MAY
Robin Hood
Bon Ton

SAT. 7 MAY
The Grecian Daughter
The Irish Widow

MON. 9 MAY
The Roman Father   C/FF
The Rival Candidates

TUES. 10 MAY
The Natural Son   C/G

WED. 11 MAY
The Roman Father
Rosina

SAT. 14 MAY
Robin Hood

MON. 16 MAY
Robin Hood   C/FF
Who's the Dupe?

MON. 23 MAY
The Natural Son   C/FF
The Agreeable Surprise

TUES. 24 MAY
Mahomet   C/G, BC,
The Two Misers   b: Miss Brunton

SAT. 28 MAY
A Bold Stroke for a Husband C/BC b: Mrs. Didier
The Old Maid

MON. 30 MAY
The Roman Father   C/FF
Old Robin Gray
The Lying Valet

TUES. 31 MAY
The Merchant of Venice   C/G, BC b: Bernard
The Dead Alive

THURS. 2 JUNE
The Way to Keep Him   C/BC b: Rowbotham
The Note of Hand

SAT. 4 JUNE
The Merchant of Venice   C/BC b: Miss Cleland
The Dead Alive

MON. 6 JUNE
Robin Hood   C/FF
The Old Maid

TUES. 7 JUNE
The Fashionable Lover   C/BC b: Miss Twist

THURS. 9 JUNE
Much Ado About Nothing   C/BC b: Lloyd
Midas   (Treasurer) & Phillips
                              (Box Book-Keeper)

SAT. 11 JUNE
The Beaux Stratagem   C/G, BC
Like Master Like Man   b: Miss Harvey

MON. 13 JUNE
The Grecian Daughter   C/FF, BC, G
The Dead Alive   b: Miss Brunton

FRI. 17 JUNE
The Duenna   b: Servants of the
                              House

MON. 20 JUNE
A Bold Stroke for a Husband C/FF b: Mrs. Didier
The Deserter   & Miss Twist

WED. 22 JUNE
As You Like It   C/FF b: Miss Stanton
The Gentle Shepherd

FRI. 24 JUNE
The Spanish Barber   C/FF b: Winstone
The Dead Alive

MON. 27 JUNE
Oroonoko   C/FF, G b: Dimond
The Romance of an Hour

WED. 29 JUNE
Lionel and Clarissa   C/FF b: Miss Wright
The Lying Valet

FRI. 1 JULY
The Chapter of Accidents   C/FF b: Part of Servants
                              of House
The Poor Soldier

MON. 4 JULY
Hamlet   C/FF b: Keasberry
The Critic

WED. 6 JULY
King Lear   C/FF b: Wordsworth
The Flitch of Bacon

FRI. 8 JULY
The Beaux Stratagem   C/FF b: Walker
The Two Misers

SAT. 9 JULY
The Grecian Daughter   C/FF, G
Rosina

MON. 11 JULY
Know Your Own Mind   C/FF b: Mr. & Mrs.
The Apprentice   Bernard

WED. 13 JULY
The School for Scandal   C/FF b: Jackson
Lethe

MON. 18 JULY
The Conscious Lovers   C/G b: Blissett
The Upholsterer

WED. 20 JULY
She Stoops to Conquer   C/FF b: T. Blanchard
The Contrivances

FRI. 22 JULY
The Follies of a Day   C/FF b: Rowbotham,
Rosina   Floor & Lloyd

MON. 25 JULY
Richard III   C/FF b: Mrs. Keasberry
Tom Thumb the Great

End of Season

Season 1785/86

Company

Mr: Bernard, Blanchard, T. Blanchard, Blisset, Bush, Congdon, Dimond, Floor, Incledon, Jackson, Keasberry, Murray, Pindar, Powell, Rowbotham, Summers, G. Summers, Wordsworth.

Mrs: Barnard, Didier, Esten, Keasberry, Murray, Powell, Summers.

Miss: Brunton, Harvey, Jackson, Stanton, Summers, Twist, Wright.

Master: Keasberry, J. Keasberry.

Treasurer: Lloyd   *Box Book Keepers:* Phillips (Bath), Walker (Bristol)   *Prompter:* Floor

1785

MON. 3 OCT.
A New Way to Pay Old Debts C/FF
Rosina

SAT. 8 OCT.
A New Way to Pay Old Debts C/G
The Dead Alive

MON. 10 OCT.
The Follies of a Day   C/FF
The Two Misers

SAT. 15 OCT.
The Follies of a Day
The Poor Soldier

MON. 17 OCT.
Robin Hood   C/FF
The Romance of an Hour

SAT. 22 OCT.
Robin Hood
The Deaf Lover

MON. 24 OCT.
Percy   C/FF
The Deserter

SAT. 29 OCT.
The Suspicious Husband
The Gentle Shepherd

MON. 31 OCT.
The Provok'd Husband   C/FF
Thomas and Sally

SAT. 5 NOV.
The Jealous Wife
The Rival Candidates

MON. 7 NOV.
Rule a Wife and have a Wife   C/FF
The Deaf Lover

TUES. 8 NOV.
Percy
The Old Maid

THURS. 10 NOV.
The Belle's Stratagem

MON. 14 NOV.
The School for Scandal   C/FF
The Anatomist

TUES. 15 NOV.
The School for Scandal   C/G
The Anatomist

THURS. 17 NOV.
Douglas
The Anatomist

SAT. 19 NOV.
The Chapter of Accidents

MON. 21 NOV.
Othello   C/FF
Appearance is Against Them

TUES. 22 NOV.
Appearance is Against Them   C/G

THURS. 24 NOV.
The Merchant of Venice
Midas

SAT. 26 NOV.
The Follies of a Day
Appearance is Against Them

MON. 28 NOV.
She Wou'd and She Wou'd Not   C/FF
The Anatomist

THURS. 1 DEC.
She Stoops to Conquer
The Agreeable Surprise

SAT. 3 DEC.
Werter   C/G

MON. 5 DEC.
Werter   C/FF
Midas

TUES. 6 DEC.
Werter

THURS. 8 DEC.
Robin Hood
Between 8–19 Dec. various performances
by The Little Devil and Troupe, at both
Houses

SAT. 10 DEC.
Hamlet

MON. 12 DEC.
Werter   C/FF

THURS. 15 DEC.
The Duenna

SAT. 17 DEC.
Werter

MON. 19 DEC.
Which is the Man?   C/FF

THURS. 22 DEC.
Which is the Man?
Thomas and Sally

MON. 26 DEC.
The Castle of Andalusia   C/FF
The Old Maid

WED. 28 DEC.
Venice Preserv'd
The Deaf Lover

THURS. 29 DEC.
The West Indian
The Agreeable Surprise

FRI. 30 DEC.
George Barnwell
Hob in the Well

SAT. 31 DEC.
Werter

1786

MON. 2 JAN.
The West Indian   C/FF
The Padlock

TUES. 3 JAN.
The Provok'd Husband   C/BJ
Old Robin Gray

THURS. 5 JAN.
The Mysterious Husband

SAT. 7 JAN.
The Follies of a Day

MON. 9 JAN.
I'll Tell You What   C/FF
Appearance is Against Them

TUES. 10 JAN.
I'll Tell You What   C/BJ, G
The Poor Soldier

MON. 16 JAN.
The Natural Son   C/FF
The Necromancer

TUES. 17 JAN.
A New Way to Pay Old Debts C/BJ, BC b: The Little
Tom Thumb the Great   Devil

WED. 18 JAN.
Hamlet   C/FF b: The Little
The Contrivances   Devil & Troupe

THURS. 19 JAN.
Robin Hood
The Old Maid

SAT. 21 JAN.
The Contrivances   C/G

MON. 23 JAN.   C/FF
Werter
The Son in Law

TUES. 24 JAN.
Werter   C/BJ
The Rival Candidates

THURS. 26 JAN.
Percy
The Quaker   C/BJ

SAT. 28 JAN.
I'll Tell You What
The Son in Law

TUES. 31 JAN.
Othello   C/BJ
The Whim, or Magician's
   Triumph

WED. 1 FEB.
I'll Tell You What   C/FF
The Quaker

THURS. 2 FEB.
The Jealous Wife
The Whim

SAT. 4 FEB.
The Natural Son

MON. 6 FEB.
The Follies of a Day   C/FF
The Poor Soldier

TUES. 7 FEB.
The Follies of a Day   C/BJ
The Whim

THURS. 9 FEB.
Merope
The Whim

MON. 13 FEB.
Fontainbleau   C/FF
The Anatomist

TUES. 14 FEB.
Werter   C/BJ, BC b: Keasberry
A Humourous Description of a Post haste
   Journey to Paris
The Flitch of Bacon   C/BJ

THURS. 16 FEB.
Love Makes a Man   C/BJ
The Scheming Lieutenant   b: Mr & Miss Summers

SAT. 18 FEB.
Cymbeline   C/BJ, BC b: Dimond
The Lyar

MON. 20 FEB.
Werter   C/FF
The Whim

TUES. 21 FEB.
As You Like It   C/BJ b: Miss Stanton
The Citizen

THURS. 23 FEB.
The Inconstant   C/BJ, BC b: Jackson
Lethe

SAT. 25 FEB.
A Word to the Wise   C/BJ, BC b: Mrs. Bernard
Bon Ton

MON. 27 FEB.
Love Makes a Man   C/FF
The Whim

TUES. 28 FEB.
Macbeth   C/G, BC b: Blissét
Three Weeks after Marriage

THURS. 2 MAR.
Much Ado About Nothing   C/BJ, BC
The Son-in-Law   b: Mrs Didier

SAT. 4 MAR.
Rule a Wife and Have a Wife   C/BJ, BC b; Murray
The Lyar

MON. 6 MAR.
Rule a Wife and Have a Wife   C/FF
The Whim

TUES. 7 MAR.
She Stoops to Conquer   C/BJ, BC
High Life Below Stairs   b: T. Blanchard

THURS. 9 MAR.
Richard III   C/BJ, BC
The Quaker   b: Rowbotham

SAT. 11 MAR.
The Wonder   C/BC
The Agreeable Surprise

MON. 13 MAR.
Much Ado About Nothing   C/FF
The Lyar

TUES. 14 MAR.
The Maid of the Mill   C/BJ, BC
All the World's a Stage   b: Miss Wright

THURS. 16 MAR.
Know Your Own Mind (Mrs. Nunns) C/BJ, BC b: Lloyd
The Gentle Shepherd   Phillips (Box
                                       Book-keeper)

SAT. 18 MAR.
The Chapter of Accidents
The Whim

MON. 20 MAR.   C/FF
The Heiress
All the World's a Stage

TUES. 21 MAR.
The Heiress   C/BJ, G
The Rival Candidates

THURS. 23 MAR.
The Mysterious Husband
The Whim

SAT. 25 MAR.
The Chapter of Accidents

MON. 27 MAR.
The Revenge   C/FF
The British Sailor

TUES. 28 MAR.
The Heiress   C/BJ
The Poor Soldier

THURS. 30 MAR.
Robin Hood
The Whim

SAT. 1 APR.
The Follies of a Day

MON. 3 APR.
The Heiress   C/FF
Rosina

TUES. 4 APR.
The Heiress   C/BJ
The Gentle Shepherd

THURS. 6 APR.
The Orphan
Rosina

MON. 17 APR.
Werter   C/FF
The British Sailor

TUES. 18 APR.
The Heiress   C/BJ
The British Sailor
The Whim

WED. 19 APR.
Werter
The Whim

THURS. 20 APR.
The Tragedy of George   C/BJ
  Barnwell
The Whim

SAT. 22 APR.
I'll Tell you What
The British Sailor

MON. 24 APR.
The Heiress   C/FF
The Whim

TUES. 25 APR.
The Heiress   C/BJ
Appearance is Against Them

THURS. 27 APR.
Fontainebleau
The Old Maid

SAT. 29 APR.
Which is the Man?

MON. 1 MAY
Robin Hood   C/FF
Appearance is Against Them

TUES. 2 MAY
The Heiress   C/BJ
Rosina

WED. 3 MAY
Romeo and Juliet   C/FF b: Boyton &
The British Sailor   Bernard

THURS. 4 MAY
Macbeth   (Seymour)   C/BJ
The Quaker

SAT. 6 MAY
The Grecian Daughter (Miss Brunton) C/G

MON. 8 MAY
The Distress'd Mother (Miss Brunton)   C/BJ, G, BC
The Whim

TUES. 9 MAY
The Distress'd Mother   C/BJ, G, BC
The British Sailor

WED. 10 MAY
Romeo and Juliet   PB/Ba, C/BJ, G
The Padlock   b: Miss Brunton

SAT. 13 MAY
The Heiress
Patrick in Prussia   C/G

MON. 15 MAY	**MON. 12 JUNE**
The Heiress C/FF	*Braganza* C/FF b: Keasberry
Patrick in Prussia	*Peeping Tom of Coventry*

MON. 15 MAY
The Heiress   C/FF
Patrick in Prussia

TUES. 16 MAY
The School for Scandal   C/BJ b: Bernard
The Mock Doctor

WED. 17 MAY
The School for Wives   C/BJ b: Floor (Prompter)
The Critic

SAT. 20 MAY
Oroonoko   C/BJ, BC
Poor Vulcan   b: Mrs. Keasberry

MON. 22 MAY
Which is the Man?   C/FF
Poor Vulcan

TUES 23 MAY
Cymbeline   C/BJ b: Wordsworth
The Honest Yorkshireman

WED. 24 MAY
The Heiress   C/BJ
The Lyar

SAT. 27 MAY
The Suspicious Husband   C/BJ b: Powell &
               Miss Cleland
Barataria

MON. 29 MAY
The Clandestine Marriage   C/FF, PB/R
Barataria

THURS. 1 JUNE
Love Makes a Man   C/BJ, BC
The Agreeable Surprise   b: Lloyd (Treas.) &
               Phliips (Box Book-
               keeper)

SAT. 3 JUNE
The Follies of a Day   C/BJ

TUES. 6 JUNE
Henry IV (i)   C/FF, G b: Blisset
The Deserter

WED. 7 JUNE
Werter   C/FF b: Miss Cleland,
Rosina   Miss Harvey,
             Mrs Powell

FRI. 9 JUNE
Love Makes a Man   C/FF, PB/R
Rosina   b: Servants of the
             House

MON. 12 JUNE
Braganza   C/FF b: Keasberry
Peeping Tom of Coventry

WED. 14 JUNE
The Beaux' Stratagem   C/FF, G b: Mr. & Mrs.
Hob in the Well   Murray

FRI. 16 JUNE
King Richard III   b: Servants of the
             House

MON. 19 JUNE
Jane Shore   C/FF, G b: Dimond
High Life Below Stairs

WED. 21 JUNE
The School for Scandal   C/FF b: Rowbotham,
The Whim   G. Summers,
             Miss Summers

FRI. 23 JUNE
The Conscious Lovers   C/FF b: Walker
The Irish Widow   (Box Book-keeper)

MON. 26 JUNE
The Belle's Stratagem   C/FF, G b: Mr. & Mrs.
The Waterman   Bernard

WED. 28 JUNE
The Hypocrite   C/FF, G b: Wordsworth
A Beggar on Horseback   & Miss Stanton

MON. 3 JULY
Cymbeline   PB/R b: Miss Wright
The Students' Frolic

WED. 5 JULY
The Rivals   C/FF b: Jackson
The Flitch of Bacon

MON. 10 JULY
Venice Preserv'd   C/FF b: Mrs. Didier
The Chaplet   & Miss Twist

WED. 12 JULY
The West Indian   C/FF b: T. Blanchard
The Honest Yorkshireman

FRI. 14 JULY
George Barnwell
? Rosina

MON. 17 JULY
The Married Man   C/FF b: Mrs. Keasberry
The Poor Soldier

End of Season

Season 1786—87

Company

Mr: Ashley, Bernard, Bignal, Blanchard, T. Blanchard, Blisset, Bloomfield, Bristowe, Dimond, Egan, Incledon, Jackson, Keasberry, Murray, Owens, Pindar, Powell, Rowbotham, Summers, G. Summers, Waterhouse, Wordsworth

Mrs: Bernard, Didier, Esten, Keasberry, Murray, Powell, Summers

Miss: Cleland, Jackson, Keasberry, Michel, Sharrock, Stanton, Summers, Twist, Williams, Wright

Master: J. Keasberry, Michel

Treasurer: Lloyd   *Box Book Keeper:* Phillips   *Prompter:* Floor

1786

MON. 2 OCT.
The School for Scandal   C/FF
The Son-in-Law
     Box Prices reduced to 4s.

SAT. 7 OCT.
The Heiress   C/BJ, BC
The Son-in-Law

MON. 9 OCT.
The Heiress   C/FF
The Gentle Shepherd

SAT. 14 OCT.
The Belle's Stratagem   C/BJ, BC, G
The Poor Soldier

MON. 16 OCT.
The Belle's Stratagem   C/FF
The Poor Soldier

SAT. 21 OCT.
Venice Preserv'd   C/BJ, BC
Patrick in Prussia

MON. 23 OCT.
I'll Tell you what   C/FF
Peeping Tom of Coventry

SAT. 28 OCT.
I'll Tell you what   C/BJ, BC
Peeping Tom of Coventry

MON. 30 OCT.
Venice Preserv'd   C/FF
The Widow's Vow

TUES. 31 OCT.
The Belle's Stratagem   C/BJ, G
The Widow's Vow

WED. 1 NOV.
Douglas   C/BJ
The Ghost

SAT. 4 NOV.
The Times
Peeping Tom of Coventry

MON. 6 NOV.
The Way to keep him   C/FF
Patrick in Prussia

TUES. 7 NOV.
Henry IV   C/BJ
The Widow's Vow

MON. 13 NOV.
The Way to keep him   C/FF
Patrick in Prussia

TUES. 14 NOV.
Hamlet   C/BJ, G
The Humorist

THURS. 16 NOV.
Henry IV
The Whim

SAT. 18 NOV.
The Miser   (Moss)   C/G, BC
Patrick in Prussia

MON. 20 NOV.
The Miser   (Moss)   C/FF
The Deserter

TUES. 21 NOV.
The Clandestine Marriage   C/BJ
The Maid of the Oaks

THURS. 23 NOV.
The School for Scandal
The Deserter

SAT. 25 NOV.
Love in a Village (Moss)

MON. 27 DEC.
The Merchant of Venice   C/FF
The Agreeable Surprise   (Moss)

TUES. 28 NOV.

Percy
The Agreeable Surprise   C/BJ

THURS. 30 NOV.

She Stoops to Conquer
The Humourist

SAT. 2 DEC.

The Heiress
The Widow's Vow

MON. 4 DEC.

The Gamester   C/FF
The Humourist

TUES. 5 DEC.

The Gamester   C/BJ
The Maid of the Oaks

THURS. 7 DEC.

Robin Hood
The Whim

SAT. 9 DEC.

The Chapter of Accidents   C/BJ

MON. 11 DEC.

The Chapter of Accidents   C/FF
The Maid of the Oaks

TUES. 12 DEC.

Which is the Man?   C/BJ
The Humourist

THURS. 14 DEC.

Macbeth
The Padlock

SAT. 16 DEC.

Much Ado about Nothing   C/BJ

MON. 18 DEC.

Hamlet   C/FF
The Humourist

TUES. 19 DEC.

Venice Preserv'd   C/BJ
Rosina

THURS. 21 DEC.

The Merchant of Venice
Patrick in Prussia

SAT. 23 DEC.

The Way to Keep Him
The Humourist

TUES. 26 DEC.

Romeo and Juliet   C/BJ
Midas

WED. 27 DEC.

Romeo and Juliet   C/FF
The Whim

THURS. 28 DEC.

The Maid of the Mill
Robinson Crusoe

FRI. 29 DEC.

George Barnwell
Robinson Crusoe

SAT. 30 DEC.

Henry IV

1787

MON. 1 JAN.

He would be a soldier   C/FF
Midas

TUES. 2 JAN.

He Would be a Soldier   C/BJ, G
Patrick in Prussia

THURS. 4 JAN.

Robin Hood
Robinson Crusoe

SAT. 6 JAN.

Werter

MON. 8 JAN.

Henry IV (i)   C/FF
Peeping Tom of Coventry

TUES. 9 JAN.

He Would be a Soldier   C/BJ
The Two Misers

THURS. 11 JAN.

The Way to Keep Him   C/G, BC
Bon Ton   b: Mrs. Esten

SAT. 13 JAN.

The Follies of a Day
The Humourist

MON. 15 JAN.

He Would be a Soldier   C/FF
Robinson Crusoe

TUES. 16 JAN.

Richard III   C/BJ
The Maid of the Oaks

THURS. 18 JAN.

As You Like It   C/BJ, BC
The Irish Widow   (b: Master Bryson)

SAT. 20 JAN.
Rule a Wife and Have a Wife

MON. 22 JAN.
The Heiress   C/FF
The Humourist

TUES. 23 JAN.
He Would be a Soldier   C/BJ
The Dead Alive

THURS. 25 JAN.
The Gamester
The Lyar

SAT. 27 JAN.
The Heiress
The Deaf Lover

MON. 29 JAN.
Robin Hood   C/FF
Appearance is against them

WED. 31 JAN.
Cymbeline   C/BJ
The Poor Soldier

THURS. 1 FEB.
The Rivals
The Poor Soldier

SAT. 3 FEB.
A Bold Stroke for a Husband

MON. 5 FEB.
He Would be a Soldier   C/FF
The Two Misers

TUES. 6 FEB.
He Would be a Soldier   C/BJ
Rosina

THURS. 8 FEB.
The School for Scandal
The Rival Candidates

SAT. 10 FEB.
Eloisa   C/G
The Humourist

MON. 12 FEB.
Eloisa   C/FF
Rosina

TUES. 13 FEB.
The West Indian   C/BJ, BC b: Dimond
The Citizen

THURS. 15 FEB.
Cymbeline   C/BJ, BC b: Floor
The Maid of the Oaks

SAT. 17 FEB.
The Fashionable Lover   C/BJ, BC b: Keasberry
The First Floor

MON. 19 FEB.
The West Indian   C/FF
The First Floor

TUES. 20 FEB.
The Conscious Lovers   C/BJ, BC b: Murray
Hob in the Well

THURS. 22 FEB.
The Belle's Stratagem   C/BJ, BC b: Jackson
Tom Thumb the Great

SAT. 24 FEB.
The Chances   C/BC b: Bernard
The Scheming Lieutenant

MON. 26 FEB.
Eloisa   C/FF
The First Floor

TUES. 27 FEB.
Love Makes a Man   b: Blisset

THURS. 1 MAR.
The Suspicious Husband   C/BJ, BC
Hunt the Slipper   b: Miss Stanton

SAT. 3 MAR.
The Natural Son   C/BJ, BC, G
The Sultan   b: Mr. G. & Miss
                               Summers

MON. 5 MAR.
As you Like It   C/FF
The Humourist

TUES. 6 MAR.
The Wonder   C/BJ, BC
The Lying Valet   b: T. Blanchard

THURS. 8 MAR.
Know Your Own Mind   C/BJ, BC
The Deuce is in Him   b: Mrs. Didier

SAT. 10 MAR.
The Jealous Wife   C/BJ, BC
The Ingenious Valet   b: Powell & Miss
                               Cleland

MON. 12 MAR.
The Suspicious Husband   C/FF
Hunt the Slipper

TUES. 13 MAR.
The Heiress   C/BJ b: Miss Wright
The Students' Frolic

THURS. 15 MAR.	**TUES. 17 APR.**
I'll Tell You What C/BJ, BC	Such Things Are C/BJ
The Devil to Pay b: Lloyd & Phillips	The Widow's Vow
SAT. 17 MAR.	**THURS. 19 APRIL**
Eloisa	She Wou'd and She Wou'd Not
The First Floor	The Old Maid
MON. 19 MAR.	**SAT. 21 APRIL**
The Chances C/FF	Much Ado About Nothing C/G
The Sultan	
	MON. 23 APRIL
TUES. 20 MAR.	*Much Ado About Nothing* C/FF
He Would be a Soldier C/BJ	*The First Floor*
The Humourist	
	TUES. 24 APRIL
THURS. 22 MAR.	The Heiress C/BJ
The Rivals	Patrick in Prussia
The Irish Widow	
	WED. 25 APRIL
SAT. 24 MAR.	Such Things Are
The Chapter of Accidents C/BC	
Rosina	**SAT. 28 APRIL**
	The Follies of a Day
MON. 26 MAR.	
Such Things are C/FF	**MON. 30 APRIL**
The Deuce is in him	*Seduction* C/FF
	The Old Maid
TUES. 27 MAR.	
Such Things Are C/BJ, G	**TUES. 1 MAY**
The Waterman	Seduction C/BJ, G
	The Lyar
THURS. 29 MAR.	
Robin Hood	**WED. 2 MAY**
The Scheming Lieutenant	Such Things Are
	All The World's a Stage
SAT. 31 MAR.	
Such Things Are	**SAT. 5 MAY**
Hunt the Slipper	He Would Be a Soldier
	The Flitch of Bacon
MON. 9 APRIL	
Cymbeline C/FF	**MON. 7 MAY**
The Irish Widow	*Such Things Are* C/FF
	Patrick in Prussia
TUES. 10 APR.	
He Would be a Soldier C/BJ	**TUES. 8 MAY**
Peeping Tom of Coventry	Seduction C/BJ
	The Critic
WED. 11 APR.	
Such Things Are	**WED. 9 MAY**
	Such Things Are
THURS. 12 APR.	The Quaker
The Beggars' Opera	
	SAT. 12 MAY
SAT. 14 APR.	The Beaux Stratagem
The Provok'd Husband C/BC	The Humourist
MON. 16 APR.	**MON. 14 MAY**
Such Things Are C/FF	*Seduction* C/FF
The Widow's Vow	*Rosina*

TUES. 15 MAY

The School for Scandal   C/BJ
Patrick in Prussia

WED. 16 MAY

The Castle of Andalusia   C/BJ b: Incledon
The Romance of an Hour

SAT. 19 MAY

Such Things Are

MON. 21 MAY

The Revenge   C/FF
The Gentle Shepherd

TUES. 22 MAY

The English Merchant   C/BJ, BC
The Gentle Shepherd   b: Mrs Keasberry

WED. 23 MAY

The Heiress   C/BJ b: Rowbotham
The Positive Man

SAT. 26 MAY

The Revenge   C/BJ, BC b: Owens
The Mogul Tale

MON. 28 MAY

Seduction   C/FF
Robinson Crusoe

TUES. 29 MAY

Jane Shore   C/BJ
The Reprisal   b: Mrs Bernard

WED. 30 MAY

The School for Wives   C/BJ
The Sultan   b: Egan & Miss
                                 Sharrock

SAT. 2 JUNE

The Foundling   C/BJ, BC
A Beggar on Horseback   b: Wordsworth

MON. 4 JUNE

Such Things Are   C/FF
Robinson Crusoe

TUES. 5 JUNE

The Natural Son   C/BJ
The Mogul Tale

THURS. 7 JUNE

The West Indian   C/BJ, BC
High Life Below Stairs   b: Lloyd & Phillips

SAT. 9 JUNE

The Maid of the Mill

MON. 11 JUNE

The Merry Wives of Windsor C/FF, G b: Dimond
The Mogul Tale

WED. 13 JUNE

Cymbeline   C/FF
The Humourist   b: Servants of the
                                 House

FRI. 15 JUNE

He Would Be a Soldier   C/FF
The Quaker   b: Servants of the
                                 House

SAT. 16 JUNE

The Merry Wives of Windsor   C/BJ
Peeping Tom of Coventry

TUES. 19 JUNE

The English Merchant   C/FF b: Keasberry
The Reprisal

WED. 20 JUNE

The Rivals   C/FF b: T. Blanchard
The Positive Man

FRI. 22 JUNE

The Beggar's Opera

SAT. 23 JUNE

The Wonder   C/BJ
Robinson Crusoe

MON. 25 JUNE

Jane Shore   C/FF b: Murray
The Padlock

WED. 27 JUNE

The Heiress   C/FF
Gretna Green   b: Wordsworth &
                                 Miss Stanton

FRI. 29 JUNE

The Gamester   C/FF
The Flitch of Bacon   b: Miss Summers
                                 Mrs. Powell, Master
                                 & Miss Michel

MON. 2 JULY

Isabella   b: Mrs. Esten
The Sultan

WED. 4 JULY

The West Indian   C/FF
Gretna Green   b: Miss Cleland,
                                 Miss Williams,
                                 Master & Miss
                                 Michel

FRI. 6 JULY

The School for Scandal   C/FF b: Floor

MON. 9 JULY

The Hypocrite   C/FF
The Two Misers   b: Jackson & Blissett

WED. 11 JULY	
Know Your Own Mind	C/FF b: Mrs. Didier
The Register Office	

FRI. 13 JULY	
King Lear	
The Gentle Shepherd	

MON. 16 JULY	
The Castle of Andalusia	C/FF b: Mrs Blanchard
Three weeks after Marriage	

WED. 18 JULY	
Macbeth	C/SF
The Devil to Pay	b: Mr. & Mrs. Bernard

FRI. 20 JULY	
Richard III	C/FF
The Son-in-Law	b: Rowbotham & Lloyd

MON. 23 JULY	
Such Things Are	C/FF b: Mrs. Keasberry
Robinson Crusoe	

End of Season

Season 1787—88

Company

Mr: Ashley, Blisset, Bloomfield, Bristow, Dimond, Egan, Floor, Fox, Incledon, Jackson, Keasberry, Knight, Murray, Powell, Rowbotham, Summers, Ward, Waterhouse, Wordsworth

Mrs: Barnes, Berrisford, Didier, Goodall (formerly Miss Stanton), Keasberry, Knight, Powell, Simpson, Warrell

Miss: Cleland, Harley, Jackson, Michel, Sharrock, Summers, Warrell.

Master: Michel

Treasurer: Lloyd   *Box Book-keepers:* Phillips (Bath), Walker (Bristol)   *Prompter:* Floor

1787

MON. 1 OCT.	
The Busy Body	C/FF, PB/R
The Devil to Pay	

WED. 3 OCT.	
Love in a Village	PB/R
The Deuce is in Him	

FRI. 5 OCT.	
The Beaux Stratagem	PB/R
The Waterman	

SAT. 6 OCT.	
The Busybody	C/BJ, BC, G
The Devil to Pay	

MON. 8 OCT.	
She Wou'd and She Wou'd Not	C/FF
Three Weeks After Marriage	

WED. 10 OCT.	
She Stoops to Conquer	PB/R
The Flitch of Bacon	

FRI. 12 OCT	
Love in a Village	PB/R
The Citizen	

SAT. 13 OCT.	
The Foundling	PB/H, C/BJ
The Waterman	

MON. 15 OCT.	
The Foundling	C/FF, PB/R
The Padlock	

WED. 17 OCT.	
The West Indian	PB/R
The Rival Candidates	

FRI. 19 OCT.	
As You Like It	PB/R
The Old Maid	

SAT. 20 OCT.	
Love in a Village	PB/H, C/BJ, BC
The Deuce is in Him	

MON. 22 OCT.
The Conscious Lovers   C/FF, PB/R
Robinson Crusoe

WED. 24 OCT.
Rule a Wife and Have a Wife   PB/R
The Quaker

FRI. 26 OCT.
The School for Scandal   PB/R
Robinson Crusoe

SAT. 27 OCT.
Rule a Wife and Have a Wife   PB/H, C/BJ, G
The Rival Candidates

MON. 29 OCT.
The Maid of the Mill   PB/R, C/FF
The Guardian

TUES. 30 OCT.
She Stoops to Conquer   PB/H, C/BJ
The Quaker

WED. 31 OCT.
The Maid of the Mill   PB/H
Three Weeks After Marriage

SAT. 3 NOV.
Macbeth   PB/H
The Padlock

MON. 5 NOV.
Henry IV (i)   PB/R, C/FF
Robinson Crusoe

TUES. 6 NOV.
Venice Preserv'd   C/BJ, G
The Flitch of Bacon

THURS. 8 NOV.
As You Like It   PB/H
The Old Maid

SAT. 10 NOV.
Much Ado About Nothing   PB/H
The Agreeable Surprise

MON. 12 NOV.
Venice Preserv'd   PB/R, C/FF
The Agreeable Surprise

TUES. 13 NOV.
The Young Quaker   PB/H, C/BJ, G
The Guardian

THURS. 15 NOV.
Jane Shore   PB/H
The Citizen

SAT. 17 NOV.
The Heiress   PB/H, C/G
The Maid of the Oaks

MON. 19 NOV.
The Young Quaker   C/FF
Midas

TUES. 20 NOV.
The Young Quaker   PB/H, C/BJ
The Deaf Lover

THURS. 22 NOV.
Henry IV   PB/H
The Devil to Pay

SAT. 24 NOV.
The West Indian   PB/H
The Deserter

MON. 26 NOV.
Such Things are   PB/R, C/FF
The Deserter

TUES. 27 NOV.
Such Things are   PB/H, C/BJ
The Agreable Surprise

THURS. 29 NOV.
The Miser   PB/H, C/G
Cross Purposes

SAT. 1 DEC.
The Young Quaker   PB/H
Midas

MON. 3 DEC.
The Young Quaker   C/FF
Midas

TUES. 4 DEC.
The Wonder   PB/H, C/BJ
The Humourist

THURS. 6 DEC.
The Beaux Stratagem   PB/H
The Irish Widow

SAT. 8 DEC.
The Provok'd Husband   PB/H
The Two Misers

MON. 10 DEC.
Macbeth   (Mrs. Barnes) PB/R, C/FF
The Deaf Lover

TUES. 11 DEC.
The New Peerage   PB/H, C/BJ, BC
The Quaker

THURS. 13 DEC.
The Heiress   PB/H
Who's The Dupe?

SAT. 15 DEC.
The School for Scandal   PB/H
The Flitch of Bacon

MON. 17 DEC.
The New Peerage   PB/R, C/FF
The Humourist

TUES. 18 DEC.
Such Things are   PB/H, C/BJ
Cross Purposes

THURS. 20 DEC.
She Wou'd and She Wou'd Not   PB/H
Thomas and Sally

SAT. 22 DEC.
The New Peerage   PB/H
The Gentle Shepherd

WED. 26 DEC.
Jane Shore   (Mrs. Barnes) PB/R, C/FF
The Gentle Shepherd

THURS. 27 DEC.
The London Merchànt   PB/H, C/BJ
Robinson Crusoe

FRI. 28 DEC.
The New Peerage   PB/H
Robinson Crusoe

SAT. 29 DEC.
She Stoops to Conquer   PB/H
The Humourist

MON. 31 DEC.
The New Peerage   PB/R, C/FF
Cross Purposes

1788

TUES. 1 JAN.
Such Things Were   PB/H, C/BJ, BC, G
The Rival Candidates

THURS. 3 JAN.
The Young Quaker   PB/H
Robinson Crusoe

SAT. 5 JAN.
Love in a Village
Three Weeks After Marriage   PB/H

MON. 7 JAN.
Such Things Were   C/FF
The Rival Candidates

TUES. 8 JAN.
Such Things Were   PB/H
The Waterman

THURS. 10 JAN.
The Busybody   PB/H
Robinson Crusoe

SAT. 12 JAN.
The Suspicious Husband   PB/H
The Agreeable Surprise

MON. 14 JAN.
The Suspicious Husband   PB/R, C/BG
Who's the Dupe?

TUES. 15 JAN.
Such Things Were   PB/H, C/BJ
Robinson Crusoe

THURS. 17 JAN.
The Maid of the Mill   PB/H, C/BJ, BC
The Deuce is in Him

SAT. 19 JAN.
Such Things Were   PB/H, C/G
The Midnight Hour

MON. 21 JAN.
Such Things Were   PB/R, C/BG
The Midnight Hour

TUES. 22 JAN.
Such Things Were   PB/H, C/BJ
The Midnight Hour

THURS. 24 JAN.
Such Things Were   PB/H
The Midnight Hour

SAT. 26 JAN.
The New Peerage   PB/H
The First Floor

MON. 28 JAN.
Such Things Were   PB/R, C/BG
The Midnight Hour

TUES. 29 JAN.
The Conscious Lovers   PB/H, C/BJ
The Midnight Hour

THURS. 31 JAN.
Othello   PB/H, C/G, BC
The Whim

SAT. 2 FEB.
Know Your Own Mind   PB/H
The Whim

MON. 4 FEB.
Robin Hood   PB/R, C/BG
The First Floor

TUES. 5 FEB.
Such Things Were   PB/H, C/BJ
The Whim

THURS. 7 FEB.
Robin Hood   PB/H
The Deaf Lover

SAT. 9 FEB.
Othello   PB/H
The Midnight Hour

MON. 11 FEB.
Othello   PB/R, C/BG
Thomas and Sally

TUES. 12 FEB.
Hamlet   C/BJ, BC, b: Dimond
The Upholsterer

THURS. 14 FEB.
The Jealous Wife (Didier) PB/H, C/BJ, BC, G
High Life Below Stairs   b: Mrs Didier

SAT.16 FEB.
The Clandestine Marriage   PB/H, C/BJ, BC
The Gentle Shepherd   b: Wordsworth

MON. 18 FEB.
Such Things Were   PB/R, C/BG
The Midnight Hour

TUES. 19 FEB.
He Would be a Soldier   PB/H, C/BJ, BC
Selima and Azor   b: Keasberry

THURS. 21 FEB.
King Lear   PB/H, C/BJ, BC
The Quaker   b: Murray

SAT. 23 FEB.
The Fashionable Lover   PB/H, C/BJ, BC
The Son-in-Law   b: Rowbotham

MON. 25 FEB.
He Would be a Soldier   PB/R, C/BG
Selima and Azor

TUES. 26 FEB.
Cymbeline   PB/H, C/BJ, BC
A Trip to Scotland   b: Mrs. Simpson

THURS. 28 FEB.
The Hypocrite   PB/H, C/BJ, BC
Bon Ton   b: Mrs. Goodall

SAT. 1 MAR.
The Chapter of Accidents   PB/H, C/BC b: Blisset
The Humourist

MON. 3 MAR.
Othello   PB/R, C/BG, TC
The Midnight Hour

TUES. 4 MAR.
Romeo and Juliet   C/BJ, BC b: Ward
The Apprentice

THURS. 6 MAR.
The Wonder   PB/H, C/BJ, BC
Tom Thumb the Great   b: Jackson

SAT. 8 MAR.
The Duenna   PB/H, C/BJ, BC
All the World's a Stage   b: Mrs. Warrell

MON. 10 MAR.
The Clandestine Marriage   PB/R
Selima and Azor

TUES. 11 MAR.
The School for Scandal   PB/H, C/BJ, BC
The Maid of the Oaks   b: Miss Prideaux

THURS. 13 MAR.
Much Ado about Nothing   C/BJ, BC
Midas   b: Lloyd & Phillips

SAT. 15 MAR.
The Funeral   PB/H, C/BJ, BC
The Deserter   b: Knight

MON. 24 MAR.
Romeo and Juliet   PB/R, C/BG
The Apprentice

TUES. 25 MAR.
Such Things Are   PB/H, C/BJ
The Whim

WED. 26 MAR.
The Suspicious Husband   PB/H
The Midnight Hour

THURS. 27 MAR.
Romeo and Juliet   PB/H, C/BJ, BC
Thomas and Sally

SAT. 29 MAR.
Know Your Own Mind   PB/H, C/BJ
Selima and Azor

MON. 31 MAR.
The Funeral   PB/R
The Midnight Hour

TUES. 1 APRIL
Such Things Were   PB/H, C/BJ
The Midnight Hour

THURS. 3 APRIL
The Belle's Stratagem   PB/H, C/BJ, BC
The Flitch of Bacon   b: Floor

SAT. 5 APRIL	
Inkle and Yarico	PB/H
Who's the Dupe?	

MON. 7 APRIL	
Inkle and Yarico	PB/R, C/BG
Who's the Dupe?	

TUES. 8 APRIL	
The Rivals	PB/H, C/BJ
All the World's a Stage	

WED. 9 APRIL	
Inkle and Yarico	PB/H
The Deaf Lover	

SAT. 12 APRIL	
He Would be a Soldier	PB/H
The Agreable Surprise	

MON. 14 APRIL	
Inkle and Yarico	PB/R, C/BG
The Citizen	

TUES. 15 APRIL	
Inkle and Yarico	PB/H, C/BJ
The Midnight Hour	

THURS. 17 APRIL	
Love Makes a Man	PB/H
The First Floor	

SAT. 19 APRIL	
The West Indian	PB/H
The Gentle Shephard	

MON. 21 APRIL	
Hamlet	PB/R, C/BG
All the World's a Stage	

TUES. 22 APRIL	
The Country Girl	PB/H, C/G
The Padlock	

WED. 23 APRIL	
Robin Hood	PB/H, C/BJ
Bon Ton	b: Incledon

SAT. 26 APRIL	
Inkle and Yarico	PB/H
The Humourist	

MON. 28 APRIL	
The Country Girl	C/BG, PB/R
The Agreeable Surprise	

TUES. 29 APRIL	
The Country Girl	PB/H, C/BJ
The Midnight Hour	

WED. 30 APRIL	
The Provok'd Husband	PB/H
The Romp	

SAT. 3 MAY	
Rule a Wife and Have a Wife	PB/H
The Romp	

MON. 5 MAY	
Inkle and Yarico	PB/R, C/BG
The Midnight Hour	

TUES. 6 MAY	
Inkle and Yarico	C/BJ
Cross Purposes	

WED. 7 MAY	
Inkle and Yarico	PB/H
The Romp	

SAT. 10 MAY	
The Country Girl	PB/H
The Midnight Hour	

MON. 12 MAY	
Much Ado About Nothing	PB/R, C/BG
The Romp	

TUES. 13 MAY	
Such Things Were	PB/H, C/BJ
The Virgin Unmask'd	

WED. 14 MAY	
The Castle of Andalusia	PB/H, C/BJ, b: Fox
The Apprentice	

SAT. 17 MAY	
The Young Quaker	PB/H, C/BJ, BC
The Romp	b: Mrs. Keasberry

MON. 19 MAY	
The Country Girl	PB/R, C/BG
The Rival Candidates	

TUES. 20 MAY	
Which is the Man?	PB/H, C/BJ
The Register Office	b: Mrs. Powell
	Miss Cleland

WED. 21 MAY	
The Fashionable Lover	PB/H, C/BJ
The Devil to Pay	b: Master & Miss
	Michel

SAT. 24 MAY	
The Heiress	PB/H, C/BJ, BC
The Agreeable Surprise	b: Miss Harley

MON. 26 MAY	
The Young Quaker	PB/R, C/BG,
The Romp	b: Keasberry

TUES. 27 MAY
The Beggar's Opera (Bannister) PB/H, C/BJ
The Humourist   b: Mr. & Miss
                                   Summers

WED. 28 MAY
Venice Preserv'd (Mrs. Kemble) PB/H, C/BJ
The Virgin Unmask'd   b: Miss Sharrock

SAT. 31 MAY
She Stoops to Conquer   PB/H, C/BJ, BC, G
The Man of Quality   b: Mrs. Knight

MON. 2 JUNE
Such Things Were   C/FF b: Dimond
The Midnight Hour

TUES. 3 JUNE
Henry II   PB/H, C/BJ
The Man of Quality

THURS. 5 JUNE
I'll Tell you What   PB/H, C/BJ
The Two Misers   b: Lloyd & Phillips

SAT. 7 JUNE
The Maid of the Mill (Blanchard)   PB/H, C/BJ, BC
Hob in the Well   b: Egan

MON. 9 JUNE
Cymbeline   PB/R, C/BG
A Trip to Scotland   b: Mrs. Simpson

WED. 11 JUNE
The Heiress   PB/R b: Mrs. Didier
Catherine and Petruchio

FRI. 13 JUNE
Henry II   PB/R, C/BG
The Man of Quality   b: Part of Servants
                                   of House

SAT. 14 JUNE
Such Things Are   PB/H
Catherine and Petruchio

MON. 16 JUNE
Such Things Are   PB/R, C/BG
The Devil to Pay   b: Murray

WED. 18 JUNE
She Stoops to Conquer   PB/R, C/BG
The Romp   b: Part of Servants of
                                   House

FRI. 20 JUNE
He Would be a Soldier   C/BG
The Virgin Unmask'd   b: Part of Servants
                                   of House

SAT. 21 JUNE
Inkle and Yarico   PB/H, C/BJ
The Midnight Hour

MON. 23 JUNE
The Country Girl   PB/R
The Man of Quality   b: Mr. & Mrs. Knight

WED. 25 JUNE
The Gamester   PB/R b: Miss Harley
High Life Below Stairs

FRI. 27 JUNE
The Busybody   PB/R
The Apprentice   b: Walker (Box
                                   Book-keeper)

SAT. 28 JUNE
The Man of Quality   PB/H, C/BJ
The Old Maid
The Gentle Shepherd

MON. 30 JUNE
Tancred and Sigismunda PB/R b: Ward
Transformation

WED. 2 JULY
I'll Tell You What   C/FF
The Gentle Shepherd   b: Bloomfield,
                                   Bristow, Miss
                                   Sharrock, Mrs.
                                   Powell, Master &
                                   Miss Michel

FRI. 4 JULY
Inkle and Yarico   PB/R
The Humourist   b: Fox, Mr. & Miss
                                   Summers, Miss
                                   Cleland, Mrs.
                                   Berrisford

MON. 7 JULY
Richard III   PB/R
The Honest Yorkshireman   b: Wodsworth &
                                   Mrs. Warrell

WED. 9 JULY
The Fair Penitent   PB/R b: Mrs. Goodall
The Reprisal

FRI. 11 JULY
The Grecian Daughter   PB/R b: Floor
Catherine and Petruchio

MON. 14 JULY
A Bold Stroke for a Wife PB/R
Chrononhotonthologos   b: Blisset & Jackson

WED. 16 JULY
The Countess of Salisbury   PB/R b: Murray
The King and the Miller of
Mansfield

MON. 21 JULY
The Merry Wives of Windsor   C/BG, PB/R
The Romp   b: Mrs. Keasberry

FRI. 18 JULY
The West Indian   PB/R
The Brave Irishman   b: Rowbotham &
                                 Lloyd (Treasurer)

End of Season

Season 1788/89

Company

Mr: Ashley, Bates, Blisset, Bloomfield, Bygrove, Dimond, Durravan Snr. and Jnr., Eastmure, Egan, Fox, Incledon, Keasberry, Knight, Murray, Pearce, Pindar, Rowbotham, Summers, Taylor, Ward, Waterhouse. Wordsworth.

Mrs: Berrisford, Didier, Keasberry, Knight, Powell, Reidford, Simpson, Smith, Warrell.

Miss: Cleland, Harley, Michel, Sharrock, Summers, Tittore (Later Mrs. Colls), Warrell.

Master: Michel, Warrell

Treasurer: Lloyd   *Box Book-keeper:* Bartley (Bath)   *Prompter:* Floor

1788

WED. 1 OCT.
The Gamester
Brystowe

MON. 15 SEPT.
The Country Girl   C/FF
The Lying Valet

FRI. 3 OCT.
Brystowe

WED. 17 SEPT.
The Beaux Stratagem

SAT. 4 OCT.
The Beaux' Stratagem   PB/H, C/BJ, BC
The Romp

FRI. 19 SEPT.
Inkle and Yarico

MON. 6 OCT.
The Wonder   C/FF
Brystowe

SAT. 20 SEPT.
The Country Girl   PB/H, C/BJ, BC
The Lying Valet

WED. 8 OCT.
Brystowe

MON. 22 SEPT.
Hamlet   C/FF
The Romp

FRI. 10 OCT.
George Barnwell   C/BG
Brystowe

FRI. 26 SEPT.
The Maid of the Mill   C/BG
Who's the Dupe?

SAT. 11 OCT.
The Wonder   PB/H, C/BJ, BC
The Poor Soldier

SAT. 27 SEPT.
Inkle and Yarico   PB/H, C/BC
The Midnight Hour

MON. 13 OCT.
The Rivals   C/FF
Brystowe

MON. 29 SEPT.
He Would be a Soldier   C/FF
The Deserter

FRI. 17 OCT.
The Castle of Andalusia   C/BG
Brystowe

SAT. 18 OCT.

The Rivals   PB/H, Ba, C/BJ, BC
The Quaker

MON. 20 OCT.

The Busybody   C/FF
The Poor Soldier

FRI. 24 OCT.

Richard III   C/BG
Brystowe

SAT. 15 OCT.

The Suspicious Husband   PB/H, C/BH, BC
The Midnight Hour

MON. 27 OCT.

The Mourning Bride   C/FF
Brystowe

TUES. 28 OCT.

The Clandestine Marriage   PB/H, C/BJ
The First Floor

THURS. 30 OCT.

The Mourning Bride   PB/H, C/BC
Who's the Dupe?

SAT. 1 NOV.

Rule a Wife and Have a Wife   PB/H
The Romp

MON. 3 NOV.

Rule a Wife and Have a Wife   C/FF
Animal Magnetism

TUES. 4 NOV.

The Conscious Lovers   PB/H, C/BJ
Animal Magnetism

THURS. 6 NOV.

The Gamester   PB/H, C/BC
Animal Magnetism

SAT. 8 NOV.

The Busy Body   PB/H
The Man of Quality

MON. 10 NOV.

Cymbeline   C/FF
Animal Magnetism

TUES. 11 NOV.

The West Indian   PB/H, C/BJ
Brystowe

THURS. 13 NOV.

Richard III   PB/H, C/BC
Brystowe

SAT. 15 NOV.

Inkle and Yarico   PB/H, C/BC
The Deaf Lover

MON. 17 NOV.

Inkle and Yarico   C/FF
The Midnight Hour

TUES. 18 NOV.

The Regent   PB/H, C/BJ, G
The Poor Soldier

THURS. 20 NOV.

She Stoops to Conquer   PB/H
Brystowe

SAT. 22 NOV.

Lionel and Clarissa   PB/H, C/BJ, BC, G
The Lying Valet

MON. 24 NOV.

The Regent   C/FF
The Poor Soldier

TUES. 25 NOV.

He Would be a Soldier   PB/H, C/BJ
The Agreeable Surprise

THURS. 27 NOV.

Venice Preserv'd   PB/H
Brystowe

SAT. 30 NOV.

The Chapter of Accidents   PB/H
Brystowe

MON. 1 DEC.

Lionel and Clarissa   C/FF
The Lying Valet

TUES. 2 DEC.

Such Things Were   PB/H, C/BJ
Animal Magnetism

THURS. 4 DEC.

Robin Hood   PB/H
Brystowe

SAT. 6 DEC.

The School for Scandal   PB/H
The Virgin Unmask'd

MON. 8 DEC.

Such Things Were   C/FF
The Romp

TUES. 9 DEC.

The Provok'd Husband   PB/H, C/BJ, BC
The Rival Candidates

THURS. 11 DEC.

The Country Girl   PB/H
Brystowe

SAT. 13 DEC.

The Suspicious Husband   PB/H, C/BC
Midas

MON. 15 DEC.
The School for Scandal   C/FF
The Virgin Unmask'd

TUES. 16 DEC.
Inkle and Yarico   PB/H, C/BJ
The Midnight Hour

THURS. 18 DEC.
The Merry Wives of Windsor   PB/H
Brystowe

SAT. 20 DEC.
Such Things Are   PB/H
The Farmer

MON. 22 DEC.
The Provok'd Husband   C/FF
The Farmer

TUES. 23 DEC.
The Heiress   PB/H, C/BJ, BC
The Farmer

FRI. 26 DEC.
George Barnwell   PB/H
Brystowe

SAT. 27 DEC.
Know Your Own Mind   PB/H
Brystowe

MON. 29 DEC.
Robin Hood   C/FF
*The King and the Miller of
Mansfield*

TUES. 30 DEC.
Robin Hood   PB/H, C/BJ
The King and the Miller of
Mansfield.

1789

THURS. 1 JAN.
Cymbeline   PB/H
Brystowe

SAT. 3 JAN.
I'll Tell you What   PB/H, BM
Animal Magnetism

MON. 5 JAN.
The Merry Wives of Windsor (Moses Kean)   C/FF
Thomas and Sally

TUES. 6 JAN.
The Young Quaker   PB/H, BM, C/BJ
Brystowe

THURS. 8 JAN.
Jane Shore   (Moses Kean) PB/BM, C/BJ, G
The Waterman

SAT. 10 JAN.
The Wonder   PB/BM, H
The Farmer

MON. 12 JAN.
Tancreed and Sigismunda (Moses Kean)   C/FF
Brystowe

TUES. 13 JAN.
Inkle and Yarico (Moses Kean)   C/BJ
Cross Purposes

THURS. 15 JAN.
The Fair Penitent   PB/H
Robinson Crusoe

SAT. 17 JAN.
The Jealous Wife (Moses Kean)
The Midnight Hour

MON. 19 JAN.
The Merry Wives of Windsor (Moses Kean)   C/FF
Brystowe

TUES. 20 JAN.
Hamlet   PB/F, C/BJ
The Waterman

THURS. 22 JAN.
Lionel and Clarissa   PB/H
The Farmer

SAT. 24 JAN.
The Clandestine Marriage   PB/H
Robinson Crusoe

MON. 26 JAN.
Jane Shore   C/FF
The Farmer

TUES. 27 JAN.
The Busybody   PB/H, C/BJ
The Farmer

THURS. 29 JAN.
The Castle of Andalusia   PB/H
The Humourist

SAT. 31 JAN.
Love Makes a Man   PB/H
Marian

MON. 2 FEB.
Love Makes a Man   C/FF
Marian

TUES. 3 FEB.
The Beggar's Opera   PB/H, C/BJ, BC
The Lying Valet

THURS. 5 FEB.
The School for Wives   PB/H
Marian

SAT. 7 FEB.
The School for Scandal   PB/H
The Poor Soldier

MON. 9 FEB.
Hamlet   C/FF
The Romp

TUES. 10 FEB.
Tancred and Sigismunda   C/BJ, BC, G
Rosina   b: Dimond

THURS. 12 FEB.
Romeo and Juliet   PB/H, C/BJ, BC
Robinson Crusoe   b: Floor

SAT. 14 FEB.
The Folllies of a Day   PB/H, C/BJ, BC, G
Marian   b: Keasberry

MON. 16 FEB.
The Country Girl   C/FF
Marian

TUES. 17 FEB.
The Fashionable Lover   PB/H, C/BJ, BC
The Gentle Shepherd   b: Blisset

THURS. 19 FEB.
Macbeth   PB/H, C/BJ, BC b: Fox
The Flitch of Bacon

SAT. 21 FEB.
Much Ado About Nothing   PB/H, C/BJ, BC
The Romp   b: Mrs. Simpson

MON. 23 FEB.
The Follies of a Day   C/FF
The Flitch of Bacon

TUES. 24 FEB.
A Word to the Wise   PB/H, C/BJ, BC, G
Catherine and Petruchio   b: Murray

THURS. 26 FEB.
Such Things Are   PB/H, C/BJ, BC
A Trip to Scotland   b: Mrs. Didier

SAT. 28 FEB.
The English Merchant   PB/H, C/BJ, BC, G
The Devil to Pay   b: Mrs. Knight

MON. 2 MAR.
A Word to the Wise   C/FF
Brystowe

TUES. 3 MAR.
Love in a Village   C/BJ, BC b: Incledon
The Citizen

THURS. 5 MAR.
Such Things Were   PB/H, C/BJ, BC
                            b: Miss Cleland
The Midnight Hour

SAT. 7 MAR.
The School for Scandal   PB/H, C/BJ, BC
A Touch of the Times   b: Ward
Transformation

MON. 9 MAR.
Inkle and Yarico   C/FF
Brystowe

TUES. 10 MAR.
Inkle and Yarico   PB/H, C/BJ, BC
The Poor Soldier   b: Wordsworth

THURS. 12 MAR.
The Young Quaker   PB/H, C/BJ, BC
Peeping Tom of Coventry   b: Miss Harley

SAT. 14 MAR.
The Foundling   PB/H, C/BJ, BC
The Golden Pippin   b: Mrs. Warrell

MON. 16 MAR.
The English Merchant   C/FF
The Farmer

TUES. 17 MAR.
The Merchant of Venice   PB/H, C/BJ, BC
St. Patrick's Day   b: Bloomfield

THURS. 19 MAR.
The Chapter of Accidents   PB/H, C/BJ, BC
The Lyar   b: Lloyd & Bartley

SAT. 21 MAR.
Know Your Own Mind   PB/Ba, H
The Romp

MON. 23 MAR.
Know Your Own Mind   PB/R, C/FF
The Golden Pippin

TUES. 24 MAR.
The Follies of a Day   PB/H, C/BJ
The Farmer

THURS. 26 MAR.
The Maid of the Mill   PB/H
Who's the Dupe?

SAT. 28 MAR.
Which is the Man?   PB/H
Rosina

MON. 30 MAR.

Love in a Village   C/FF
Animal Magnetism

TUES. 31 MAR.

The Beaux Stratagem   PB/H, C/BJ
The Virgin Unmask'd

THURS. 2 APRIL

Tancred and Sigismunda   PB/H
The Quaker

SAT. 4 APRIL

The West Indian   PB/H
Marian

MON. 13 APRIL

The Merchant of Venice   C/FF
Brystowe

TUES. 14 APRIL

Inkle and Yarico   PB/H, C/BJ
The Farmer

WED. 15 APRIL

The Merchant of Venice   PB/H
The Romp

THURS. 16 APRIL

The Country Girl   PB/H
Brystowe

SAT. 18 APR.

The Wonder   PB/H
   (Bryson's Musical Children)
The Poor Soldier

MON. 20 APR.

Cymbeline   C/FF
The Poor Soldier

TUES. 21 APR.

The Disbanded Officer   PB/H, C/BJ, G
   (Bryson's Musical Children)
The Agreeable Surprise

THURS. 23 APR.

The Young Quaker   PB/H
Brystowe

SAT. 25 APR.

The Disbanded Officer   PB/H
The Farmer

MON. 27 APR.

The Disbanded Officer   C/FF
   (Bryson's Musical Children)
The Farmer

TUES. 28 APR.

The Regent   PB/H, C/BJ
Brystowe

THURS. 30 APR.

Robin Hood   PB/H
Animal Magnetism

SAT. 2 MAY

The English Merchant   PB/H
   (Bryson's Musical Children)
Rosina

MON. 4 MAY

Love in a Village   C/FF
   (Bryson's Musical Children)
Animal Magnetism

TUES. 5 MAY

Inkle and Yarico   PB/H, C/BJ
   (Bryson's Musical Children)
The Deaf Lover

THURS. 7 MAY

The Rivals   PB/H, C/BJ, BC
Midas   b: Miss Tittore

SAT. 9 MAY

I'll Tell You What   PB/H
The Farmer

MON. 11 MAY

The Regent   C/FF
   (Bryson's Musical Children)
Rosina

TUES. 12 MAY

The Regent   PB/H, C/BJ
   (Bryson's Musical Children)
Comus

THURS. 14 MAY

The Duenna   PB/H
Brystowe

SAT. 16 MAY

The Disbanded Officer   PB/H
Comus

MON. 18 MAY

The Disbanded Officer   C/FF
Comus

TUES. 19 MAY

Inkle and Yarico   PB/H, C/BJ, BC
The Romp   b: Knight

THURS. 21 MAY

A Word to the Wise   PB/H, C/BJ
The Gentle Shepherd

SAT. 23 MAY

The Pilgrim   PB/H, C/BJ, BC
Poor Vulcan   b: Mrs. Keasberry

MON. 25 MAY

The Pilgrim   C/FF b: Keasberry
Poor Vulcan

TUES. 26 MAY

Cymbeline   PB/H, C/BJ
All's Well that End's Well   b: Rowbotham

THURS. 28 MAY

Such Things Are   PB/H, C/BJ, BC
The Whim   b: Miss Summers

SAT. 30 MAY

The Spanish Barber   PB/H, C/G
The Guardian   b: Durravan Jnr.
The Poor Soldier

MON. 1 JUNE

The Jealous Wife   C/FF
The Gentle Shepherd

TUES. 2 JUNE

Twelfth Night   PB/H, C/BJ b: Bates
Robinson Crusoe

WED. 3 JUNE

The Jealous Wife   PB/H, C/BJ
  (Bryson's Musical Children)
The Quaker

SAT. 6 JUNE

The Young Quaker   PB/H, C/BJ
Miss in her Teens   b: Master & Miss Michel

MON. 8 JUNE

Matilda   C/FF, G b: Dimond
All's Well that ends Well

TUES. 9 JUNE

Love Makes a Man   PB/H, C/BJ,
The Man of Quality   b: Lloyd & Bartley

THURS. 11 JUNE

The Pilgrim   PB/H, C/BJ
The Midnight Hour

SAT. 13 JUNE

The School for Scandal   PB/H, C/BJ
The Whim

MON. 15 JUNE

King John   C/FF b: Mrs. Simpson
The Citizen

WED. 17 JUNE

Twelfth Night   C/SF b: Fox & Bates
The Siege of Gibraltar

SAT. 20 JUNE

King John   PB/H, C/BJ,
The Poor Soldier   b: Warrell and children

MON. 22 JUNE

Macbeth   C/BG b: Ward
The What d'ye call It?

THURS. 25 JUNE

The Young Quaker   C/FF b: Part of Servants
The Whim   of the House

FRI. 26 JUNE

The Merchant of Venice   C/BG
The Midnight Hour

MON. 29 JUNE

The Spanish Barber   C/FF b: Blissett
The Guardian
The Virgin Unmask'd

WED. 1 JULY

Romeo and Juliet   C/FF b: Mrs. Colls
Bon Ton

FRI. 3 JULY

The Rivals   C/BG b: Part of Servants
The Whim   of House

MON. 6 JULY

The Unhappy Favourite   b: Murray
Don Quixote in England

WED. 8 JULY

The Wonder   C/SF b: Miss Harley
The Maid of the Oaks

FRI. 10 JULY

The School for Scandal   C/BG b: Bloomfield
The King and the Miller of Mansfield

MON. 13 JULY

Inkle and Yarico   C/FF b: Mr. and
The Poor Soldier   Mrs. Knight

WED. 15 JULY

The Grecian Daughter   C/FF b: Wordsworth
The Dead Alive   & Durravan Jnr.

FRI. 17 JULY

The Winter's Tale   PB/BM b: Fox & Bates
The Guardian
The Siege of Gibraltar

MON. 20 JULY

The Countess of Salisbury   C/FF b: Mrs. Didier
A Bold Stroke for a Wife   & Miss Summers

WED. 22 JULY

Inkle and Yarico   C/FF b: Floor (Prompter)
Brystowe   and Miss Cleland

FRI. 24 JULY

The Padlock   C/FF b: Rowbotham
The Man of Quality   & Lloyd (Treasurer)

Werter
Rosina

MON. 27 JULY

C/FF b: Mrs. Keasberry

End of Season

Season 1789/90

Company

Mr: Ashley, Bates, Blisset, Bloomfield, Bristow, Dimond, Durravan Snr. and Jnr., Eastmure, Fox, Incledon, Keasberry, Knight, Murray, Pindar, Rowbotham, Smith, Summers, Taylor, Ward, Wordsworth.

Mrs: Didier, Keasberry, Knight, Malloy, Powell, Simpson, Smith.

Miss: Brett, Cleland, Floor, Sharrock, Summers, Wallis.

Master: Keasberry.

Treasurer: Lloyd.   *Box Book Keeper:* Bartley, (Bath).   *Prompter:* Floor.

1789

MON. 21 SEPT.

Inkle and Yarico   C/FF
The Midnight Hour

WED. 23 SEPT.

Rule a Wife and Have a Wife
The Padlock

SAT. 26 SEPT.

Inkle and Yarico   PB/H
The Midnight Hour

MON. 28 SEPT.

The Chapter of Accidents   C/FF
The Padlock

FRI. 2 OCT.

The Country Girl   C/BG
The Farmer

SAT. 3 OCT.

Rule a Wife and Have a Wife   C/BJ, G
The Padlock

MON. 5 OCT.

Such Things Are   C/FF
Rosina

FRI. 9 OCT.

The Provok'd Husband   C/BG
Gil Blas of Santillane

SAT. 10 OCT.

The Country Girl   PB/H, C/BJ
The Farmer

MON. 12 OCT.

Hamlet   C/FF
Gil Blas of Santillane

FRI. 16 OCT.

The Wonder   C/BG
Gil Blas of Santillane

SAT. 17 OCT.

As You Like It   PB/H, C/BJ, BC, G
Rosina

MON. 19 OCT.

As You Like It   C/FF
The Lying Valet

SAT. 24 OCT.

Love in a Village   PB/H, C/BJ, BC, G
Bon Ton

MON. 26 OCT.

The Mourning Bride   C/FF
Gil Blas of Santillane

TUES. 27 OCT.

She Stoops to Conquer   PB/H, C/BJ
The Poor Soldier

WED. 28 OCT.

The Chapter of Accidents   PB/H
Cross Purposes

SAT. 31 OCT.

The Wonder   PB/H
The Romp

MON. 2 NOV.
Earl Goodwin   C/FF
The Farmer

TUES. 3 NOV.
Earl Goodwin   PB/H, C/BJ, G
The Padlock

WED. 4 NOV.
Earl Goodwin   PB/H
The Farmer

SAT. 7 NOV.
The Provok'd Husband   PB/H, C/G
The Farmhouse

MON. 9 NOV.
Earl Goodwin   C/FF
Gil Blas of Santillane

TUES. 10 NOV.
Venice Preserv'd   PB/H, C/BJ, BC
The Farmhouse

THURS. 12 NOV.
The School for Scandal PB/H
The Romp

SAT. 14 NOV.
The Pilgrim   PB/H
The Agreeable Surprise

MON. 16 NOV.
Venice Preserv'd   C/FF
The Farmhouse

TUES. 17 NOV.
Such Things Are   PB/H, C/BJ
The Farmhouse

THURS. 19 NOV.
The Young Quaker   PB/H
Gil Blas of Santillane

SAT. 21 NOV.
The Bell's Stratagem   PB/H, C/BJ, BC
The Humorist

MON. 23 NOV.
The Belle's Stratagem C/FF
The Farmhouse

TUES. 24 NOV.
Earl Goodwin   PB/H, C/BJ
The Farmer   b: Mrs Yearsley
                       (Author)

THURS. 26 NOV.
The Country Girl   PB/H
Gil Blas of Santillane

SAT. 28 NOV.
Inkle and Yarico   PB/H
Who's the Dupe?

MON. 30 NOV.
Earl Goodwin   C/FF
The Poor Soldier

TUES. 1 DEC.
The Conscious Lovers   PB/H, C/BJ
The Poor Soldier

THURS. 3 DEC.
The Duenna
Gil Blas of Santillane

SAT. 5 DEC.
The West Indian   PB/H
Rosina

MON. 7 DEC.
Earl Goodwin   C/FF b: Mrs. Yearsley
The Romp

TUES. 8 DEC.
The Clandestine Marriage C/BJ
The Rival Candidates

THURS. 10 DEC.
The Merchant of Venice
The Farmhouse

SAT. 12 DEC.
The Heiress

MON. 14 DEC.
The Conscious Lovers C/FF
The Farmhouse

TUES. 15 DEC.
Cymbeline   C/BJ
The Farmer

THURS. 17 DEC.
The Busybody
Gil Blas of Santillane

SAT. 19 DEC.
The Follies of a Day
Cymon

MON. 21 DEC.
The Heiress   C/FF
Cymon

TUES. 22 DEC.
The Conscious Lovers   C/BJ
The Quaker

WED. 23 DEC.
Hamlet
The Romp

SAT. 26 DEC.
Know Your Own Mind

MON. 28 DEC.
George Barnwell   C/FF
Brystowe

TUES. 29 DEC.
George Barnwell   C/BJ
Gil Blas of Santillane

WED. 30 DEC.
Inkle and Yarico
Cymon

THURS. 31 DEC.
Venice Preserv'd
Gil Blas of Santillane

1790

SAT. 2 JAN.
Much Ado about Nothing   PB/Ba
The Midnight Hour

MON. 4 JAN.
Know Your Own Mind   C/FF
Brystowe

TUES. 5 JAN.
The Dramatist   C/G

THURS. 7 JAN.
The Young Quaker
Cymon

SAT. 9 JAN.
The Suspicious Husband
Gil Blas of Santillane

MON. 11 JAN.
The Dramatist   C/FF
The Poor Soldier

THURS. 14 JAN.
As You Like It
Brystowe

SAT. 16 JAN.
The Dramatist
The Farmer

MON. 18 JAN.
The Dramatist   C/FF
The Farmer

THURS. 21 JAN.
The Child of Nature   C/G
Bristowe

MON. 25 JAN.
The Child of Nature   C/FF
The Midnight Hour

TUES. 26 JAN.
The Sultan   C/G b: Miss Wallis

THURS. 28 JAN.
Inkle and Yarico   PB/H
Brystowe

FRI. 29 JAN.
The Heiress
The Gentle Shepherd

MON. 1 FEB.
Thomas and Sally   C/FF
The Child of Nature
The Farmhouse

THURS. 4 FEB.
Much Ado about Nothing
Gil Blas

SAT. 6 FEB.
The Child of Nature
Thomas and Sally

MON. 8 FEB.
The Fair Penitent   C/FF
Cymon

TUES. 9 FEB.
The Earl of Essex   C/BC b: Dimond
Hobby Horses
Cymon

THURS. 11 FEB.
Romeo and Juliet   C/BC b: Floor
Brystowe

SAT. 13 FEB.
The Dramatist   C/BC b: Keasberry
The Sultan

MON. 15 FEB.
The Dramatist   C/FF
The Romp

TUES. 16 FEB.
Twelfth Night   C/BC b: Murray
Gallick Gratitude

THURS. 18 FEB.
The School for Scandal   C/BC b: Bloomfield
The Farmer

SAT. 20 FEB.
The Jealous Wife   C/BC b: Mrs. Simpson
Selima and Azor

MON. 22 FEB.
The Earl of Essex   C/FF
Selima and Azor

THURS. 25 FEB.
The Rivals   C/BC b: Mrs Didier
A Bold Stroke for a Wife

SAT. 27 FEB.
Robin Hood   C/BC b: Miss Brett
All the World's a Stage

MON. 1 MAR.
The School for Scandal   C/FF
All the World's a Stage

THURS. 4 MAR.
A Word to the Wise   C/BC b: Incledon
The Deserter

SAT. 6 MAR.
The Winter's Tale   C/BC, G b: Ward
The Drummer

MON. 8 MAR.
Robin Hood   C/FF
The Son in Law

THURS. 11 MAR.
The Beaux Stratagem   C/BC b: Eastmure
The Devil on Two Sticks

SAT. 13 MAR.
Lionel and Clarissa   C/BC b: Durravan Jnr.
High Life below Stairs

MON. 15 MAR.
Such Things Are   C/FF
The Gentle Shepherd

TUES. 16 MAR.
Love Makes a Man   b: Wordsworth
The Devil to Pay

THURS. 18 MAR.
The English Merchant   C/BC
The Drummer   b: Lloyd & Bartley

SAT. 20 MAR.
Fontainebleau   C/BC b: Knight
The Dramatist

MON. 22 MAR.
The Dramatist   C/FF
The Devil upon Two Sticks

THURS. 25 MAR.
Such Things Were
The Padlock

SAT. 27 MAR.
The Highland Reel   C/G
The Midnight Hour

MON. 5 APRIL
The Highland Reel   C/FF
The Drummer

TUES. 6 APRIL
The Child of Nature
Gil Blas of Santillane

WED. 7 APRIL
The Highland Reel

THURS. 8 APRIL
The Belle's Stratagem
The Romp

SAT. 10 APRIL
The Dramatist
Cymon

MON. 12 APRIL
Thomas and Sally   C/FF
The Child of Nature
The Romp

THURS. 15 APRIL
Inkle and Yarico
The Son in Law

SAT. 17 APRIL
A Bold Stroke for a Wife
The Highland Reel

MON. 19 APRIL
Such Things Were   C/FF
The Highland Reel

SAT. 24 APRIL
Tancred and Sigismunda   C/BC
The Farmhouse

MON. 26 APRIL
Much Ado about Nothing   C/FF
The Farmer

THURS. 29 APRIL
False Appearances
The Devil upon Two Sticks   C/G

SAT. 1 MAY
The Follies of a Day
The Highland Reel

MON. 3 MAY
False Appearances   C/FF
The Highland Reel

THURS. 6 MAY
Othello   C/BC
The Druids

SAT. 8 MAY
The Child of Nature   C/G
The Pannel

MON. 10 MAY
Macbeth   C/FF b: Incledon
The Deserter

SAT. 15 MAY
False Appearances   C/BC
Lethe

MON: 17 MAY
Tancred and Sigismunda   C/FF
The Pannel

THURS. 20 MAY
The Fashionable Lover
The Druids

SAT. 22 MAY
Which is the Man?   C/BC
The Highland Reel   b: Mrs. Keasberry

MON. 24 MAY
Othello   C/FF
The Farmhouse

TUES. 25 MAY
The School for Wives   C/BC b: Mrs Smith
The Register Office

THURS. 27 MAY
Fontainebleau   C/BC, G
High Life Below Stairs   b: Mr. & Miss Summers

SAT. 29 MAY
The School for Scandal   C/BC b: Miss Cleland
The Poor Soldier

MON. 31 MAY
Fontainbleau   C/FF b: Keasberry
The Drummer

TUES. 1 JUNE
The Natural Son   C/BC b: Rowbotham
Don Quixote in England

THURS. 3 JUNE
The Suspicious Husband   C/BC b: Pindar
The Miller of Mansfield

SAT. 5 JUNE
Know Your Own Mind   C/BC, b: Mrs. Mallory

MON. 7 JUNE
Hamlet   b: Blisset
The Devil to Pay

TUES. 8 JUNE
The Castle of Andalusia   C/BC b: Miss Sharrock
The Druids

THURS. 10 JUNE
Fontainebleau   C/BC b: Lloyd &
The Siege of Gibraltar   Bartley

SAT. 12 JUNE
The Heiress
The Pannel

MON. 14 JUNE
Trudge and Wowski   b: Mr. & Mrs. Knight
She Wou'd and She Wou'd Not
The Romp

WED. 16 JUNE
Cymbeline   b: Bloomfield
The Siege of Gibraltar

SAT. 19 JUNE
The Dramatist
The Druids

MON. 21 JUNE
The Unhappy Favourite   PB/U
High Life Below Stairs   b: Mrs. Didier &
                                    Miss Summers

WED. 23 JUNE
Henry IV (i)   b: Eastmure
The Farmhouse

FRI. 25 JUNE
The Castle of Andalusia
The Humorist

MON. 28 JUNE
Edward and Eleonora   b: Murray
The Poor Soldier

WED. 30 JUNE
Jane Shore   b: Bates
The Druids

FRI. 2 JULY
Love in a Village
The Midnight Hour

MON. 5 JULY
Mahomet   C/FF b: Mrs. Simpson
The Adventurers

WED. 7 JULY
Romeo and Juliet   b: Wordsworth &
The Milesian   Rowbotham

FRI. 9 JULY
He Would be a Soldier
The Devil to Pay

MON. 12 JULY
The Dramatist   b: Bloomfield
Gil Blas of Santillane

MON. 19 JULY
The Distress'd Mother   b: Dimond
The Pannel

WED. 21 JULY		**FRI. 30 JULY**	
Lionel and Clarissa	b: Miss Brett	*The West Indian*	C/BG b: Lloyd
The Milesian		*Rosina*	
FRI. 23 JULY		**MON. 2 AUGUST**	
The Fashionable Lover		*Henry II*	b: Mrs. Keasberry
The Adventurers		*The Highland Reel*	

MON. 26 JULY

Percy   C/FF

The Man of Quality   b: Fox & Durravan
                          Jnr.

WED. 28 JULY

Inkle and Yarico   b: Floor &

Gil Blas of Santillane   Miss Cleland   *End of Season*

Season 1790/91

Company

Mr: Ashley, Blisset, Bloomfield, Dimond, Durravan Snr. and Jnr., Eastmure, Hindes, Hodgkinson, Huttley, H. Keasberry, Knight, Murray, Pindar, Richardson, Rowbotham, Smith, Summers, Taylor, Wordsworth.

Mrs: Brett, Didier, Hodgkinson, Keasberry, Knight, Simpson, Smith.

Miss: Brett, Floor, Hopkins, Monk, Sharrock, Summers, Wallis.

Treasurer: Paul.   Box Book-keepers: Bartley, (Bath), Walker, (Bristol).   Prompter: Floor.

1790		**MON. 11 OCT.**	
		The Wonder	C/FF
MON. 27 SEPT.		*The Highland Reel*	
WED. 29 SEPT.			
Cancelled because of death of		**WED. 13 OCT.**	
Duke of Cumberland		*Know Your Own Mind*	
FRI. 1 OCT.		**FRI. 15 OCT.**	
The Dramatist	PB/H	*Othello*	PB/H
The Adventurers		*The Druids*	
SAT. 2 OCT.		**SAT. 16 OCT.**	
The West Indian	PB/H, C/BC	The Child of Nature	C/BC, G
The Devil to Pay		The Highland Reel	
MON. 4 OCT.		**MON. 18 OCT.**	
The Child of Nature	PB/H, C/FF	*The Provok'd Husband*	C/FF
The Lyar		*The Druids*	
WED. 6 OCT.		**WED. 20 OCT.**	
Love in a Village		*Love in a Village*	PB/H
? *The Deaf Lover*		*Who's the Dupe?*	
FRI. 8 OCT.		**FRI. 22 OCT.**	
The Young Quaker		*The Country Girl*	PB/H
Cross Purposes		*The Druids*	
SAT. 9 OCT.		**SAT. 23 OCT.**	
The Young Quaker	C/BC	Love in a Village	PB/H, C/BC
The Lyar		Who's the Dupe	

MON. 25 OCT.
The Suspicious Husband   PB/H, C/FF
The Romp

WED. 27 OCT.
As You Like It   PB/H
The Druids

FRI. 29 OCT.
The Castle of Andalusia
The Adventurers

SAT. 30 OCT.
Know Your Own Mind   PB/H, C/BC
The Romp

MON. 1 NOV.
Venice Preserv'd   PB/H, C/FF
The Rival Candidates

TUES. 2 NOV.
The Child of Nature   PB/H
The Highland Reel

THURS. 4 NOV.
Othello   PB/H
The Druids

SAT. 6 NOV.
The Wonder   C/G, BC
The Waterman

MON. 8 NOV.
The Fashionable Lover   PB/H, C/FF
The Waterman

THURS. 11 NOV.
The Battle of Hexham   PB/H, C/G, BC
The Deaf Lover

SAT. 13 NOV.
The Country Girl

MON. 15 NOV.
The Battle of Hexham   C/FF
The Adventurers

TUES. 16 NOV.
The Dramatist   PB/H
The Adventurers

THURS. 18 NOV.
As You Like It
The Farm House

SAT. 20 NOV.
The Country Girl   PB/H
The Gentle Shepherd

MON. 22 NOV.
The Recruiting Officer   PB/H, C/FF
The Farm House

TUES. 23 NOV.
The Battle of Hexham

THURS. 25 NOV.
The Recuiting Officer   C/G, BC
The Drummer

SAT. 27 NOV.
The Provok'd Husband   C/G, BC
The Adventurers

MON. 29 NOV.
The Battle of Hexham   C/FF
The Drummer

THURS. 2 DEC.
The Castle of Andalusia   C/G
The Midnight Hour

SAT. 4 DEC.
The Suspicious Husband   PB/H
The Highland Reel

MON. 6 DEC.
Cymbeline   PB/H, C/FF
The First Floor

THURS. 9 DEC.
Cymbeline   PB/H, C/G, BC
The Romp

SAT. 11 DEC.
Inkle and Yarico
The Lyar

MON. 13 DEC.
Inkle and Yarico   C/FF
The Midnight Hour

THURS. 16 DEC.
Know Your Own Mind
The Virgin Unmask'd

SAT. 18 DEC.
The West Indian   PB/H
No Song, No Supper

MON. 20 DEC.
He Would be a Soldier   C/FF
The Flitch of Bacon

TUES. 21 DEC.
The Conscious Lovers   C/G

THURS. 23 DEC.
Julia de Roubigne   PB/H, C/G, BC
No Song, No Supper

MON. 27 DEC.
The Battle of Hexham   C/FF
No Song, No Supper

TUES. 28 DEC.

The Battle of Hexham

WED. 29 DEC.

Inkle and Yarico   PB/H
The Druids

THURS. 30 DEC.

The Recruiting Officer
No Song, No Supper

1791

SAT. 1 JAN.

Much Ado about Nothing   PB/H
The Flitch of Bacon

MON. 3 JAN.

Julia de Roubigne   C/FF
The Gentle Shepherd

TUES. 4 JAN.

Venice Preserv'd   C/BJ
No Song, No Supper

THURS. 6 JAN.

She Stoops to Conquer
Brystowe

SAT. 8 JAN.

The Belle's Stratagem   PB/H
The Humourist

MON. 10 JAN.

The Belle's Stratagem   C/FF
No Song, No Supper

TUES. 11 JAN.

The School for Scandal   C/BJ
No Song, No Supper

THURS. 13 JAN.

Julia de Roubigne
Brystowe

SAT. 15 JAN.

The Battle of Hexham
The Romp

MON. 17 JAN.

Julia de Roubigne   C/FF
The Highland Reel

TUES. 18 JAN.

Lionel and Clarissa   PB/H, C/BJ
The First Floor

THURS. 20 JAN.

Tancred and Sigismunda   PB/H
Brystowe

SAT. 22 JAN.

The Child of Nature
No Song, No Supper

MON. 24 JAN.

The German Hotel   PB/H, C/FF
The Poor Soldier

TUES. 25 JAN.

The German Hotel   C/G, BJ
The Highland Reel

THURS. 27 JAN.

The German Hotel   PB/H
Brystowe

SAT. 29 JAN.

Lionel and Clarissa   C/BJ
The Drummer

MON. 31 JAN.

Lionel and Clarissa   C/FF
The Deaf Lover

TUES. 1 FEB.

The Inconstant   PB/H, C/BJ, G
No Song, No Supper

THURS. 3 FEB.

The Battle of Hexham   PB/H
The Gentle Shepherd

SAT. 5 FEB.

The Wonder   PB/H
The Poor Soldier

MON. 7 FEB.

The Battle of Hexham   PB/H, C/FF
No Song, No Supper

TUES. 8 FEB.

The Young Quaker   PB/H, C/BJ
The Flitch of Bacon

THURS. 10 FEB.

Isabella
Brystowe

SAT. 12 FEB.

The Suspicious Husband
No Song, No Supper

MON. 14 FEB.

Isabella   PB/H, C/FF
The Flitch of Bacon

TUES. 15 FEB.

The Belle's Stratagem   PB/H, C/BJ
The Highland Reel

THURS. 17 FEB.

The School for Scandal   PB/H
No Song, No Supper

SAT. 19 FEB.
The Inconstant
Rosina

MON. 21 FEB.
The Inconstant   C/FF
The Humourist

TUES. 22 FEB.
The Way to Keep Him   C/BJ, G, BH
The Farmer   b: Dimond

THURS. 24 FEB.
The Funeral   PB/H, C/BJ, BC
The Poor Soldier   b: Mrs. Didier

SAT. 26 FEB.
All in the Wrong   PB/H, C/BJ, BC
Poor Vulcan   b: Keasberry

MON. 28 FEB.
Lionel and Clarissa   PB/H, C/FF
The Drummer

TUES. 1 MAR.
The English Merchant   PB/H, C/BJ,
The Citizen   b: Mrs. Simpson

THURS. 3 MAR.
The Heiress   PB/H, C/BJ, BC
Rosina   b: Huttley

SAT. 5 MAR.
The Chapter of Accidents   C/BC, b: Blisset
St. Patrick's Day

MON. 7 MAR.
The English Merchant   PB/H, C/FF
No Song, No Supper

TUES. 8 MAR.
Fontainebleau   PB/H, C/BJ, BC
Catherine and Petruchio   b: Murray

THURS. 10 MAR.
The Jealous Wife   C/BJ, BC b: Eastmure
The Sultan

SAT. 12 MAR.
The Dramatist   PB/H, C/BC, G
The Spoil'd Child   b: Mrs. Knight

MON. 14 MAR.
Fontainebleau   PB/H, C/FF
St. Patrick's Day

TUES. 15 MAR.
The Provok'd Husband   PB/Y, C/BC, G
The Maid of the Oaks   b: Miss Wallis

THURS. 17 MAR.
A Bold Stroke for a Husband PB/Y, C/BJ, BC
The Padlock   b: Hodgkinson

SAT. 19 MAR.
The Maid of the Mill   C/BC b: Miss Brett
Ways and Means

MON. 21 MAR.
As You Like It   PB/H, C/FF
The Midnight Hour

TUES. 22 MAR.
The Way to Keep Him   PB/H, C/BJ, G
The Lying Valet   b: Mr. Durravan Jnr.

THURS. 24 MAR.
Such Things Are   C/BJ, BC
The Milesian   b: Rowbotham

SAT. 26 MAR.
The Pilgrim   C/BC, b: Mrs. Smith
Poor Vulcan

MON. 28 MAR.
The Foundling   C/FF
The Farmer

TUES. 29 MAR.
The Clandestine Marriage   PB/H, C/BJ, G
The Deserter   b: Wordsworth

THURS. 31 MAR.
The Merchant of Venice   PB/H, C/BJ, BC, G
Ways and Means   b: Paul, Bartley

SAT. 2 APRIL
The Foundling   PB/H
No Song, No Supper

MON. 4 APRIL
A Bold Stroke for a Husband PB/H, C/FF
The Spoil'd Child

TUES. 5 APRIL
The Battle of Hexham   C/BJ
The Farmer

THURS. 7 APRIL
Inkle and Yarico   C/BJ, BC
The Midnight Hour

SAT. 9 APRIL
A Bold Stroke for a Husband
The Spoil'd Child

MON. 11 APRIL
The Merchant of Venice   PB/H, C/FF
Ways and Means

TUES. 12 APRIL
Fontainebleau   PB/H, C/BJ
St. Patrick's Day

THURS. 14 APRIL
Richard III   C/G
The Romp

SAT. 16 APRIL
As You Like It   C/G, BC, BJ
No Song, No Supper

MON. 25 APRIL
King Richard III   C/FF, G
The Spoil'd Child

TUES. 26 APRIL
The Merchant of Venice   C/BJ
The Highland Reel

WED. 27 APRIL
As You Like It   C/BC, BJ
Rosina

THURS. 28 APRIL
Cymbeline   C/G
The Spoil'd Child

SAT. 30 APRIL
The School for Arrogance   PB/H, C/G
The Waterman

MON. 2 MAY
The School for Arrogance   PB/H, C/FF
No Song, No Supper

TUES. 3 MAY
Julia de Roubigne   PB/H, C/BJ
No Song, No Supper

THURS. 5 MAY
The Battle of Hexham   PB/H, C/BJ, BC
Poor Vulcan   b: Mrs. Lloyd (widow
                                   of late Treasurer)

SAT. 7 MAY
Much Ado about Nothing   PB/H, C/G
Modern Antiques

MON. 9 MAY
As You Like It   C/FF
Modern Antiques

TUES. 10 MAY
The School for Arrogance   PB/H, C/BJ
Modern Antiques

THURS. 12 MAY
The Heiress   PB/H
The Quaker

SAT. 14 MAY
The Belle's Stratagem   PB/H, C/BC, BJ
Modern Antiques

MON. 16 MAY
The School for Arrogance   C/FF
Modern Antiques

TUES. 17 MAY
She Wou'd and She Wou'd Not   PB/H, C/BJ
Love in a Camp   b: Knight

THURS. 19 MAY
Such Things Are   PB/H, C/BJ b: Floor
Brystowe

SAT. 21 MAY
Jane Shore   PB/H, C/BJ, BC
The Two Misers   b: Mrs. Keasberry

MON. 23 MAY
The Belle's Stratagem   C/FF
The Two Misers

TUES. 24 MAY
Robin Hood   PB/H, C/BJ,
The Lyar   b: Richardson &
                                   Mrs. Brett

THURS. 26 MAY
The Busybody   PB/H, C/BJ BC
Rosina   b: Miss Monk

SAT. 28 MAY
The Belle's Stratagem   PB/H, C/BJ, BC
The Deuce is in Him   b: Miss Sharrock

MON. 30 MAY
The Battle of Hexham   PB/H, C/FF
The Padlock

TUES. 31 MAY
The Clandestine Marriage   PB/H, C/BJ
The Farm House   b: Mr & Miss
                                   Summers

THURS. 2 JUNE
The School for Scandal   C/BJ
Brystowe

SAT. 4 JUNE
The School for Arrogance   PB/H, C/BJ
The Highland Reel

MON. 6 JUNE
Jane Shore   C/FF b: Dimond
Rosina

TUES. 7 JUNE
The Child of Nature   PB/H, C/BJ
The Spanish Barber   b: Bartley & Paul

THURS. 9 JUNE
The Way to Keep Him   C/BJ
The Virgin Unmask'd

SAT. 11 JUNE

As You Like It　　　　　　C/BJ, BC
The Poor Soldier　　　　　　b: Miss Hopkins

MON. 13 JUNE

Hamlet　　　　　　　　　　C/FF b: Keasberry
Poor Vulcan

WED. 15 JUNE

The Merchant of Venice　　C/FF
Ways and Means　　　　　　b: Servants of the
　　　　　　　　　　　　　　　　House

FRI. 17 JUNE

The Provok'd Husband　　　b: Walker (Box book-
The Farm House　　　　　　　keeper)

SAT. 18 JUNE

Fontainebleau　　　　　　　C/BJ
Ways and Means

MON. 20 JUNE

Trudge and Wowski　　　　b: Mr & Mrs Knight
The Dramatist
The Highland Reel

WED. 22 JUNE

The Duenna　　　　　　　　b: Hutley
The Citizen

FRI. 24 JUNE

The Way to Keep Him　　　PB/R, H
The Farmer　　　　　　　　b: Part of Servants
　　　　　　　　　　　　　　　　of House

MON. 27 JUNE

The Orphan　　　　　　　　C/G
The Maid of the Oaks　　　b: Miss Wallis

WED. 29 JUNE

The Gamester　　　　　　　PB/H, C/FF
Catherine and Petruchio　　b: Hodgkinson

FRI. 1 JULY

The School for Scandal　　PB/H
The Spoil'd Child　　　　　b: Richardson, Taylor
　　　　　　　　　　　　　　　& J. Ashley

MON. 4 JULY

The Earl of Essex　　　　　C/FF b: Mrs. Simpson
Cymon

WED. 6 JULY

All in the Wrong　　　　　b: Mr. & Mrs. Smith
The Register Office

FRI. 8 JULY

Such Things Are　　　　　b: Floor (Prompter)
Rosina

MON. 11 JULY

Macbeth　(S. Rossignol)　b: Blisset
The Cheats of Scapin

WED. 13 JULY

Mahomet　　　　　　　　　PB/R, H, C/FF
The Flitch of Bacon　　　　b: Miss Brett

FRI. 15 JULY

The Inconstant　　　　　　b: Lloyd's Widow
The Deserter

MON. 18 JULY

The Roman Father　　　　C/FF, G b: Murray
The Poor Soldier

WED. 20 JULY

The Clandestine Marriage　b: Rowbotham &
Patrick in Prussia　　　　　Wordsworth

FRI. 22 JULY

As You Like It　　　　　　b: Paul (Treasurer)
The Highland Reel

MON. 25 JULY

Inkle and Yarico (S. Rossignol) b: Mrs. Didier &
St. Patrick's Day　　　　　Miss Summers

WED. 27 JULY

Cymbeline　　　　　　　　C/G b: Durravan Jnr.
Two Strings to your Bow

FRI. 29 JULY

The Beggar's Opera　　　　PB/H, C/G
The Drummer

MON. 1 AUG.

The Countess of Salisbury　(S. Rossignol)
No Song, No Supper　　　　b: Mrs. Keasberry

End of Season

Season 1791/92

Company

Mr: Ashley, Blisset, F. Blisset, Cavana, Charlton, Dimond, Durravan Snr. and Jnr., Eastmure, Haymes, Hodgkinson, Holland, Huttley, King, Keasberry, Knight, Mackenzie, Marshall, Murray, Quick, Rowbotham, Smith, Taylor, West.

Mrs: Brett, Charlton, Didier, Hodgkinson, Keasberry, Knight, Taylor, Smith.

Miss: Brett, Floor, Gopell, Hopkins, Monk, Smith, S. Smith, Summers, Wallis.

Treasurer: Paul.   *Box-Book-keepers:* Bartley, (Bath)., Walker (Bristol).   *Prompter:* Floor.

1791

TUES. 27 SEPT.
The Wonder   C/BJ, G
Rosina

WED. 28 SEPT.
Percy   PB/H, C/BJ, BC, G
The Farmhouse

THURS. 29 SEPT.
The Child of Nature
The Farmer

FRI. 30 SEPT.
Inkle and Yarico   C/BJ, BC, G
The Scheming Lieutenant

SAT. 1 OCT.
Isabella   PB/H, C/BJ
The Poor Soldier

MON. 3 OCT.
The Wonder   PB/H
The Poor Soldier

WED. 5 OCT.
Inkle and Yarico   PB/H
The Scheming Lieutenant

FRI. 7 OCT.
The Child of Nature
The Farmer

SAT. 8 OCT.
The Merchant of Venice
Entertainments

MON. 10 OCT.
The Grecian Daughter   PB/H
The Spoil'd Child

SAT. 15 OCT.
The Way to Keep Him   PB/H
Two Strings to Your Bow

MON. 17 OCT.
Isabella
The Farmhouse

FRI. 21 OCT.
George Barnwell   PB/H
Brystowe

SAT. 22 OCT.
Know Your Own Mind   PB/Ba, C/BJ
No Song, No Supper

MON. 24 OCT.
The Conscious Lovers   PB/H
Brystowe

WED. 26 OCT.
The Beggar's Opera   PB/H
The Farmer

FRI. 28 OCT.
Venice Preserv'd
The Waterman

SAT. 29 OCT.
The Conscious Lovers   C/BJ

MON. 31 OCT.
The Haunted Tower
Two Strings to your Bow

WED. 2 NOV.
The Haunted Tower   PB/H
The Humourist

FRI. 4 NOV.
Richard III
Brystowe

SAT. 5 NOV.
Fontainebleau   C/BJ
The Romp

MON. 7 NOV.
The Inconstant
The Highland Reel

TUES. 8 NOV.

The Haunted Tower   PB/H, C/BJ, G
The Humourist

THURS. 10 NOV.

Richard III   PB/H
No Song, No Supper

SAT. 12 NOV.

The School for Scandal   PB/H
The Spoil'd Child

MON. 14 NOV.

The Haunted Tower
The Romp

TUES. 15 NOV.

The Haunted Tower   PB/H, C/BJ
The Deaf Lover

THURS. 17 NOV.

Venice Preserv'd   C/BC, BJ
The Waterman

SAT. 19 NOV.

The Fashionable Lover   C/BC, BJ
The Highland Reel

MON. 21 NOV.

The School for Scandal
The Deaf Lover

TUES. 22 NOV.

The Haunted Tower   PB/H, C/BJ
Ways and Means

THURS. 24 NOV.

The Inconstant   PB/H
The Quaker

SAT. 26 NOV.

The Country Girl   C/BC, BJ
No Song, No Supper

MON. 28 NOV.

Wild Oats   PB/H
Ways and Means

TUES. 29 NOV.

Wild Oats   C/BJ, G
The Farmhouse

THURS. 1 DEC.

The Heiress   PB/H
The Virgin Unmask'd

SAT. 3 DEC.

The Suspicious Husband
The Drummer

MON. 5 DEC.

Wild Oats
The Farmhouse

TUES. 6 DEC.

Wild Oats   C/BJ
The Padlock

THURS. 8 DEC.

The Haunted Tower   PB/H
The Midnight Hour

SAT. 10 DEC.

The Provok'd Husband   PB/H
Rosina

MON. 12 DEC.

The Haunted Tower   C/FF
The Midnight Hour

TUES. 13 DEC.

Wild Oats   C/BJ
Cross Purposes

THURS. 15 DEC.

The Haunted Tower   PB/H
Who's the Dupe?

SAT. 17 DEC.

Much Ado About Nothing   PB/H
Cymon

MON. 19 DEC.

Wild Oats   C/FF
No Song, No Supper

TUES. 20 DEC.

Inkle and Yarico   C/BJ
Ways and Means

THURS. 22 DEC.

The Rivals   PB/H
Robinson Crusoe

MON. 26 DEC.

Wild Oats   C/FF
The Highland Reel

TUES. 27 DEC.

The Haunted Tower   PB/H, C/BJ
Robinson Crusoe

WED. 28 DEC.

Wild Oats
Who's the Dupe?

THURS. 29 DEC.

George Barnwell
Robinson Crusoe

SAT. 31 DEC.

The Wonder   PB/H
The Highland Reel

1792

MON. 2 JAN.
Macbeth   C/FF
The Irish Widow

TUES. 3 JAN.
Wild Oats   PB/H, C/BJ
No Song, No Supper

THURS. 5 JAN.
Macbeth
The Irish Widow

SAT. 7 JAN.
The Child of Nature   PB/H
Robinson Crusoe

MON. 9 JAN.
Wild Oats   C/FF
Who's the Dupe?

TUES. 10 JAN.
Wild Oats   C/BJ
The Romp

THURS. 12 JAN.
The Dramatist   PB/H
The Lyar

SAT. 14 JAN.
The School for Scandal
Catherine and Petruchio

MON. 16 JAN.
Much Ado About Nothing   C/FF
Cross Purposes

TUES. 17 JAN.
Notoriety   PB/H, C/BJ, G
Cross Purposes

THURS. 19 JAN.
Richard III   PB/H, C/BC, BJ
The Spoil'd Child

SAT. 21 JAN.
The Haunted Tower   PB/H
The Irish Widow

MON. 23 JAN.
Notoriety   C/FF
The Quaker

TUES. 24 JAN.
Notoriety   PB/H, C/BJ
The Quaker

THURS. 26 JAN.
Wild Oats   PB/H
The Deaf Lover

SAT. 28 JAN.
The Chapter of Accidents   PB/H
The Poor Soldier

TUES. 31 JAN.
Love in a Village   PB/H, C/BJ, BC
The Drummer

WED. 1 FEB.
Wild Oats   PB/H, C/FF
The Spoil'd Child

THURS. 2 FEB.
Notoriety
The Rival Candidates

SAT. 4 FEB.
The Country Girl
The Deserter

MON. 6 FEB.
Richard III   C/FF
The Rival Candidates

TUES. 7 FEB.
Wild Oats   C/BJ
The Farmhouse

THURS. 9 FEB.
Douglas   PB/H, C/BC, BJ
The Highland Reel

SAT. 11 FEB.
Love in a Village   C/BC, BJ
The Humorist

MON. 13 FEB.
Notoriety   C/FF
The Deserter

TUES. 14 FEB.
Notoriety   C/BJ
Rosina

THURS. 16 FEB.
The Haunted Tower   PB/H
The Midnight Hour

SAT. 18 FEB.
The West Indian   PB/H
The Double Disguise

MON. 20 FEB.
Douglas   C/FF
The Double Disguise

TUES. 21 FEB.
Wild Oats   C/BJ
No Song, No Supper

THURS. 23 FEB.
Notoriety
The Double Disguise

SAT. 25 FEB.
The Battle of Hexham   PB/H
Two Strings to Your Bow

MON. 27 FEB.
Love in a Village   C/FF
The Drummer

TUES. 28 FEB.
Cymbeline   C/BJ, BC b: Dimond
The Capricious Lovers

THURS. 1 MAR.
The Dramatist   C/BJ, BC
The Englishman in Paris   b: Mrs. Didier

SAT. 3 MAR.
Which is the Man?   PB/H, C/BJ, BC
Robin Hood   b: Keasberry

MON. 5 MAR.
Wild Oats   C/FF
The Double Disguise

TUES. 6 MAR.
Romeo and Juliet   PB/H, C/BJ, G
The Romp   b: Miss Wallis

THURS. 8 MAR.
The Provok'd Husband   PB/H, C/BJ, BC
Selima and Azor   b: Huttley

SAT. 10 MAR.
The Clandestine Marriage   PB/H, C/BC, BJ
The Devil on Two Sticks   b: Blisset

MON. 12 MAR.
The Battle of Hexham   C/FF
The Humourist

TUES. 13 MAR.
The Merchant of Venice   b: Murray
The Highland Reel

THURS. 15 MAR.
The Belle's Stratagem   PB/H, C/BC, BJ
Mayor of Garret   b: Eastmure

SAT. 17 MAR.
The English Merchant   C/BJ b: Mrs. Taylor
The Family Party

MON. 19 MAR.
Notoriety   C/FF
The Mayor of Garret

TUES. 20 MAR.
Rule a Wife and Have a Wife   C/BJ b: Mrs. Knight
Trudge and Wowski
The Son-in-Law

THURS. 22 MAR.
Such Things Are   C/BJ b: Mrs. Smith
Edgar and Emmeline

SAT. 24 MAR.
A Bold Stroke for a Husband   PB/H
The Flitch of Bacon   b: Miss Brett

MON. 26 MAR.
Which is the Man?   PB/H, C/FF
The Family Party

TUES. 27 MAR.
Lionel and Clarissa   b: Durravan Jnr.
The Citizen

THURS. 29 MAR.
I'll Tell You What   PB/H, C/BJ
The Spoil'd Child   b: Paul & Bartley

SAT. 31 MAR.
More Ways than One   PB/H, C/BJ, BC
The Devil to Pay   b: Hodgkinson

MON. 9 APRIL
Cymbeline   C/FF
The Spoil'd Child

TUES. 10 APRIL
Inkle and Yarico   PB/H, C/BJ
The Mayor of Garret

WED. 11 APRIL
The Battle of Hexham
The Scheming Lieutenant

THURS. 12 APRIL
Notoriety
The Flitch of Bacon

SAT. 14 APRIL
The Chapter of Accidents   PB/H
No Song, No Supper

MON. 16 APRIL
More Ways than One   PB/H, C/FF
Robin Hood

TUES. 17 APRIL
Wild Oats   C/BJ
The Family Party

THURS. 19 APRIL
The Fair Penitent   PB/H
Cross Purposes

SAT. 21 APRIL
More Ways than One

MON. 23 APRIL
Wild Oats   C/FF
The Rival Candidates

TUES. 24 APRIL	
As You Like It	C/BJ b: Miss Hopkins
The Maid of the Oaks	

THURS. 26 APRIL	
The Haunted Tower	PB/H, C/BJ
The Farmhouse	

SAT. 28 APRIL	
The Road to Ruin	C/G
The Flitch of Bacon	

MON. 30 APRIL	
The Road to Ruin	C/FF
The Double Disguise	

TUES. 1 MAY	
I'll Tell you What	PB/H, C/BJ
Robin Hood	

THURS. 3 MAY	
The Road to Ruin	
The Quaker	

SAT. 5 MAY	
The Maid of the Mill	PB/H, C/BJ, BC
The Deaf Lover	

MON. 7 MAY	
The Road to Ruin	C/FF
The Flitch of Bacon	

TUES. 8 MAY	
Notoriety	PB/H, C/BJ
No Song, No Supper	

THURS. 10 MAY	
The Road to Ruin	
The Padlock	

SAT. 12 MAY	
The Haunted Tower	
Ways and Means	

MON. 14 MAY	
The Maid of the Mill	C/FF
Cross Purposes	

TUES. 15 MAY	
Wild Oats	PB/H, C/BJ
The Highland Reel	

THURS. 17 MAY	
The Road to Ruin	
The Citizen	

SAT. 19 MAY	
The Follies of a Day	PB/H, C/BJ, BC
Rosina	b: Mrs. Keasberry

MON. 21 MAY	
The Road to Ruin	C/FF
The Citizen	

TUES. 22 MAY	
Duplicity	PB/H, C/BJ,G
Jacob Gawky's Ramble	b: Knight
The Village Lawyer	

THURS. 24 MAY	
The School for Scandal	PB/H, C/BJ b: Floor
Robinson Crusoe	

SAT. 26 MAY	
The Way to Keep Him	PB/H, C/BH
The Prisoner at Large	b: Mr. & Mrs. Charlton

MON. 28 MAY	
The Road to Ruin	C/FF
The Devil to Pay	

TUES. 29 MAY	
Measure for Measure	PB/H, C/BJ, BH
A Bold Stroke for a Wife	b: Rowbotham

THURS. 31 MAY	
Much Ado About Nothing	PB/H, C/BJ b: West
The Devil to Pay	

SAT. 2 JUNE	
She Wou'd and She Wou'd Not	PB/H
The Agreeable Surprise	b: Miss Monk

MON. 4 JUNE	
Wild Oats	C/FF
Rosina	

TUES. 5 JUNE	
The Chapter of Accidents	PB/H, C/BJ, BH
The Prisoner at Large	b: Miss Summers

THURS. 7 JUNE	
The Roman Father	PB/H, C/BJ, BC
Modern Antiques	b: Paul & Bartley

SAT. 9 JUNE	
Duplicity	PB/H, C/BJ
The Highland Reel	b: Haymes & J. Ashley

MON. 11 JUNE	
Romeo and Juliet	C/FF b: Dimond
The Prisoner at large	

TUES. 12 JUNE	
He Would be a Soldier	C/BJ
The Village Lawyer	

THURS. 14 JUNE	
Measure for Measure	PB/H, C/BJ
The Spoil'd Child	

SAT. 16 JUNE	
Wild Oats	C/BJ
The Farmhouse	

MON. 18 JUNE
The Roman Father   PB/F, C/FF
The Village Lawyer   b: Keasberry

WED. 20 JUNE
Measure for Measure   C/SF
The Prisoner at Large   b: Mr. & Mrs. Charlton

FRI. 22 JUNE
Much Ado About Nothing   PB/F b: Walker
The Romp

SAT. 23 JUNE
Such Things Are   PB/H, C/BJ,
The Padlock   b: City Infirmary &
                                    Dispensary

MON. 25 JUNE
The Chapter of Accidents   b: Miss Wallis
The Bristol Tars

WED. 27 JUNE
Inkle and Yarico   PB/H, C/FF
The Padlock   b: Huttley

FRI. 29 JUNE
Such Things Are   PB/H
The Humourist   b: Servants of the
                                    House

MON. 2 JULY
The Clandestine Marriage   b: Mrs. Didier &
The Highland Reel   Miss Summers

THURS. 5 JULY
He Woud be a Soldier   PB/H
Who's the Dupe?   b: Servants of the
                                    House

MON. 9 JULY
Cymbeline   b: Blisset
The Agreeable Surprise

WED. 11 JULY
The Jealous Wife   b: Miss Smith
The Poor Soldier

FRI. 13 JULY
The Fair Penitent   PB/H
Cross Purposes   b: Mrs. Hodgkinson,
                                    Mrs. Brett,
                                    Mrs. Smith

MON. 16 JULY
The Earl of Essex   C/G b: Murray
The Guardian

WED. 18 JULY
Hamlet   PB/F b: Miss Hopkins
The Midnight Hour

FRI. 20 JULY
George Barnwell   C/BG b: Floor
Brystowe

MON. 23 JULY
Duplicity   b: Mr. & Mrs. Knight
The Son-in-Law

WED. 25 JULY
The Fashionable Lover   b: Miss Monk
A Bold Stroke for a Wife

FRI. 27 JULY
King Lear   C/ My b: Rowbotham
The Comedy of Errors

MON. 30 JULY
The Wonder   C/FF, My
Comedy of Errors   b: Durravan Jnr.

WED. 1 AUG.
Jane Shore   C/BMn b: Paul
Love a la Mode

FRI. 3 AUG.
Werter   C/G b: Mrs. Keasberry
The Gentle Shepherd

End of Season

Season 1792/93

Company

Mr: Ashley, Atkins, Blisset, F. Blisset, Charlton, Cleveland, Dimond, Durravan Snr., Durravan Jnr., Eastmure, Haymes, Holland, Hoyle, Huttley, Johnson, Kelly, Keasberry, Knight, Marshall, Murray, Rowbotham, Underwood.

Mrs: Charlton, Didier, Johnson, Keasberry, Kelly, Knight, Marshall, (formerly Miss Webb), Murray, Pinder, Smith.

Miss: Floor, Gopell, Herbert, Monk, Murray, Smith, S. Smith, Summers, Wallis, Webb.

Master: Smith.

Treasurer: Paul.   *Box Book-keepers:* Bartley (Bath), Walker (Bristol).   *Prompter:* Floor.

1792

TUES. 18 SEPT.
The Clandestine Marriage   C/BJ, G
The Spoil'd Child

WED. 19 SEPT.
Wild Oats
Who's the Dupe?

THURS. 20 SEPT.
Cymbeline
The Romp

FRI. 21 SEPT.
The Road to Ruin
The Padlock

SAT. 22 SEPT.
Love in a Village   C/BH

MON. 24 SEPT.
Cymbeline   C/FF b: Infirmary
The Padlock

WED. 26 SEPT.
Wild Oats

FRI. 28 SEPT.
The Clandestine Marriage
The Virgin Unmask'd

SAT. 29 SEPT.
The Chapter of Accidents
Rosina

MON. 1 OCT.
Love in a Village   C/FF
The Lying Valet

The Wonder
Love a la Mode

WED. 3 OCT.

SAT. 6 OCT.
The Wonder   C/BJ
Love a la Mode

MON. 8 OCT.
The Road to Ruin   C/FF
The Romp

WED. 10 OCT.
The Chapter of Accidents
The Farm House

SAT. 13 OCT.
The Road to Ruin   C/BJ
The Quaker

MON. 15 OCT.
The Merchant of Venice   C/FF
The Drummer

WED. 17 OCT.
Next-door Neighbours
The Highland Reel

FRI. 19 OCT.
The Beggar's Opera
The Guardian

SAT. 20 OCT.
Next-Door Neighbours   C/BJ, G
The Highland Reel

MON. 22 OCT.
Hamlet   C/FF
The Humourist

FRI. 26 OCT.
George Barnwell
Robinson Crusoe

SAT. 27 OCT.
The West Indian   C/BJ
The Deserter

MON. 29 OCT.
Notoriety   C/FF
The Deserter

SAT. 3 NOV.
Notoriety   C/BJ
The Flitch of Bacon

MON. 5 NOV.
King Lear   C/FF
Who's the Dupe?

TUES. 6 NOV.
She Stoops to Conquer   C/BJ
The Agreeable Surprise

THURS. 8 NOV.
King Lear
The Farm House

SAT. 10 NOV.
Wild Oats
Cross Purposes

MON. 12 NOV.
The Fugitive   C/FF
Cross Purposes

TUES. 13 NOV.
The Fugitive   C/BJ, G
The Romp

THURS. 15 NOV.
The Merchant of Venice
The Gentle Shepherd

SAT. 17 NOV.
Inkle and Yarico

MON. 19 NOV.
The Road to Ruin   C/FF
The Poor Soldier

TUES. 20 NOV.
The Fugitive   C/BJ
The Quaker

THURS. 22 NOV.
The Beggar's Opera
The Guardian

SAT. 24 NOV.
Next-Door Neighbours

MON. 26 NOV.
The Fugitive   C/FF
The Gentle Shepherd

TUES. 27 NOV.
The Road to Ruin   C/BJ
Who's the Dupe?

THURS. 29 NOV.
Richard III
The Lying Valet

SAT. 1 DEC.
The Provok'd Husband
The Prisoner at large

MON. 3 DEC.
The Grecian Daughter   C/FF
The Prisoner at large

TUES. 4 DEC.
The Fugitive   C/BJ
The Padlock

THURS. 6 DEC.
The Grecian Daughter   C/BC, BJ
The Farmer

SAT. 8 DEC.
The Clandestine Marriage
Selima and Azor

MON. 10 DEC.
Wild Oats   C/FF
The Flitch of Bacon

TUES. 11 DEC.
Wild Oats   C/BJ
The Flitch of Bacon

THURS. 13 DEC.
The Surrender of Calais   C/G

SAT. 15 DEC.
The Wonder
The Double Disguise

MON. 17 DEC.
The Surrender of Calais   C/FF
The Lying Valet

TUES. 18 DEC.
The Surrender of Calais   C/BJ
The Prisoner at Large

THURS. 20 DEC.
Venice Preserv'd
The Spoil'd Child

SAT. 22 DEC.
The School for Scandal   C/BJ
The Farmer

WED. 26 DEC.
Hamlet   C/BJ
The Romp

THURS. 27 DEC.
The Surrender of Calais   C/FF
The Romp

FRI. 28 DEC.

The Surrender of Calais

SAT. 29 DEC.

Much Ado About Nothing
The Farmer

MON. 31 DEC.

The School for Scandal   C/FF
The Farmer

1793

TUES. 1 JAN.

The Surrender of Calais   C/BJ
The Double Disguise

THURS. 3 JAN.

Inkle and Yarico
The Guardian

SAT. 5 JAN.

The Road to Ruin
The Poor Soldier

MON. 7 JAN.

The Surrender of Calais   C/FF
The Double Disguise

TUES. 8 JAN.

The Fugitive   C/BJ, G
The Irishman in London

THURS. 10 JAN.

The Surrender of Calais
The Quaker

SAT. 12 JAN.

Wild Oats

MON. 14 JAN.

The Fugitive   C/FF
The Irishman in London

TUES. 15 JAN.

Notoriety   C/BJ
The Highland Reel

THURS. 17 JAN.

The Maid of the Mill
The Irishman in London

SAT. 19 JAN.

The Fashionable Lover

MON. 21 JAN.

The Surrender of Calais   C/FF
The Irishman in London

TUES. 22 JAN.

The Surrender of Calais   C/BJ
The Prisoner at Large

THURS. 24 JAN.

Cymbeline
Ways and Means

SAT. 26 JAN.

The Suspicious Husband

MON. 28 JAN.

As You Like It   C/FF
Ways and Means

TUES. 29 JAN.

The Spoil'd Child   C/BJ
Next-Door Neighbours

THURS. 31 JAN.

King Lear
The Irishman in London

SAT. 2 FEB.

As You Like It
The Gentle Shepherd

MON. 4 FEB.

The Suspicious Husband   C/FF
The Farmer

TUES. 5 FEB.

The Surrender of Calais   C/BJ
Ways and Means

THURS. 7 FEB.

The Road to Ruin   C/G
Hartford Bridge

SAT. 9 FEB.

The West Indian

MON. 11 FEB.

The Earl of Essex   C/FF
Hartford Bridge

TUES. 12 FEB.

Macbeth   C/BJ
The Farm House

THURS. 14 FEB.

Wild Oats
Hartford Bridge

SAT. 16 FEB.

The Chapter of Accidents
The Highland Reel

MON. 18 FEB.

Wild Oats   C/FF
The Irishman in London

TUES. 19 FEB.
The Battle of Hexham   C/BJ b: Dimond
The Irishman in London

THURS. 21 FEB.
Which is the Man?   C/BJ, BC
Robin Hood   b: Mrs. Didier

SAT. 23 FEB.
The Haunted Tower   C/BJ, BC b: Keasberry
The Ghost

MON. 25 FEB.
The Battle of Hexham   C/FF
The Ghost

TUES. 26 FEB.
Percy   C/BJ, BC, G
The Devil to Pay   b: Miss Wallis

THURS. 28 FEB.
Love in a Village   C/BJ, BC b: Hutley
The Irishman in London

SAT. 2 MAR.
The Heiress   b: Blisset
Midas

MON. 4 MAR.
The Haunted Tower   C/FF
The Farm House

TUES. 5 MAR.
The Earl of Essex   C/BJ b: Murray
Robin Hood

THURS. 7 MAR.
Lionel and Clarissa   C/BJ b: Eastmure
The Prisoner at Large

SAT. 9 MAR.
The Country Girl   b: Mrs. Marshall

MON. 11 MAR.
The Earl of Essex   C/FF
Hartford Bridge

TUES. 12 MAR.
The Dramatist   b: Mrs. Knight
Peeping Tom of Coventry

THURS. 14 MAR.
Much Ado About Nothing   b: Rowbotham
The Comedy of Errors

SAT. 16 MAR.
The Road to Ruin   C/BJ, BC, G
Dead or Alive   b: Durravan

MON. 18 MAR.
The Haunted Tower   C/FF
Ways and Means

TUES. 19 MAR.
The Duenna   C/BJ b: Miss Gopell
The Maid of the Oaks

THURS. 21 MAR.
Cymbeline   b: Paul & Bartley
The Agreeable Surprise

SAT. 23 MAR.
Love Makes a Man   C/BC
The Positive Man   b: Mr. & Mrs. Charlton

MON. 1 APRIL
The Orphan   C/FF
Peeping Tom of Coventry

TUES. 2 APRIL
The Surrender of Calais   C/BJ
The Irishman in London

WED. 3 APRIL
The Merchant of Venice   C/BJ
Hartford Bridge

THURS. 4 APRIL
Inkle and Yarico
Ways and Means

SAT. 6 APRIL
The Heiress   C/BJ, BC
The Highland Reel

TUES. 9 APRIL
The Haunted Tower   C/BJ
Love a la Mode

THURS. 11 APRIL
The Battle of Hexham   C/BJ, BC, G
Cross Purposes

SAT. 13 APRIL
Columbus   C/G
The Quaker

MON. 15 APRIL
The Heiress   C/FF, G

TUES. 16 APRIL
Columbus   C/BJ
The Farm House

THURS. 18 APRIL
Columbus
The Flitch of Bacon

SAT. 20 APRIL
Notoriety   C/BJ, BC
The Poor Soldier

MON. 22 APRIL
Columbus   C/FF
The Romp

TUES. 23 APRIL

Wild Oats   C/BJ
Hartford Bridge

THURS. 25 APRIL

Columbus
The Romp

SAT. 27 APRIL

The Country Girl   C/BC
The Deserter

MON. 29 APRIL

Columbus   C/FF
Hartford Bridge

TUES. 30 APRIL

The Surrender of Calais   C/BJ
The Irishman in London

THURS. 2 MAY

Everyone has his Fault   C/G
The Humourist

SAT. 4 MAY

Columbus

MON. 6 MAY

Everyone has his Fault   C/FF
The Irishman in London

TUES. 7 MAY

Everyone has his Fault   C/BJ
Hartford Bridge

THURS. 9 MAY

Romeo and Juliet   C/BJ, b: Floor
Robin Hood

SAT. 11 MAY

Everyone has his Fault
No Song, No Supper

MON. 13 MAY

Everyone has his Fault   C/FF
No Song, No Supper

TUES. 14 MAY

Columbus   C/BJ
No Song, No Supper

THURS. 16 MAY

Everyone has his Fault
The Gentle Shepherd

SAT. 18 MAY

A Bold Stroke for a Husband   C/BJ, BC
The Golden Pippin   b: Mrs. Keasberry

MON. 20 MAY

Columbus   C/FF
The Waterman

TUES. 21 MAY

The Natural Son   PB/Ba, C/BJ, G
The Positive Man   b: Knight

THURS. 23 MAY

The Double Falsehood   PB/Ba, C/BC, G
The King and the Miller   b: Marshall & Hoyle
of Mansfield

SAT. 25 MAY

The Lord of the Manor   b: Haymes
Catherine and Petruchio

MON. 27 MAY

Everyone has his Fault   C/FF
No Song, No Supper

THURS. 30 MAY

The Battle of Hexham   b: Miss Monk
The Midnight Hour

SAT. 1 JUNE

The Haunted Tower   b: Miss Summers
The First Floor

MON. 3 JUNE

The Law of Lombardy   C/BG, G b: Dimond
The Positive Man

WED. 5 JUNE

The Maid of the Mill   b: Kelly
Catherine and Petruchio

THURS. 6 JUNE

The Merry Wives of Windsor   C/BJ, BC
The Sultan   b: Paul & Bartley

SAT. 8 JUNE

The Road to Ruin   C/BJ
Hartford Bridge   b: Theatre Servants

MON. 10 JUNE

Henry II   C/FF b: Keasberry
The Golden Pippin

WED. 12 JUNE

Macbeth   C/FF b: Cleveland
The Padlock

FRI. 14 JUNE

The Heiress   b: Walker
The Spoil'd Child

SAT. 15 JUNE

The Natural Son   C/BJ b: Office keepers
The Poor Soldier

MON. 17 JUNE

The Merry Wives of Windsor   b: Blisset
Catherine and Petruchio

WED. 19 JUNE
The Natural Son   b: Miss Monk
Robin Hood

FRI. 21 JUNE
Wild Oats
The Deserter

SAT. 22 JUNE
Wild Oats   C/BJ b: Office Keepers
The Deserter

MON. 24 JUNE
Inkle and Yarico   C/FF, G
Cupid Turned Postillion   b: Mrs. Didier &
                                        Mrs. Smith

WED. 26 JUNE
Romeo and Juliet   C/FF b: Huttley
The Divorce

FRI. 28 JUNE
The Road to Ruin
The First Floor

SAT. 29 JUNE
Everyone has his fault   C/BJ
The Divorce

MON. 1 JULY
King John   C/FF, G
Miss in her Teens   b: Mr. & Mrs. Murray

WED. 3 JULY
Cymbeline   b: Eastmure
The Highland Reel

FRI. 5 JULY
The Double Falsehood   C/BG
Rosina

MON. 8 JULY
Notoriety   b: Durravan Jnr.
Selima and Azor

WED. 10 JULY
The Lord of the Manor   C/FF b: Haymes
The Positive Man

FRI. 12 JULY
Battle of Hexham   C/My
The Gentle Shepherd   b: Floor (Prompter)

MON. 15 JULY
Rule a Wife and have a Wife   C/G
Hob in the Well   b: Mr. & Mrs. Knight

WED. 17 JULY
The Earl of Essex   b: Miss Summers
The Prisoner at Large

FRI. 19 JULY
Jane Shore   C/My b: Rowbotham
Try Again

MON. 22 JULY
Which is the Man?   b: Miss Wallis
The Devil to Pay

WED. 24 JULY
The Duenna   b: Miss Gopell
The Sultan

FRI. 26 JULY
Tancred and Sigismunda   b: Paul (Treasurer)
Hob in the Well

MON. 29 JULY
King Henry V   PB/R, C/FF, G
No Song, No Supper   b: Mrs. Keasberry

End of Season

Season 1793/94

Company

Mr: Ashley, Atkins, Blisset, Charlton, Dimond, Durravan, Eastmure, Elliston, Galindo, Haymes, Hoyle, Huttley, Johnson, Keasberry, Kelly, Knight, Marshall, Murray, Rowbotham, Sandford, Smith, Taylor.

Mrs: Charlton, Didier, Johnson, Keasberry, Kelly, Knight, Murray, Smith

Miss: Biggs, Floor, Gopell, Harvey, Herbert, Monk, Murray, Quick, Smith, S. Smith, Summers, Wallis. Wallis.

Master: Smith.

Treasurer: Paul.   *Box Book-keepers:* Bartley, (Bath), Walker, (Bristol).   *Prompter:* Floor.

1793

TUES. 24 SEPT.
The Natural Son   C/BJ
The Highland Reel

WED. 25 SEPT.
Inkle and Yarico
Cross Purposes

THURS. 26 SEPT.
Romeo and Juliet   C/BC, G
The Romp

FRI. 27 SEPT.
The Road to Ruin
The Irishman in London

SAT. 28 SEPT.
Wild Oats   C/BJ, BC, G
The Flitch of Bacon

MON. 30 SEPT.
The Natural Son   C/FF
The Highland Reel

SAT. 5 OCT.
Everyone has His Fault   C/BJ

MON. 7 OCT.
Everyone has His Fault   C/SF
The Citizen

SAT. 12 OCT.
The School for Scandal   C/BJ, G
Rosina

MON. 14 OCT.
Wild Oats (Courtney, Bagpiper) C/FF
The Flitch of Bacon

TUES. 15 OCT.
The West Indian   C/BJ
The Flitch of Bacon

SAT. 19 OCT.
The Chapter of Accidents
No Song, No Supper

MON. 21 OCT.
The Provok'd Husband   C/FF
The Prize

WED. 23 OCT.
Columbus

SAT. 26 OCT.
The Provok'd Husband   C/BJ, G
The Prize

MON. 28 OCT.
The Wonder   C/FF
The Prize

SAT. 2 NOV.
The Wonder   C/BJ
The Prize

MON. 4 NOV.
Columbus   C/FF
The Quaker

WED. 6 NOV.
The School for Scandal
The Prize

FRI. 8 NOV.
She Stoops to Conquer
Hartford Bridge

SAT. 9 NOV.
The Suspicious Husband   C/G
Ways and Means

MON. 11 NOV.
The Surrender of Calais   C/FF
The Irishman in London

TUES. 12 NOV.
Everyone has His Fault   C/BJ
The Prize

THURS. 14 NOV.
Columbus
The Quaker

SAT. 16 NOV.
The Road to Ruin   C/G
Hartford Bridge

MON. 18 NOV.
Everyone has His Fault   C/FF
The Prize

TUES. 19 NOV.
The London Hermit   C/BJ, G
The Highland Reel

THURS. 21 NOV.
The Surrender of Calais
The Irishman in London

SAT. 23 NOV.
She Stoops to Conquer
The Midnight Hour

MON. 25 NOV.
The London Hermit   C/FF
The Midnight Hour

TUES. 26 NOV.
The Heiress   C/BJ, G
Sprigs of Laurel

THURS. 28 NOV.
Columbus
The Prize

SAT. 30 NOV.
Wild Oats
Sprigs of Laurel

MON. 2 DEC.
The Gamester   C/FF
Sprigs of Laurel

TUES. 3 DEC.
How to grow Rich   C/BJ, G
Rosina

THURS. 5 DEC.
The Gamester   C/G
Sprigs of Laurel

SAT. 7 DEC.
Everyone has His Fault
The Prize

MON. 9 DEC.
How to Grow Rich   C/FF
The Poor Soldier

TUES. 10 DEC.
How to Grow Rich   C/BJ
The Poor Soldier

THURS. 12 DEC.
Columbus
Hartford Bridge

SAT. 14 DEC.
The Merchant of Venice   C/G

MON. 16 DEC.
A Bold Stroke for a Husband   C/FF
Sprigs of Laurel

TUES. 17 DEC.
A Bold Stroke for a Husband   C/BJ
No Song, No Supper

THURS. 19 DEC.
Everyone has His Fault
The Prize

SAT. 21 DEC.
The Child of Nature   C/G
The Black Forest
The Spoil'd Child

MON. 23 DEC.
How to grow Rich   C/FF
The Prize

THURS. 26 DEC.
Richard III   C/BJ
The Prize

FRI. 27 DEC.
Columbus
Thomas and Sally
The Black Forest

SAT. 28 DEC.
How to grow Rich
Sprigs of Laurel

MON. 30 DEC.
The Child of Nature   C/FF
The Spoil'd Child
The Black Forest

TUES. 31 DEC.
The Surrender of Calais   C/BJ
The Prisoner at Large

1794

THURS. 2 JAN.
Inkle and Yarico   C/G
Ways and Means

SAT. 4 JAN.
As You Like It   C/G
The Ghost
The Black Forest

MON. 6 JAN.
The Surrender of Calais   C/FF
Thomas and Sally
The Black Forest

TUES. 7 JAN.
The Road to Ruin   C/BJ
No Song, No Supper

THURS. 9 JAN.
Everyone has His Fault
The Prize

SAT. 11 JAN.
Much Ado About Nothing
Hartford Bridge

MON. 13 JAN.
Columbus   C/FF
Sprigs of Laurel

TUES. 14 JAN.
Macbeth   C/BJ
The Black Forest

THURS. 16 JAN.
The Provok'd Husband   PB/BM
Brystowe

SAT. 18 JAN.
The Belle's Stratagem (Miss Collins) PB/BM, C/BJ, BC
The Midnight Hour

MON. 20 JAN.
The Belle's Stratagem (Miss Collins) PB/BM, C/FF
Thomas and Sally
The Black Forest

TUES. 21 JAN.
The Fashionable Lover   PB/BM, C/BJ
The Ghost
The Black Forest

THURS. 23 JAN.
The Gamester   PB/BM
Brystowe

SAT. 25 JAN.
Know Your Own Mind (Miss Collins) PB/BM,
The Deserter   C/BJ, BC

MON. 27 JAN.
Macbeth   C/FF
Hartford Bridge

TUES. 28 JAN.
Cymbeline   C/BJ
The Black Forest

WED. 29 JAN.
The West Indian   PB/BM, C/G
The Children in the Wood

SAT. 1 FEB.
The School for Scandal
Sprigs of Laurel

MON. 3 FEB.
Everyone has His Fault   C/FF
The Children in the Wood

TUES. 4 FEB.
Everyone has His Fault   C/BJ
The Children in the Wood

THURS. 6 FEB.
The Mountaineers   C/G
Cross Purposes

SAT. 8 FEB.
Wild Oats
Robin Hood

MON. 10 FEB.
Know Your Own Mind (Miss Collins) C/FF
The Children in the Wood

TUES. 11 FEB.
The Mountaineers   C/BJ
The Black Forest

THURS. 13 FEB.
The Surrender of Calais
The Prize

SAT. 15 FEB.
The Natural Son
Brystowe

MON. 17 FEB.
The Mountaineers   C/FF
Robin Hood

TUES. 18 FEB.
Such Things Are   C/BJ
The Children in the Wood

THURS. 20 FEB.
Hamlet
The Prize

SAT. 22 FEB.
The Mountaineers
The Gentle Shepherd

MON. 24 FEB.
The Mountaineers   C/FF
No Song, No Supper

TUES. 25 FEB.

Henry IV   C/BJ, G b: Dimond
Follies of a Day

THURS. 27 FEB.

The Rivals   C/BJ, G
Hartford Bridge   b: Mrs. Didier

SAT. 1 MAR.

Henry V   C/BJ, BC, G
Marian   b: Mrs. Keasberry

MON. 3 MAR.

The Surrender of Calais   C/FF
The Children in the Wood

TUES. 4 MAR.

The Law of Lombardy   C/BJ, G b: Miss Wallis

THURS. 6 MAR.

Duplicity   C/BJ, BC, G b: Elliston
The Farmer

SAT. 8 MAR.

The Young Quaker   C/G b: Blisset
Marian

MON. 10 MAR.

Cymbeline   C/FF
The Black Forest

TUES. 11 MAR.

The Funeral   C/BJ,G b: Murray
Midsummer Night's Dream

THURS. 13 MAR.

Which is the Man?   b: Eastmure
The Devil to Pay

SAT. 15 MAR.

The Haunted Tower   b: Huttley
The Follies of a Day

MON. 17 MAR.

The Mountaineers   C/FF
The Gentle Shepherd

TUES. 18 MAR.

The Spanish Barber   C/BJ, G
The Romp   b: Mrs. Knight
Hob in the Well

THURS. 20 MAR.

The Haunted Tower   PB/BM, C/G b: Haymes
The Sultan

SAT. 22 MAR.

Everyone has His Fault   b: Sandford
The Black Forest

MON. 24 MAR.

Such Things Are   C/FF
Sprigs of Laurel

TUES. 25 MAR.

Love in a Village   C/G b: Miss Gopell
Catherine and Petruchio

THURS. 27 MAR.

The Child of Nature   C/G
The Recruiting Sergeant   b: Mr. & Mrs. Charlton
The Invasion

SAT. 29 MAR.

The Guardian   C/G b: Mrs. Smith
A Midsummer Night's Dream
The Farmer

MON. 31 MAR.

Columbus   C/FF
The Prize

TUES. 1 APRIL

The Way to Keep Him   C/BJ, BC
The Highland Reel   b: Mrs. Johnson

THURS. 3 APRIL

The Battle of Hexham   C/G
Florizel and Perdita   b: Bartley & Paul

SAT. 5 APRIL

The Provok'd Husband   C/G b: Rowbotham
Rosina

MON. 7 APRIL

The Law of Lombardy   C/FF
The Invasion

TUES. 8 APRIL

The Mountaineers   C/BJ
Ways and Means

THURS. 10 APRIL

The Wonder   C/BJ, BC
No Song, No Supper   b: Brooks (Leader of Band)

SAT. 12 APRIL

Columbus

MON. 21 APRIL

The Battle of Hexham   C/FF
The Children in the Wood

TUES. 22 APRIL

The Surrender of Calais   C/BJ
The Children in the Wood

WED. 23 APRIL

Duplicity
The Black Forest
The Recruiting Sergeant

THURS. 24 APRIL
The Haunted Tower
The Prize

SAT. 26 APRIL
The Heiress   C/BJ, BC, G
The Irish Widow

MON. 28 APRIL
Romeo and Juliet   C/FF
The Purse

TUES. 29 APRIL
The Mountaineers   C/BJ
The Drummer

THURS. 1 MAY
Everyone has His Fault   b: Floor
Brystowe

SAT. 3 MAY
Inkle and Yarico   C/BJ, BC, G

MON. 5 MAY
The Mountaineers   C/FF
The Irish Widow

TUES. 6 MAY
The Road to Ruin   C/BJ, G
The Ghost
The Purse

THURS. 8 MAY
Romeo and Juliet
The Farmhouse

SAT. 10 MAY
Love's Frailties   C/G

MON. 12 MAY
Love's Frailties   C/FF
Sprigs of Laurel

TUES. 13 MAY
The Mountaineers   C/BJ
The Irish Widow

WED. 14 MAY
Love's Frailties
The Prize

THURS. 15 MAY
Columbus
The Black Forest
The Recruiting Sergeant

FRI. 16 MAY
Everyone has His Fault
The Children in the Wood

SAT. 17 MAY
Henry IV
The Spoil'd Child
The Purse

MON. 19 MAY
Hamlet   C/FF
The Irish Widow

TUES. 20 MAY
The Barber's Petition   C/BJ, G b: Knight
The Chapter of Accidents

THURS. 22 MAY
The Foundling   C/G b: Miss Herbert
Hob in the Well

SAT. 24 MAY
The Merry Wives of Windsor C/BJ, BC
Catherine and Petruchio   b: Miss Summers &
                                 Hoyle

MON. 26 MAY
Love's Frailties   C/FF
The Recruiting Sergeant
The Purse

TUES. 27 MAY
Lionel and Clarissa   C/BJ, G
Edgar and Emmeline   b: Mrs. Keasberry

THURS. 29 MAY
Macbeth   b: Mr. & Mrs. Kelly
The Highland Reel

SAT. 31 MAY
Much Ado About Nothing   C/BJ b: Marshall
Bucks Have At Ye All
The Two Misers

MON. 2 JUNE
Henry IV (i)   C/FF b: Dimond
The Follies of a Day

TUES. 3 JUNE
The Duenna   C/BJ b: Taylor
The Sultan

THURS. 5 JUNE
Henry II   C/BJ, BC
The Poor Soldier   b: Paul & Bartley

SAT. 7 JUNE
The Rivals   C/BJ
The Gentle Shepherd

MON. 9 JUNE
The Grecian Daughter   C/FF
Robin Hood

TUES. 10 JUNE

George Barnwell   C/BJ
Children in the Wood

WED. 11 JUNE

Everyone has his fault   C/FF b: Hoyle
Hartford Bridge

FRI. 13 JUNE

The Gamester   C/SF
The Gentle Shepherd   b: Walker (Box book-
                           keeper)

SAT. 14 JUNE

The Young Quaker   C/BJ, PB /BM
The Prize   b: Office keepers

MON. 16 JUNE

The Roman Father   C/FF
Edgar and Emmeline   b: Keasberry

WED. 18 JUNE

The School for Scandal   b: Sandford (Receiver
No Song, No Supper   at the boxes)

FRI. 20 JUNE

Wild Oats   C/SF
The Romp   b: Part of Office-
                  keepers

SAT. 21 JUNE

The West Indian   C/BJ, BC
Robin Hood

MON. 23 JUNE

The Provok'd Husband   b: Blisset
The Follies of a Day

WED. 25 JUNE

Henry V   b: Eastmure
The Sultan

FRI. 27 JUNE

The Way to Keep Him   C/SF
Sprigs of Laurel   b: Part of Office-
                  keepers

SAT. 28 JUNE

Hamlet   C/BJ
The Romp

MON. 30 JUNE

A Midsummer Night's Dream b: Mrs. Didier &
The Spoil'd Child   Mrs. Smith
Edgar and Emmeline

WED. 2 JULY

The Countess of Salisbury   C/G b: Elliston
The Farmer

FRI. 4 JULY

Richard III   PB/R, C/G
Rosina   b: Galindo

SAT. 5 JULY

The School for Scandal   C/BJ
The Farmer

MON. 7 JULY

The Child of Nature   b: Miss Gopell
The Ghost

WED. 9 JULY

The Haunted Tower   b: Haymes
Florizel and Perdita

FRI. 11 JULY

Duplicity   b: Atkins, Marshall,
The Recruiting Sergeant   Smith, Kelly,
The Black Forest   Durravan

SAT. 12 JULY

The Merchant of Venice   C/BJ
The Waterman

MON. 14 JULY

Revenge   C/G
The Highland Reel   b: Mr. & Mrs. Murray

WED. 16 JULY

Inkle and Yarico   b: Mr. & Mrs. Charlton
The Son-in-Law

FRI. 18 JULY

The Merchant of Venice   C/My
Miss in her Teens   b: Brooks & Boyton
                           (musicians)

MON. 21 JULY

The Prodigal   C/G
The Spanish Barber   b: Mr. & Mrs. Knight
Midas

WED. 23 JULY

King Lear   C/G b: Rowbotham
The Two Misers

FRI. 25 JULY

Everyone has his fault   b: Floor

MON. 28 JULY

Isabella   C/G b: Miss Wallis
The Deserter

WED. 30 JULY

The Merry Wives of Windsor   b: Miss Summers
Marian

FRI. 1 AUG.

Jane Shore   b: Paul
The Positive Man

MON. 4 AUG.

Columbus   C/SF, G
The Quaker   b: Mrs. Keasberry

End of Season

Season 1794/95

Company

Mr: Ashley, Atkins, Betterton, Biggs, Blisset, Charlton, Crompton, Dimond, Durravan, Elliston, Eyre, Galindo, Hoyle, Keasberry, Kerridge, Knight, Marshall, Murray, Rowbotham, Simpson, Smith, Taylor, Turpin, Williamson.

Mrs: Charlton, Didier, Eyre, Haynes, Keasberry, Knight, Murray, Pollock, Smith, Twistleton.

Miss: Bateman, Betterton, Biggs, Gopell, Harvey, Herbert, Murray, Quick, Summers, S. Smith.

Treasurer: Paul.   *Box Book-keepers:* Bartley, (Bath), Walker, (Bristol).   *Prompter:* Floor.

1794

MON. 29 SEPT.		
The West Indian	C/FF	
The Padlock	b: Lord Howe's Fleet Fund	

SAT. 4 OCT.	
Everyone has His Fault	C/BJ, BC
The Padlock	

MON. 6 OCT.	
The Road to Ruin	C/FF
The Deserter	

WED. 8 OCT.
The Conscious Lovers

SAT. 11 OCT.	
The Conscious Lovers	PB/BM, H, C/BJ,
The Poor Soldier	BC, G

MON. 13 OCT.	
Henry IV (i)	C/FF
The Children in the Wood	

SAT. 18 OCT.	
She Stoops to Conquer	PB/H
Britain's Glory	

MON. 20 OCT.	
Hamlet	C/FF
Britain's Glory	

SAT. 25 OCT.	
Henry IV	C/BJ, BC
The Children in the Wood	

MON. 27 OCT.	
Columbus	C/FF
Hartford Bridge	

WED. 29 OCT.	
As You Like It	PB/H
My Grandmother	

SAT.1 NOV.	
The Chapter of Accidents	PB/H, C/BJ, BC
The Prize	

MON. 3 NOV.	
Wild Oats	C/FF
My Grandmother	

TUES. 4 NOV.	
Wild Oats	PB/H, C/BJ, G
My Grandmother	

THURS. 6 NOV.	
Douglas	PB/H, C/G
Britain's Glory	

SAT. 8 NOV.	
As You Like It	
Sprigs of Laurel	

MON. 10 NOV.	
The Box Lobby Challenge	C/FF
Sprigs of Laurel	

TUES. 11 NOV.	
The Box Lobby Challenge	PB/H, C/BJ, G
Hartford Bridge	

THURS. 13 NOV.	
The Road to Ruin	PB/H
My Grandmother	

SAT. 15 NOV.	
The Wonder	PB/H
No Song, No Supper	

MON. 17 NOV.	
The Jew	C/FF
The Agreeable Surprise	

TUES. 18 NOV.	
The Jew	PB/H, C/BJ, G
The Agreeable Surprise	

THURS. 20 NOV.	
Inkle and Yarico	PB/Ba, H
The Prisoner at Large	

SAT. 22 NOV.
The Mountaineers   PB/H
My Grandmother

MON. 24 NOV.
The Jew   C/FF
The Lyar

TUES. 25 NOV.
The Jew   C/BJ
The Farm House

THURS. 27 NOV.
The Box Lobby Challenge   PB/H
The Irishman in London

SAT. 29 NOV.
The West Indian   PB/H
The Children in the Wood

MON. 1 DEC.
The Mountaineers   C/FF
My Grandmother

TUES. 2 DEC.
Rule a Wife and Have a Wife   PB/H, C/BJ
My Grandmother

THURS. 4 DEC.
The Jew   PB/H
The Prize

SAT. 6 DEC.
The Surrender of Calais   PB/H, C/BJ
The Flitch of Bacon

MON. 8 DEC.
Columbus   PB/H, C/FF
The Prize

TUES. 9 DEC.
Everyone has His Fault   PB/H, C/BJ
The Quaker

THURS. 11 DEC.
Love in a Village   PB/H
The Spoil'd Child

SAT. 13 DEC.
The School for Scandal
My Grandmother

MON. 15 DEC.
The Jew   PB/H, C/FF
The Flitch of Bacon

TUES. 16 DEC.
The Jew   PB/H, C/BJ
The Highland Reel

THURS. 18 DEC.
Columbus   PB/H
The Prize

SAT. 20 DEC.
The Rage   PB/H, C/G
The Agreeable Surprise

MON. 22 DEC.
The Rage   C/FF
No Song, No Supper

TUES. 23 DEC.
The Rage   PB/H, C/BJ
Sprigs of Laurel

FRI. 26 DEC.
The Grecian Daughter   PB/Ba, BM, H, C/BJ,
                        BC, G
The Children in the Wood

SAT. 27 DEC.
The Mountaineers   PB/BM, H
My Grandmother

MON. 29 DEC.
The Rage   C/FF
The Children in the Wood

TUES. 30 DEC.
The Jew   PB/BM, H, C/BJ
The Deserter

1795

THURS. 1 JAN.
Romeo and Juliet   C/BJ, BC
Ways and Means

SAT. 3 JAN.
Much Ado About Nothing   PB/BA, H
The Ghost

MON. 5 JAN.
The Grecian Daughter   C/FF
My Grandmother

TUES. 6 JAN.
Richard III   PB/Ba, C/BJ
Cross Purposes

THURS. 8 JAN.
Columbus   PB/H
The Children in the Wood

SAT. 10 JAN.
The Provok'd Husband   PB/H
My Grandmother

MON. 12 JAN.
The Rage   C/FF
Ways and Means

TUES. 13 JAN.
The Rage   C/BJ
The Waterman

THURS. 15 JAN.

Macbeth

SAT. 17 JAN.

The Jew   PB/H
The Lyar

MON. 19 JAN.

Romeo and Juliet   C/FF
The Ghost

TUES. 20 JAN.

She Stoops to Conquer   C/BJ
Don Juan

THURS. 22 JAN.

Othello   C/BJ
The Spoil'd Child

SAT. 24 JAN.

The Rivals
The Prize

MON. 26 JAN.

(Performance cancelled because of bad weather)

TUES. 27 JAN.

The Rage   C/BJ
Don Juan

THURS. 29 JAN.

Jane Shore   PB/H
Don Juan

SAT. 31 JAN.

The Box Lobby Challenge   PB/Ba, H
The Children in the Wood

MON. 2 FEB.

Jane Shore   C/FF
The Prize

TUES. 3 FEB.

Hamlet   PB/F, C/BJ
The Quaker

THURS. 5 FEB.

Wild Oats   PB/H
Don Juan

SAT. 7 FEB.

The Jew   PB/Ba, H
My Grandmother

MON. 9 FEB.

The Jew   C/FF
My Grandmother

TUES. 10 FEB.

Everyone has His Fault   C/BJ
Don Juan

THURS. 12 FEB.

The Earl of Warwick   PB/H, C/BJ, BC, G
No Song, No Supper

SAT. 14 FEB.

The Battle of Hexham   C/BJ, BC
Edgar and Emmaline   b: Mrs. Pollock

MON. 16 FEB.

The Provok'd Husband   C/FF
Don Juan

TUES. 17 FEB.

Columbus   PB/BM, H, C/BJ
Who's the Dupe?

THURS. 19 FEB.

Fontainville Forest   C/G
Hartford Bridge

SAT. 21 FEB.

The Rage   PB/H
My Grandmother

MON. 23 FEB.

The Battle of Hexham   C/FF
Don Juan

TUES. 24 FEB.

The Mountaineers   C/BC, BJ,
The Recruiting Sergeant   b: Dimond
The Black Forest

THURS. 26 FEB.

Duplicity   PB/F, C/BJ, G
The Romantic Lady   b: Mrs. Didier

SAT. 28 FEB.

Such Things Are   C/BJ, BC, G
The Farmer   b: Keasberry

MON. 2 MAR.

Othello   C/FF
The Spoil'd Child

TUES. 3 MAR.

The Earl of Warwick   b: Murray
The Little Hunchback

THURS. 5 MAR.

The Merchant of Venice   C/BJ, BC b: Williamson
The Purse

SAT. 7 MAR.

The Road to Ruin   C/BC, G b: Elliston
The Love of Fame

MON. 9 MAR.

The Earl of Warwick   C/FF
Don Juan

TUES. 10 MAR.
Henry IV   PB/H b: Blisset
The Dreamer Awake

THURS. 12 MAR.
The Duenna   PB/F, C/BJ, G b: Biggs
The Irish Widow

SAT. 14 MAR.
As You Like It   C/BJ, BC, G
High Life Below Stairs   b: Mrs. Knight

MON. 16 MAR.
Fontainville Forest   C/FF
The Farmer

TUES. 17 MAR.
The Haunted Tower   PB/H, C/BJ
Caernarvon Castle   b: Miss Gopell

THURS. 19 MAR.
The Suspicious Husband   PB/H, C/BJ b: Taylor
Robin Hood

SAT. 21 MAR.
Cymbeline   PB/Ba, H
Two Strings to Your Bow   b: Miss Briggs

MON. 23 MAR.
The Rage   C/FF
My Grandmother

TUES. 24 MAR.
The Spanish Barber   PB/BM, H, C/BJ
The Virgin Unmask'd   b: Knight
Hunt the Slipper

THURS. 26 MAR.
The Pilgrim   PB/H, b: Bartley & Paul
Poor Vulcan

SAT. 28 MAR.
Venice Preserv'd   PB/H, C/BJ, BC
The Lying Valet   b: Mrs. Twistleton

MON. 6 APRIL
Fontainville Forest   C/FF
Don Juan

TUES. 7 APRIL
Fontainville Forest   PB/H, C/BJ
The Children in the Wood

THURS. 9 APRIL
The Jew   PB/H
My Grandmother

SAT. 11 APRIL
The Belle's Stratagem   PB/H, C/BC
The Poor Soldier

MON. 13 APRIL
The Spanish Barber   C/FF
The Virgin Unmask'd
Hunt the Slipper

TUES. 14 APRIL
The Rage   PB/H, C/BJ
Don Juan

THURS. 16 APRIL
The School for Scandal   PB/H
The Flitch of Bacon

SAT. 18 APRIL
The Rivals   PB/H
Crochet Lodge

MON. 20 APRIL
The Belle's Stratagem   C/FF
Crochet Lodge

TUES. 21 APRIL
Macbeth   PB/H, C/BJ
The Prisoner at Large

THURS. 23 APRIL
The Mountaineers   PB/H, C/BJ b: Floor
The Little Hunchback

SAT. 25 APRIL
Fontainville Forest   PB/H
Crochet Lodge

MON. 27 APRIL
The Jew   C/FF
The Highland Reel

TUES. 28 APRIL
Columbus   PB/H, C/BJ
The Black Forest

WED. 29 APRIL
The Belle's Stratagem   PB/H
The Highland Reel

THURS. 30 APRIL
The Rage   PB/H
Don Juan

FRI. 1 MAY
The Road to Ruin   PB/H
The Children in the Wood

SAT. 2 MAY
The Wheel of Fortune   C/G
No Song, No Supper

MON. 4 MAY
The Wheel of Fortune   C/FF
Crochet Lodge

TUES. 5 MAY
The Wheel of Fortune   C/BJ
My Grandmother

THURS. 7 MAY
Richard III   C/BJ.
The Poor Soldier   b: Bath City
                                    Infirmary &
                                    Sunday Schools

SAT. 9 MAY
Percy   C/BC, BJ, G
The Prize

MON. 11 MAY
The Wheel of Fortune   C/FF
My Grandmother

TUES. 12 MAY
The Wheel of Fortune   PB/H, C/BJ
Rosina

THURS. 14 MAY
The Clandestine Marriage   PB/H, C/BJ
The Deuce is in Him

SAT. 16 MAY
The Heiress   PB/H, b: Mrs. Smith
Lilliput

MON. 18 MAY
Fontainville Forest   C/FF
The Prize

TUES. 19 MAY
The Fugitive   PB/H, C/BC, BJ
Netley Abbey   b: Mrs. Keasberry

THURS. 21 MAY
The West Indian   PB/H, C/BJ, BC
The Follies of a Day   b: Rowbotham

SAT. 23 MAY
Everyone has his fault   PB/H b: Miss Herbert
The Cooper

MON. 25 MAY
The Wheel of Fortune   PB/H, C/FF
The Black Forest

TUES. 26 MAY
The Dramatist   PB/H, C/BJ
Hob in the Well   b: Mr. & Mrs. Charlton

THURS. 28 MAY
The Mountaineers   PB/H b: Hoyle & Miss
The Telegraph   Summers
The Black Forest

SAT. 30 MAY
The Chapter of Accidents   C/BC b: Galindo
Midas

MON. 1 JUNE
Everyone has his fault   C/FF
The Children in the Wood

TUES. 2 JUNE
The Miser   PB/H, C/BJ
France as it was   b: Mr. & Mrs. Eyre
Lilliput

WED. 3 JUNE
The Jew   PB/H, b: Marshall
Catherine and Petruchio

SAT. 6 JUNE
Such Things Are   PB/H, C/BC, BJ
The Romp   b: Miss Harvey

MON. 8 JUNE
The Mountaineers   C/FF b: Dimond
The Little Hunchback

TUES. 9 JUNE
The Child of Nature   PB/F b: Paul & Bartley
The Purse
Midas

THURS. 11 JUNE
The Merchant of Venice   PB/H, C/BJ
Crochet Lodge   b: Office Keepers

SAT. 13 JUNE
She Stoops to Conquer   PB/H, C/BJ
The Children in the Wood   b: Office Keepers

MON. 15 JUNE
The Child of Nature   b: Blisset
The Telegraph
The Miser

WED. 17 JUNE
Henry IV (i)   b: Galindo
The Purse
The Black Forest

FRI. 19 JUNE
The Merchant of Venice   PB/F
The Romp   b: Part of Keepers of
                                     the House

SAT. 20 JUNE
Rule a Wife and Have a Wife   C/BJ, G
The Prisoner at Large   b: Office Keepers

MON. 22 JUNE
Cymbeline   b: Mr. & Miss Biggs
France as it was

FRI. 26 JUNE

The Dramatist   PB/F b: Walker
The Spoil'd Child

MON. 29 JUNE

Wild Oats   C/G b: Elliston
Hob in the Well

WED. 1 JULY

The Pilgrim   PB/F
The Old Maid   b: Charlton & Mrs.
                            Didier

FRI. 3 JULY

The Road to Ruin   PB/F
My Grandmother   b: Part of Keepers of
                            the House

MON. 6 JULY

Venice Preserv'd   b: Mrs. Twistleton
The Dreamer Awake

WED. 8 JULY

The School for Scandal PB/F b: Mrs. Pollock
Rosina

FRI. 10 JULY

The Mountaineers   b: Floor & Sanders
The Purse   (Receiver at the
The Black Forest   Boxes)

MON. 13 JULY

All in good humour   b: Mr. & Mrs. Knight
The Country Girl
High Life below Stairs

WED. 15 JULY

Macbeth   b: Hoyle & Miss
The Highland Reel   Summers

FRI. 17 JULY

The Pilgrim   PB/R b: Marshall
The Children in the Wood

MON. 20 JULY

A Quarter of an Hour   C/FF, G
  Before Dinner   b: Mr. & Mrs. Murray
Henry VIII
The Cooper

WED. 22 JULY

The Provok'd Husband PB/R b: Rowbotham
Midas

FRI. 24 JULY

King Lear   PB/R b: Paul
The Positive Man

MON. 27 JULY

Columbus   b: Mrs. Keasberry
Netley Abbey

End of Season

Season 1795/96

Company

Mr: Atkins, Betterton, Biggs, Blisset, Charlton, Cooper, Crumpton, Cunningham, Dimond, Doyle, Elliston, Eyre, Galindo, Hoyle, Marshall, Murray, Pinder, Rowbotham, Simpson, Smith, Taylor, Williamson.

Mrs: Charlton, Didier, Eyre, Murray, Pollock, Yates.

Miss: Bateman, Betterton, Biggs, Gopell, Harvey, Herbert, Loder, Murray, Quick, Smith, Summers, Tebay, Warrell.

Master: Betterton, Tebay.

Treasurer: Paul   *Box Book Keepers:* Bartley (Bath)   *Prompter:* Floor

1795

MON. 21 SEPT

Percy   PB/R, C/FF
The Old Maid

WED. 23 SEPT.

The Dramatist   PB/R
The Flitch of Bacon

FRI. 25 SEPT.
The Clandestine Marriage   PB/R
The Black Forest

SAT. 26 SEPT.
Percy   C/BJ
The Old Maid

MON. 28 SEPT.
Fontainville Forest   PB/R, C/FF
Rosina

WED. 30 SEPT.
Columbus   PB/R
The Prize

FRI. 2 OCT.
The Fashionable Lover   PB/R
The Sultan

SAT. 3 OCT.
The Dramatist   PB/H, C/BJ, G
Rosina

MON. 5 OCT.
The Jew   PB/R, C/FF
Don Juan

WED. 7 OCT.
Cymbeline   PB/R
My Grandmother

SAT. 10 OCT
The Clandestine Marriage   C/BJ
My Grandmother

MON. 12 OCT.
Know Your Own Mind   C/FF
The Quaker

WED. 14 OCT.
Life's Vagaries   PB/R
No Song, No Supper

FRI. 16 OCT.
The Fair Penitent   PB/R
Don Juan

SAT. 17 OCT.
Life's Vagaries   PB/H, C/BJ, G
The Quaker

MON. 19 OCT.
The Road to Ruin   PB/R, C/FF
Hartford Bridge

WED. 21 OCT.
The Mountaineers   PB/H
The Deserter

FRI. 23 OCT.
Love in a Village   PB/R
The Deuce is in Him

SAT. 24 OCT.
Know Your Own Mind   PB/H, C/BJ
No Song, No Supper

MON. 26 OCT.
Life's Vagaries   PB/R
The Children in the Wood

WED. 28 OCT.
The Grecian Daughter   PB/R
The Padlock

FRI. 30 OCT.
Columbus   PB/R
Netley Abbey

SAT. 31 OCT.
Life's Vagaries   C/BJ
The Deserter

MON. 2 NOV.
Isabella   PB/R
The Agreeable Surprise

WED. 4 NOV.
The School for Scandal   PB/R
Rosina

FRI. 6 NOV.
King Lear   PB/R
Don Juan

SAT. 7 NOV.
The Mountaineers   PB/H, C/BJ
My Grandmother

MON. 9 NOV.
Everyone has His Fault   PB/R
My Grandmother

TUES. 10 NOV.
The Jew   PB/H, C/BJ
The Agreeable Surprise

THURS. 12 NOV.
Isabella   C/BJ, BC

MON. 16 NOV.
The Busy Body   PB/R
The Waterman

TUES. 17 NOV.
The Busy Body   PB/H, C/BJ, BC
The Irish Mimic

THURS. 19 NOV.
The Rage   PB/H
Don Juan

SAT. 21 NOV.
Life's Vagaries   PB/H
Rosina

MON. 23 NOV.
The Wheel of Fortune   PB/R
The Irish Mimic

TUES. 24 NOV.
The Wheel of Fortune   PB/H, C/BJ
The Padlock

THURS. 26 NOV.
Columbus   PB/H
The Prize

FRI. 27 NOV.
The Rage
The Children in the Wood

SAT. 28 NOV.
The Suspicious Husband
The Children in the Wood

MON. 30 NOV.
The Suspicious Husband   PB/R
The Prize

TUES. 1 DEC.
The West Indian   PB/H, C/BJ
The Black Forest
(Richer performs on the tight rope at both theatres
till 4 Jan)

THURS. 3 DEC.
Love in a Village   PB/H
The Irish Mimic

SAT. 5 DEC.
The Provok'd Husband   PB/H
The Prize

MON. 7 DEC.
The West Indian   PB/R
The Deuce is in Him

TUES. 8 DEC.
The Clandestine Marriage   PB/H, C/BJ
Hartford Bridge

THURS. 10 DEC.
The School for Scandal   PB/H
No Song, No Supper

SAT. 12 DEC.
The Rivals   PB/H
The Deuce is in Him

MON. 14 DEC.
The Provok'd Husband   PB/R
The Irish Mimic

TUES. 15 DEC.
The Road to Ruin   PB/H, C/BJ
The Cooper
William Tell

THURS. 17 DEC.
The Fashionable Lover   PB/H
William Tell

SAT. 19 DEC.
She Stoops to Conquer
The Irish Mimic

MON. 21 DEC.
The Stoops to Conquer   PB/R
William Tell

TUES. 22 DEC.
The Bank Note   C/BJ
Don Juan

WED. 23 DEC.
Everyone has His Fault   PB/H
Ways and Means

SAT. 26 DEC.
Know your own Mind   PB/H
Rosina

MON. 28 DEC.
The Rivals   PB/R
The Cooper
William Tell

TUES. 29 DEC.
The Mountaineers   PB/H, C/BJ
The Cooper
William Tell

WED. 30 DEC.
The Bank Note   PB/H
My Grandmother

THURS. 31 DEC.
Cymbeline   PB/H
William Tell

1796

SAT. 2 JAN.
The Wonder   PB/H
Bon Ton

MON. 4 JAN.
The Wonder   PB/R
The Children in the Wood

TUES. 5 JAN.
The Grecian Daughter   PB/H, C/BJ, BC
The Agreeable Surprise

THURS. 7 JAN.
Columbus   PB/H
Catherine and Petruchio

SAT. 9 JAN.

The Dramatist   PB/H
The Deserter

MON. 11 JAN.

The Bank Note   PB/R
Ways and Means

TUES. 12 JAN.

As You Like It   PB/H, C/BJ, BC, G
The Romp

THURS. 14 JAN.

Hamlet
William Tell

SAT. 16 JAN.

The Belle's Stratagem   PB/H
The Prisoner at Large

MON. 18 JAN.

Hamlet   PB/R
The Prisoner at Large

TUES. 19 JAN.

The Chapter of Accidents   PB/H, C/BJ, BC
The Poor Soldier

THURS. 21 JAN.

The Bank Note   PB/H
The Children in the Wood

SAT. 23 JAN.

The Pilgrim   PB/H
The Adopted Child

MON. 25 JAN.

The Pilgrim   PB/R
The Adopted Child

TUES. 26 JAN.

The Deserted Daughter   PB/H, C/BJ, G
The Flitch of Bacon

THURS. 28 JAN.

Henry IV
The Purse
William Tell

FRI. 29 JAN.

The Deserted Daughter
The Adopted Child

MON. 1 FEB.

The Deserted Daughter   PB/R
The Poor Soldier

TUES. 2 FEB.

The Mountaineers   C/BJ
The Adopted Child

THURS. 4 FEB.

She Stoops to Conquer   PB/H
Valentine and Orson

SAT. 6 FEB.

The Deserted Daughter   PB/H
The Gentle Shepherd

MON. 8 FEB.

The Deserted Daughter   PB/R
The Adopted Child

TUES. 9 FEB.

Othello   (H. Siddons)   PB/F, C/BJ, BC, G
Valentine and Orson

THURS. 11 FEB.

The Deserted Daughter   PB/H
Valentine and Orson

SAT. 13 FEB.

Columbus   PB/H
The Adopted Child

MON. 15 FEB.

Othello   (H. Siddons)   PB/R
The Gentle Shepherd

TUES. 16 FEB.

The Purse   b: Dimond
Fountainville Forest
Selima and Azor

THURS. 18 FEB.

A Word to the Wise   PB/H, C/G, b:Mrs.Didier
The Double Disguise

SAT. 20 FEB.

Wild Oats   PB/H, C/G, B:
Robin Hood   b: Miss Betterton

MON. 22 FEB.

A Word to the Wise   PB/R
Valentine and Orson

TUES. 23 FEB.

The Maid of the Mill   C/BJ, G, b:Blisset
The Highland Reel

THURS. 25 FEB.

The Child of Nature   C/G, BJ, BC. b:Elliston
Bath Theatricals
The Children in the Wood

SAT. 27 FEB.

Every Man in his Humour   PB/H, C/BJ, BC,
Poor Vulcan   b: Williamson

MON. 29 FEB.

The Deserted Daughter   PB/R
Valentine and Orson

TUES. 1 MAR.
A Quarter of an Hour   PB/H, C/G, b: Murray
  before Dinner
Lionel and Clarissa
All in Good Humour

THURS. 3 MAR.
The Follies of a Day   PB/H, b: Taylor
Bath Theatricals
Midas

SAT. 5 MAR.
The Earl of Warwick   PB/H, C/BC
The Midnight Hour   b: Mrs. Yates

MON. 7 MAR.
Every Man in His Humour   PB/R
The Adopted Child

TUES. 8 MAR.
The Battle of Hexham   PB/H, C/G, BJ
The Farmer   b: Biggs

THURS. 10 MAR.
The Surrender of Calais   PB/H, C/BC
Edgar and Emmeline   b: Miss Herbert

SAT. 12 MAR.
The Merry Wives of Windsor   PB/H, C/BC, BJ
Sprigs of Laurel   b: Galindo

MON. 14 MAR.
A Quarter of an Hour before PB/R
  Dinner
The Child of Nature
Valentine and Orson

TUES. 15 MAR.
The Beggar's Opera   C/BJ, BC
The Prize   b: Miss Gopell

THURS. 17 MAR.
Henry VIII   C/BJ,
St. Patrick's Day   b: Paul & Bartley

SAT. 19 MAR.
A Bold Stroke for a Husband   PB/H, C/BJ
Cymon   b: Charlton

MON. 28 MAR.
The Provok'd Husband (Miss Wallis)   PB/R
My Grandmother

TUES. 29 MAR.
The Child of Nature (Miss Wallis) PB/H, C/G
The Sultan

WED. 30 MAR.
The Jew   PB/H
Valentine and Orson

THURS. 31 MAR.
Romeo and Juliet (Miss Wallis)   C/BJ, BC
The Quaker

SAT. 2 APRIL
The Provok'd Husband (Miss Wallis)   PB/H, C/BJ, BC
The Irish Mimic

MON. 4 APRIL
Romeo and Juliet (Miss Wallis)   PB/R
The Quaker

TUES. 5 APRIL
Much Ado About Nothing (Miss Wallis)   PB/H,
The Poor Soldier   C/BJ

THURS. 7 APRIL
Everyone has His Fault (Miss Wallis) PB/H, C/BJ, BC
Poor Vulcan

FRI. 8 APRIL
Everyone has His Fault (Miss Wallis) PB/R, H
Edgar and Emmeline

SAT. 9 APRIL
The Wonder   (Miss Wallis)   C/BJ, BC
Rosina

MON. 11 APRIL
Hamlet   PB/R
The Romp

TUES. 12 APRIL
Hamlet   PB/F, C/BJ
My Grandmother

THURS. 14 APRIL
The Busybody   PB/H
Valentine and Orson

SAT. 16 APRIL
The Pilgrim   PB/H
The Adopted Child

MON. 18 APRIL
Speculation   PB/R
The Double Disguise

TUES. 19 APRIL
Speculation   C/BJ
The Old Maid

THURS. 21 APRIL
A Quarter of an Hour before   PB/H, C/BJ
  Dinner
Fontainville Forest
Valentine and Orson

SAT. 23 APRIL
The Deserter Daughter   PB/H
The Romp

MON. 25 APRIL	
Macbeth	PB/R
St. Patrick's Day	

TUES. 26 APRIL	
Speculation	C/BJ
Selima and Azor	

THURS. 28 APRIL	
Macbeth	PB/F, C/BJ, BC
No Song, No Supper	

SAT. 30 APRIL	
The Rage	PB/H
Lock and Key	

MON. 2 MAY	
Speculation	PB/R
Lock and Key	

TUES. 3 MAY	
The Haunted Tower	PB/H, C/BJ
The Irish Widow	b: Miss Biggs

THURS. 5 MAY	
Love Makes a Man	PB/H, C/BC,BJ
Marian	b: Floor

SAT. 7 MAY	
Lock and Key	C/BJ, C
The Lyar	

MON. 9 MAY	
The Wheel of Fortune	PB/R
Lock and Key	

TUES. 10 MAY	
The Wheel of Fortune	C/BJ
Valentine and Orson	

THURS. 12 MAY	
Tamerlane	PB/H
Lock and Key	

SAT. 14 MAY	
A Word to the Wise	PB/H
The Adopted Child	

MON. 16 MAY	
A Quarter of an Hour before Dinner	PB/R
Fontainville Forest	
Cymon	

TUES. 17 MAY	
The Guardian	PB/F, C/BJ b: Hoyle
The Comedy of Errors	
The Devil to Pay	

THURS. 19 MAY	
Douglas	C/BJ, G
Lethe	b: Mrs. Murray
The Cooper	

SAT. 21 MAY	
Which is the Man?	C/BJ, BC
The Apparition	b: Mr. & Mrs. Eyre

MON. 23 MAY	
The Deserted Daughter	
The Adopted Child	

TUES. 24 MAY	
More Ways than One	PB/H, C/BJ
Cymon	b: Rowbotham

THURS. 26 MAY	
Inkle and Yarico	PB/H, C/BJ
The Recruiting Sergeant	b: Miss Warrell
Damon and Phillida	

SAT. 28 MAY	
The Beaux Stratagem	PB/H, C/BJ, BC
The Purse	b: Betterton
Harlequin's Frolics	

MON. 30 MAY	
More Ways than One	PB/R
Lock and Key	

TUES. 31 MAY	
The Maid of the Mill	PB/H, C/BJ
The Irishman in London	b: Miss Summers & Miss Harvey

WED. 1 JUNE	
The Young Quaker	C/BJ
Lock and Key	

THURS. 2 JUNE	
George Barnwell	C/G b: Atkins
The Little Hunchback	
Thomas and Sally	

SAT. 4 JUNE	
Tamerlane	PB/H
My Grandmother	

MON. 6 JUNE	
The Maid of the Mill	PB/R
The Irishman in London	

TUES. 7 JUNE	
The Merchant of Venice	PB/H, C/BJ
Bath Theatricals	b: Marshall
Love and Money	

THURS. 9 JUNE

The Mountaineers   C/BJ, BC
The Apparition   b: Paul & Bartley

SAT. 11 JUNE

The Young Quaker   C/BJ, BC, G
The Adopted Child   b: Office Keepers

MON. 13 JUNE

A Bold Stroke for a Husband PB/R b: Blisset
Damon and Phillida
Love and Money

WED. 15 JUNE

The Battle of Hexham   PB/R b: Galindo
Lethe
The Recruiting Sergeant

FRI. 17 JUNE

George Barnwell   PB/BM, R
The Children in the Wood   b: Floor (Prompter)

SAT. 18 JUNE

The Jew   C/BJ, G
The Highland Reel   b: Office Keepers

MON. 20 JUNE

The Belle's Stratagem   PB/R
Poor Vulcan   b: Miss Betterton

WED. 22 JUNE

Richard III   PB/R b: Taylor
Bristol Theatricals
Thomas and Sally

FRI. 24 JUNE

Love Makes a Man   PB/R
Rosina   b: Part of Servants of
                         the Theatre

SAT. 25 JUNE

The Belle's Stratagem   PB/H, C/BJ
Hartford Bridge   b: Office Keepers

MON. 27 JUNE

Robin Hood   PB/R b: Biggs
The Farmer
The Irish Widow

WED. 29 JUNE

Jane Shore   PB/R b: Mrs. Yates
British Fortitude and
   Hibernian Friendship
The Purse

SAT. 2 JULY

Columbus   PB/H, C/BJ
Lock and Key

MON. 4 JULY

The Surrender of Calais   PB/R b: Williamson
The Irish Mimic

WED. 6 JULY

Lionel and Clarissa   PB/R
The Devil to Pay   b: Miss Warrell &
                         Miss Herbert

FRI. 8 JULY

Inkle and Yarico   PB/R
The Adopted Child

SAT. 9 JULY

A Bold Stroke for a Husband PB/H, C/BJ
The Adopted Child

MON. 11 JULY

The Mountaineers   PB/R, C/G b: Elliston
Bristol Theatricals
The Siege of Quebec

WED. 13 JULY

The Natural Son   b: Eyre & Miss Biggs
The Apparition

FRI. 15 JULY

The Gamester   b: Hoyle & Miss
True Blue   Summers
Rose and Colin

SAT. 16 JULY

The Wonder
Lock and Key

MON. 18 JULY

The Brothers   PB/R
The Mariners   b: Charlton & Mrs.
                         Didier

WED. 20 JULY

The Beaux Stratagem   PB/R
Rosina   b: Part of the Servants
                         of the Theatre

FRI. 22 JULY

The Chapter of Accidents   PB/R
Don Juan   b: Part of Servants of
                         the Theatre

SAT. 23 JULY

The Brothers   C/BJ
The Apparition

MON. 25 JULY

Zara   b: Mr. & Mrs. Murray
Florizel and Perdita

WED. 27 JULY

The Haunted Tower   PB/R
Tit for Tat   b: Miss Gopell

FRI. 29 JULY	**FRI. 5 AUG.**
The West Indian PB/R b: Rowbotham	The Mountaineers PB/R b: Paul
The Positive Man	Bristol Theatricals
	The Siege of Quebec
MON. 1 AUG.	
Tamerlane C/FF b: Dimond	**MON. 8 AUG.**
Selima and Azor	Columbus C/SF
	Lock and Key
WED. 3 AUG.	
The Jew PB/R b: Betterton	
The Siege of Valenciennes	End of Season

Season 1796/97

Company

Mr: Atkins, Betterton, Biggs, Blisset, Charlton, Cook, Crumpton, Cunningham, Dimond, Doyle, Elliston, Eyre, Galindo, Harley, Hill, Hoyle, Rowbotham, Sedley, Smith, J. Smith, Taylor, Williamson.

Mrs: Atkins, (formerly Miss Warrell), Charlton, Didier, Eyre, Smith, J. Smith, Taylor, (formerly Miss Herbert), Wilson.

Miss: Bateman, Betterton, Biggs, Gopell, Loder, Quick, Summers, Tebay.

Master: I. Tebay, T. Tebay.

Treasurer: Paul.   *Box Book-keeper:* Bartley, (Bath).   *Prompter:* Floor.

1796	**SAT. 15 OCT.**
	The Merchant of Venice C/BJ, BC, G
MON. 26 SEPT.	The Poor Sailor
Richard III C/FF	
Rosina	**MON. 17 OCT.**
	The Road to Ruin C/FF
WED. 28 SEPT.	The Poor Sailor
The Merchant of Venice	
	TUES. 18 OCT.
SAT. 1 OCT.	The Jew PB/BM, C/BJ
Richard III C/BJ, BC, G	Lock and Key
Rosina	
	WED. 19 OCT.
MON. 3 OCT.	The Mountaineers
The Provok'd Husband C/FF	The Poor Sailor
Don Juan	
	THURS. 20 OCT.
WED. 5 OCT.	The Road to Ruin
The Jew	My Grandmother
SAT. 8 OCT.	**SAT. 22 OCT.**
The Jew C/BJ, BC	First Love
Lock and Key	The Children in the Wood
MON. 10 OCT.	**MON. 24 OCT.**
Tamerlane C/FF	First Love C/FF
Robin Hood	The Children in the Wood
	SAT. 29 OCT.
WED. 12 OCT.	Know Your Own Mind C/BJ
Know Your Own Mind	The Adopted Child
The Poor Sailor	

MON. 31 OCT.
The Surrender of Calais   C/FF
Lock and Key

WED. 2 NOV.
First Love
My Grandmother

FRI. 4 NOV.
The Fair Penitent
Valentine and Orson

SAT. 5 NOV.
The Clandestine Marriage   C/BJ
The Prize

MON. 7 NOV.
Henry IV (i)   C/FF
The Prize

TUES. 8 NOV.
First Love   C/BJ
The Double Disguise

THURS. 10 NOV.
Tamerlane the Great
Robin Hood

SAT. 12 NOV.
As You Like It
No Song, No Supper

MON. 14 NOV.
The Way to Get Married   C/FF
No Song, No Supper

TUES. 15 NOV.
The Way to Get Married   C/BJ, G
The Double Disguise

THURS. 17 NOV.
Which is the Man?
The Poor Sailor

SAT. 19 NOV.
First Love
My Grandmother

MON. 21 NOV.
The Way to Get Married   C/FF
The Poor Sailor

TUES. 22 NOV.
The Way to Get Married   C/BJ
The Padlock

THURS. 24 NOV.
The Deserted Daughter
The Smugglers

SAT. 26 NOV.
Everyone has his fault
Cymon

MON. 28 NOV.
Philaster   PB/R, C/FF
The Old Maid

THURS. 29 NOV.
The Wonder   C/BJ
Lock and Key

THURS. 1 DEC.
Philaster   C/G
The Smugglers

MON. 5 DEC.
The Way to Get Married   C/FF
The Smugglers

TUES. 6 DEC.
The Surrender of Calais   C/BJ
The Old Maid

THURS. 8 DEC.
The Way to Get Married
The Adopted Child

SAT. 10 DEC.
The Suspicious Husband
The Prize

MON. 12 DEC.
Jane Shore   (Miss Wallis)   PB/P, C/FF
The Adopted Child

TUES. 13 DEC.
Jane Shore   (Miss Wallis)   C/BJ, G
Rosina

THURS. 15 DEC.
Much Ado About Nothing (Miss Wallis)   C/BJ, BC
The Sultan

SAT. 17 DEC.
The Provok'd Husband (Miss Wallis)   C/BJ
The Prize

MON. 19 DEC.
The Mountaineers   PB/R, C/FF
The Agreeable Surprise

TUES. 20 DEC.
Inkle and Yarico   C/BJ
The Lyar

THURS. 22 DEC.
Much Ado About Nothing (Miss Wallis)   C/BC
Lock and Key

SAT. 24 DEC.
The Conscious Lovers (Miss Wallis)   C/BC
No Song, No Supper

MON. 26 DEC.
The Jealous Wife (Miss Wallis) C/FF
My Grandmother

TUES. 27 DEC.
George Barnwell   C/BJ
Valentine and Orson

WED. 28 DEC.
The Jealous Wife
My Grandmother

THURS. 29 DEC.
The Chapter of Accidents   PB/BM, C/BJ
Follies of a Day   b: Miss Wallis

FRI. 30 DEC.
The Merchant of Venice
Don Juan

SAT. 31 DEC.
The West Indian (Miss Wallis) C/BJ, BC
The Sultan

1797
MON. 2 JAN.
The Way to Get Married   C/FF
Lock and Key

TUES. 3 JAN.
The Deuce is in Him (Signora Storace)   C/BJ, BC
No Song, No Supper
The Highland Reel

THURS. 5 JAN.
The Haunted Tower (Signora Storace) C/BJ, BC
The Old Maid

SAT. 7 JAN.
The Way to Get Married
Valentine and Orson

MON. 9 JAN.
The Haunted Tower (Signora Storace) C/FF
The Lyar

TUES. 10 JAN.
The Mountaineers   C/BJ
No Song, No Supper

THURS. 12 JAN.
The Haunted Tower   C/BC, BJ
My Grandmother   b: Signora Storace

SAT. 14 JAN.
The Suspicious Husband
The Old Maid

MON. 16 JAN.
The Surrender of Calais (Signora Storace) C/FF
The Prize

TUES. 17 JAN.
The Haunted Tower (Signora Storace)   C/BJ
The Prize

THURS. 19 JAN.
First Love
Pantomime

SAT. 21 JAN.
The Deserted Daughter
The Irishman in London

MON. 23 JAN.
The Mountaineers (Signora Storace) C/FF
My Grandmother

TUES. 24 JAN.
The Surrender of Calais (Signora Storace) C/BJ
My Grandmother

THURS. 26 JAN.
The Duenna (Signora Storace) C/BJ, BC
Catherine and Petruchio

FRI. 27 JAN.
The Duenna (Signora Storace) PB/P, R
No Song, No Supper

SAT. 28 JAN.
The Way to Get Married
The Cave of Hecate

TUES. 31 JAN.
The Maid of the Mill (Signora Storace)   C/BJ
No Song, No Supper

THURS. 2 FEB.
The Duenna (Signora Storace) C/BJ
Lock and Key

FRI. 3 FEB.
The Maid of the Mill   C/FF
Lock and Key   b: Signora Storace

SAT. 4 FEB.
First Love   C/BJ, BC
The Two Misers

MON. 6 FEB.
?   C/FF
The Irishman in London

TUES. 7 FEB.
The Jew   C/BJ
The Children in the Wood

THURS. 9 FEB.
Fortune's Fool
The Cave of Hecate

SAT. 11 FEB.
The School for Scandal   C/BJ, BC
The Two Misers

MON. 13 FEB.
Fortune's Fool   C/FF
The Highland Reel

TUES. 14 FEB.
Fortune's Fool   C/BJ
The Smugglers

THURS. 16 FEB.
The Road to Ruin
The Cave of Hecate

SAT. 18 FEB.
The Wheel of Fortune
Poor Vulcan

MON. 20 FEB.
The Deserted Daughter   C/FF
The Two Misers

TUES. 21 FEB.
Henry IV   C/BJ
The Quaker

THURS. 23 FEB.
Zorinski   C/G
The Agreeable Surprise

SAT. 25 FEB.
Wild Oats
The Poor Soldier

MON. 27 FEB.
Zorinski   C/FF
The Quaker

TUES. 28 FEB.
Wild Oats   C/BJ
The Two Misers

THURS. 2 MAR.
Hamlet
The Cave of Hecate

SAT. 4 MAR.
Zorinski

MON. 6 MAR.
Zorinski   (M'Donnell, piper)   C/FF
The Poor Soldier

TUES. 7 MAR.
Cymbeline   C/BJ b: Dimond
The Doctor and the Apothecary

THURS. 9 MAR.
The Rage   b: Mrs. Didier
The Mariners

SAT. 11 MAR.
The Pilgrim   b: Hartley
The Farmer

MON. 13 MAR.
The Wheel of Fortune   C/FF
The Cave of Hecate

TUES. 14 MAR.
Everyone has His Fault   PB/Ba b: Blisset
The Scheming Lieutenant

THURS. 16 MAR.
Macbeth   C/BJ, BC, G
Rose and Colin   b: Elliston
Sylvester Daggerwood

SAT. 18 MAR.
Such Things Are   b: Williamson
The Brave Irishman

MON. 20 MAR.
Tamerlane   C/FF
The Cave of Hecate

TUES. 21 MAR.
The Belle's Stratagem   C/BJ b: Miss Betterton
Modern Antiques

THURS. 23 MAR.
More Ways than One   b: Mrs. Atkins
The Padlock

SAT. 25 MAR.
The Way to Get Unmarried   b: Charlton
The Battle of Hexham
Bantry Bay

MON. 27 MAR.
Rose and Colin   C/FF
Such Things Are
Bantry Bay

TUES. 28 MAR.
The Brothers   C/BJ b: Biggs
The Spoil'd Child

THURS. 30 MAR.
A Bold Stroke for a Husband b: Taylor
The Son-in-Law

SAT. 1 APRIL
The Mask'd Friend   C/BJ
Edgar and Emmeline   b: Mr. & Mrs. Eyre
The Apprentice

MON. 3 APRIL
Macbeth   C/FF
The Recruiting Sergeant
Bantry Bay

TUES. 4 APRIL
The Castle of Andalusia   C/BJ b: Miss Gopell
My Grandmother

THURS. 6 APRIL
The School for Wives   b: Paul & Bartley
Lubin and Annette
Sylvester Daggerwood

SAT. 8 APRIL
He Would be a Soldier   C/G b: Miss Biggs
The Drummer

MON. 17 APRIL
Zorinski   C/FF
The Cave of Hecate

TUES. 18 APRIL
Zorinski   C/BJ
The Cooper
Bantry Bay

THURS. 20 APRIL
George Barnwell
Valentine and Orson

SAT. 22 APRIL
The Way to Get Married
The Doctor and the
    Apothecary

MON. 24 APRIL
The Way to Get Married   C/FF
The Doctor and the
    Apothecary

TUES. 25 APRIL
The Wheel of Fortune   C/BJ
The Poor Sailor

THURS. 27 APRIL
Percy

SAT. 29 APRIL
A Cure for the Heartache   C/G

MON. 1 MAY
A Cure for the Heartache   C/FF
The Spoil'd Child

TUES. 2 MAY
A Cure for the Heartache   C/BJ
The Deuce is in Him

THURS. 4 MAY
The Mountaineers   b: Floor
My Grandmother

SAT. 6 MAY
A Cure for the Heartache

MON. 8 MAY
A Cure for the Heartache   C/FF
Lock and Key

TUES. 9 MAY
The Provok'd Husband   C/BJ b: Mrs. Smith
Miss in her Teens

THURS. 11 MAY
A Cure for the Heartache   C/BJ
Valentine and Orson

FRI. 12 MAY
Othello   b: Betterton
Three Weeks before Marriage
Three Weeks after Marriage

SAT. 13 MAY
A Cure for the Heartache

MON. 15 MAY
The School for Wives   C/FF
The Cave of Hecate

TUES. 16 MAY
A Word to the Wise
Three Weeks after Marriage

THURS. 18 MAY
The Suspicious Husband   b: Rowbotham
The Apparition

SAT. 20 MAY
The Jew   C/BC b: Hill
Bon Ton

MON. 22 MAY
A Cure for the Heartache   C/FF
The Apparition

TUES. 23 MAY
The Child of Nature   C/BJ b: Mrs. Taylor
The Cooper
The Devil to Pay

THURS. 25 MAY
Fontainville Forest   C/BJ b: Galindo
High Life Below Stairs

SAT. 27 MAY
Romeo and Juliet   C/BJ, b: Miss Summers
The Apprentice

MON. 29 MAY
Romeo and Juliet   C/FF
The Doctor and the
    Apothecary

TUES. 30 MAY

The Wonder   b: Cunningham
Harlequin's Eulogium
Catherine and Petruchio

THURS. 1 JUNE

The Lyar   C/BJ b: Atkins
Sylvester Daggerwood
The Children in the Wood

SAT. 3 JUNE

The Way to Get Married   C/BJ
The Doctor and the
    Apothecary

MON.5 JUNE

A Cure for the Heartache   C/FF
My Grandmother

TUES. 6 JUNE

The Rivals   C/BJ
The Highland Reel

THURS. 8 JUNE

Othello   C/BJ, BC, G
The School for Arrogance   b: Paul & Bartley

SAT. 10 JUNE

Wild Oats
The Apparition

MON. 12 JUNE

Wild Oats (Mr. & the Misses D'Egville) C/FF b: Dimond
The Shipwreck

FRI. 16 JUNE

The Wonder   b: Part of Servants of
Don Juan   House

SAT. 17 JUNE

Inkle and Yarico   C/BJ b: Office Keepers
Rosina

MON. 19 JUNE

Cymbeline   C/FF b: Blisset
Rosina

WED. 21 JUNE

The Pilgrim   b: Mr. & Mrs. Taylor
Sylvester Daggerwood
The Cooper

SAT. 24 JUNE

The Mountaineers   C/BJ
Lock and Key

MON. 26 JUNE

Othello   b: Miss Betterton
Poor Vulcan

WED. 28 JUNE

The Beggar's Opera   C/FF b: Mrs. Atkins
Catherine and Petruchio

SAT. 1 JULY

Zorinski   C/BJ
The Shipwreck

MON. 3 JULY

The Brothers   C/FF b: Biggs
The Rival Soldiers

WED. 5 JULY

The Earl of Warwick   C/FF
Modern Antiques   b: Eyre & Miss
                             Summers

FRI. 7 JULY

The Mountaineers   b: Part of Servants of
The Quaker   House

SAT. 8 JULY

The Beggar's Opera   C/BJ, G
Valentine and Orson

MON. 10 JULY

The Castle of Andalusia   b: Miss Gopell
The Follies of a Day

WED. 12 JULY

Macbeth   b: Rowbotham
Rosina

FRI. 14 JULY

The Clandestine Marriage   b: Galindo
The Poor Soldier

MON. 17 JULY

Richard III   PB/R, C/G b: Harley
Cymon

FRI. 21 JULY

The Jew   b: Part of Servants of
Lock and Key   House

MON. 24 JULY

The Life of the Day   C/BG
The Old Maid   b: Charlton & Mrs.
Comus   Didier

ERI. 28 JULY

Everyone has his fault   b: Floor
Comus

WED. 2 AUG.

School for Scandal   b: Miss Biggs

MON. 7 AUG.

A Cure for the Heartache   C/FF
The Shipwreck

End of Season

Season 1797/98

Company

Mr: Atkins, Biggs, Blisset, Charlton, Crumpton, Cunningham, Dimond, Doyle, Edwin, Elliston, Eyre, Galindo, Harley, Hill, Sedley, Smith, Rowbotham, Taylor, Tebay, Williamson.

Mrs: Atkins, Charlton, Cunningham, Didier, Edwin, Eyre, Sedley, Smith, Taylor.

Miss: Allingham, Benson, Galindo, Gopell, Loder, Mitchell, Murray, Quick, Summers, Tebay,

Master: I. Tebay, T. Tebay.

Treasurer: Paul.   *Box Book-keeper:* Bartley, (Bath).   *Prompter:* Floor.

1797

MON. 25 SEPT.
She Stoops to Conquer (Quick)   C/FF, G
The Miser

WED. 27 SEPT.
The Duenna   (Quick)   C/G

FRI. 29 SEPT.
The Brothers   (Quick)   C/G
The Quaker

SAT. 30 SEPT.
She Stoops to Conquer (Quick)   C/BJ, BC
The Miser

MON. 2 OCT.
The Belle's Stratagem (Quick)   C/FF, G
The Lying Valet

WED. 4 OCT.
Love Makes a Man (Quick)   C/G

FRI. 6 OCT.
The Castle of Andalusia (Quick) C/G
Barnaby Brittle

SAT. 7 OCT.
The Castle of Andalusia (Quick)   C/BJ, BC
Barnaby Brittle

MON. 9 OCT.
The Way to Get Married   C/G b: Quick
Hartford Bridge

WED. 11 OCT.
The Child of Nature
My Grandmother
The Sultan

FRI. 13 OCT.
As You Like It
The Prize

SAT. 14 OCT.
The Child of Nature   C/BJ, BC, G
My Grandmother
The Sultan

MON. 16 OCT.
The Roman Father
Lock and Key

WED. 18 OCT.
The Road to Ruin
The Padlock

SAT. 21 OCT.
As You Like It   C/BJ, BC, G
The Prize

MON. 23 OCT.
A Cure for the Heartache   C/FF
The Cave of Hecate

WED. 25 OCT.
The Grecian Daughter
The Cooper
Britons Triumphant

SAT. 28 OCT.
A Cure for the Heartache   C/BJ
The Cooper
Britons Triumphant

MON. 30 OCT.
The Heir at Law   C/FF
The Cave of Hecate

WED. 1 NOV.
First Love   PB/R
The Jubilee

FRI. 3 NOV.
Much Ado About Nothing
Rose and Colin
Britons Triumphant

SAT. 4 NOV.
Much Ado About Nothing   C/BJ, BC
Rosina

MON. 6 NOV.
The Heir at Law   C/FF
The Romp

TUES. 7 NOV.
The Roman Father   C/BJ, BC, G
Lock and Key

THURS. 9 NOV.
The Heir at Law   C/G
The Rival Soldiers

SAT. 11 NOV.
The Battle of Hexham   C/BJ, BC
The Romp

MON. 13 NOV.
The Battle of Hexham   C/FF
The Wedding Day

TUES. 14 NOV.
The Heir at Law   C/BJ
The Spoil'd Child

THURS. 16 NOV.
The Grecian Daughter
The Cave of Hecate

SAT. 18 NOV.
Zorinski
The Wedding Day

MON. 20 NOV.
The Heir at Law   C/FF
The Children in the Wood

TUES. 21 NOV.
The Heir at Law   C/BJ
The Children in the Wood

THURS. 23 NOV.
The Wheel of Fortune   C/BJ, BC, G
The Jubilee

SAT. 25 NOV.
The Belle's Stratagem
The Shipwreck

MON. 27 NOV.
The Will   C/FF
Lock and Key

TUES. 28 NOV.
The Will   C/BJ
The Cave of Hecate

THURS. 30 NOV.
The Way to Get Married
The Jubilee

SAT. 2 DEC.
The School for Scandal
The Sultan

MON. 4 DEC.
The Will   C/FF
The Midnight Hour

TUES. 5 DEC.
The Will   C/BJ, G
The Midnight Hour

THURS. 7 DEC.
The Maid of the Mill   C/BC
The Wedding Day

SAT. 9 DEC.
Wild Oats
The Shipwreck

MON. 11 DEC.
The Maid of the Mill   C/FF
The Wedding Day

TUES. 12 DEC.
The Heir at Law   C/BJ
Rosina

THURS. 14 DEC.
The Provok'd Husband   C/G
Raymond and Agnes

SAT. 16 DEC.
The Maid of the Mill   C/BC

MON. 18 DEC.
Hamlet   C/FF
The Old Maid

TUES. 19 DEC.
The Will   C/BJ
The Lyar

THURS. 21 DEC.
The Wonder
Raymond and Agnes

SAT. 23 DEC.
A Cure for the Heartache
The Prize

TUES. 26 DEC.
The Road to Ruin   C/BJ, G
Raymond and Agnes

WED. 27 DEC.
The Heir at Law   C/FF
The Children in the Wood

THURS. 28 DEC.
The Mountaineers
The Jubilee

FRI. 29 DEC.
The Heir at Law
Raymond and Agnes

SAT. 30 DEC.
Know Your Own Mind

1798

MON. 1 JAN.
The Will   C/FF
The Doctor and the Apothecary

TUES. 2 JAN.
The Will   C/BJ
Raymond and Agnes

THURS. 4 JAN.
She Stoops to Conquer
Lock and Key

MON. 8 JAN.
A Cure for the Heartache   PB/R, C/FF
Rosina

TUES. 9 JAN.
Love in a Village (Incledon)   C/BJ
Raymond and Agnes

THURS. 11 JAN.
The Beggar's Opera (Incledon) C/BJ, BC
The Spoil'd Child

FRI. 12 JAN.
Love in a Village   (Incledon)
The Waterman

SAT. 13 JAN.
The Duenna   (Incledon)   C/BC
Rosina

MON. 15 JAN.
The Beggar's Opera   C/FF
The Old Maid

TUES. 16 JAN.
The Castle of Andalusia (Incledon)   C/BJ
The Farmer

THURS. 18 JAN.
The Haunted Tower   C/BJ, BC
The Waterman

SAT. 20 JAN.
Know Your Own Mind
Raymond and Agnes

MON. 22 JAN.
The Heir at Law   C/FF
Catherine and Petruchio

TUES. 23 JAN.
The Provok'd Husband   C/BJ
The Sultan

THURS. 25 JAN.
Henry IV
Raymond and Agnes

SAT. 27 JAN.
Zorinski
The Shipwreck

MON. 29 JAN.
The Will   C/FF
The Farmer

THURS. 1 FEB.
Henry IV   C/BJ
The Cave of Hecate

FRI. 2 FEB.
George Barnwell
Bon Ton

SAT. 3 FEB.
The Fop's Fortune

MON. 5 FEB.
Love in a Village (Mme. Mara) PB/R, C/FF
Bon Ton

TUES. 6 FEB.
The Wheel of Fortune   C/BJ
The Chimney Corner

THURS. 8 FEB.
The Will
The Chimney Corner

SAT. 10 FEB.
The Jew   PB/BM
Raymond and Agnes

MON. 12 FEB.
The Beggar's Opera (Mme Mara) C/FF
The Old Maid

TUES. 13 FEB.
The Heir at Law   C/BJ
The Chimney Corner

THURS. 15 FEB.
The Beggar's Opera (Mme Mara) C/BJ, BC
Catherine and Petruchio

SAT. 17 FEB.
Abroad and at Home   C/BJ, BC
No Song, No Supper

MON. 19 FEB.
The Will   C/FF b: The Infirmary
No Song, No Supper

TUES. 20 FEB.

The Will   C/BJ
Raymond and Agnes

THURS. 22 FEB.

Abroad and at Home
The Shipwreck

SAT. 24 FEB.

The Heir at Law
The Chimney Corner

MON. 26 FEB.

The Provok'd Husband   C/FF
Raymond and Agnes

TUES. 27 FEB.

Cymbeline   b: Voluntary Sub-
The Rival Soldiers   scription for
                      Defence Forces

THURS. 1 MAR.

Rule a Wife and Have a Wife   PB/BM b: Dimond
The Jubilee

FRI. 2 MAR.

Cymbeline   b: Voluntary Sub-
Voluntary Contributions   scriptions Fund
The Rival Soldiers

SAT. 3 MAR.

The Deserted Daughter   b: Mrs. Didier
Comus

MON. 5 MAR.

Rule a Wife and Have a Wife
Raymond and Agnes

TUES. 6 MAR.

The West Indian   C/G b: Blisset
Don Juan

THURS. 8 MAR.

Zorinski   b: Elliston
The Cooper

SAT. 10 MAR.

Lionel and Clarissa   b: Miss Gopell
The Follies of a Day

MON. 12 MAR.

The Heir at Law   C/FF
The Chimney Corner

TUES. 13 MAR.

The Rivals   C/BJ b: Mrs. Edwin
The Recruiting Sergeant
The Virgin Unmask'd

THURS. 15 MAR.

Fashionable Levities   C/BJ b: Harley
The Adopted Child
Who's the Dupe?

SAT. 17 MAR.

The Spanish Barber   C/BJ b: Taylor
St. Patrick's Day
The Deserter

MON. 19 MAR.

Abroad and at Home   C/FF
Raymond and Agnes

TUES. 20 MAR.

Inkle and Yarico   b: Biggs
Jabal's Travels
Blunders at Brighton

THURS. 22 MAR.

The Fugitive   b: Mrs. Atkins
The Ladies Catch Club
Peeping Tom of Coventry

SAT. 24 MAR.

The Life of the Day   b: Charlton
The Farmhouse
Barataria

MON. 26 MAR.

The Fashionable Lover   C/FF
Voluntary Contributions
The Chimney Corner

TUES. 27 MAR.

The Surrender of Calais   C/BJ b: Williamson
Rose and Colin
The Soldiers Festival

THURS. 29 MAR.

The Way to Keep Him   C/BJ, BC
The Highland Reel   b: Paul & Bartley

SAT. 31 MAR.

Everyone has His Fault   b: Miss Allingham
Poor Vulcan

MON. 9 APRIL

The Deserted Daughter   C/FF
Raymond and Agnes

TUES. 10 APRIL

The Beggar's Opera (Mme Mara)   C/BJ, BC
The Mayor of Garret

THURS. 12 APRIL

Love in a Village (Mme Mara)   PB/Ba, C/BJ, BC
The Citizen

SAT. 14 APRIL
Much Ado About Nothing
Raymond and Agnes

MON. 16 APRIL
Abroad and at Home   C/FF
Poor Vulcan

TUES. 17 APRIL
The Duenna   (Mme Mara)   C/BJ
The Lying Valet

THURS. 19 APRIL
Lionel and Clarissa   C/BJ b: Mme Mara
Bon Ton

SAT. 21 APRIL
The Castle Spectre   C/G
The Agreeable Surprise

MON. 23 APRIL
The Castle Spectre   C/FF
My Grandmother

TUES. 24 APRIL
The Castle Spectre   C/BJ
The Waterman

THURS. 26 APRIL
The Castle Spectre
Rosina

SAT. 28 APRIL
The Chapter of Accidents   b: Miss Mitchell
Robin Hood

MON. 30 APRIL
The Castle Spectre   C/FF
The Adopted Child

TUES. 1 MAY
The Castle Spectre   C/BJ
The Adopted Child

THURS. 3 MAY
The Deserted Daughter   C/BJ b: Floor
Lock and Key

SAT. 5 MAY
The Heir at Law
Raymond and Agnes

MON. 7 MAY
The Castle Spectre   C/FF
The Ghost

TUES. 8 MAY
The Castle Spectre   C/BJ
The Ghost

THURS. 10 MAY
Othello   b: Galindo
The Poor Soldier

SAT. 12 MAY
The Castle Spectre   C/BC

MON. 14 MAY
The Heir at Law   C/FF
My Grandmother

TUES. 15 MAY
The Purse   C/G b: Edwin
The Child of Nature
Midas

THURS. 17 MAY
A Cure for the Heartache   C/BJ, BC b: Rowbotham
Cymon

SAT. 19 MAY
The Dramatist   C/BJ, BC b: Hill
The Son in Law

MON. 21 MAY
The Castle Spectre   C/FF
The Rival Soldiers

TUES. 22 MAY
The Rage   C/G b: Mrs. Taylor
The Two Misers

THURS. 24 MAY
The Count of Narbonne   PB/BM, C/BJ, BC
British Fortitude   b: Eyre
Sylvester Daggerwood

SAT. 26 MAY
Macbeth   C/BJ, BC
The Soldier's Festival   b: Mr. & Mrs. Sedley

MON. 28 MAY
The Dramatist   C/FF
Raymond and Agnes

TUES. 29 MAY
The Chances   PB/BM
The Deserter   b: Mrs. Charlton

THURS. 31 MAY
The Jealous Wife   C/BJ, BC
The Cave of Hecate   b: Mrs. Cunningham

SAT. 2 JUNE
The School for Scandal   PB/BM
Comus   b: Atkins & Miss
Summers

MON. 4 JUNE
The Castle Spectre   C/FF
The Son in Law

TUES. 5 JUNE
Inkle and Yarico
My Grandmother

THURS. 7 JUNE
Henry V   C/G b: Paul & Bartley
The Padlock

SAT. 9 JUNE
The Wonder
Don Juan

MON. 11 JUNE
The Count of Narbonne (Murray)   C/FF b: Dimond
Midas

WED. 13 JUNE
Henry V (Murray)   C/FF
The Farmhouse   b: Charlton & Mrs.
                             Didier

FRI. 15 JUNE
The Merchant of Venice (Murray)   C/FF
My Grandmother   b: Part of Office
                             Keepers

SAT. 16 JUNE
The Heir at Law   C/BJ
Rosina   b: Office Keepers

MON. 18 JUNE
The Jealous Wife (Murray)   b: Blisset
Don Juan

WED. 20 JUNE
Macbeth   (Murray)   PB/R
The Deserter   b: Mr. & Mrs. Taylor

SAT. 23 JUNE
The Merchant of Venice (Murray) C/BJ
The Farmhouse

FRI. 29 JUNE
The Heir at Law   b: Part of Office
Lock and Key   Keepers

SAT. 30 JUNE
The Castle Spectre (Murray)   C/BJ
The Guardian

MON. 2 JULY
The Recruiting Sergeant (Murray)   PB/R
The Child of Nature   b: Mr. & Mrs.
Cymon   Edwin

WED. 4 JULY
Everyone has His Fault (Murray)   PB/R
The Deserter   b: Eyre & Hill

FRI. 6 JULY
The West Indian   b: Mr. & Mrs. Sedley
Cymon

SAT. 7 JULY
The Child of Nature   C/BJ
The Prize
Florizel and Perdita

MON. 9 JULY
A Cure for the Heartache   PB/R, TC b: Biggs
The Irish Widow

FRI. 13 JULY
Othello (Murray)   PB/R
Robin Hood   b: Part of Office
                             Keepers

SAT. 14 JULY
The Heir at Law   C/BJ
Raymond and Agnes

MON. 16 JULY
King Lear   PB/R b: Murray
Comus

WED. 18 JULY
The Clandestine Marriage   PB/R
The Generous Tars   b: Cunningham &
The Virgin Unmask'd   Miss Summers

FRI. 20 JULY
The Jealous Wife   PB/R b: Rowbotham
The Adopted Child

SAT. 21 JULY
The Mountaineers   C/BJ
The Adopted Child

MON. 23 JULY
The Lie of the Day   C/G b: Elliston
Edgar and Emmeline

WED. 25 JULY
The Rivals   PB/R, TC
The Wandering Jew   b: Charlton &
                             Mrs. Didier

SAT. 28 JULY
The Rivals   C/BJ b: Williamson
No Song, No Supper

MON. 30 JULY
The Castle Spectre
No Song, No Supper

End of Season

Season 1798/99

Company

Mr: Asker, Atkins, Campbell, Charlton, Cherry, Crumpton, Cunningham, Dimond, Doyle, Edwin, Elliston, Eyre, Galindo, Harley, Leslie, Richardson, Rowbotham, Sedley, J. Smith, W. Smith, Taylor, Tebay, Williamson.

Mrs: Atkins, Charlton, Cherry, Cooke, Didier, Dumont, Edwin, Eyre, Mountain, Sedley, Smith, J. Smith, Taylor.

Miss: Allingham, (later Mrs. Ricketts), Cherry, F. Cherry, Smith, Summers, Tebay, S. Tebay.

Master: Quick, T. Tebay.

Treasurer: Paul.　　　*Box Book-keeper:* Bartley, (Bath).　　　*Prompter:* Floor

1798

MON. 24 SEPT.
The Will　　　　　　　　　PB/R
The Wedding Day

WED. 26 SEPT.
Henry IV (i)　　　　　　　PB/R, TC
No Song, No Supper

FRI. 28 SEPT.
The Castle Spectre　　　　PB/TC
Catherine and Petruchio

SAT. 29 SEPT.
The Will

MON. 1 OCT.
The Way to Keep Him　　　PB/TC, C/FF
Two Strings to your Bow

WED. 3 OCT.
Everyone has his fault　　　PB/TC
The Padlock

FRI. 5 OCT.
Othello　　　　　　　　　PB/R
Two Strings to your Bow

SAT. 6 OCT.
The Way to Keep Him　　　C/BJ, BC, G
Two Strings to your Bow

MON. 8 OCT.
A Cure for the Heartache　PB/TC, C/FF
The Quaker

WED. 10 OCT.
The Haunted Tower　　　　PB/TC
The Farm House

FRI. 12 OCT.
George Barnwell　　　　　PB/TC
Raymond and Agnes

SAT. 13 OCT.
The Castle Spectre　　　　C/BJ, G
The Quaker

MON. 15 OCT.
Hamlet　　　　　　　　　C/FF
The Prize

FRI. 19 OCT.
The Heir at Law　　　　　PB/TC
Raymond and Agnes

SAT. 20 OCT.
The Heir at Law　　　　　C/BJ
Two Strings to your Bow

MON. 22 OCT.
Love Makes a Man (Quick)　C/FF
The Lying Valet

SAT. 27 OCT.
Love Makes a Man (Quick)　C/BJ, BC
Modern Antiques

MON. 29 OCT.
The Belle's Stratagem (Quick)　C/FF
The Miser

WED. 31 OCT.
The Brothers (Quick)　　　PB/TC
Barataria

SAT. 3 NOV.
The Brothers (Quick)　　　C/BJ, BC, G
Animal Magnetism

TUES. 6 NOV.
Inkle and Yarico　　　　　C/BJ
Catherine and Petruchio

WED. 7 NOV.
The Beaux Stratagem　　　C/FF b: Quick
The Mistake

THURS. 8 NOV.
A Cure for the Heartache (Neyler)   C/BJ, BC
The Waterman

SAT. 10 NOV.
The Castle of Andalusia   BC
The Farm House

MON. 12 NOV.
Wives as they Were   PB/TC, C/FF
  and Maids as they Are
Raymond and Agnes

TUES. 13 NOV.
Wives as they Were and   C/BJ, G
  Maids as they Are
The Irishman in London

THURS. 15 NOV.
The Will
Raymond and Agnes

SAT. 17 NOV.
The Castle Spectre
The Padlock

MON. 19 NOV.
Wives as they Were   C/FF
  and Maids as they Are
The Irishman in London

TUES. 20 NOV.
Wives as they Were   C/BJ
  and Maids as they Are
Rosina

THURS. 22 NOV.
The Castle Spectre
The Padlock

SAT. 24 NOV.
The Beaux Stratagem   C/G
Raymond and Agnes

MON. 26 NOV.
The Castle Spectre   PB/TC, C/FF
The Waterman

TUES. 27 NOV.
The Fair Penitent (Miss Gough)   C/BJ, BC, G
The Deserter

THURS. 29 NOV.
The Gamester (Miss Gough)   C/BC
The Sultan
Britons Triumphant

SAT. 1 DEC.
The Rivals (Miss Gough)   C/BC

MON. 3 DEC.
The Fair Penitent (Miss Gough)   PB/TC, C/FF
The Mouth of the Nile

TUES. 4 DEC.
Lovers'Vows   C/BJ, G
The Ghost

THURS. 6 DEC.
Lovers' Vows
The Poor Soldier

SAT. 8 DEC.
Everyone has His Fault (Miss Gough)   C/BJ, BC
The Mouth of the Nile

MON. 10 DEC.
Lovers' Vows   PB/TC, C/FF
The Poor Soldier

TUES. 11 DEC.
Lovers' Vows   C/BJ
Ways and Means

THURS. 13 DEC.
Douglas   (Miss Gough)   C/BJ, BC
The Virgin Unmask'd
The Mouth of the Nile

SAT. 15 DEC.
Wives as they Were and
  Maids as they Are
The Midnight Hour

MON. 17 DEC.
Lovers' Vows   PB/R, C/FF
Ways and Means

TUES. 18 DEC.
Tamerlane (Miss Gough)   C/BJ, BC
Raymond and Agnes

THURS. 20 DEC.
Lovers' Vows
The Flitch of Bacon

SAT. 22 DEC.
The Will
The Jew and the Doctor

WED. 26 DEC.
The Castle Spectre   PB/R, TC, C/FF
The Mouth of the Nile

THURS. 27 DEC.
The Castle Spectre   C/BJ
The Mouth of the Nile

FRI. 28 DEC.
Jane Shore   (Miss Gough)   C/BJ, BC
The Jew and the Doctor

SAT. 29 DEC.
The Way to Keep Him
The Quaker

MON. 31 DEC.
Lovers' Vows   C/FF
The Jew and the Doctor

1799

TUES. 1 JAN.
The Hair at Law   C/BC, BJ
Raymond and Agnes

THURS. 3 JAN.
Macbeth
Animal Magnetism

FRI. 4 JAN.
Lovers' Vows
The Jew and the Doctor

SAT. 5 JAN.
Love in a Village (Mrs. Mountain) C/BJ, BC
The Prize

MON. 7 JAN.
The Gamester   C/FF
The Ghost
The Mouth of the Nile

THURS. 10 JAN.
Lovers' Vows
Raymond and Agnes

SAT. 12 JAN.
The Way to get Married (Mrs. Mountain) C/BC
No Song, No Supper

MON. 14 JAN.
Lovers' Vows   C/FF
The Jew and the Doctor

TUES. 15 JAN.
The Stranger   C/G
The Sultan

THURS. 17 JAN.
The Count of Narbonne   C/BC
Robin Hood   (Miss Gough & Mrs. Mountain)

FRI. 18 JAN.
Lovers' Vows
Animal Magnetism

SAT. 19 JAN.
The Castle Spectre
The Padlock

MON. 21 JAN.
The Stranger   C/FF
Raymond and Agnes

TUES. 22 JAN.
The Distress'd Mother   C/BH b: Miss Gough
Edgar and Emmeline

THURS. 24 JAN.
The Stranger

SAT. 26 JAN.
Lionel and Clarissa (Mrs. Mountain)   C/BC
The Jew and the Doctor

MON. 28 JAN.
Love in a Village   C/FF
The Jew and the Doctor

TUES. 29 JAN.
The Grecian Daughter (Mrs. Siddons)   C/G

THURS. 31 JAN.
Douglas (Mrs. Siddons)   C/BC
The Lyar

FRI. 1 FEB.
The Grecian Daughter (Mrs. Siddons)
The Wedding Day

SAT. 2 FEB.
The Fair Penitent (Mrs. Siddons)   C/G, BC
The Midnight Hour

MON. 4 FEB.
Jane Shore   (Mrs. Siddons) C/FF
The Midnight Hour

TUES. 5 FEB.
Jane Shore (Mrs. Siddons)   C/G

THURS. 7 FEB.
Isabella (Mrs. Siddons)   C/BC, G

SAT. 9 FEB.
The Mourning Bride   C/BC, G
Ways and Means   b: Mrs Siddons

MON. 11 FEB.
Isabella   (Mrs. Siddons)   C/FF
My Grandmother

TUES. 12 FEB.
The Gamester (Mrs. Siddons)   C/G

THURS. 14 FEB.
Macbeth   (Mrs. Siddons) C/BC, G
Two Strings to your Bow

SAT. 16 FEB.
Isabella   (Mrs. Siddons)   C/BC, G

MON. 18 FEB.
Macbeth   (Mrs. Siddons) C/FF
Ways and Means

TUES. 19 FEB.
The Merchant of Venice (Mrs. Siddons)   PB/BM, C/G
No Song, No Supper

THURS. 21 FEB.
The Distress'd Mother (Mrs. Siddons)   C/BC, G

SAT. 23 FEB.
The Provok'd Husband (Mrs. Siddons)   C/BC, G
The Jew and the Doctor

MON. 25 FEB.
Douglas   (Mrs. Siddons)   PB/P, C/FF
Two Strings to your Bow

TUES. 26 FEB.
George Barnwell   C/BC, BH b: Dimond
   (Mrs. Siddons & Mrs. Mountain)
Comus

THURS. 28 FEB.
The School for Scandal   C/BC, BH
The Double Disguise   b: Mrs. Didier

SAT. 2 MAR.
Wild Oats   C/BH, b: Cherry
The Blue Devils
Interludes

MON. 4 MAR.
Laugh When You Can   C/FF
No Song, No Supper

TUES. 5 MAR.
Hamlet   C/BC, G b: Elliston
The Wandering Jew

THURS. 7 MAR.
The Surrender of Calais   b: Harley
The Shipwreck

SAT. 9 MAR.
Cymbeline   C/BH
The Irish Widow   b: Miss Allingham

MON. 11 MAR.
Laugh When You Can   C/FF
The Padlock

TUES. 12 MAR.
The Will   C/BC b: Edwin
The Sicilian Romance

THURS. 14 MAR.
A Cure for the Heartache   b: Charlton
Lock and Key

SAT. 16 MAR.
The Heir at Law   C/BC b: Taylor
Hartford Bridge

MON. 25 MAR.
Lovers' Vows   C/FF
Raymond and Agnes

TUES. 26 MAR.
The Castle Spectre
The Quaker

THURS. 28 MAR.
Laugh When You Can
Comus

SAT. 30 MAR.
The Stranger
The Jew and the Doctor

MON. 1 APRIL
The Stranger   PB/TC, C/FF
Comus

THURS. 4 APRIL
Zorinski   b: Paul & Hartley
The Doctor and the
   Apothecary

SAT. 6 APRIL
Blue Beard
The Lyar

MON. 8 APRIL
The Heir at Law   PB/P, C/FF
Robin Hood

THURS. 11 APRIL
Laugh When You Can
Blue Beard

SAT. 13 APRIL
The Child of Nature
Blue Beard

MON. 15 APRIL
Zorinski   PB/TC, C/FF
The Doctor and the
   Apothecary

THURS. 18 APRIL
Wives as they Were
   and Maids as they Are
Blue Beard

SAT. 20 APRIL
The Wonder
Blue Beard

MON. 22 APRIL
The Stranger   C/FF
The Poor Soldier

THURS. 25 APRIL
The Stranger
Blue Beard

SAT. 27 APRIL
?
Blue Beard

MON. 29 APRIL
Lionel and Clarissa   C/FF
The Follies of a Day   b: Mrs. Mountain

TUES. 30 APRIL
?
Blue Beard

THURS. 2 MAY
The Wheel of Fortune   C/BC b: Miss Smith
The Highland Reel

SAT. 4 MAY
The Castle Spectre

MON. 6 MAY
Blue Beard   PB/TC, C/FF
The Midnight Hour

THURS. 9 MAY
A Cure for the Heartache   b: Floor
The Children in the Wood

SAT. 11 MAY
Five Thousand a Year   C/BC b: Eyre
The Cooper
Lovers' Quarrels

MON. 13 MAY
The Wonder   PB/TC, C/FF
Blue Beard

TUES. 14 MAY
The Deserted Daughter   b: Mrs. Taylor
Honest Thieves

THURS. 16 MAY
The Belle's Stratagem   b: Rowbotham
Edgar and Emmeline

SAT. 18 MAY
The Haunted Tower   b: Mrs. Cooke
My Grandmother

MON. 20 MAY
Five Thousand a Year   C/FF
Blue Beard

TUES. 21 MAY
The Volunteer   C/BC, b: Galindo
The Heir at Law
Swordsmanship Displays

THURS. 23 MAY
The Jew   PB/Ba, C/BC
The Horse and the Widow   b: Sedley

SAT. 25 MAY
Know Your Own Mind   b: Cunningham
Lethe
A Pantomime Galimaufry

MON. 27 MAY
The Stranger   C/FF
Blue Beard

TUES. 28 MAY
The Birthday   b: Mrs. Charlton
Hampton Court Frolicks

THURS. 30 MAY
The Clandestine Marriage   C/G

SAT. 1 JUNE
The Will   b: Miss Summers
The Deserter

MON. 3 JUNE
The Birthday   C/FF
Blue Beard

SAT. 8 JUNE
The Young Quaker   b: Williamson (ill)
The Jew and the Doctor

MON. 10 JUNE
The Castle Spectre   C/FF, b: Dimond
The Horse and the Widow
The Mouth of the Nile

THURS. 13 JUNE
The Suspicious Husband
No Song, No Supper

SAT. 15 JUNE
The Stranger
The Doctor and the Apothecary

MON. 17 JUNE
The Will   b: Eyre & Richardson
Naval Revels
Lock and Key

WED. 19 JUNE
The Child of Nature   b: Sedley
The Honest Thieves

FRI. 21 JUNE
Laugh When You Can   PB/TC, b: Part of
Animal Magnetism   Office Keepers

SAT. 22 JUNE
The Birthday
Blue Beard

MON. 24 JUNE
The Merchant of Venice   PB/TC
The Sultan   b: Mrs. Ricketts

WED. 26 JUNE

Hamlet	PB/TC, b: Mrs. Cooke
The Shipwreck	

MON. 1 JULY

The Sicilian Romance	b: Mr. & Mrs. Cherry
Blue Devils	(Mrs. Parker)
Two Strings to Your Bow	

WED. 3 JULY

The Young Quaker	b: Galindo
Rosina	

FRI. 5 JULY

The West Indian	b: Part of Office
The Jew and the Doctor	Keepers

SAT. 6 JULY

The Birthday
Blue Beard

MON. 8 JULY

The Birthday	b: Charlton &
The Spanish Barber	Mrs. Didier
The Spoil'd Child	

WED. 10 JULY

Inkle and Yarico	PB/R, TC
Sylvester Daggerwood	b: Cunningham &
Edgar and Emmeline	Miss Summers

FRI. 12 JULY

Romeo and Juliet	b: Part of Servants
The Doctor and the	of House
Apothecary	

MON. 15 JULY

Know Your Own Mind	C/FF, b: Mr. & Mrs.
Fortune's Frolic	Edwin

WED. 17 JULY

The Belle's Stratagem	PB/BM, C/FF
The Purse	b: Rowbotham
The Cooper	

FRI. 19 JULY

The Mountaineers	b: Crumpton, Doyle,
Raymond and Agnes	Campbell, J. Tebay,
	Mrs. J. Smith

FRI. 26 JULY

Macbeth	b: Paul
The Highland Reel	

MON. 29 JULY

The Birthday	C/FF
Blue Beard	

End of Season

Season 1799/1800

Company

Mr: Campbell, Charlton, Cherry, Crumpton, Cunningham, D'Arcy, Dimond, Doyle, Edwin, Elliston, Eyre, Parsons, Phillips, Richardson, Rowbotham, Sedley, J. Smith, W. Smith, Stanwix, Taylor, Tebay, J. Tebay, Turner.

Mrs: Charlton, Cherry, Cooke, Cunningham, D'Arcy, Davey, Didier, Edwin, Eyre, Johnstone, Sedley, J. Smith, W. Smith, Taylor.

Miss: Atkins, Cherry, F. Cherry, Daniels (formerly Mrs. Cooke), Grimani, Quick, Smith, S. Smith, Summers, Taylor, Tebay, S. Tebay.

Master: S. Tebay, Quick.

Treasurer: Paul (died during season)   *Box Book-keeper:* Bartley (Bath).

New Prompter: Glassington   *New Treasurer:* Smith.

1799

MON. 23 SEPT.

The Birthday	C/FF
The Quaker	
The Sultan	

SAT. 28 SEPT.

Richard III	C/BC
The Sultan	

MON. 30 SEPT.

The West Indian	PB/TC, C/FF
Blue Beard	

FRI. 4 OCT.

Lovers' Vows   PB/R, TC
Blue Beard

SAT. 5 OCT.

The Birthday   C/BC
Rosina
The Purse

MON. 7 OCT.

Wives as they Were   (Quick)   PB/TC, C/FF
Who's the Dupe?

WED. 9 OCT.

The Way to Keep Him   (Quick)   PB/TC
Animal Magnetism

FRI. 11 OCT.

The Beaux Stratagem   (Quick)   PB/TC
Animal Magnetism

SAT. 12 OCT.

The Way to Keep Him   (Quick)   C/BC
The Lovers' Mistake

MON. 14 OCT.

Secrets worth knowing   (Quick)   C/FF
The Mistake

WED. 16 OCT.

Love in a Village   (Quick)   C/G

FRI. 18 OCT.

Secrets worth knowing   (Quick)   PB/TC
Blue Beard

SAT. 19 OCT.

Wives as they Were   (Quick)   C/BC, G
    Maids as they Are
The Commissary

MON. 21 OCT.

The Maid of the Mill   PB/TC b: Quick
The Author

WED. 23 OCT.

The Castle Spectre   C/FF

FRI. 25 OCT.

(Closed for rehearsals for Pizarro)

SAT. 26 OCT.

Secrets Worth Knowing   C/BC, G
The Flitch of Bacon

MON. 28 OCT.

Pizarro   C/FF
The Purse

TUES. 29 OCT.

Pizarro

WED. 30 OCT.

Pizarro

FRI. 1 NOV.

Pizarro

SAT. 2 NOV.

The Will
The Jew and the Doctor

MON. 4 NOV.

Pizarro   C/FF
My Grandmother

WED. 6 NOV.

Pizarro

FRI. 8 NOV.

Pizarro   PB/P
The Waterman

SAT. 9 NOV.

The Castle Spectre   C/BC
The Rival Soldiers

MON. 11 NOV.

Pizarro   C/FF
The Ghost

THURS. 14 NOV.

The Heir at Law
Blue Beard

SAT. 16 NOV.

Pizarro   C/G

MON. 18 NOV.

Everyone Has His Fault   C/FF
The Jew and the Doctor

THURS. 21 NOV.

Pizarro
The Flitch of Bacon

SAT. 23 NOV.

Pizarro

MON. 25 NOV.

False and True   C/FF
The Midnight Hour

THURS. 28 NOV.

Pizarro
The Ghost

SAT. 30 NOV.

Everyone has His Fault   C/BC
The Highland Reel

MON. 2 DEC.

The Stranger   C/FF
The Highland Reel

THURS. 5 DEC.

False and True
The Midnight Hour

SAT. 7 DEC.

The Stranger
Blue Beard

MON. 9 DEC.   C/FF

Pizarro
Two Strings to your Bow

TUES. 10 DEC.

The Castle Spectre
The Deserter

THURS. 12 DEC.

Pizarro
Two Strings to Your Bow

SAT. 14 DEC.   C/G

The West Indian
The Castle of Sorrento

MON. 16 DEC.   C/FF

Pizarro
The Deserter

TUES. 17 DEC.   C/BC

Lovers' Vows
Blue Beard

THURS. 19 DEC.

Pizarro
Ways and Means

SAT. 21 DEC.   C/G

Sighs
The Castle of Sorrento

MON. 23 DEC.   C/FF

Sighs
The Castle of Sorrento

THURS. 26 DEC.

Pizarro
The Doctor and the Apothecary

FRI. 27 DEC.

The Grecian Daughter
The Children in the Wood

SAT. 28 DEC.

The Stranger
Blue Beard

MON. 30 DEC.   C/FF

Pizarro
The Children in the Wood

TUES. 31 DEC.

Sighs
Blue Beard

1800

THURS. 2 JAN.

Pizarro
Rosina

FRI. 3 JAN.

George Barnwell
The Children in the Wood

SAT. 4 JAN.

Know Your Own Mind
False and True

MON. 6 JAN.   PB/R, C/FF

The Stranger
Blue Beard

TUES. 7 JAN.

The Birthday
Raymond and Agnes

THURS. 9 JAN.

Pizarro
The Purse

(From 9 Jan. – 18 Feb. Richer performs on
the Tightrope at both Theatres)

SAT. 11 JAN.

The Provok'd Husband
The Prize

MON. 13 JAN.   C/FF

The Provok'd Husband
False and True

THURS. 16 JAN.   C/G

The Wonder
The Turnpike Gate

SAT. 18 JAN.

The Way to Get Married
Raymond and Agnes

MON. 20 JAN.   PB/R, C/FF

Lovers' Vows
The Prize

TUES. 21 JAN.   C/BJ

Lovers' Vows
Turnpike Gate

THURS. 23 JAN.

Pizarro
Lock and Key

SAT. 25 JAN.

The Mountaineers
Lock and Key

MON. 27 JAN.
The Birthday   C/FF
Blue Beard

TUES. 28 JAN.
The Stranger   C/BJ
The Padlock

FRI. 31 JAN.
The Castle Spectre
My Grandmother

SAT. 1 FEB.
The Rivals
False and True

MON. 3 FEB.
Pizarro   PB/R
My Grandmother

TUES. 4 FEB.
The Will   C/BJ
Turnpike Gate

THURS. 6 FEB.
Pizarro
The Cooper

SAT. 8 FEB.
The Chapter of Accidents
The Farmhouse

MON. 10 FEB.
The Mountaineers   C/FF
The Turnpike Gate

TUES. 11 FEB.
The Wheel of Fortune   C/BJ, G
The Castle of Sorrento

THURS. 13 FEB.
Macbeth
The Romp

SAT. 15 FEB.
Management   C/G
The Farmer

MON. 17 FEB.
Management   C/FF
The Farmer

TUES. 18 FEB.
Lovers' Vows   C/BJ
Raymond and Agnes

THURS. 20 FEB.
Pizarro
The Poor Soldier

SAT. 22 FEB.
The Haunted Tower (Mrs. Mountain)   C/BC, BJ
The Flitch of Bacon

MON. 24 FEB.
The Haunted Tower   C/FF
The Flitch of Bacon

TUES. 25 FEB.
Lionel and Clarissa (Mrs. Mountain)   C/BJ
No Song, No Supper

THURS. 27 FEB.
Management
The Jew and the Doctor

SAT. 1 MAR.
The Duenna   (Mrs. Mountain)   C/BC, BJ
Robin Hood

MON. 3 MAR.
Lionel and Clarissa   PB/R, TC, C/FF
Robin Hood

TUES. 4 MAR.
Management   C/BJ
Raymond and Agnes

THURS. 6 MAR.
Pizarro
The Spoil'd Child

SAT. 8 MAR.
The Wise Man of the East   C/G
The Children in the Wood

MON. 10 MAR.
Management (Fernando, lyre)   C/FF
Blue Beard

TUES. 11 MAR.
The Stranger   (Fernando, lyre)   C/BC, BJ, G
The Shipwreck   b: Dimond

THURS. 13 MAR.
The Heir at Law   b: Mrs. Didier
The London Hermit

SAT. 15 MAR.
A Cure for the Heartache   b: Cherry
Daphne and Amintor
Botheration

MON. 17 MAR.
Pizarro   C/FF, PB/R
The Spoil'd Child

TUES. 18 MAR.
Macbeth   C/G b: Elliston
The Pannel

THURS. 20 MAR.
Zorinski   C/BC, BJ, b: Eyre
Silvester Daggerwood
The Doldrum

SAT. 22 MAR.

Douglas	PB/BM, C/BC
The Highland Reel	b: Mrs. Johnstone

MON. 24 MAR.

The Wise Man of the East	C/FF
The Castle of Sorrento	

TUES. 25 MAR.

The Country Girl	C/BJ, G b: Mrs. Edwin
The Purse	
Arthur and Emmeline	

THURS. 27 MAR.

The School for Scandal	b: Charlton
The Chimney Corner	

SAT. 29 MAR.

The Italian Monk	b: Richardson
The Recruiting Sergeant	
Lovers' Quarrels	

MON. 31 MAR.

A Cure for the Heartache (S. Rossignol)	C/FF
Blue Beard	

TUES. 1 APRIL

The Belle's Stratagem (S. Rossignol)	C/BJ
Comus	b: Mrs. Cooke

THURS. 3 APRIL

Rule a Wife and Have a Wife	C/G
Arthur and Emmeline	b: Bartley & Widow Paul

SAT. 5 APRIL

The Young Quaker	C/BJ, G b: Taylor
The Virgin Unmask'd	
The Naval Pillar	

MON. 14 APRIL

Pizarro	C/FF
The Romp	

TUES. 15 APRIL

Lovers' Vows	C/BJ
Blue Beard	

WED. 16 APRIL

The Grecian Daughter	C/BJ, G
The Poor Soldier	

SAT. 19 APRIL

Pizarro	
The Naval Pillar	

MON. 21 APRIL

Lovers' Vows	
Raymond and Agnes	

TUES. 22 APRIL

Speed the Plough	C/BJ, G
The Jew and the Doctor	

THURS. 24 APRIL

Hamlet	C/BJ b: Turner
The Doctor and the Apothecary	

SAT. 26 APRIL

Much Ado About Nothing	C/BC
Blue Beard	

MON. 28 APRIL

Speed the Plough	C/FF
The Poor Soldier	

TUES. 29 APRIL

Speed the Plough	C/BJ
The Children in the Wood	

THURS. 1 MAY

The Wise Man of the East	
Blue Beard	

SAT. 3 MAY

Speed the Plough	C/BC
The Adopted Child	

MON. 5 MAY

Speed the Plough	C/FF
The Doctor and the Apothecary	

TUES. 6 MAY

Management	C/BJ, BC
The Quaker	

THURS. 8 MAY

Pizarro	
Lock and Key	

SAT. 10 MAY

Speed the Plough	C/BJ
The Farmhouse	

MON. 12 MAY

Speed the Plough	C/FF
The Quaker	

TUES. 13 MAY

The Birthday	b: Edwin
The Agreeable Surprise	
Edgar and Emmeline	

THURS. 15 MAY

The Mountaineers	C/BC b: Mrs. Taylor
The Follies of a Day	

SAT. 17 MAY

The Suicide	C/BJ, G
A Peep behind the Curtain	b: Mr. & Mrs. Sedley

MON. 19 MAY

Pizarro　　　　　　　　C/FF
The Naval Pillar

TUES. 20 MAY

The Inconstant　　　　C/BJ, BC, G
The Pannel　　　　　　b: Cunningham

THURS. 22 MAY

Romeo and Juliet　　　C/BJ, BC
The Son-in-Law　　　　b: Glassington

SAT. 24 MAY

Cymbeline　　　　　　C/BJ, BC, G
The School for Arrogance　b: Smith (new
　　　　　　　　　　　　　　Treasurer) & Miss
　　　　　　　　　　　　　　Smith

MON. 26 MAY

Speed the Plough　　C/FF
The Pannel

TUES. 27 MAY

The Surrender of Calais　C/BJ, BC
No Song, No Supper　　b: Rowbotham

THURS. 29 MAY

The Battle of Hexham　C/BJ,
The Citizen　　　　　b: Mr. & Mrs. d'Arcy

SAT. 31 MAY

Percy　　　　　　　　C/BJ, BC
Florizel and Perdita　　b: Charlton & Miss
　　　　　　　　　　　　Grimani

MON. 2 JUNE

Romeo and Juliet　　C/FF
The Devil to Pay

TUES. 3 JUNE

The Wise Man of the East　C/BJ b: Miss Summers
The King and the Miller of
　Mansfield

THURS. 5 JUNE

The Will　　　　　　b: Bartley & Floor
False and True　　　　(ex-Prompter)

SAT. 7 JUNE

The Heir at Law　　　C/BJ
The Devil to Pay

MON. 9 JUNE

The Stranger　　　　b: Dimond
Arthur and Emmeline

WED. 11 JUNE

The Castle Spectre　　b: Part of the Servants
The King and the Miller of　of the House
　Mansfield

FRI. 13 JUNE

The Gamester　　　PB/R b: Turner
Animal Magnetism

SAT. 14 JUNE

Speed the Plough　(Miss Griffiths)　C/BJ, BC
Musical Entertainment

MON. 16 JUNE

The Earl of Warwick　　b: Mrs. Johnstone
Rosina

SAT. 21 JUNE

Management　(Miss Griffiths)　C/BJ
Rosina

MON. 23 JUNE

The Desert Island　　C/FF
The Romance of an Hour　b: Mr. & Mrs. & Miss
The Irishman's Vagaries

FRI. 27 JUNE

The Inconstant　　　b: Part of the Office
The Jew and the Doctor　　Keepers

SAT. 28 JUNE

The Castle Spectre　　C/BJ
The Romance of an Hour　b: The Office
　　　　　　　　　　　　Keepers

MON. 30 JUNE

The School for Scandal　b: Charlton & Mrs.
St. David's Day　　　　Didier

FRI. 4 JULY

The Mountaineers　　b: Part of the Office
The Padlock　　　　　Keepers

SAT. 5 JULY

Speed the Plough　　　C/BJ
Blue Beard

MON. 7 JULY

The Red Cross Knights　b: Mr. & Mrs. Edwin
The Country Girl

FRI. 11 JULY

The West Indian　　　b: Glassington, Tebay
Arthur and Emmeline　　Jnr., Mr. & Mrs.
　　　　　　　　　　　　J. Smith, Widow
　　　　　　　　　　　　Paul

SAT. 12 JULY

She Stoops to Conquer　(Blisset)　C/G, BJ, BC
　　　　　　　　　　　　b: Theatrical
　　　　　　　　　　　　Benevolent Fund

MON. 21 JULY

Speed the Plough　　C/FF
Blue Beard

End of Season

Season 1800/01

Company

Mr: Bartley, Campbell, Charlton, Cherry, Cunningham, D'Arcy, Dimond, Doyle, Edwin, Elliston, Eyre, Faulkner, Parsons, Phillips, Richardson, Rowbotham, Sedley, J. Smith, W. Smith, Stanwix, Taylor, Tebay, Turner, Williams.

Mrs: Charlton, Cherry, Cooke, Didier, Edwin, Johnstone, Phillips, Samuels, Sedley, J. Smith, Taylor.

Miss: Cherry, F. Cherry, Daniels, Every, Grimani, Smith, J. Smith, S. Smith, Summers, Tebay, S. Tebay.

Master: Charlton, Quick.

Treasurer: Smith   *Box Book-keeper:* Bartley (Bath), Sanders (Bristol).   *Prompter:* Glassington

1800

MON. 29 SEPT.
Speed the Plough   C/FF
Blue Beard

WED. 1 OCT.
The Stranger   PB/R
The Padlock

FRI. 3 OCT.
Hamlet   PB/R
Rosina

SAT. 4 OCT.
Speed the Plough   C/BJ, BC
The Prize

MON. 6 OCT.
Romeo and Juliet   PB/R
Edgar and Emmeline

WED. 8 OCT.
The West Indian   PB/R, U
Blue Beard

FRI. 10 OCT.
Macbeth   (Faulkner)   PB/R
The Romp

SAT. 11 OCT.
Hamlet   C/BJ, BC
The Padlock

MON. 13 OCT.
Lovers' Vows   (Faulkner)   P/BR
The Jew and the Doctor

WED. 15 OCT.
Pizarro   PB/R
Ways and Means

FRI. 17 OCT.
The Heir at Law   PB/R
Blue Beard

SAT. 18 OCT.
The Stranger   C/BJ, BC
Rosina

MON. 20 OCT.
The School for Scandal   PB/R
Robin Hood

WED. 22 OCT.
The Point of Honour   PB/R
Two Strings to your Bow
Blue Beard

SAT. 25 OCT.
Lovers' Vows   C/BJ, BC
Ways and Means

MON. 27 OCT.
Pizarro   PB/R
My Grandmother

WED. 29 OCT.
The Point of Honour   PB/R
The Sultan
The Quaker

FRI. 31 OCT.
The Wonder   PB/R
Obi

SAT. 1 NOV.
The Point of Honour   C/BJ, BC
Blue Beard

MON. 3 NOV.
The Birthday   C/FF
Obi

WED. 5 NOV.
The Point of Honour   PB/TC
Obi

THURS. 6 NOV.
?
Obi

FRI. 7 NOV.

?
Obi

SAT. 8 NOV.

Speed the Plough   C/BJ
Ways and Means

MON. 10 NOV.

The Point of Honour   C/FF
Obi

TUES. 11 NOV.

The Point of Honour   C/BJ
Blue Beard

THURS. 13 NOV.

The Castle Spectre

SAT. 15 NOV.

The School for Scandal

MON. 17 NOV.

Speed the Plough   C/FF
The Children in the Wood

TUES. 18 NOV.

The Wonder   C/BJ
Obi

THURS. 20 NOV.

The Will   C/BC
Obi

SAT. 22 NOV.

Pizarro
The Spoil'd Child

MON. 24 NOV.

The Mountaineers   C/FF
The Midnight Hour

TUES. 25 NOV.

The Point of Honour   C/BJ, G
Obi

THURS. 27 NOV.

Isabella   C/BC
Obi

SAT. 29 NOV.

The Heir-at-Law
No Song, No Supper

MON. 1 DEC.

Pizarro   C/FF
The Spoiled Child

TUES. 2 DEC.

The Iron Chest   C/BJ
The Old Maid

THURS. 4 DEC.

Romeo and Juliet   C/BC, BJ
The Romp

SAT. 6 DEC.

The Stranger
Lock and Key

MON. 8 DEC.

The Iron Chest   (Faulkner) PB/R
Catherine and Petruchio

TUES. 9 DEC.

Speed the Plough   C/BJ
Obi

THURS. 11 DEC.

The Secret   C/G
No Song, No Supper

FRI. 12 DEC.

Every One has His Fault   C/BJ, G
The Midnight Hour   b: Widow and
                                   children of the
                                   late Rowbotham

SAT. 13 DEC.

The Iron Chest   C/G
Catherine and Petruchio

MON. 15 DEC.

The Secret   C/FF
Obi

TUES. 16 DEC.

The Secret
Blue Beard

THURS. 18 DEC.

Pizarro   C/G
The Old Maid

SAT. 20 DEC.

The Point of Honour
Obi

MON. 22 DEC.

The Duenna   (Incledon)   C/FF
Rosina

TUES. 23 DEC.

The Duenna   (Incledon)   C/BJ
Rosina

FRI. 26 DEC.

The Beggar's Opera (Incledon) C/BJ, BC
Obi

SAT. 27 DEC.

Love in a Village (Incledon)   C/BC
Lock and Key

MON. 29 DEC.
The Beggar's Opera (Incledon) C/FF
The Lying Valet

TUES. 30 DEC.
Lionel and Clarissa (Incledon) C/BJ

1801

THURS. 1 JAN.
The Stranger   (Incledon)   C/BJ
Robin Hood

FRI. 2 JAN.
The Castle of Andalusia   b: Incledon
The Quaker

SAT. 3 JAN.
Inkle and Yarico   C/G
The Farmer

MON. 5 JAN.
Love in a Village (Incledon)   C/FF
The Waterman

TUES. 6 JAN.
The Duenna   (Incledon)   C/BJ
The Flitch of Bacon

THURS. 8 JAN.
The Beggar's Opera (Incledon) C/BJ, BC
Obi

SAT. 10 JAN.
The Castle Spectre (Incledon)   C/BJ
The Waterman

MON. 12 JAN.
The Castle of Andalusia (Incledon) PB/R, C/FF
The Farmer

TUES. 13 JAN.
Lovers' Vows (Incledon)   C/BJ
The Highland Reel

THURS. 15 JAN.
The Point of Honour   (Incledon)   C/BJ, BC
The Turnpike Gate

FRI. 16 JAN.
Lionel and Clarissa   PB/R b: Incledon
The Turnpike Gate

SAT. 17 JAN.
The Heir-at-Law   C/G

TUES. 20 JAN.
Speed the Plough   C/BJ
Blue Beard

WED. 21 JAN.
The Point of Honour   PB/R, C/FF
Obi

THURS. 22 JAN.
Life   C/G
Edgar and Emmeline

SAT. 24 JAN.
Pizarro

MON. 25 JAN.
Life   PB/R, C/FF
The Lyar

TUES. 27 JAN.
The Provok'd Husband   C/BJ
Paul and Virginia

THURS. 29 JAN.
Life   C/BJ
The Doctor and the Apothecary

SAT. 31 JAN.
The Suspicious Husband   C/G
Paul and Virginia

MON. 2 FEB.
Life   PB/R, C/FF
The Doctor and the Apothecary

TUES. 3 FEB.
Richard III   C/BJ
Paul and Virginia

THURS. 5 FEB.
Life
Follies of a Day

SAT. 7 FEB.
The Way to Get Married   C/G
Paul and Virginia

MON. 9 FEB.
The Provok'd Husband   PB/R, C/FF
Paul and Virginia

TUES. 10 FEB.
King John   C/BJ, G
The Deserter

THURS. 12 FEB.
The Stranger
Paul and Virginia

SAT. 14 FEB.
Life
The Lyar

MON. 16 FEB.
Richard III   PB/R, C/FF
Paul and Virginia

TUES. 17 FEB.
Speed the Plough   C/BJ
Paul and Virginia

THURS. 19 FEB.
The Point of Honour
Blue Beard

SAT. 21 FEB.
Pizarro

MON. 23 FEB.
Speed the Plough   PB/R, C/FF
Blue Beard

TUES. 24 FEB.
Life   C/BJ
Paul and Virginia

THURS. 26 FEB.
The Stranger
Paul and Virginia

SAT. 28 FEB.
The School for Prejudice   C/BJ, G
The Review

MON. 2 MAR.
Life   PB/R, C/FF
Paul and Virginia

TUES. 3 MAR.
Rule a Wife and Have a Wife C/BJ, BC, G
The Spanish Barber   b: Dimond

THURS. 5 MAR.
The Rivals   C/BJ, G
The Spoil'd Child   b: Mr. & Mrs. Didier

SAT. 7 MAR.
Know Your Own Mind   C/BJ, BC, G b: Cherry
The Poor Soldier

MON. 9 MAR.
Pizarro   PB/R, C/FF
The Review

TUES. 10 MAR.
Henry V   C/BJ, BC, G
Bath Theatricals   b: Elliston
False and True

SAT. 12 MAR.
A Word to the Wise   C/BJ, BC, G b: Eyre
Arthur and Emmeline

SAT. 14 MAR.
A Bold Stroke for a Husband C/BJ, BC, G
Comus   b: Mrs. Johnstone

MON. 16 MAR.
The School for Prejudice   PB/R, C/FF
Paul and Virginia

TUES. 17 MAR.
Cheap Living   C/BJ, BC, G
The Cooper   b: Mrs. Edwin
The Maid of the Oaks

THURS. 19 MAR.
Wild Oats   C/BJ, BC b: Charlton
St. David's Day

SAT. 21 MAR.
Richard III   C/BJ, BC
Bath Theatricals   b: Richardson
The Old Maid

MON. 23 MAR.
Life   PB/R, C/FF
Paul and Virginia

TUES. 24 MAR.
The Surrender of Calais   C/BJ, b: Miss Daniels
The Veteran Tar

THURS. 26 MAR.
The Earl of Warwick   C/BJ, BC, G
The Recruiting Sergeant   b: Smith and Bartley
The True-Born Irishman

SAT. 28 MAR.
The Maid of the Mill   C/BJ, BC, b: Taylor
The Farmhouse

MON. 6 APRIL
Jane Shore   (Mrs. Siddons) PB/R, C/FF
The Prize

TUES. 7 APRIL
Jane Shore   (Mrs. Siddons) C/BJ, BC, G
The Spoiled Child

THURS. 9 APRIL
Douglas   (Mrs. Siddons) C/BJ, BC, G
The Children in the Wood

FRI. 10 APRIL
Isabella   (Mrs. Siddons)   PB/R
The Children in the Wood

SAT. 11 APRIL
The Mourning Bride (Mrs. Siddons)   C/BJ, BC, G
Lock and Key

MON. 13 APRIL
The Mourning Bride (Mrs. Siddons) PB/R, C/FF
Lock and Key

TUES. 14 APRIL
The Gamester (Mrs. Siddons) C/BJ, G
My Grandmother

THURS. 16 APRIL
Isabella   (Mrs. Siddons)   C/BJ, BC, G
The Romp

FRI. 17 APRIL
Macbeth   C/BJ, BC, G
Animal Magnetism   b: Mrs. Siddons

SAT. 18 APRIL
King John   (Mrs. Siddons)   C/BJ, BC, G

MON. 20 APRIL
The Stranger   (Mrs. Siddons)   PB/R
The Poor Soldier

TUES. 21 APRIL
The Stranger (Mrs. Siddons)   C/BJ, BC, G
Rosina

THURS. 23 APRIL
Life
Paul and Virginia

SAT. 25 APRIL
The Distress'd Mother   C/BJ, BC, G
The Deaf Lover   b: Miss Grimani

MON. 27 APRIL
Speed the Plough   PB/R, C/FF
Paul and Virginia

TUES. 28 APRIL
Speed the Plough   C/BJ
My Grandmother

THURS. 30 APRIL
The Poor Gentleman   C/G
Paul and Virginia

SAT. 2 MAY
Lovers' Vows   C/BC
No Song, No Supper

MON. 4 MAY
The Poor Gentleman   PB/R, C/FF
The Review

TUES. 5 MAY
Zorinski   C/BJ, G
The Purse   b: Miss Taylor
The Wedding Day

THURS. 7 MAY
The Road to Ruin   C/BJ, G
The Castle of Sorrento   b: Cunningham

SAT. 9 MAY
The Fugitive   C/G
Tristram Shandy   b: Mr. & Mrs. Sedley

MON. 11 MAY
Pizarro   PB/R, C/FF
The Wedding Day

TUES. 12 MAY
The Chapter of Accidents   C/BJ, G b: Edwin
The Shipwreck

THURS. 14 MAY
The Point of Honour   C/BJ b: Glassington
Paul and Virginia

SAT. 16 MAY
The Pilgrim   C/G, Miss Smith
The Young Actress
All the World's a Stage

MON. 18 MAY
The Poor Gentleman   PB/R, C/FF
Blue Beard

TUES. 19 MAY
The Will   C/BJ,
The Register Office   b: Mrs. Charlton &
Cymon   Miss Every

THURS. 21 MAY
Speed the Plough   b: Miss Summers
The Pannel

SAT. 23 MAY
The Castle Spectre
The Review

MON. 25 MAY
Lovers' Vows   PB/R, C/FF
Paul and Virginia

TUES. 26 MAY
The School for Prejudice   b: Stanwix
Blue Beard

THURS. 28 MAY
The Inconstant   C/G b: Smith & Barltey
Paul and Virginia

SAT. 30 MAY
A Cure for the Heartache
Lock and Key

MON. 1 JUNE
The Stranger   PB/R b: Mrs. Johnstone
The Shipwreck

WED. 3 JUNE
The Inconstant   PB/R
Animal Magnetism   b: Part of Office
                Keepers

FRI. 5 JUNE
The Castle Spectre   PB/R
The Rival Soldiers   b: Part of Office
                Keepers

SAT. 6 JUNE
The Poor Gentleman   C/BJ, BC
The Rival Soldiers

MON. 8 JUNE
As You Like It   PB/R
Peeping Tom of Coventry   b: Mr. & Mrs. Cherry

WED. 10 JUNE
The Surrender of Calais   PB/R, TC
Arthur and Emmeline   b: Eyre & Miss Every

FRI. 12 JUNE
The School for Scandal   PB/R
The Jew and the Doctor   b: Sanders (Box
                                 -keeper)

SAT. 13 JUNE
Life   C/BJ, BC
The Flitch of Bacon

MON. 15 JUNE
Cheap Living   PB/R
The Purse   b: Mr. & Mrs. Edwin
Maid of the Oaks

WED. 17 JUNE
Zorinski   PB/R
Sylvester Daggerwood   b: Widow Rowbotham
The Pannel   & Family; Miss
                               Summers

FRI. 19 JUNE
Life   PB/R
The Padlock   b: Bath & Bristol
                               Theatrical Fund

SAT. 20 JUNE
The Poor Gentleman   C/BJ
Blue Beard

MON. 22 JUNE
The Dramatist   PB/R b: Elliston
The Dear Lover

WED. 24 JUNE
The Point of Honour   PB/R, C/FF
The Recruiting Sergeant   b: Parsons, Stanwix,
Edgar and Emmeline   Campbell, Tebay,
                               Doyle, Mr. &
                               Mrs. J. Smith,
                               Williams

FRI. 26 JUNE
A Cure for the Heartache PB/R
The Midnight Hour   b: Part of the Office
                               keepers

MON. 29 JUNE
Cymbeline   C/FF, PB/R b: Dimond
The Seaside Story

WED. 1 JULY
King Lear   PB/R
Paul and Virginia   b: Taylor & Smigh
                               (Treasurer)

FRI. 3 JULY
Speed the Plough   PB/R
The Spanish Barber   b: Charlton & Mrs.
                               Didier

MON. 6 JULY
The Poor Gentleman   PB/R
Obi

End of Season

Season 1801/02

Company

Mr: Campbell, Chalmers, Chambers, Charlton, Cherry, Cunningham, Doyle, Edwin, Egan, Elliston, Evans, Eyre, Parsons, Sedley, J. Smith, Smith, Stanwix, Talbot, Taylor, J. Tebay, Williams.

Mrs: Charlton, Cunningham, Didier, Edwin, Egan, Johnstone, Summers, Taylor.

Miss: Cherry, Daniels, Every, Godfrey, Grimani, Quick, Smith, S. Smith, Summers, Tebay, S. Tebay.

Master: Rowbotham, T. Tebay.

Treasurer: Smith *Box book-keepers:* Bartley (Bath), Sanders (Bristol) *Prompter:* Williamson

1801

MON. 31 AUG.
Douglas (Mrs. Siddons) PB/R, C/FF
The Deserter

WED. 2 SEPT.
Jane Shore (Mrs. Siddons) PB/R
The Lyar

FRI. 4 SEPT.
Isabella (Mrs. Siddons) PB/R
The Midnight Hour

SAT. 5 SEPT.
Jane Shore (Mrs. Siddons) C/BJ, BC, G
The Lyar

MON. 7 SEPT.
Macbeth (Mrs. Siddons) PB/R
No Song, No Supper

WED. 9 SEPT.
The Distressed Mother (Mrs. Siddons) PB/R
Obi

FRI. 11 SEPT.
The Mourning Bride (Mrs. Siddons) PB/R
The Citizen

SAT. 12 SEPT.
Macbeth (Mrs. Siddons) C/BJ, BC, G
The Citizen

MON. 14 SEPT.
Pizarro (Mrs. Siddons) PB/R, C/FF
The Sultan

WED. 16 SEPT.
Tamerlane (Mrs. Siddons) PB/R
The Flitch of Bacon

FRI. 18 SEPT.
King John PB/R b: Mrs. Siddons
Catherine and Petruchio

SAT. 19 SEPT.
Pizarro C/BJ, BC, G
(Mrs. Siddons' additional night)
The Sultan

MON. 21 SEPT.
The Poor Gentleman PB/R, C/FF
The Farm House

WED. 23 SEPT.
Lovers' Vows PB/R
The Poor Soldier

FRI. 25 SEPT.
The Suspicious Husband PB/R
Paul and Virginia

SAT. 26 SEPT.
The Way to Get Married (Miss Biggs) C/BJ, BC
The Old Maid

MON. 28 SEPT.
The Way to Get Married PB/R, C/FF
The Old Maid

WED. 30 SEPT.
Speed the Plough PB/R
Blue Beard

FRI. 2 OCT.
Deaf and Dumb PB/R
The Quaker

SAT. 3 OCT.
Speed the Plough C/BJ, BC
The Poor Soldier

MON. 5 OCT.
Deaf and Dumb PB/R, U, C/FF
The Spoil'd Child

WED. 7 OCT.
A Cure for the Heartache PB/R
Paul and Virginia

FRI. 9 OCT.
The Castle Spectre   PB/R
The Waterman

SAT. 10 OCT.
Deaf and Dumb
The Spoil'd Child

MON. 12 OCT.
Bristol Performance (Probably cancelled)

WED. 14 OCT.
Deaf and Dumb   PB/R
The Seaside Story

FRI. 16 OCT.
Life   PB/R
Blue Beard

SAT. 17 OCT.
Deaf and Dumb   C/BJ
The Seaside Story

MON. 19 OCT.
Othello   PB/R, C/FF
The Romp

WED. 21 OCT
The Heir-at-Law   PB/R
Paul and Virginia

FRI. 23 OCT.
Othello   PB/R
The Gypsy Prince

SAT. 24 OCT.
A Cure for the Heartache   C/BJ, BC
The Gipsy Prince

MON. 25 OCT.
Deaf and Dumb   PB/R, C/FF
The Gypsy Prince

TUES. 27 OCT.
The Poor Gentleman   C/BJ
The Gipsy Prince

THURS. 29 OCT.
Deaf and Dumb
Obi

SAT. 31 OCT.
Life
Paul and Virginia

MON. 2 NOV.
The Point of Honour   PB/R, C/FF
Sylvester Daggerwood
The Prize

TUES. 3 NOV.
The Stranger   C/BJ
The Prize

THURS. 5 NOV.
King Lear   C/BJ, BC, G
Animal Magnetism

SAT. 7 NOV.
Lovers' Vows
The Adopted Child

MON. 9 NOV.
King Lear   C/FF
The Adopted Child

TUES. 10 NOV.
The Point of Honour   C/BJ
Sylvester Daggerwood
Blue Beard

THURS. 12 NOV.
The Castle Spectre
The Deserter

SAT. 14 NOV.
The Stranger   C/BJ
Lock and Key

MON. 16 NOV.
The Stranger   PB/R, C/FF
Lock and Key

TUES. 17 NOV.
Deaf and Dumb   C/BJ
The Children in the Wood

THURS. 19 NOV.
Speed the Plough
My Grandmother

SAT. 21 NOV.
Folly as it Flies
The Flitch of Bacon

MON. 23 NOV.
Folly as it Flies   PB/R, C/FF
The Children in the Wood

TUES. 24 NOV..
Folly as it Flies   C/BJ
No Song No Supper

THURS. 26 NOV.
Pizarro
The Romp

SAT. 28 NOV.
The Heir-at-Law
Paul and Virginia

MON. 30 NOV.
Folly as it Flies   PB/R, C/FF
The Doctor and Apothecary

TUES. 1 DEC.
Cyrus, Prince of Medea   C/BJ, G
The Seaside Story

THURS. 3 DEC.
Deaf and Dumb   C/G
The Seaside Story

SAT. 5 DEC.
Folly as it Flies
Blue Beard

MON. 7 DEC.
Cymon   PB/R, C/FF
The Seaside Story

TUES. 8 DEC.
Life   C/BJ
Paul and Virginia

THURS. 10 DEC.
Richard III   C/BJ, BC
The Black Forest

SAT. 12 DEC.
The Suspicious Husband   C/BJ, BC, G
Catherine and Petruchio

MON. 14 DEC.
Deaf and Dumb   PB/R
Paul and Virginia

TUES. 15 DEC.
Everyone has his Fault   C/BJ
The Doctor and the Apothecary

THURS. 17 DEC.
Richard III   (G.F.Cooke) C/BC, G
Animal Magnetism

FRI. 18 DEC.
Richard III (G.F.Cooke)   PB/R
Animal Magnetism

SAT. 19 DEC.
Othello   (G.F.Cooke)   C/BH, BC, G
The Old Maid

MON. 21 DEC.
(Probably cancelled because of Cooke's illness)

TUES. 22 DEC.
The Merchant of Venice (G.F.Cooke)   C/BJ, BC, G
Love a la Mode

WED. 23 DEC.
Richard III   (G.F.Cooke)   C/G

SAT. 26 DEC.
The Poor Gentleman
Obi

MON. 28 DEC.
Pizarro   C/FF
The Black Forest

TUES. 29 DEC.
Folly as it Flies   C/BJ
The Recruiting Sergeant
The Black Forest

WED. 30 DEC.
George Barnwell
The Spoil'd Child
The Devil to Pay

THURS. 31 DEC.
Richard Coeur de Lion
The Purse
The Children in the Wood

1802

SAT. 2 JAN.
Speed the Plough
Lock and Key

MON. 4 JAN.
Folly as it Flies   C/FF
Paul and Virginia

TUES. 5 JAN.
Richard Coeur de Lion   C/BJ
The Jew and the Doctor
The Virgin Unmask'd

THURS. 7 JAN.
Richard Coeur de Lion
The Cooper
The Farmhouse

SAT. 9 JAN.
The Jew   C/BH
Paul and Virginia

MON. 11 JAN.
Richard Coeur de Lion   PB/R, C/FF
The Purse
The Children in the Wood

TUES. 12 JAN.
Othello   C/BJ, BJ
The Black Forest

THURS. 14 JAN.
Pizarro
No Song no Supper

SAT. 16 JAN.
The Mountaineers
Blue Beard

TUES. 19 JAN.
Percy   C/BJ
Paul and Virginia

WED. 20 JAN.
The Jew   PB/R, C/FF
Richard Coeur de Lion

THURS. 21 JAN.
Speed the Plough
Comus

SAT. 23 JAN.
Deaf and Dumb
Richard Coeur de Lion

MON. 25 JAN.
The Mountaineers   PB/R, C/FF
Comus

TUES. 26 JAN.
Folly as it Flies   C/BJ
Richard Coeur de Lion

THURS. 28 JAN.
The Birthday
The Padlock

FRI. 29 JAN.
The Will

SAT. 30 JAN.
(No performance – anniversary of Charles I
        martyrdom)

MON. 1 FEB.
The Poor Gentleman   PB/R
No Song no Supper
Throughout February presentations of
The Phantasmagoria at both Theatres

TUES. 2 FEB.
A Cure for the Heartache   C/BJ
The Quaker

THURS. 4 FEB.
The Point of Honour

SAT. 6 FEB.
Life
Richard Coeur de Lion

MON. 8 FEB.
The Point of Honour   PB/R, C/FF
Paul and Virginia

TUES. 9 FEB.
The Dramatist   C/BJ
The Agreeable Surprise

THURS. 11 FEB.
The Mountaineers
Richard Coeur de Lion

SAT. 13 FEB.
Lovers' Vows
Paul and Virginia

MON. 15 FEB.
The Birthday   PB/R, C/FF
Richard Coeur de Lion

TUES. 16 FEB.
Deaf and Dumb   C/BJ
The Children in the Wood

THURS. 18 FEB.
Alfonso King of Castile
The Devil to Pay

SAT. 20 FEB.
The Jew
The Farmer

MON. 22 FEB.
Alfonso, King of Castile   PB/R, C/FF
The Devil to Pay

TUES. 23 FEB.
Alfonso, King of Castile   C/BJ
Robin Hood

THURS. 25 FEB.
Folly as it Flies
The Agreeable Surprise

SAT. 27 FEB.
Life
Blue Beard

MON. 1 MAR.
Alfonso, King of Castile   PB/R, C/FF
The Black Forest

TUES. 2 MAR.
Wild Oats   C/BJ
Comus

THURS. 4 MAR.
Alfonso, King of Castile   C/G
Fortune's Frolics

SAT. 6 MAR.
Speed the Plough
Paul and Virginia

MON. 8 MAR.
Folly as it Flies   PB/R
Blue Beard

TUES. 9 MAR.
Oroonoko   C/G b: Elliston
The Son-in-Law
The Jew and the Doctor

THURS. 11 MAR.
Secrets Worth Knowing   PB/BM b: Mrs. Didier
The Deaf Lover

SAT. 13 MAR.
The School for Scandal   C/BC b: Cherry
False and True

MON. 15 MAR.
Oroonoko   PB/R
The Romp
The Agreeable Surprise

TUES. 16 MAR.
The Haunted Tower   PB/R b: Miss Daniels
Sylvester Daggerwood
Lock and Key

THURS. 18 MAR.
Red Cross Knights   C/G b: Eyre
The Irish Mimic

SAT. 20 MAR.
Cymbeline   C/BJ, BC
Arthur and Emmeline   b: Mrs. Johnstone

MON. 22 MAR.
The School for Scandal   C/FF
The Son-in-Law

TUES. 23 MAR.
The West Indian   C/G, BJ b: Taylor
Rosina
Abednego's Trip to Bath

THURS. 25 MAR.
The Castle Spectre   C/BJ, BC
Sylvester Daggerwood   b: Charlton
Midas

SAT. 27 MAR.
The Surrender of Calais   C/BJ b: Sedley
The Country Girl

MON. 29 MAR.
Alfonso, King of Castile   PB/R
Rosina

TUES. 30 MAR.
Which is the Man?   C/BJ, G, BH, BC
Of Age Tomorrow   b: Mrs. Edwin

THURS. 1 APR.
The Poor Gentleman   b: Smith & Bartley
Selima and Azor

SAT. 3 APR.
The Child of Nature   C/BJ, BC
Catherine and Petruchio   b: Miss Grimani
Abednego's Trip to Bath

MON. 5 APR.
The Merchant of Venice (G.F.Cooke)   PB/R
Love a la Mode

TUES. 6 APR.
The Merchant of Venice (G.F.Cooke)   C/BJ, BC, G
Love a La Mode

THURS. 8 APR.
Alfonso, King of Castile
Paul and Virginia

SAT. 10 APR.
The Heir-at-Law
Sadek and Kalasrade

MON. 19 APR.
Deaf and Dumb   PB/R
Blue Beard

TUES. 20 APR.
Folly as it Flies   C/G
Sadek and Kalasrade

THURS. 22 APR.
Lovers' Vows
Sadak and Kalasrade

SAT. 24 APR.
Deaf and Dumb
Richard Coeur de Lion

MON. 26 APR.
Wild Oats   PB/R
Of Age Tomorrow

TUES. 27 APR.
Life
Sadak and Kalasrade

THURS. 29 APR.
Speed the Plough
Of Age Tomorrow

SAT. 1 MAY
The Stranger   C/G
Sadak and Kalasrade

MON. 3 MAY
The Stranger   PB/R
Of Age Tomorrow

TUES. 4 MAY
As You Like It   C/G, BJ
Sadak and Kalasrade

THURS. 6 MAY
The Wheel of Fortune
Sadak and Kalasrade

SAT. 8 MAY

Pizarro
The Quaker

MON. 10 MAY

Life
Sadak and Kalasrade

TUES. 11 MAY

The Young Quaker   b: Edwin
The Two Misers

THURS. 13 MAY

The Suspicious Husband   C/BJ, G b: Miss Smith &
Of Age Tomorrow   widow of late
                             Rowbotham

SAT. 15 MAY

Wives as they Were   C/G b: Cunningham
A Bold Stroke for a Wife

MON. 17 MAY

As You Like It   PB/R
Sadak and Kalasrade

TUES. 18 MAY

The Wonder   C/G b: Mrs. Taylor
Paul and Virginia

THURS. 20 MAY

The Woodman   b: Mrs. Charlton &
Of Age Tomorrow   Miss Every

SAT. 22 MAY

Henry IV   (Blisset)   C/BJ, BC, BH, G
The Doctor and the Apothecary   b: Egan

MON. 24 MAY

Folly as it Flies   PB/R
Sadak and Kalasrade

TUES. 25 MAY

Much Ado About Nothing   C/BJ, BH, G
Rosina   b: Miss Summers

THURS. 27 MAY

A Word to the Wise   b: Smith/Bartley
The Review

SAT. 29 MAY

The Maid of the Mill (Blisset) C/BC, BJ, G
The Poor Soldier

MON. 31 MAY

Macbeth   PB/R b: Johnstone
Of Age Tomorrow

WED. 2 JUNE

Henry IV (i)   PB/R b: Cunningham
The Poor Soldier

THURS. 3 JUNE

The West Indian   PB/R b: Part of the
The Devil to Pay   Office Keepers

SAT. 5 JUNE

The Stranger   C/BJ, BH, b: Part of
The Deaf Lover   Office Keepers

MON. 7 JUNE

The Beaux Stratagem   PB/R b: Mr., Mrs. &
Robin Hood   Miss Cherry

WED. 9 JUNE

The Castle Spectre   PB/R b: Part of the
No Song, No Supper   Office Keepers

FRI. 11 JUNE

Speed the Plough   PB/R b: Sanders
The Deaf Lover

SAT. 12 JUNE

Richard III (G.F. Cooke)   C/BJ, BC, G b: Bath &
Of Age Tomorrow   Bristol Theatrical Fund

MON. 14 JUNE

The Haunted Tower   PB/R b: Charlton &
The Spoil'd Child   Mrs. Didier
Sylvester Daggerwood

WED. 16 JUNE

The Jealous Wife   PB/R b: Williamson
Lock and Key

FRI. 18 JUNE

Romeo and Juliet   PB/R b: Miss Grimani
The Deserter

SAT. 19 JUNE

The Poor Gentleman   C/BJ, BC b: Part of
     (Mrs. St. John)   Office Keepers etc.
Robin Hood

MON. 21 JUNE

Which is the Man?   PB/R b: Mr. & Mrs.
Paul and Virginia   Edwin

WED. 23 JUNE

The Rivals   PB/R b: Eyre &
The Hottentots   Miss Every

FRI. 25 JUNE

The Wonder   b: Miss Summers,
Rosina   Stanwix, Doyle

SAT. 26 JUNE

Deaf and Dumb (Mrs. St. John)   C/BJ, BC b: Office
No Song, No Supper   Keepers etc.

MON. 28 JUNE

The Poor Gentleman   PB/R b: Elliston
Of Age Tomorrow

WED. 30 JUNE		**SAT. 3 JULY**
The Suspicious Husband	PB/R b: Mr. &	Folly as it Flies C/BJ b: Part of Office
The Farmer	Mrs. Taylor	Paul and Virginia Keepers etc.

FRI. 2 JULY

The Mountaineers   PB/R b: Smith &

The Young Actress   Miss Smith

Midas

MON. 5 JULY

Folly as it Flies

Sadak and Kalasrade

End of Season

Season 1802/03

Company

Mr: Bennett, Bew, Charlton, Cunningham, Doyle, Edwin, Egan, Elliston, Evans, Eyre, Langdon, Lee, Lovegrove, Parsons, Sedley, Smith, J. Smith, Taylor, Tebay, Webber, Williams.

Mrs: Charlton, Cunningham, Didier, Edwin, Egan, Johnstone, Lee, Sedley, Taylor.

Miss: Daniels, Every, Grimani, Owen, J. Quick, Smith, S. Smith, Summers, Tebay, S. Tebay.

Master: T. Tebay, Quick

Treasurer: Smith   *Box Book-keeper:* Bartley (Bath), Sanders (Bristol)

1802

MON. 30 AUG.

Richard III   (G.F.Cooke) PB/BM, R

The Romp

WED. 1 SEPT.

Macbeth   (G.F.Cooke) PB/R

The Devil to Pay

FRI. 3 SEPT.

Alfonso, King of Castile (G.F.Cooke) PB/R

Love a la Mode

SAT. 4 SEPT.

Alfonso King of Castile   C/BJ, BC

Love a La Mode

MON. 6 SEPT.

The Man of the World (G.F.Cooke) PB/BM, R

Of Age Tomorrow

WED. 8 SEPT.

Tamerlane the Great (G.F.Cooke) PB/BM, R

Lock and Key

THURS. 9 SEPT.

The Man of the World (G.F.Cooke) C/BJ, BC

Of Age Tomorrow

FRI. 10 SEPT.

The Man of the World (G.F.Cooke) PB/BM, R

The Deaf Lover

SAT. 11 SEPT.

Tamerlane the Great (G.F.Cooke) C/BC, BJ

MON. 13 SEPT.

Richard III (G.F.Cooke)   PB/BM, R

Catherine and Petruchio

WED. 15 SEPT.

The Castle Spectre   PB/BM, R

The Farmer

FRI. 17 SEPT.

The School for Scandal   PB/R

The Agreeable Surprise

SAT. 18 SEPT.

The Cabinet   C/BJ, BC

The Jew and the Doctor

MON. 20 SEPT.

The Cabinet   PB/R

The Jew and the Doctor

WED. 22 SEPT.

The Cabinet   PB/BM, R

Of Age Tomorrow

FRI. 24 SEPT.

The Haunted Tower (Sga. Storace) PB/R

The Midnight Hour

SAT. 25 SEPT.

The Haunted Tower (Sga. Storace) C/BJ, BC

The Agreeable Surprise

MON. 27 SEPT.

The Mountaineers (Sga. Storace) PB/R

No Song, No Supper

WED. 29 SEPT.
The Maid of the Mill   (Sga. Storace) PB/R
My Grandmother

FRI. 1 OCT.
The Cabinet   (Sga. Storace) PB/R
The Follies of a Day

SAT. 2 OCT.
The Cabinet (Sga. Storace) C/BJ, BC, G
The Midnight Hour

MON. 4 OCT.
The Surrender of Calais (Sga. Storace) PB/R
My Grandmother

WED. 6 OCT.
The Duenna (Sga. Storace) PB/R
The Prize

THURS. 7 OCT.
No Song, No Supper   C/BJ, BC, G
My Grandmother   b: Sga. Storace
The Prize

FRI. 8 OCT.
The West Indian   PB/R
The Deserter   b: Office-keepers

MON. 11 OCT.
Pizarro   PB/R
The Black Forest

WED. 13 OCT.
The Phantasmagoria
presented at both theatres until 23 Oct.
Speed the Plough   PB/R
Of Age Tomorrow

FRI. 15 OCT.
The Point of Honour   PB/R
Sadak and Kalasrade

SAT. 16 OCT.
Othello
The Black Forest

MON. 18 OCT.
Hamlet   PB/BM, R
Paul and Virginia

WED. 20 OCT.
Deaf and Dumb   PB/BM, R
The Padlock

FRI. 22 OCT.
George Barnwell   PB/BM, R
Blue Beard

SAT. 23 OCT.
Folly as It Flies   PB/BM, C/BJ
Of Age Tomorrow

TUES. 26 OCT.
Speed the Plough   PB/BM, Ba, C/BJ
Paul and Virginia

WED. 27 OCT.
Folly as it Flies
The Sixty-Third Letter

THURS. 28 OCT.
Hamlet   PB/BM, C/BC
The Devil to Pay

SAT. 30 OCT.
The Castle Spectre   PB/BM
The Sixty-Third Letter

MON. 1 NOV.
Hamlet   PB/R
The Sixty-Third Letter

TUES. 2 NOV.
She Stoops to Conquer (Blisset) PB/BM, Ba, C/BJ, G
Richard Coeur de Lion

THURS. 4 NOV.
The Heir-at-Law (Blisset)   PB/BM
The Sixty-Third Letter

SAT. 6 NOV.
The West Indian

MON. 8 NOV.
She Stoops to Conquer (Blisset) PB/R
Sadak and Kalasrade

TUES. 9 NOV.
Hamlet   PB/BM, C/BJ, G
Two Strings to Your Bow

THURS. 11 NOV.
The Stranger   PB/BM
Sadak and Kalasrade

SAT. 13 NOV.
Lovers' Vows (Blisset) PB/BM, C/BC, BJ
Follies of a Day

MON. 15 NOV.
Henry IV (i)   (S. Kemble) PB/R
The Waterman

TUES. 16 NOV.
Henry IV (i)   (S. Kemble)   C/BJ, BC, G
The Waterman

THURS. 18 NOV.
Henry IV (i)   (S. Kemble) PB/BM, C/BJ, BC, G
The Citizen

SAT. 20 NOV.
A Cure for the Heartache (Blisset) PB/BM, Ba, C/BC
Paul and Virginia

MON. 22 NOV.
The Merry Wives of Windsor   PB/R
The Citizen   (S. Kemble)

TUES. 23 NOV.
The Merry Wives of Windsor   PB/BM, Ba, C/BJ, G
(S. Kemble)
The Quaker

THURS. 25 NOV.
The Castle Spectre   PB/BM, C/BJ, BC
The Recruiting Sergeant
The Purse

SAT. 27 NOV.
Much Ado About Nothing   (Blisset)   C/BJ, BC, G
Who's The Dupe?

MON. 29 NOV.
The Heir-at-Law   (Blisset)   PB/R
Blue Beard

TUES. 30 NOV.
The Cabinet   PB/BM, Ba, C/BJ
Of Age Tomorrow

THURS. 2 DEC.
The Way to get Married   (Blisset)   PB/BM, Ba, C/BJ, BC
Sadak and Kalasrade

SAT. 4 DEC.
Delays and Blunders   PB/BM, Ba, C/G
Lock and Key

MON. 6 DEC.
Delays and Blunders   PB/R
Paul and Virginia

TUES. 7 DEC.
Henry IV (i)   (Blisset) PB/BM, C/BJ, BC, G
The Children in the Wood

THURS. 9 DEC.
Delays and Blunders   PB/BM
Blue Beard

SAT. 11 DEC.
The Mountaineers   PB/BM, Ba
Richard Coeur de Lion

MON. 13 DEC.
Delays and Blunders   PB/R
The Children in the Wood

TUES. 14 DEC.
The Heir at Law   (Blisset)   PB/BM, C/BJ
Sadak and Kalasrade

THURS. 16 DEC.
Speed the Plough   PB/BM
Midas

SAT. 18 DEC.
The Poor Gentleman
Comus

MON. 20 DEC.
Much Ado About Nothing   (Blisset) PB/R
Who's the Dupe?

TUES. 21 DEC.
Everyone has His Fault   (Blisset)   PB/BM, C/BJ, G
Bon Ton

THURS. 23 DEC.
Love in a Village   (Blisset)   PB/BM, C/BJ, BC
Paul and Virginia

MON. 27 DEC.
Pizarro   PB/R
Midas

TUES. 28 DEC.
Macbeth   PB/BM, C/BJ
Blue Beard

WED. 29 DEC.
George Barnwell   PB/BM, C/G
Sadak and Kalasrade

THURS. 30 DEC.
A Cure for the Heartache   (Blisset)   PB/BM, C/BJ, G
The Children in the Wood

FRI. 31 DEC.
Othello   PB/BM
The Old Maid

1803

SAT. 1 JAN.
The Provok'd Husband   (Blisset)   C/G
Who's the Dupe?

MON. 3 JAN.
The Provok'd Husband   (Blisset)   C/FF
Bon Ton

TUES. 4 JAN.
Delays and Blunders   PB/BM, C/BJ
Of Age Tomorrow

FROM 4 JAN.–12 FEB.
Richer performs on the
Tight Rope at both Theatres

WED. 5 JAN.
Point of Honour   PB/BM
Sadak and Kalasrade

THURS. 6 JAN.
Hamlet   PB/BM
The Devil to Pay

SAT. 8 JAN.
The Battle of Hexham   PB/BM
Blue Beard

MON. 10 JAN.
The Battle of Hexham   PB/R, C/FF
Comus

TUES. 11 JAN.
The Maid of the Mill   PB/BM, C/BJ, G
The Drummer   b: Blisset

THURS. 13 JAN.
Pizarro   PB/BM, Ba
Ways and Means

FRI. 14 JAN.
Merchant of Venice (Foote) PB/BM, C/BJ, BC, G
Sadak and Kalasrade

SAT. 15 JAN.
The Stranger   PB/BM, Ba
Paul and Virginia

MON. 17 JAN.
Henry IV (i)   (Blisset)   PB/R, C/FF
The Black Forest

TUES. 18 JAN.
The Will   PB/BM, C/BJ
Richard Coeur de Lion

THURS. 20 JAN.
Folly as It Flies   PB/BM
A Tale of Mystery

FRI. 21 JAN.
King Lear   PB/BM, C/G
The Black Forest

SAT. 22 JAN.
Delays and Blunders   PB/BM, Ba
A Tale of Mystery

MON. 24 JAN.
The Stranger   PB/R, C/FF
Ways and Means

TUES. 25 JAN.
Deaf and Dumb   PB/BM, Ba, C/BJ
Robin Hood

THURS. 27 JAN.
The Mountaineers   PB/BM
A Tale of Mystery

FRI. 28 JAN.
Lovers' Vows   PB/BM
Sadak and Kalasrade

SAT. 29 JAN.
The Jew   PB/BM
A Tale of Mystery

MON. 31 JAN.
The Will   PB/BM, R, C/FF
Robin Hood

TUES. 1 FEB.
The Cabinet   PB/BM, Ba, C/BJ
Follies of a Day

THURS. 3 FEB.
The Surrender of Calais   PB/BM, C/G
A Tale of Mystery

FRI. 4 FEB.
Rule a Wife and Have a Wife PB/BM
The Midnight Hour

SAT. 5 FEB.
Wild Oats
Richard Coeur de Lion

MON. 7 FEB.
Wild Oats   PB/R, C/FF
A Tale of Mystery

TUES. 8 FEB.
Pizarro   PB/BM, C/BJ
The Farmer

THURS. 10 FEB.
Inkle and Yarico   PB/BM
Blue Beard

FRI. 11 FEB.
Life   PB/BM
A Tale of Mystery

SAT. 12 FEB.
Much Ado About Nothing   PB/BM
Paul and Virginia

MON. 14 FEB.
Life   PB/R, C/FF
A Tale of Mystery

TUES. 15 FEB.
The Poor Gentleman   PB/BM, Ba, C/BJ
Lock and Key

THURS. 17 FEB.
Battle of Hexham   PB/BM, C/G
A Tale of Mystery

FRI. 18 FEB.
Othello   PB/BM
The Guardian

SAT. 19 FEB.
The Suspicious Husband   PB/BM
A Tale of Mystery

MON. 21 FEB.
The Woodman   (Incledon) PB/R, C/FF
The Guardian

TUES. 22 FEB.

The Woodman   (Incledon)   PB/BM, C/BJ, BC
The Waterman

THURS. 24 FEB.

Love in a Village   (Incledon)   PB/BM, Ba, C/BC, G
Paul and Virginia   (Blisset)

SAT. 26 FEB.

The Beggar's Opera   (Incledon)   PB/BM, C/BC
Two Strings to Your Bow

MON. 28 FEB.

Love in a Village   (Incledon)   PB/R, C/FF
Paul and Virginia

TUES. 1 MAR.

The Duenna   PB/BM, C/BJ
Rosina   b: Incledon

THURS. 3 MAR.

The Wonder   PB/BM, Ba, C/BJ
A Tale of Mystery
(Band of Bohemian Silver Miners)

SAT. 5 MAR.

Speed the Plough   PB/BM
A Tale of Mystery (Silver Miners Band)

MON. 7 MAR.

The Wonder   PB/R, C/FF
A Tale of Mystery

TUES. 8 MAR.

The Three and Deuce   C/BJ, G b: Elliston
The Spoil'd Child
The Agreeable Surprise

THURS. 10 MAR.

The Road to Ruin   b: Mrs. Didier
Sylvester Daggerwood
My Grandmother

SAT. 12 MAR.

Such Things Are   PB/BM, C/G
The Recruiting Sergeant
Of Age Tomorrow   b: Mrs. Johnstone

MON. 14 MAR.

Speed the Plough   PB/R
Of Age Tomorrow

TUES. 15 MAR.

Know Your Own Mind   C/BJ, BC, G
Il Bondocani   b: Mrs. Edwin

THURS. 17 MAR.

The Jealous Wife   (Blisset) C/BJ, BC, G b: Eyre
Arthur and Emmeline

SAT. 19 MAR.

The Busybody   (Blisset)   C/BJ, BC, G b: Sedley
Catherine and Petruchio

MON. 21 MAR.

Such Things Are   PB/R
A Tale of Mystery

TUES. 22 MAR.

Lionel and Clarissa   PB/BM, C/BJ, BC
The Deaf Lover   b: Taylor

THURS. 24 MAR.

She Wou'd and She Wou'd   PB/BM, C/BJ, G, BC
   Not   (Blisset)
Blue Beard

FRI. 25 MAR.

The School of Reform   PB/TC

SAT. 26 MAR.

The Rivals   (Blisset)   PB/BM, C/BJ, BC, G
The Prisoner at Large   b: Cunningham

MON. 28 MAR.

Pizarro
Two Strings to Your Bow

TUES. 29 MAR.

The Cabinet   PB/BM, C/BJ
The Prize   b: Miss Daniels

THURS. 31 MAR.

The Heiress   PB/BM, C/BJ, G
The Son-in-Law   b: Smith & Bartley

SAT. 2 APRIL

The Belle's Stratagem   PB/BM, Ba, C/BJ, BC, G
Edgar and Emmeline   b: Miss Grimani

MON. 11 APRIL

Macbeth   (J.P.Kemble)   PB/R
The Devil to Pay

TUES. 12 APRIL

Macbeth   (Kemble)   PB/BM, C/BJ, BC, G
The Devil to Pay

THURS. 14 APRIL

Hamlet   (Kemble)   PB/BM, C/BJ, BC, G
The Deserter

SAT. 16 APRIL

The Stranger   (Kemble)   PB/BM, C/BJ, BC, G
Midas

MON. 18 APRIL

Pizarro   (Kemble)   PB/R, C/FF
Two Strings to Your Bow

TUES. 19 APRIL
The Merchant of Venice   (Kemble) PB/BM, C/BJ, G
Of Age Tomorrow

THURS. 21 APRIL
Pizarro   (Kemble)   PB/BM, C/BJ, BC, G
The Romp

SAT. 23 APRIL
The Wheel of Fortune   (Kemble) PB/BM, Ba,
Paul and Virginia   C/BJ, BC, G

MON. 25 APRIL
Hamlet   (Kemble)   PB/R, C/FF
The Prisoner at Large

TUES. 26 APRIL
The Distress'd Mother (Kemble) PB/BM, C/BJ,
The Prisoner at Large   BC, G

THURS. 28 APRIL
Hamlet   (Kemble)   PB/BM, C/BJ, BC, G
Ways and Means

FRI. 29 APRIL
Much Ado About Nothing   PB/R, C/BJ, BC, G
Paul and Virginia   b: Elliston

SAT. 30 APRIL
Rule a Wife and Have a Wife PB/BM, C/BJ, BC, G
   (Kemble)
A Tale of Mystery

MON. 2 MAY
The Distress'd Mother (Kemble) PB/BM, R, C/FF
Lock and Key

TUES. 3 MAY
The Mountaineers (Kemble) PB/BM, Ba, C/BJ,
Lock and Key   BC, G

THURS. 5 MAY
Pizarro (Kemble)   PB/BM, C/BJ, BC, G
The Ghost

SAT. 7 MAY
Richard III   (Kemble)   PB/BM, C/BJ, BC, G
The Children in the Wood

MON. 9 MAY
Richard III   (Kemble)   PB/BM, R
The Ghost

TUES. 10 MAY
Hamlet   (Kemble)   PB/BM, C/BJ, BC, G
No Song, No Supper

THURS. 12 MAY
John Bull   PB/BM, C/G
The Padlock

SAT. 14 MAY
John Bull   PB/BM, Ba
A Tale of Mystery

MON. 16 MAY
John Bull   PB/R, C/FF
The Children in the Wood

TUES. 17 MAY
The Poor Gentleman   C/BJ, G b: Edwin
The Agreeable Surprise
The Rival Soldiers

THURS. 19 MAY
Which is the Man?   C/BJ
High Life Below Stairs   b: Miss Smith,
                            Mrs. Rowbotham

SAT. 21 MAY
The School for Scandal   C/BC b: Bennett
The Shipwreck

MON. 23 MAY
John Bull   PB/R
The Rival Soldiers

TUES. 24 MAY
Chapter of Accidents   PB/BM, C/BJ, BC, G
Poor Vulcan   b: Mrs. Taylor

THURS. 26 MAY
The West Indian   PB/BM, Ba, C/BJ, BC
The Quaker   b: Mrs. Charlton &
                                Miss Every

SAT. 28 MAY
Venice Preserv'd   PB/BM, C/BJ
The Adopted Child   b: Mr. & Mrs. Egan

MON. 30 MAY
John Bull   PB/R, C/FF
A Tale of Mistery

TUES. 31 MAY
The Way to Keep Him   PB/BM, Ba, C/BJ
The Poor Soldier   BC, G
                            b: Miss Summers

THURS. 2 JUNE
Lovers' Vows   PB/BM, Ba, C/BJ, BC
The Gentle Shepherd   G
                           b: Smith & Bartley

SAT. 4 JUNE
Speed the Plough   PB/BM
A Tale of Mystery

MON. 6 JUNE
John Bull
The Black Forest

TUES. 7 JUNE

The Battle of Hexham   PB/BM
Paul and Virginia

THURS. 9 JUNE

The Castle Spectre
The Black Forest

SAT. 11 JUNE

Life   PB/BM
Sadak and Kalasrade

MON. 13 JUNE

Lovers' Vows (Mingaud)   b: Eyre
The Poor Soldier

WED. 15 JUNE

The Battle of Hexham   b: Part of Office
High Life below Stairs   Keepers

FRI. 17 JUNE

The Poor Gentleman   b: Part of Office
Paul and Virginia   Keepers

SAT. 18 JUNE

John Bull
A Tale of Mystery

MON. 20 JUNE

The Way to Keep Him   PB/R
Poor Vulcan   b: Mr. & Mrs. Taylor

WED. 22 JUNE

Look before you Leap   PB/R
The Child of Nature   b: Bath & Bristol
Blue Beard   Theatrical Fund

FRI. 24 JUNE

The Belle's Stratagem   PB/R b: Sanders
Rosina

SAT. 25 JUNE

The Mountaineers   C/BJ, BC, G
Rosina

MON. 27 JUNE

The Heir-at-Law   PB/R
Of Age Tomorrow   b: Charlton & Mrs.
    Didier

WED. 29 JUNE

Speed the Plough   b: Doyle, Langdon,
Look Before you Leap   Master Quick,
    Miss Summers,
    Miss Owen

FRI. 1 JULY

The Castle Spectre   PB/R
The Agreeable Surprise   b: Part of Office
    Keepers

SAT. 2 JULY

John Bull   C/G
Look Before you Leap

MON. 4 JULY

Know your Own Mind   b: Mr. & Mrs. Edwin
Sylvester Daggerwood
Edgar and Emmeline

WED. 6 JULY

Venice Preserv'd   PB/R b: Mrs. Johnstone
The Recruiting Sergeant
The Gentle Shepherd

SAT. 9 JULY

John Bull
Look Before you Leap

MON. 11 JULY

John Bull
A Tale of Mystery

End of Season

Season 1803−04

Company

Mr: Bennet, Branton, Charlton, Cunningham, Doyle, Edwin, Egan, Egerton, Elliston, Evans, Eyre, Griffin, Langdon, Lodge, Lovegrove, Parsons, Sedley, J. Smith Jnr., Taylor, Tebay, Thompson, Watson Jnr., Webber, Woodley.

Mrs: Charlton, Cunningham, Didier, Edwin, Egan, Johnstone, Second, Sedley, Taylor, Tebay.

Miss: Daniels, Every, Fisher, Loder, Owen, J. Quick, Smith, Summers, Tebay, S. Tebay.

Master: Quick

Treasurer: Smith   *Box Book-keepers:* Bartley, (Bath), Sanders (Bristol)   *Prompter:* Woodley

1803

MON. 19 SEPT.
Speed the Plough   C/FF, PB/R
Of Age Tomorrow   b: Military Fund

WED. 21 SEPT.
The Mountaineers
A Tale of Mystery

FRI. 23 SEPT.
George Barnwell   PB/R
The Recruiting Sergeant
No Song, No Supper

SAT. 24 SEPT.
Pizarro   C/BJ
No Song, No Supper   b: Bath Military Fund

MON. 26 SEPT.
John Bull   PB/R
The Quaker

WED. 28 SEPT.
The Way to Keep Him   PB/R
The Poor Soldier

FRI. 30 SEPT.
Macbeth   PB/R
The Volunteers

SAT. 1 OCT.
John Bull   C/BJ
Of Age Tomorrow

MON. 3 OCT.
Pizarro
Look Before you Leap

WED. 5 OCT.
The Stranger

FRI. 7 OCT.
The Battle of Hexham

SAT. 8 OCT.
The Mountaineers   C/BJ, BC, G
Britons Strike Home

MON. 10 OCT.
The Voice of Nature   C/FF
The Recruiting Sergeant
The Midnight Hour

FRI. 14 OCT.
The Heir-at-Law   (St. Pierre & Mme
Of Age Tomorrow   Volange − dancers)

SAT. 15 OCT.
The Voice of Nature   C/BJ, BC
The Millers   (St. Pierre & Mme
The Poor Soldier   Volange)

MON. 17 OCT.
The Voice of Nature   C/FF
  (St. Pierre & Mme. Volange)
The Birthday

TUES. 18 OCT.
Henry V
The Children in the Wood

FRI. 21 OCT.
Lovers' Vows
Love Laughs at Locksmiths

SAT. 22 OCT.
The Stranger   C/BJ, BC
The Millers   (St. Pierre & Mme
Love Laughs at Locksmiths   Volange)

MON. 24 OCT.
Hamlet
  (St. Pierre & Mme. Volange)
The Romp

FRI. 28 OCT.
The Maid of Bristol
The Voice of Nature

SAT. 29 OCT.
The Voice of Nature   C/BJ, BC
    (St. Pierre & Mme. Volange)
Love Laughs at Locksmiths
Rose and Colin
The Recruiting Sergeant

MON. 31 OCT.
Cymbeline
    (St. Pierre & Mme. Volange)
My Grandmother

WED. 2 NOV.
The Wonder   b: St. Pierre & Mme.
Paul and Virginia   Volange

SAT. 5 NOV.
The Maid of Bristol   C/BJ, BC
    (St. Pierre & Mme. Volange)
Rose and Colin
Love Laughs at Locksmiths

MON. 7 NOV.
John Bull
    (St. Pierre & Mme. Volange)
Ways and Means

TUES. 8 NOV.
John Bull   C/BJ
Ways and Means

THURS. 10 NOV.
The Way to Get Married   C/BJ, BC
    (St. Pierre & Mme. Volange)
Paul and Virginia
Rose and Colin

SAT. 12 NOV.
The Wonder   C/BJ
The Deserter of Naples   b: St. Pierre & Mme.
A Spanish Ballet   Volange

MON. 14 NOV.
Pizarro
The Deserter of Naples

TUES. 15 NOV.
The Deserter of Naples   C/BJ
    (St. Pierre & Mme Volange last night)
The West Indian
The Error of the Moment

THURS. 17 NOV.
The Birthday   C/G
The Maid of Bristol
Love Laughs at Locksmiths

SAT. 19 NOV.
Lovers' Vows
A Tale of Mystery

MON. 21 NOV.
The Wheel of Fortune
Love Laughs at Locksmiths

TUES. 22 NOV.
The Haunted Tower (Mrs. Second)   C/BJ, BC
Blue Beard

THURS. 24 NOV.
Hamlet   C/BJ, BC
The Children in the Wood

SAT. 26 NOV.
Love in a Village (Mrs. Second) C/BC
The Midnight Hour

MON. 28 NOV.
The Haunted Tower (Mrs. Second) C/FF
A Tale of Mystery

TUES. 29 NOV.
The Marriage Promise   C/BJ
Love Laughs at Locksmiths

THURS. 1 DEC.
The Beggar's Opera   (Mrs. Second) C/BC, BJ
Of Age Tomorrow

SAT. 3 DEC.
The Marriage Promise   PB/Ba, C/BC, G
The Highland Reel

MON. 5 DEC.
The Marriage Promise   C/FF
The Highland Reel

TUES. 6 DEC.
The Duenna   (Mrs. Second) PB/Ba, C/BJ, BC
The Deaf Lover

THURS. 8 DEC.
Pizarro
Bon Ton

SAT. 10 DEC.
The Marriage Promise
The Camp

MON. 12 DEC.
Love in a Village (Mrs. Second)C/FF
Bon Ton

TUES. 13 DEC.
John Bull   C/BJ
Of Age Tomorrow

THURS. 15 DEC.
Macbeth   C/BJ, BC, G
The Camp

SAT. 17 DEC.

The Birthday   PB/Ba
The Voice of Nature
A Tale of Mystery

MON. 19 DEC.

The Marriage Promise   C/FF
The Camp

TUES. 20 DEC.

The Maid of the Mill   PB/Ba, C/BJ
The Jew and the Doctor   b: Mrs. Second

THURS. 22 DEC.

The Castle Spectre   PB/Ba
Rosina

FRI. 23 DEC.

The Marriage Promise   PB/Ba
Blue Beard

MON. 26 DEC.

John Bull   C/FF
The Devil to Pay

TUES. 27 DEC.

John Bull   PB/Ba, C/BJ
A Tale of Mystery

WED. 28 DEC.

John Bull
Raising the Wind

THURS. 29 DEC.

Wild Oats   C/G
Raising the Wind

FRI. 30 DEC.

George Barnwell   PB/Ba, C/BC
Love Laughs at Locksmiths

SAT. 31 DEC.

The Wheel of Fortune
Raising the Wind

1804

MON. 2 JAN.

Wild Oats   C/FF
Love Laughs at Locksmiths

TUES. 3 JAN.

Hamlet   C/BJ
The Devil to Pay

THURS. 5 JAN.

The Heir-at-Law   PB/Ba
The Highland Reel

FRI. 6 JAN.

George Barnwell
Love Laughs at Locksmiths

SAT. 7 JAN.

The Hero of the North   PB/Ba
The Ghost

MON. 9 JAN.

Othello   C/FF
Raising the Wind

TUES. 10 JAN.

The Hero of the North   C/BJ
Raising the Wind

THURS. 12 JAN.

The Hero of the North   PB/Ba, C/BC
My Grandmother

FRI. 13 JAN.

Othello
Ways and Means

SAT. 14 JAN.

The Mountaineers   PB/Ba
Blue Beard

MON. 16 JAN.

The Hero of the North   C/FF
Raising the Wind

TUES. 17 JAN.

The Suspicious Husband   PB/Ba, C/BJ
Love Laughs at Locksmiths

THURS. 19 JAN.

The Hero of the North   PB/Ba, C/BC
Raising the Wind

FRI. 20 JAN.

The Stranger   PB/Ba
Of Age Tomorrow

SAT. 21 JAN.

The Marriage Promise   PB/Ba
Lock and Key

MON. 23 JAN.

The Hero of the North   C/FF
Raising the Wind

TUES. 24 JAN.

Henry V   PB/F, C/BJ
The Children in the Wood

THURS. 26 JAN.

The Hero of the North   PB/Ba
Raising the Wind

SAT. 28 JAN.

A Cure for the Heartache   PB/Ba
Sadak and Kalasrade

TUES. 31 JAN.

John Bull   PB/Ba, C/BJ
The Doctor and the
Apothecary

WED. 1 FEB.

The Suspicious Husband   C/FF
Love Laughs at Locksmiths

THURS. 2 FEB.

The Hero of the North   PB/Ba
The Spoiled Child

SAT. 4 FEB.

She Stoops to Conquer   PB/Ba
Love Laughs at Locksmiths

MON. 6 FEB.

The Hero of the North   C/FF
Of Age Tomorrow

TUES. 7 FEB.

Richard III   (Caulfield)   PB/Ba, C/BJ, G
The Romp

THURS. 9 FEB.

Know your Own Mind   PB/Ba
Sadak and Kalasrade

SAT. 11 FEB.

The Hero of the North   PB/Ba
Raising the Wind

MON. 13 FEB.

A Cure for the Heartache
Raising the Wind

TUES. 14 FEB.

Hamlet   (Caulfield)   PB/Ba, C/BJ, G
The Rival Soldiers

THURS. 16 FEB.

The Mountaineers (Caulfield) PB/Ba, C/BJ, BC
A Tale of Mystery

SAT. 18 FEB.

The Hero of the North   PB/Ba
Raising the Wind

MON. 20 FEB.

Hamlet   C/FF
The Lyar

TUES. 21 FEB.

Henry V   PB/Ba, C/BJ, BC
Love Laughs at Locksmiths

THURS. 23 FEB.

Henry IV (i)   (Partly Amateur Cast) PB/Ba, C/BJ,
The Review   BC, G
                             b: Bath & Bristol
                             Theatrical Fund

SAT. 25 FEB.

The Suspicious Husband   (Caulfield)   C/BC, G
The Lyar

MON. 27 FEB.

The Mountainers   C/FF
Paul and Virginia

TUES. 28 FEB.

The West Indian   C/BJ, BC, G
Sylvester Daggerwood   b: Elliston
Love Laughs at Locksmiths

THURS. 1 MAR.

The Dramatist   C/BC, BJ b: Mrs.Didier
Paul and Virginia
Abednego's Trip to Bath

SAT. 3 MAR.

Pizarro   C/BJ, BC, G
Peeping Tom   b: Mrs. Johnstone

MON. 5 MAR.

Henry IV (i) (partly amateur cast)   C/FF
The Children in the Wood

TUES. 6 MAR.

The Provok'd Husband (Blisset) C/BJ, Bc, G
Blue Beard   b: Mrs. Edwin

THURS. 8 MAR.

Lionel and Clarissa   C/BC, BJ, G b: Eyre
A Tale of Terror

SAT. 10 MAR.

Henry VIII   C/BJ, BC, G
The Spanish Barber   b: Sedley

MON. 12 MAR.

The Hero of the North   C/FF
Raising the Wind

TUES. 13 MAR.

The Belle's Stratagem   C/BJ, BC
Robin Hood   b: Miss Daniels

THURS. 15 MAR.

Much Ado About Nothing   PB/Ba, C/BJ, BC
The Cabinet   b: Charlton (Deputy
                                Manager)

SAT. 17 MAR.

The Heir-at-Law   C/BJ, BC, G
St. Patrick's Day   b: Bennett

MON. 19 MAR.

King John   C/FF
The Review

TUES. 20 MAR.
The Poor Gentleman   C/BJ, BC
The Country Girl   b: Mr. & Mrs.Taylor

THURS. 22 MAR.
Life   C/BC, BJ
Of Age Tomorrow   b: Smith & Bartley

FRI. 23 MAR.
Henry IV (i) (Partly Amateur Cast) C/BG b: Infirmary
The Prize

SAT. 24 MAR.
The Road to Ruin   C/BJ, BC, G
The Deserter of Naples   b: Egerton

MON. 2 APR.
Love in a Village   (Incledon) C/FF
Ways and Means

TUES. 3 APR.
Love in a Village   (Incledon) PB/Ba, C/BC, BJ
Ways and Means

THURS. 5 APR.
The Beggars Opera   C/BC, BJ
  (Incledon)
The Jew and the Doctor

SAT. 7 APR.
Rosina   (Incledon)   PB/Ba, C/BC
The Voice of Nature
The Waterman

MON. 9 APRIL
The Beggar's Opera (Incledon) C/FF
A Tale of Mystery

TUES. 10 APRIL
The Duenna   C/BC, BJ b: Incledon
Paul and Virginia

THURS. 12 APRIL
King John   PB/Ba, C/BC
The Review

SAT. 14 APRIL
Speed the Plough   PB/Ba
Love Laughs at Locksmiths

MON. 16 APRIL
The Wife of Two Husbands PB/R, C/FF
Love Laughs at Locksmiths

TUES. 17 APRIL
The Wife of Two Husbands   PB/Ba, C/BJ
Sadak and Kalasrade

THURS. 19 APRIL
The School for Scandal   PB/Ba, C/BC, BJ
The Padlock

SAT. 21 APRIL
The Wife of Two Husbands   C/G
Of Age Tomorrow

MON. 23 APRIL
The Hero of the North   PB/R, C/FF
Raising the Wind

TUES. 24 APRIL
Know Your Own Mind   PB/Ba, C/BJ
The Doctor and the Apothecary

THURS. 26 APRIL
Othello
A Tale of Mystery

SAT. 28 APRIL
The Hero of the North   C/G
Raising the Wind

MON. 30 APRIL
The Wheel of Fortune   PB/TC, C/FF
Of Age Tomorrow

TUES. 1 MAY
Macbeth   C/BJ, BC
Lock and Key

THURS. 3 MAY
The Wheel of Fortune   C/BJ, BC
Blue Beard

FRI. 4 MAY
The Stranger   b: Elliston
The Lyar

SAT. 5 MAY
The Stranger   C/BJ, BC
Love Laughs at Locksmiths

MON. 7 MAY
Speed the Plough   PB/R, C/FF
Sylvester Daggerwood
Love Laughs at Locksmiths

TUES. 8 MAY
Pizarro   C/BJ, G
The Lyar

THURS. 10 MAY
The Soldier's Daughter   C/BJ, BC, G
Rosina

MON. 14 MAY
The Soldier's Daughter   C/FF
Paul and Virginia

TUES. 15 MAY
John Bull   C/BJ b: Edwin
The Old Maid

THURS. 17 MAY	
The Jealous Wife	C/BC
A Tale of Mystery	b: Miss Smith &
	Mrs. Rowbotham

SAT. 19 MAY	
Cymbeline	PB/Ba, C/BC, BJ
Paul and Virginia	b: Miss Fisher

MON. 21 MAY	
The Soldier's Daughter	PB/R, C/FF
The Farmhouse	

TUES. 22 MAY	
The Clandestine Marriage	PB/Ba, C/BJ, BC, G
The Wedding Day	b: Lovegrove &
	Miss Loder

THURS. 24 MAY	
The Will　(Blisset)	PB/Ba, C/BJ, BC, G
Who's the Dupe?	b: Mrs. Charlton

SAT. 26 MAY	
As You Like It	C/BC b: Woodley
The Agreeable Surprise	

MON. 28 MAY	
John Bull	PB/R, C/FF
The Wedding Day	

TUES. 29 MAY	
The Rivals	C/BJ, BC b: Evans
The Turnpike Gate	

THURS. 31 MAY	
The Point of Honour	b: Miss Summers &
The Farm House	Webber
The Devil to Pay	

SAT. 2 JUNE	
The Castle Spectre	b: Door keepers etc.
Catherine and Petruchio	

TUES. 5 JUNE	
The Heir-at-Law　(Blisset)	PB/Ba, H, C/BJ, BC, G
A Tale of Mystery	b: Smith & Bartley

WED. 6 JUNE	
A Cure for the Heartache (Blisset)　PB/R, C/FF	
Who's the Dupe?	

THURS. 7 JUNE	
Wild Oats	C/BJ
The Midnight Hour	b: Part of the Office
	Keepers

SAT. 9 JUNE	
The Way to Keep Him	PB/H, C/BJ, BC
The Children in the Wood	b: Part of the Office
	Keepers etc.

MON. 11 JUNE	
The Point of Honour	PB/R
The Child of Nature	b: Eyre & Mrs.
The Rival Soldiers	Johnstone

WED. 13 JUNE	
The Heir-at-Law	b: Part of Office
The Padlock	Keepers

FRI. 15 JUNE	
The Castle Spectre	b: Part of Office
A Tale of Mystery	Keepers

SAT. 16 JUNE	
The Soldier's Daughter	C/BJ
Raising the Wind	

MON. 18 JUNE	
Pizarro	b: Egerton & Bennett
The Farmer	

WED. 20 JUNE	
The Merry Wives of Windsor	b: Mr. & Mrs. Sedley
The Spanish Barber	

FRI. 22 JUNE	
Lovers' Vows	b: Sanders
The Agreeable Surprise	

SAT. 23 JUNE	
Lovers' Vows	C/BJ, BC
The Farmer	

MON. 25 JUNE	
The Clandestine Marriage	PB/R
Inkle and Yarico	b: Charlton &
	Mrs. Didier

WED. 27 JUNE	
Wild Oats	PB/R, C/FF
The Poor Soldier	b: Doyle, Langdon,
	Thompson, Lodge

FRI. 29 JUNE	
The Rivals	PB/R
Of Age Tomorrow	b: Part of Office
	Keepers

SAT. 30 JUNE	
Inkle and Yarico	b: Part of Office
The Voice of Nature	Keepers etc.
The Rival Soldiers	

MON. 2 JULY	
The Will	PB/R
The Deserter of Naples	b: Mr. & Mrs. Edwin

	WED. 4 JULY		MON. 9 JULY	
John Bull	PB/R		*The Soldier's Daughter*	PB/R
Paul and Virginia	b: Smith &		*Raising the Wind*	
	Cunningham			
	FRI. 6 JULY			
Cymbeline	PB/R			
The Prize	b: Lovegrove &			
	Miss Fisher		*End of Season*	

Season 1804–05

Company

Mr: Bateson, Bennett, Caulfield, Charlton, W. Charlton, Cunningham, Doyle, Edwards, Egan, Egerton, Evans, Gattie, Gomery, Herbert, Kelly, Langdon, Lovegrove, Lodge, Magrath, Mallinson, Ridgway, Sedley, Sims, Smith, J. Smith, Tebay, Thompson, Webber, Woodley, Wrench.

Mrs: Charlton, Cunningham, Didier, Egan, Lee, Ridgway (formerly Miss Loder), Sims, Sedley, Windsor, (formerly Miss Daniels), Worthington.

Miss: Chapman, Fisher, Jameson, Loder, Martin, Owen, L. Quick, Smith, Summers, Tebay, S. Tebay.

Master: Cooke, Quick.

Treasurer: Smith.   *Box Book-keepers:* Bartley (Bath), Sanders (Bristol)   *Prompter:* Woodley

1804

MON. 24 SEPT.

The Soldier's Daughter	PB/R
Raising the Wind	

WED. 26 SEPT.

Cymbeline	PB/R
Lock and Key	

FRI. 28 SEPT.

The Castle Spectre	PB/R
The Citizen	

SAT. 29 SEPT.

The Soldier's Daughter	C/BJ, BC, G
Raising the Wind	

MON. 1 OCT.

The Child of Nature	C/FF
The Farm House	
My Grandmother	

WED. 3 OCT.

The Stranger	PB/R
The Rival Soldiers	

In OCT. and NOV.

Richer appears frequently on the
Tight Rope at both Theatres

FRI. 5 OCT.

Henry IV (i)	(S. Kemble)	PB/R
The Padlock		

SAT. 6 OCT.

The Child of Nature	PB/H, C/BJ, BC, G
Lock and Key	

MON. 8 OCT.

The Merry Wives of Windsor (S. Kemble)	PB/R
Paul and Virginia	

WED. 10 OCT.

The Child of Nature	PB/R
The Birthday	

FRI. 12 OCT.

John Bull	(S. Kemble)	PB/R
Of Age Tomorrow		

SAT. 13 OCT.

Henry IV	(S. Kemble)	C/BJ, BC, G
Paul and Virginia		

MON. 15 OCT.
The Merchant of Venice   PB/P, R
No Song, No Supper   b: S. Kemble

WED. 17 OCT.
The Mountaineers   PB/R
The Farmer

FRI. 19 OCT.
The Clandestine Marriage   PB/R, TC
Alonzo and Imogene

SAT. 20 OCT.
The Child of Nature   C/BJ, BC, G
The Mountaineers

MON. 22 OCT.
The West Indian   PB/R
Alonzo and Imogene

WED. 24 OCT.
Romeo and Juliet   PB/R
Alonzo and Imogene

FRI. 26 OCT.
The Will for the Deed   PB/R
The Prize

SAT. 27 OCT.
The Will for the Deed   C/BJ, BC, G
Of Age Tomorrow

MON. 29 OCT.
Pizarro   PB/R
Raising the Wind

WED. 31 OCT.
The Jealous Wife   PB/R
The Will for the Deed

FRI. 2 NOV.
George Barnwell   PB/R
The Rival Soldiers
Alonzo and Imogene

SAT. 3 NOV.
The West Indian   PB/BM, H, C/BJ,
The Rival Soldiers   BC, G

MON. 5 NOV.
Romeo and Juliet   PB/R
Alonzo and Imogene

TUES. 6 NOV.
The Jealous Wife   C/BJ, BC
The Paragraph

THURS. 8 NOV.
Romeo and Juliet   C/BJ, BC, G
The Paragraph

SAT. 10 NOV.
John Bull
Alonzo and Imogene

MON. 12 NOV.
Lover's Vows   PB/R
The Paragraph

TUES. 13 NOV.
Venice Preserv'd (Holman)   PB/BM, C/BJ, BC, G
Alonzo and Imogene

THURS. 15 NOV.
Macbeth   (Holman)   PB/BM, C/BC, G
Alonzo and Imogene

SAT. 17 NOV.
Much Ado About Nothing (Holman) C/BC, G
The Paragraph

MON. 19 NOV.
Venice Preserv'd (Holman)   PB/R
The Paragraph

TUES. 20 NOV.
The Soldier's Daughter   PB/BM, C/BJ
The Will for the Deed

THURS. 22 NOV.
The Earl of Essex   (Holman) PB/BM, C/BC, BJ, G
The Paragraph

SAT. 24 NOV.
The Wonder   PB/H, C/BC, G
Catherine and Petruchio   b: Holman

MON. 26 NOV.
The Earl of Essex   (Holman) PB/R
Rosina

TUES. 27 NOV.
The Blind Bargain   PB/BM, C/BJ, G
Rosina

THURS. 29 NOV.
The Blind Bargain   PB/BM
The Gretna Blacksmith
The Farmer

SAT. 1 DEC.
The Poor Gentleman   PB/BM, C/G
A Tale of Mystery

MON. 3 DEC.
The Blind Bargain   PB/R
A Tale of Mystery

TUES. 4 DEC.
The Blind Bargain   PB/BM, C/BJ
The Gretna Blacksmith
The Paragraph

THURS. 6 DEC.
John Bull   C/BC
The Sultan

SAT. 8 DEC.
The Castle Spectre   PB/BM, C/G
Love Laughs at Locksmiths

MON. 10 DEC.
The Blind Bargain   PB/R
The Paragraph

TUES. 11 DEC.
The Blind Bargain   PB/BM, C/BJ
The Gretna Blacksmith
The Paragraph

THURS. 13 DEC.
The Will   PB/BM, C/G
The Hunter of the Alps

SAT. 15 DEC.
The Belle's Stratagem   PB/BM, C/BC
The Hunter of the Alps

MON. 17 DEC.
The Belle's Stratagem   PB/R
Love Laughs at Locksmiths

TUES. 18 DEC.
Speed the Plough   C/BJ
The Hunter of the Alps

THURS. 20 DEC.
The Blind Bargain   PB/BM, Ba
Love Laughs at Locksmiths

SAT. 22 DEC.
The Heir-at-Law   PB/BM, Ba, C/G
The Hunter of the Alps

WED. 26 DEC.
Jane Shore   PB/BM, C/BJ, G
The Magic of Hope

THURS. 27 DEC.
Jane Shore   PB/R
The Hunter of the Alps

FRI. 28 DEC.
The Blind Bargain   PB/BM
The Magic of Hope

SAT. 29 DEC.
Love in a Village (Incledon)   PB/BM, C/BC, BJ
The Quaker

MON. 31 DEC.
Love in a Village (Incledon)   PB/R, TC
The Quaker

1805

TUES. 1 JAN.
Rosina   (Incledon)   PB/BM, C/BJ
The Child of Nature
The Waterman

WED. 2 JAN.
George Barnwell (Incledon)   PB/BM
The Magic of Hope

THURS. 3 JAN.
Pizarro (Local gentlemen   PB/H
            amateurs performing)
The Minor

FRI. 4 JAN.
The Castle Spectre   PB/BM
The Magic of Hope

SAT. 5 JAN.
The Blind Bargain   PB/Ba
The Magic of Hope

MON. 7 JAN.
The Heir-at-Law   PB/R
The Hunter of the Alps

    Throughout January Richer again
    appears at both Theatres

TUES. 8 JAN.
Pizarro   (Gentlemen amateurs)   PB/BM, C/BJ
The Review

WED. 9 JAN.
The Blind Bargain   PB/BM
The Magic of Hope

THURS. 10 JAN.
The Mountaineers   PB/BM, C/BC
The Paragraph

SAT. 12 JAN.
The Good-Natured Man   PB/BM
The Hunter of the Alps

MON. 14 JAN.
The Blind Bargain   PB/R
The Magic of Hope

TUES. 15 JAN.
Othello   PB/BM, C/BJ
The Hunter of the Alps

WED. 16 JAN.
Othello   PB/R
The Magic of Hope

THURS. 17 JAN.
Lovers' Vows   PB/BM
Love Laughs at Locksmiths

SAT. 19 JAN.
The Inconstant PB/BM
The Gretna Blacksmith
The Hunter of the Alps

MON. 21 JAN.
The Good Natured Man PB/R
The Magic of Hope

TUES. 22 JAN.
The Battle of Hexham PB/BM, C/BJ
Don Juan

WED. 23 JAN.
The Battle of Hexham PB/R
The Magic of Hope

THURS. 24 JAN.
The Blind Bargain PB/BM
Don Juan

SAT. 26 JAN.
The Stranger C/BC, G

MON. 28 JAN.
The Blind Bargain PB/R
The Magic of Hope

TUES. 29 JAN.
The Good Natured Man PB/BM, Ba, C/BJ
The Hunter of the Alps

THURS. 31 JAN.
The Surrender of Calais PB/BM, Ba
Don Juan

SAT. 2 FEB.
The Provok'd Husband PB/BM, Ba, C/G
Of Age Tomorrow

MON. 4 FEB.
The Inconstant PB/R
Don Juan

TUES. 5 FEB.
Laugh when you can PB/Ba, C/BJ, G
The Children in the Wood

THURS. 7 FEB.
The Inconstant PB/BM, Ba, C/G
The Magic of Hope

SAT. 9 FEB.
John Bull PB/Ba, C/BC
Raising the Wind
The Coat and Badge

MON. 11 FEB.
Laugh when you can PB/R
The Children in the Wood

TUES. 12 FEB.
The School of Reform PB/BM, Ba, C/BJ
A Tale of Mystery

THURS. 14 FEB.
The School of Reform PB/BM, Ba
The Magic of Hope

SAT. 16 FEB.
Wild Oats PB/BM, C/G
The Hunter of the Alps
The Coat and Badge

MON. 18 FEB.
The School of Reform PB/R
Don Juan

TUES. 19 FEB.
The School of Reform PB/BM, Ba, C/BJ
The Paragraph

THURS. 21 FEB.
Speed the Plough PB/BM, Ba, C/BC
The Magic of Hope

SAT. 23 FEB.
The Blind Bargain PB/Ba
Robin Hood

MON. 25 FEB.
The School of Reform PB/R
The Hunter of the Alps

TUES. 26 FEB.
The School of Reform PB/BM, Ba, C/BJ
The Magic of Hope

THURS. 28 FEB.
Love in a Village (Incledon) PB/BM, Ba, C/BC, BJ
The Quaker

SAT. 2 MAR.
The Beggar's Opera (Incledon) PB/BM, Ba, C/BC, BJ
Don Juan

MON. 4 MAR.
Lionel and Clarissa (Incledon) PB/R
The Quaker

TUES. 5 MAR.
Lionel and Clarissa (Incledon) PB/BM, Ba, C/BJ
Paul and Virginia

THURS. 7 MAR.
The Duenna (Incledon) PB/BM, Ba, C/BC, BJ
The Poor Soldier

SAT. 9 MAR.
The Castle of Andalusia PB/BM, Ba, C/BC
Lock and Key b: Incledon

MON. 11 MAR.
The Duenna (Incledon)   PB/R
The Poor Soldier

TUES. 12 MAR.
The Jealous Wife   PB/BM, C/BJ, G
The Devil to Pay   b: Miss Smith

THURS. 14 MAR.
The Deserter Daughter (Blisset)   PB/BM, C/BC, BJ
The Old Maid   b: Mrs. Didier

SAT. 16 MAR.
Barbarossa   (Incledon)   PB/BM, C/BJ, BC
The Farmer   b: Charlton — Deputy
                              Manager

MON. 18 MAR.
The Castle of Andalusia   PB/R b: Incledon
Lock and Key

TUES. 19 MAR.
Pizarro   PB/BM, C/BC
The Lie of the Day   b: Egerton

THURS. 21 MAR.
She Wou'd and She Wou'd Not   PB/BM, C/BJ
The Paragraph   b: Lovegrove

SAT. 23 MAR.
A Cure for the Heartache   PB/BM b: Sedley
Edgar and Emmeline

MON. 25 MAR.
The School of Reform   PB/R, TC
The Magic of Hope

TUES. 26 MAR.
The Haunted Tower   PB/BM, C/BJ
The Deaf Lover   b: Mrs. Windsor

THURS. 28 MAR.
Know your own Mind   PB/BM, C/BJ, BC
A Tale of Mystery   b: Miss Fisher

SAT. 30 MAR.
The Belle's Stratagem   C/BC b: Miss Jameson
No Song, No Supper

MON. 1 APRIL
The Honey Moon   PB/R
The Magic of Hope

TUES. 2 APRIL
The Young Quaker   PB/BM b: Mallinson
The Apparition

THURS. 4 APRIL
Douglas (Bartley Jnr., from   PB/Ba, C/BJ, BC
       D.L.)   b: Smith & Bartley
Inkle and Yarico

SAT. 6 APRIL
The Honeymoon   PB/BM, Ba, C/BJ, BC
The Magic of Hope

MON. 15 APRIL
The Honey Moon   PB/R
Of Age Tomorrow

TUES. 16 APRIL
The Honeymoon   PB/Ba, C/BJ
Of Age Tomorrow

THURS. 18 APRIL
The Rivals   PB/BM, C/BJ, BC
The Gretna Blacksmith   b: Gomery
The Magic of Hope

SAT. 20 APRIL
The Blind Bargain   PB/Ba
Love Laughs at Locksmiths

MON. 22 APRIL
The Provok'd Husband   PB/R
Love Laughs at Locksmiths

TUES. 23 APRIL
The Honeymoon   PB/BM, Ba, C/BJ
The Paragraph

THURS. 25 APRIL
The Provok'd Husband (Blisset)   PB/Ba, C/BJ, BC
Who's the Dupe?

SAT. 27 APRIL
The School of Reform   PB/BM, Ba
The Magic of Hope

MON. 29 APRIL
The Honeymoon   PB/R
Inkle and Yarico

TUES. 30 APRIL
To Marry or Not to Marry   PB/BM, Ba, C/BJ
The Will for the Deed

THURS. 2 MAY
The Honeymoon   PB/BM, Ba
The Magic of Hope

SAT. 4 MAY
To Marry or Not to Marry   PB/BM, Ba
The Register Office
The Black Forest

MON. 6 MAY
To Marry or Not to Marry   PB/R
The Paragraph

TUES. 7 MAY
The Soldier's Daughter   PB/BM, C/BJ
The Doctor and the   b: Bennett
   Apothecary

THURS. 9 MAY

The Maid of the Mill (Blisset)   PB/BM, Ba, C/BC
Ways and Means   b: Mr & Mrs.
             Cunningham

SAT. 11 MAY

Everyone has His Fault   PB/BM, C/BC b: Gattie
The Prisoner at Large

MON. 13 MAY

To Marry or Not to Marry   PB/R
The Magic of Hope

TUES. 14 MAY

The Castle Spectre   PB/BM, Ba, C/BJ
The Register Office   b: Herbert
Robin Hood

THURS. 16 MAY

Matrimony   PB/BM b: Evans
The Point of Honour
Hob in the Well

SAT. 18 MAY

Henry IV   (Blisset)   PB/BM, Ba, C/BJ, BC
The Purse   b: Woodley
Miss in Her Teens

MON. 20 MAY

The Honeymoon   PB/R
The Purse
The Black Forest

TUES. 21 MAY

The School for Wives   PB/BM, Ba
The Shipwreck   b: Mr. & Mrs. Egan

THURS. 23 MAY

Barbarossa   C/BJ, BC
False and True   b: Mrs. Charlton

SAT. 25 MAY

Which is the Man?   PB/BM
A Tale of Mystery   b: Miss Summers,
             Webber

MON. 27 MAY

Who wants a Guinea?   PB/R
The Magic of Hope

TUES. 28 MAY

Pizarro   (Blisset)   PB/H, C/BJ, BC
Miss in her Teens   b: Smith & Barltey

THURS. 30 MAY

The Venetian Outlaw   C/BJ, BC
The Sultan   b: Miss Chapman &
Matrimony   Smith

FRI. 31 MAY

To Marry or Not to Marry   PB/BM, Ba, C/BJ
Love Laughs at Locksmiths

MON. 3 JUNE

Who wants a Guinea?   PB/R
Love Laughs at Locksmiths

WED. 5 JUNE

John Bull   b: Office Keepers etc.
The Romp

THURS. 6 JUNE

The School of Reform   C/G
Raising the Wind   b: Office-keepers etc.

SAT. 8 JUNE

Speed the Plough   b: Office-keepers etc
The Review

MON. 10 JUNE

Robin Hood   PB/R b: Mrs. Windsor
Lovers' Quarrels
Paul and Virginia

WED. 12 JUNE

To Marry or not to Marry   PB/R
The Will for the Deed   b: Part of Office
             keepers

FRI. 14 JUNE

John Bull   PB/R
The Review   b: Part of Office-
             keepers

SAT. 15 JUNE

Who Wants a Guinea?   PB/BM, C/G
Lock and Key

MON. 17 JUNE

The Venetian Outlaw   PB/R, b: Egerton
Spanish Dollars
The Village Lawyer

WED. 19 JUNE

Know your own Mind   PB/R b: Miss Fisher
The Midnight Hour

FRI. 21 JUNE

The Will   PB/R.b: Sanders
The Follies of a Day

SAT. 22 JUNE

The Venetian Outlaw   C/BJ
Spanish Dollars
The Village Lawyer

MON. 24 JUNE

The Soldier's Daughter   PB/R b: Miss Smith
Lovers' Quarrels
Three weeks after marriage

WED. 26 JUNE

Douglas   PB/R, b: Miss Jameson
Sylvester Daggerwood
The Romp

FRI. 28 JUNE

The Blind Bargain   PB/R
The Rival Soldiers   b: Part of Office-
                      keepers

SAT. 29 JUNE

The Honeymoon   PB/Ba, C/BJ, G
Three weeks after Marriage

MON. 1 JULY

Barbarossa   PB/R b: Charlton
A House to be Sold

WED. 3 JULY

The Maid of the Mill   PB/R
Edgar and Emmeline   b: Mr. & Mrs.
Miss in her Teens   Sedley

FRI. 5 JULY

Who wants a Guinea?   PB/R
The Register Office   b: Cunningham, Egan,
Raising the Wind   Miss Summers,
                      Miss Chapman

TUES. 9 JULY

The Venetian Outlaw   PB/R b: Lovegrove
Matrimony
The Dead Alive

WED. 10 JULY

Lovers' Vows   PB/R b: Mallinson
It's all a Farce

FRI. 12 JULY

The Point of Honour   PB/R
The Apparition   b: Gattie & Smith
The Prisoner at Large   (Treasurer)

SAT. 13 JULY

Venice Preserv'd   PB/Ba, C/BJ, BC, G
Collins' Ode on the Passions
Matrimony

Last night at Orchard Street and
Miss Smith's farewell to Bath,
on going to Covent Garden. BJ
and BC had announced the play
as Which is the Man?

MON. 15 JULY

The Honeymoon   PB/R
Matrimony

*End of Season – and of the Theatre Royal in
Orchard Street, Bath.*

Index of Actors

Note

Members of the Company are indexed under the seasons during which they appeared. Where a positive identification can be made, forenames are given in clear; where the identification is conjectural, in square brackets. An asterisk indicates a guest appearance. If from dates or type of roles played a name appears to refer to two different people, as yet unidentifiable, this is indicated by a number after the name. Where ladies married, cross references are given to both names.

Actors, singers and dancers are not differentiated unless they were special guests. Though a few members of the Stock Company did specialise, often they had to be all three as occasion required. The chief members of the theatre staff who took regular benefits are recorded, with their function. Some had been actors, though not all. Musicians and other occasionally known theatre staff are not listed.

ADAMS, Mr.
1759–60
ADAMS, Mrs.
1759–60
ADCOCK, Mr. [?William]
1766–67
ADCOCK, Mrs. [?Mary]
1766–67
ADCOCK, Miss [?Sarah Maria]
1766–67
ADCOCK, Miss P.
1766–67
ALLINGHAM, Miss Maria Caroline [later Mrs. RICKETTS, *q.v.*]
1797–98, 1798–99
AMBROSE, Miss
1759–69, 1760–61
AMBROSE, Miss Caroline
1759–60
ARTHUR, Mr. John
1759–60, 1760–61, 1761–62, 1762–63, 1763–64, 1764–65, 1765–66, 1766–67, 1767–68, 1771–72
ARTHUR, Mrs. Grace [formerly Miss READ, *q.v.*]
1771–72, 1772–73

ASHLEY, Mr. John
1786–87, 1787–88, 1788–89, 1789–90, 1790–91, 1791–92, 1792–93, 1793–94, 1794–95
ASKER, Mr.
1798–99
ATKINS, Mr. (1)
1759–60, 1760–61
ATKINS, Mr. (2) William
1792–93, 1793–94, 1794–95, 1795–96, 1796–97, 1797–98, 1798–99
ATKINS, Mrs. Eliza [formerly Miss WARRELL, *q.v.*]
1795–96, 1796–97, 1797–98, 1798–99
ATKINS, Master
1760–61
ATKINS, Miss
1799–1800

BAKER, Mr.
1767–68
BAKER, Mrs.
1760–61, 1761–62
BANNISTER, Mr. [?Charles]
1763–64, 1764–65, 1765–66, 1766–67, 1787–88*

BARNES, Mrs.
1787–88*
BARNETT, Mr.
1777–78
BARNETT, Mrs.
1777–78
BARRETT, Mr.
1770–71, 1771–72, 1772–73
BARRY, Mr.
1757–58
BARTLEY, Mr. (Box Book Keeper, Bath)
1788–89, 1789–90, 1790–91, 1791–92,
1792–93, 1793–94, 1794–95, 1795–96,
1796–97, 1797–98, 1798–99, 1799–1800,
1800–01, 1801–02, 1802–03, 1803–04,
1804–05
BARTLEY, Mr. G.
1803*
BATEMAN, Miss
1794–95, 1795–96, 1796–97
BATES, Mr. Robert
1763–64, 1764–65
BATES, Mr. William
1788–89, 1789–90
BATES, Master [not William above: ?James]
1764–65
BATESON, Mr.
1804–05
BECKHAM, Mr.
1756–57
BELLFIELD, Mrs. Anne [stage name of Mrs Anne
Turner. Variant spellings, e.g. Belfille, Belville]
1778–79, 1782–83*
BENNETT, Mr.
1802–03, 1803–04, 1804–05
BERESFORD, Mrs. [or Berrisford]
1787–88
BERNARD, Mr. John
1784–85, 1785–86, 1786–87
BERNARD, Mrs.
1783–84, 1784–85, 1785–86, 1786–87
BETTERTON, Mr. Thomas William
1794–95, 1795–96, 1796–97
BETTERTON, Master John
1794–95, 1795–96, 1796–97
BETTERTON, Miss Julia
1794–95, 1795–96, 1796–97
BEW, Mr. Charles
1802–03
BIGGS, Mr. James
1794–95, 1795–96, 1796–97, 1797–98
BIGGS, Miss Anne
1793–94, 1794–95, 1795–96, 1796–97,
1801–02*
BIGNAL, Mr.
1786–87
BISHOP, Mr.
1753–54

BISHOP, Mrs.
1750–51, 1751–52, 1752–53, 1753–**54**,
1756–57, 1757–58, 1758–59, 1759–60,
1760–61, 1761–62
BLAKEY, Mr.
1751–52, 1752–53, 1753–54
BLAND, Mr.
1751–52
BLANCHARD, Mr. Thomas
1781–82, 1782–83, 1783–84, 1784–85,
1785–86, 1786–87, 1787–88*
BLANCHARD, Mr. T. [Thomas Jnr.]
1782–83, 1783–84, 1784–85, 1785–86,
1786–87
BLANCHARD, Mrs. [formerly Miss WRIGHT, q.v.]
1786–87
BLAND, Mr.
1751–52
BLISSET, Mr. Francis
1773–74, 1774–75, 1775–76, 1776–77,
1777–78, 1778–79, 1779–80, 1780–81,
1781–82, 1782–83, 1783–84, 1784–85,
1785–86, 1786–87, 1787–88, 1788–89,
1789–90, 1790–91, 1791–92, 1792–93,
1793–94, 1794–95, 1795–96, 1796–97,
1797–98, 1799–1800,* 1802–03,* 1803–04,*
1804–05*
BLISSET, Mr. Francis White (Jnr.)
1791–92, 1792–93
BLOOMFIELD, Mr.
1787–88, 1788–89, 1789–90, 1790–91
BONNOR, Mr. Charles
1777–78, 1778–79, 1779–80, 1780–81,
1781–82, 1782–83, 1783–84
BOOTH, Mr.
1762–63
BRANTON, Mr.
1803–04
BRETT, Mr. William
1773–74, 1774–75, 1775–76, 1776–77,
1777–78, 1778–79, 1780–81, 1781–82
BRETT, Mrs. Hannah
1774–75, 1775–76, 1776–77, 1777–78,
1778–79, 1780–81, 1781–82, 1790–91,
1791–92
BRETT, Master William
1780–81, 1781–82
BRETT, Miss Frances
1789–90, 1790–91, 1791–92
BRISTOW, Mr.
1786–87, 1787–88, 1789–90
BRODERICK, Master
1780–81
BROOKES, Mr.
1750–51, 1751–52, 1752–53, 1753–54,
1754–55, 1755–56, 1756–57, 1757–58,
1758–59, 1759–60, 1760–61, 1761–62,
1762–63, 1763–64, 1764–65, 1765–66,

BROOKES, Mr. (*cont.*)
1766–67, 1767–68, 1768–69, 1769–70,
1770–71, 1771–72, 1772–73, 1773–74,
1774–75, 1775–76, 1776–77, 1777–78,
1778–79, 1779–80, 1780–81, 1781–82
BROOKES, Mrs. Sarah
1750–51, 1752–53, 1761–62
BROWN, Mr. Henry
1753–54, 1754–55, 1755–56, 1756–57
BROWN, Mr. J.
1778–79, 1782–83, 1783–84
BROWN, Mrs. J.
1782–83, 1783–84
BROWNE, Mr.
1777–78, 1778–79, 1779–80, 1780–81,
1781–82, 1782–83, 1783–84
BROWNE, Mrs.
1783–84
BROWNSMITH, Mr. John
1759–60
BRUNSDON, Mr. John
1770–71, 1771–72, 1774–75, 1775–76,
1776–77, 1781–82
BRUNSDON, Mrs.
1770–71
BRUNTON, Mr. John
1780–81, 1781–82, 1782–83, 1783–84,
1784–85
BRUNTON, Master John
1782–83
BRUNTON, Miss Anne
1784–85, 1785–86*
BRUNTON, Misses Elizabeth and Harriet
1782–83
BRYAN, Mr. (Prompter)
1763–64, 1764–65
BRYSON'S MUSICAL CHILDREN
1788–89*
BUSH, Mr.
1785–86
BYGROVE, Mr.
1788–89
BYRNE, Master James
1778–79, 1779–80
BYRNE, Miss Eleanor
1778–79, 1779–80

CAMPBELL, Mr. J.
1798–99, 1799–1800, 1800–01, 1801–02
CAMPBELL, Mrs.
1753–54
CANTELO, Miss
1776–77, 1777–78
CARMICHAEL, Mrs.
1757–58
CARTHY, Mr.
1751–52

CARTWRIGHT, Mr.
1752–53, 1753–54
CASTLE, Mr. Richard
1751–52, 1752–53, 1753–54, 1755–56,
1756–57, 1758–59
CATCHPOLE, Miss
1782–83
CAULFIELD, Mr. Henry E.
1803–04,* 1804–05
CECIL, Mr.
1765–66
CHALMERS, Mr.
1801–02
CHAMBERS, Mr.
1801–02
CHAPMAN, Miss
1804–05
CHARLTON, Mr. Charles
1791–92, 1792–93, 1793–94, 1794–95,
1795–96, 1796–97, 1797–98, 1798–99,
1799–1800, 1800–01, 1801–02, 1802–03,
1803–04, 1804–05
CHARLTON, Master [later Mr. W.]
1800–01, 1802–03, 1803–04, 1804–05
CHARLTON, Mrs. Elizabeth
1791–92, 1792–93, 1793–94, 1794–95,
1795–96, 1796–97, 1797–98, 1798–99,
1799–1800, 1800–01, 1801–02, 1802–03,
1803–04, 1804–05
CHERRY, Mr. Andrew
1798–99, 1799–1800, 1800–01, 1801–02
CHERRY, Mrs.
1798–99, 1799–1800, 1800–01, 1801–02
CHERRY, Miss
1798–99, 1799–1800, 1800–01, 1801–02
CHERRY, Miss F.
1798–99, 1799–1800, 1800–01, 1801–02
CLAGET, Mr.
1757–58
CLAGGETT, Master [These two may be the same
person]
1751–52
CLARKE, Mr. Matthew
1778–79, 1779–80
CLAYTON, Mrs.
1751–52
CLELAND, Miss
1784–85, 1785–86, 1786–87, 1787–88,
1788–89, 1789–90
CLEVELAND, Mr. Thomas
1792–93
COLLINS, Mr. John
1759–60, 1762–63, 1767–68
COLLINS, Miss Clementina
1791–92, 1793–94*
COLLS, Mrs. [formerly Miss TITTORE, *q.v.*]
1788–89

222

COOKE, Mr. (1)
1769–70
COOKE, Mr. (2)
1782–83, 1783–84
COOKE, Mr. George Frederick
1801–02,* 1802–03*
COOKE, Mrs. Alicia [later Miss DANIELS and Mrs. WINDSOR, q.v.]
1798–99, 1799–1800, 1800–01
COOKE, Master (1)
1782–83, 1783–84
COOKE, Master (2)
1804–05
COOPER, Mr.
1795–96
COSTELLO, Mr.
1753–54
COURTENAY, Mr. [Pseudonym of JOHN HENDERSON, q.v.]
1772–73
COURTNEY, Mr. (Bagpiper)
1793–94*
COX, Mr.
1750–51, 1751–52, 1752–53, 1753–54, 1754–55
CRESWICK, Mr.
1761–62, 1762–63
CRUMPTON, Mr.
1794–95, 1795–96, 1796–97, 1797–98, 1798–99
CUNNINGHAM, Mr. [?Thomas]
1795–96, 1796–97, 1797–98, 1798–99, 1799–1800, 1800–01, 1801–02, 1802–03, 1803–04, 1804–05
CUNNINGHAM, Mrs.
1797–98, 1799–1800, 1801–02, 1802–03, 1803–04, 1804–05,
CURTIS, Miss
1771–72, 1772–73, 1773–74, 1774–75

DALY, Mr.
1756–57, 1757–58
DALY, Mrs.
1756–57, 1757–58
DANCER. Mr.
1750–51, 1751–52, 1752–53
DANIELS, Miss Alicia [v. Mrs. COOKE and Mrs. WINDSOR]
1800–01, 1801–2, 1802–03, 1803–04
D'ARCY, Mr.
1799–1800, 1800–01
D'ARCY, Mrs.
1799–1800
DAVEY, Mrs.
1799–1800
DEATH, Mr. Thomas
1763–64, 1770–71

DELANE, Mrs.
1773–74
DENEUVILLE, Master
1771–72, 1772–73, 1773–74, 1774–75
DENEUVILLE, Master Lewis
1774–75
DIBBENS, Mr.
1765–66
DIDIER, Mr. Abraham J.
1767–68, 1768–69, 1769–70, 1770–71, 1771–72, 1772–73, 1773–74, 1774–75, 1775–76, 1776–77, 1777–78, 1778–79, 1779–80, 1780–81, 1787–88*
DIDIER, Mrs. Margaret
1767–68, 1768–69, 1769–70, 1770–71, 1771–72, 1772–73, 1773–74, 1774–75, 1775–76, 1776–77, 1777–78, 1778–79, 1779–80, 1780–81, 1781–82, 1782–83, 1783–84, 1784–85, 1785–86, 1786–87, 1787–88, 1788–89, 1789–90, 1790–91, 1791–92, 1792–93, 1793–94, 1794–95, 1795–96, 1796–97, 1797–98, 1798–99, 1799–1800, 1800–01, 1801–02, 1802–03, 1803–04, 1804–05
DIMOND, Mr. William Wyatt
1774–75, 1775–76, 1776–77, 1777–78, 1778–79, 1779–80, 1780–81, 1781–82, 1782–83, 1783–84, 1784–85, 1785–86, 1786–87, 1787–88, 1788–89, 1789–90, 1790–91, 1791–92, 1792–93, 1793–94, 1794–95, 1795–96, 1796–97, 1797–98, 1798–99, 1799–1800, 1800–01. Continued in management 1801–05
DODD, Mr. James William
1764–65
DODD, Mrs. Martha
1764–65
DOYLE, Mr. (1) [?John]
1761–62, 1762–63
DOYLE, Mr. (2) John Colston
1795–96, 1796–97, 1797–98, 1798–99, 1799–1800, 1800–01, 1801–02, 1802–03, 1803–04, 1804–05
DU BELLAMY, Charles Clementine [EVANS]
1778–79, 1779–80
DURRAVAN, Mr. (Snr.) [?Malachy]
1788–89, 1789–90, 1790–91, 1791–92, 1792–93, 1793–94, 1794–95
DURRAVAN, Mr. James (Jnr.)
1788–89, 1789–90, 1790–91, 1791–92, 1792–93
DUTTON, Mr. Frederick
1782–83

EASTMURE, Mr.
1788–89, 1789–90, 1790–91, 1791–92, 1792–93, 1793–94

ESTEN, Mrs.
1785–86, 1786–87
EDWARDS, Mr.
1804–05
EDWIN, Mr. John (Snr.)
1768–69, 1769–70, 1770–71, 1771–72,
1772–73, 1773–74, 1774–75, 1775–76,
1776–77, 1777–78, 1778–79
EDWIN, Mr. John (Jnr.) [v. also Master EDWIN]
1797–98, 1798–99, 1799–1800, 1800–01,
1801–02, 1802–03, 1803–04
EDWIN, Mrs.
1777–78, 1778–79
EDWIN, Mrs Elizabeth Rebecca
1797–98, 1798–99, 1799–1800, 1800–01,
1801–02, 1802–03, 1803–04
EDWIN, Master
1776–77, 1777–78, 1778–79
EGAN, Mr. (1)
1772–73, 1773–74, 1774–75, 1775–76,
1777–78, [?2], 1786–87, 1787–88, 1788–89,
1801–02, 1802–03, 1803–04, 1804–05
EGAN, Mrs.
1801–02, 1802–03, 1803–04, 1804–05
EGAN, Miss
1777–78
EGERTON, Mr.
1803–04, 1804–05
D'EGVILLE, Mr. and the Misses
1796–97
ELLISTON, Mr. Robert William
1790–01 (brief appearance), 1793–94, 1794–95,
1795–96, 1796–97, 1797–98, 1798–99,
1799–1800, 1800–01, 1801–02, 1802–03,
1803–04
ELRINGTON, Mr. [?Richard]
1751–52
ELRINGTON, Mrs. [?Elizabeth Grace]
1751–52
ELRINGTON, Master
1762–63
EVANS, Mr. Thomas
1801—02, 1802–03, 1803–04, 1804–05
EVANS, Miss
1784–85
EVERY, Miss Ann
1800–01, 1801–02, 1802–03, 1803–04
EYRE, Mr. Edmund
1794–95, 1795–96, 1796–97, 1797–98,
1798–99, 1799–1800, 1800–01, 1801–02,
1802–03, 1803–04
EYRE, Mrs.
1794–95, 1795–96, 1796–97, 1797–98,
1798–99, 1799–1800

FARRAN, Mrs.
1759–60, 1760–61, 1769–70, 1783–84

FARRAN, Miss
1769–70, 1770–71
FARREN, Mrs. [formerly Miss MANSELL, q.v.]
1783–84
FAULKNER, Mr.
1800–01*
FAWKES, Mr.
1754–55, 1755–56, 1756–57, 1757–58
FAWKES, Mrs.
1756–57, 1757–58
FERCI, Sgr. (Tight-rope)
1772–73*
FERNANDO, Sgr. (Lyre-player)
1799–1800*
FISHER, Mr.
1757–58
FISHER, Mr. (Box Book Keeper)
1760–61, 1761–62, 1762–63, 1764–65,
1765–66, 1767–68, 1768–69, 1769–70,
1770–71, 1771–72, 1772–73, 1774–75,
1775–76, 1776–77, 1777–78, 1778–79,
1779–80, 1780–81, 1781–82, 1782–83,
1783–84
FISHER, Miss
1803–04, 1804–05
FISHER, Master
1757–58
FLOOR, Mr. Andrew (Actor—later Prompter)
1768–69, 1769–70, 1770–71, 1771–72,
1772–73, 1773–74, 1774–75, 1775–76,
1776–77, 1778–79, 1779–80, 1780–81,
1783–84, 1784–85, 1785–86, 1786–87,
1787–88, 1788–89, 1789–90, 1790–91,
1791–92, 1792–93, 1793–94, 1794–95,
1795–96, 1796–97, 1797–98, 1798–99
FLOOR, Miss
1789–90, 1790–91, 1791–92, 1792–93,
1793–94
FOOTE, Mr.
1802–03*
FOX, Mr. (1)
1765–66
FOX, Mr. (2)
1787–88, 1788–89, 1789–90
FREEMAN, Mr.
1759–60
FURNIVAL, Mr.
1751–52, 1752–53, 1753–54, 1755–56,
1756–57, 1757–58, 1758–59, 1759–60,
1760–61, 1762–63, 1763–64, 1764–65,
1765–66, 1766–67, 1767–68, 1768–69,
1769–70, 1770–71, 1771–72, 1772–73

GALINDO, Mr. Thomas
1793–94, 1794–95, 1795–96, 1796–97,
1797–98, 1798–99
GALINDO, Miss
1797–98

GATTIE, Mr. Henry
1804–05
GAUDRY, Mr.
1766–67, 1767–68, 1768–69, 1769–70
GIFFARD, Mr.
1757–58
GLASSINGTON, Mr. (Prompter)
1799–1800, 1800–01
GLOVER, Mrs.
1768–69
GODFREY, Miss
1801–02
GOMERY, Mr. Robert
1804–05
GOODALL, Mrs. Charlotte [formerly Miss
STANTON, q.v.]
1787–88
GOODWIN, Mrs.
1763–64
GOPELL, Miss
1792–93, 1793–94, 1794–95, 1795–96,
1796–97, 1797–98
GORDON, Mrs.
1766–67
GOUGH, Miss Kitty
1798–99*
GREEN, Mr.
1751–52
GREEN, Mrs.
1751–52, 1755–56
GRIFFIN, Mr.
1777–78, 1778–79, 1779–80, 1880–81,
1803–04
GRIFFIN, Mrs.
1780–81
GRIFFITH, Mr.
1756–57, 1757–58, 1758–59, 1759–60
GRIFFITHS, Mr.
1799–1800
GRIMANI, Miss Julia Ann
1799–1800, 1800–01, 1801–02, 1802–03
GRIST, Mr. Thomas
1777–78, 1778–79
GRIST, Mrs.
1778–79
GUION, Mr.
1768–69, 1769–70, 1770–71

HAMILTON, Mrs
1762–63
HACKET, Mr.
1755–56
HARLEY, Mr. G. D.
1796–97, 1797–98, 1798–99
HARLEY, Miss
1787–88, 1788–89

HARPER, Mr.
1756–57, 1757–58, 1758–59, 1759–60,
1760–61, 1762–63, 1765–66, 1766–67,
1767–68, 1768–69, 1769–70
HARTLEY, Mr. (Prompter)
1762–63, 1765–66, 1766–67, 1767–68
HARTLEY, Mrs. Elizabeth
1761–62, 1762–63
HARTRY, Mr.
1760–61
HARVEY, Miss
1784–85, 1785–86, 1793–94, 1794–95,
1795–96
HASKER, Mr.
1782–83, 1783–84
HASKER, Mrs.
1782–83
HAUGHTON, Mr. Jack
1764–65, 1765–66, 1766–67, 1767–68,
1768–69, 1769–70, 1770–71, 1771–72,
1772–73, 1773–74, 1774–75, 1775–76,
1776–77, 1777–78, 1778–79, 1779–80,
1780–81, 1781–82
HAYMES, Mr.
1791–92, 1792–93, 1793–94
HAYNES, Mrs.
1794–95
HEDGES, Mrs.
1780–81
HENDERSON, Mr. John [introduced as
COURTENAY, q.v.]
1772–73, 1773–74, 1774–75, 1775–76,
1776–77, 1777–78,* 1778–79*
HERBERT, Mr. [?Joseph]
1804–05
HERBERT, Miss S. T. [later Mrs. TAYLOR, q.v.]
1793–94, 1794–95, 1795–96
HIBBERT, Mr.
1752–53
HILL, Mr.
1796–97, 1797–98
HINDES, Mr.
1790–91
HIPPISLEY, Mrs.
1751–52
HITCHCOCK, Mr. Robert
1776–77
HITCHCOCK, Master
1776–77
HITCHCOCK, Mrs.
1776–77
HITCHCOCK, Miss
1776–77
HODGKINSON, Mr. John
1789–90, 1790–91, 1791–92
HOLLAND, Mr. Charles
1762–63

LEE, Mr. (1) John
1758–59, 1759–60, 1760–61, 1768–69,
1769–70, 1770–71, 1779–80
LEE, Mr. (2) [?Henry]
1802–03
LEE, Mrs. (1)
1758–59, 1759–60, 1760–61, 1761–62,
1762–63, 1763–64, 1764–65, 1765–66,
1768–69, 1769–70, 1770–71
LEE, Mrs. (2)
1802–03, 1804–05
LEONELLI, Signora
1783–84*
LESSINGHAM, Mrs. Jane
1765–66
LEWKENOR, Mr. Robert
1757–58
LINDLEY, Mrs.
1751–52
LITTLE DEVIL, The [Paulo REDIGE] and Mm.
DUPRÉE (or DUPUIS) and MERIMÉE (or MEUNIS)
(Tightrope walker)
1783–84,* 1785–86*
LLOYD, Mr.
1779–80, 1780–81 (Treasurer), 1781–82,
1782–83, 1783–84, 1784–85, 1785–86,
1786–87, 1787–88, 1788–89, 1789–90
LODER, Miss Ann [later Mrs. RIDGWAY, q.v.]
1803–04, 1804–05
LODER, Miss Mary
1795–96, 1796–97, 1797–98
LODGE, Mr. James
1803–04, 1804–05
LOVEGROVE, Mr. William
1802–03, 1803–04, 1804–05
LOVEMORE, Mrs.
1778–79
LOWE, Miss
1753–54, 1754–55, 1755–56, 1756–57

McGEORGE, Mr.
1770–71
McGEORGE, Mrs.
1770–71
MACKENZIE, Mr.
1791–92
MACLELAN, Mr.
1753–54
MAGRATH, Mr.
1804–05
MAHON, Mrs.
1768–69
MALLINSON, Mr. Joseph
1804–05
MALLORY, Mrs.
1789–90
MALONE, Mr.
1750–51

MANSELL, Miss [later Mrs. FARREN, q.v.]
1773–74, 1774–75, 1775–76, 1776–77
MANWARING, Miss
1755–56
MARA, Madame Gertrude Elizabeth
1797–98*
MARSHALL, Mr. Thomas
1791–92, 1792–93, 1793–94, 1794–95,
1795–96
MARSHALL, Mrs. [formerly Miss WEBB, q.v.]
1792–93
MARTIN, Mr. Stephen
1754–55, 1755–56, 1756–57, 1757–58,
1758–59, 1759–60, 1760–61, 1761–62,
1762–63, 1763–64, 1764–65, 1765–66
MARTIN, Mrs.
1754–55, 1755–56, 1763–64, 1764–65,
1765–66, 1766–67, 1767–68, 1768–69,
1769–70, 1770–71, 1771–72, 1772–73,
1773–74, 1774–75, 1775–76, 1776–77,
1777–78, 1778–79, 1779–80, 1780–81
MARTIN, Miss
1804–05
MASON, Mr.
1752–53
MATTHEWS, Mr.
1778–79, 1782–83, 1783–84
MELMOTH, Mr. Courtenay [Samuel Jackson
PRATT]
1778–79*
MICHEL, Master and Miss L.
1786–87, 1787–88, 1788–89
MILLS, Mr.
1782–83, 1783–84
MINGAUD, M.
1802–03*
MITCHELL, Miss (1)
1776–77
MITCHELL, Miss (2)
1797–98
MONK, Miss
1790–91, 1791–92, 1792–93, 1793–94
MONTAGUE, Mrs.
1777–78
MOODY, Mr. [?John]
1753–54
MOOR, Mr.
1768–69, 1769–70, 1770–71, 1771–72,
1772–73, 1773–74
MORGAN, Mr.
1750–51, 1751–52, 1752–53
MORRISON, Miss
1753–54, 1754–55, 1755–56, 1756–57,
1757–58, 1758–59
MOSS, Mr. William Henry
1786–87*
MOUNTAIN, Mrs. Rosemond
1798–99,* 1799–1800*

MURRAY, Mr. Charles
  1785–86, 1786–87, 1787–88, 1788–89,
  1789–90, 1790–91, 1791–92, 1792–93,
  1793–94, 1794–95, 1795–96, 1797–98*
MURRAY, Mrs.
  1785–86, 1786–87, 1792–93, 1793–94,
  1794–95, 1795–96
MURRAY, Miss Harriet
  1792–93, 1793–94, 1794–95, 1795–96,
  1797–98

NEPECKER, Mr.
  1766–67
NEPECKER, Mrs.
  1766–67
NEYLER, Mr.
  1798–99*
NUNNS, Mrs.
  1785–86*

O'HARA, Mrs.
  1759–60
OTWAY, Mr.
  1751–52
OWEN, Miss
  1802–03, 1803–04, 1804–05
OWENS, Mr.
  1784–85, 1786–87

PALMER, Mr. (Box Keeper)
  1756–57
PALMER, Mr. Samuel (Treasurer)
  1760–61, 1761–62, 1762–63, 1765–66,
  1767–68, 1768–69, 1769–70, 1770–71,
  1771–72, 1772–73, 1774–75, 1775–76,
  1776–77, 1777–78, 1778–79, 1779–80
PARKER, Mrs.
  1798–99*
PARSONS, Mr.
  1799–1800, 1800–01, 1801–02, 1802–03,
  1803–04
PAUL, Mr. Peter (Treasurer)
  1790–91, 1791–92, 1792–93, 1793–94,
  1794–95, 1795–96, 1796–97, 1797–98,
  1798–99, 1799–1800
PAYNE, Mr.
  1776–77, 1777–78, 1778–79, 1779–80,
  1780–81, 1781–82, 1782–83, 1784–85
PAYNE, Master
  1776–77, 1777–78, 1778–79, 1779–80,
  1780–81
PENN, Mr.
  1771–72, 1773–74
PHANTASMAGORIA, The
  1801–02*
PHILLIPS, Mr. [?Thomas]
  1799–1800, 1800–01

PHILLIPS, Mrs. (1)
  1767–68
PHILLIPS, Mrs. (2)
  1800–01
PHILLIPS, Mr. (Box Book Keeper)
  1784–85, 1785–86, 1786–87, 1787–88
PINDAR, Mr.
  1785–86, 1786–87, 1788–89, 1789–90,
  1790–91, 1795–96
PINDER, Mrs.
  1792–93
PITT, Mr.
  1753–54
PLYM, Miss
  1756–57
POLLETT, Mr.
  1783–84
POLLOCK, Mrs.
  1794–95, 1795–96
POWELL, Mr. John
  1781–82, 1784–85, 1785–86, 1786–87,
  1787–88
POWELL, Mrs.
  1781–82, 1784–85, 1785–86, 1786–87,
  1787–88, 1788–89, 1789–90
PRESTON, Mr.
  1765–66
PRICE, Mr.
  1759–60, 1760–61
PRICE, Mrs.
  1755–56
PRIDEAUX, Miss
  1787–88
PYNE, Mr.
  1769–70
PYNE, Mrs.
  1769–70

QUELCH, Mrs.
  1763–64, 1764–65, 1765–66, 1766–67
QUICK, Mr. John
  1797–98,* 1798–99,* 1799–1800*
QUICK, Master
  1798–99, 1799–1800, 1800–01, 1802–03,
  1803–04, 1804–05
QUICK, Miss
  1793–94, 1794–95, 1795–96, 1796–97,
  1797–98, 1799–1800, 1801–02, 1802–03,
  1803–04, 1804–05
QUICK, Miss J.
  1802–03, 1803–04
QUICK, Miss L.
  1804–05

READ, Mrs.
  1769–70

READ, Miss Grace [later Mrs. ARTHUR, q.v.]
1763–64, 1764–65, 1765–66, 1766–67,
1767–68

REIDFORD, Mrs.
1788–89

REDDISH, Mr. Samuel
1766–67

REDDISH, Mrs. Polly
1766–67

REYNOLDS, Miss
1759–60, 1760–61, 1761–62, 1762–63,
1764–65, 1765–66

RICHARDS, Mr.
1768–69

RICHARDSON, Mr. (1)
1752–53, 1753–54, 1754–55, 1756–57 [?(2)],
1790–91 [?(3)], 1798–99, 1799–1800, 1800–01

RICHARDSON, Mrs.
1752–53, 1753–54, 1754–55, 1755–56,
1756–57, 1757–58, 1758–59, 1759–60

RICHER, Mr. Jack (Tight Rope Walker)
1795–96,* 1799–1800,* 1802–03,* 1804–05*

RICKETTS, Mrs. [formerly Miss ALLINGHAM, q.v.]
1798–99

RIDGWAY, Mr.
1804–05

RIDGWAY, Mrs. [formerly Miss Ann LODER, q.v.]
1804–05

ROBINSON, Mrs.
1776–77

ROBSON, Mr.
1771–72, 1772–73

ROCHE, Miss
1752–53, 1753–54

ROSCO, Miss
1758–59

ROSIGNOL, Sgr. [?GAETANO]
1782–83,* 1790–91,* 1799–1800*

ROTHERY, Mr.
1764–65, 1765–66

ROWBOTHAM, Mr. Samuel
1776–77, 1777–78, 1778–79, 1779–80,
1780–81, 1781–82, 1782–83, 1783–84,
1784–85, 1785–86, 1786–87, 1787–88,
1788–89, 1789–90, 1790–91, 1791–92,
1792–93, 1793–94, 1794–95, 1795–96,
1796–97, 1797–98, 1798–99, 1799–1800,
1800–01

ROWBOTHAM, Master
1801–02

ROWLEY, Mrs.
1755–56

ROWSWELL, Mr.
1773–74, 1774–75, 1775–76

SALISBURY, Mr.
1767–68

SAMUELS, Mrs.
1800–01

SANDERS, Mr.
1753–54

SANDERS, Mrs.
1753–54

SANDERS, Mr. (Box Book Keeper, Bristol)
1794–95, 1801–02, 1802–03, 1803–04,
1804–05

SANDFORD, Mr.
1793–94, 1794–95

SAUNDERS, Mrs.
1770–71, 1771–72

SCRACE, Miss Patty Ann
1775–76, 1778–79, 1780–81, 1781–82,
1782–83

SCUDDER, Miss
1760–61

SECOND, Mrs. Sarah
1803–04*

SEDLEY, Mr.
1796–97, 1797–98, 1798–99, 1799–1800,
1800–01, 1801–02, 1802–03, 1803–04,
1804–05

SEDLEY, Mrs.
1797–98, 1798–99, 1799–1800, 1800–01,
1802–03, 1803–04, 1804–05

SEYMOUR, Mr.
1785–86*

SHARROCK, Miss
1786–87, 1787–88, 1788–89, 1789–90,
1790–91

SHERRIFFE, Mr.
1759–60, 1760–61, 1761–62, 1762–63,
1763–64, 1764–65, 1765–66, 1766–67,
1767–68, 1768–69, 1769–70, 1770–71,
1771–72, 1772–73, 1773–74

SHERRIFFE, Mrs.
1760–61, 1761–62, 1762–63, 1763–64,
1764–65, 1765–66, 1766–67, 1767–68,
1768–69, 1769–70, 1770–71, 1771–72,
1772–73, 1773–74, 1774–75, 1775–76,
1776–77, 1777–78

SHERRIFFE, Master
1775–76, 1776–77

SHERWOOD, Mrs.
1768–69

SIDDONS, Mr. William
1778–79, 1779–80, 1780–81, 1781–82

SIDDONS, Mrs Sarah
1778–79, 1779–80, 1780–81, 1781–82,
1798–99, 1800–01, 1801–02

SIDDONS, Mr. Henry
1795–96*

SIMPSON, Mr. (1)
1782–83, 1783–84

SIMPSON, Mr. [?(2)]
1794–95, 1795–96

SIMPSON, Mrs.
1782–83, 1783–84, 1787–88, 1788–89,
1789–90, 1790–91
SIMS, Mr.
1804–05
SIMS, Mrs.
1804–05
SMITH, Mr. J.
1796–97, 1798–99, 1799–1800, 1800–01,
1801–02, 1802–03, 1803–04, 1804–05
SMITH, Mrs. J.
1796–97, 1799–1800, 1800–01
SMITH, Mr. W.
1789–90, 1790–91, 1791–92, 1793–94,
1794–95, 1795–96, 1796–97, 1797–98,
1798–99, (Treasurer), 1799–1800, 1800–01,
1801–02, 1802–03, 1803–04, 1804–05
SMITH, Mrs. W.
1788–89, 1789–90, 1790–91, 1792–93,
1793–94, 1794–95, 1796–97, 1797–98,
1798–99, 1799–1800
SMITH, Mr. (Jnr.)
1803–04 [also probably 1801–02, 1802–03,
1804–05 as Mr. SMITH]
SMITH, Miss J.
1800–01
SMITH, Miss Sarah
1791–92, 1792–93, 1793–94, 1798–99,
1800–01, 1801–02, 1802–03, 1803–04,
1804–05
SMITH, Miss S.
1791–92, 1792–93, 1793–94, 1794–95,
1799–1800, 1800–01, 1801–02, 1802–03
SMITH, Mr. (Treasurer) [probably W. SMITH, q.v.]
1799–1800, 1800–01, 1801–02, 1802–03,
1803–04, 1804–05
SMYTH, Mr.
1757–58
SMYTH, Mrs.
1757–58
ST. JOHN, Mrs.
1801–02*
ST. PIERRE, M.
1803–04*
STANTON, Miss Charlotte [later Mrs. GOODALL,
q.v.]
1783–84, 1784–85, 1785–86, 1786–87
STANWIX, Mr. William Robbins
1799–1800, 1800–01, 1801–02
STEPHENS, Mr. Samuel
1751–52, 1752–53, 1753–54, 1754–55,
1755–56, 1756–57, 1757–58, 1758–59,
1759–60, 1760–61
STORACE, Signora Ann Selina ("Nancy")
1796–97,* 1802–03*
STORER, Miss
1780–81

STOW, Mr.
1771–72
STRADDER, Miss
1759–60
SULLIVAN, Mr.
1756–57, 1757–58, 1759–60, 1762–63
SUMMERS, Mr. G.
1775–76, 1776–77, 1777–78, 1778–79,
1779–80, 1780–81, 1781–82, 1782–83,
1783–84, 1784–85, 1785–86, 1786–87
SUMMERS, Mr. Robert
1769–70, 1770–71, 1771–72, 1772–73,
1773–74, 1774–75, 1775–76, 1776–77,
1777–78, 1778–79, 1779–80, 1780–81,
1781–82, 1782–83, 1783–84, 1784–85,
1785–86, 1786–87, 1787–88, 1788–89,
1789–90, 1790–91
SUMMERS, Mrs.
1769–70, 1770–71, 1771–72, 1772–73,
1773–74, 1774–75, 1775–76, 1776–77,
1777–78, 1778–79, 1779–80, 1780–81,
1781–82, 1782–83, 1783–84, 1784–85,
1785–86, 1786–87
SUMMERS, Master [probably later G. SUMMERS]
1772–73, 1774–75, 1776–77
SUMMERS, Miss
1769–70, 1770–71, 1771–72, 1772–73,
1773–74, 1774–75, 1775–76, 1776–77,
1777–78, 1778–79, 1779–80, 1780–81,
1781–82, 1782–83, 1783–84, 1784–85,
1785–86, 1786–87, 1787–88, 1788–89,
1789–90, 1790–91, 1791–92, 1792–93,
1793–94, 1794–95, 1795–96, 1796–97,
1797–98, 1798–99, 1799–1800, 1800–01,
1801–02, 1802–03, 1803–04, 1804–05

TALBOT, Mr. Montague
1801–02
TAYLOR, Mr. (1)
1788–89, 1789–90, 1790–91, 1791–92
TAYLOR, Mr. (2) Charles
1793–94, 1794–95, 1795–96, 1796–97,
1797–98, 1798–99, 1799–1800, 1800–01,
1801–02, 1802–03, 1803–04
TAYLOR, Mrs. (1)
1772–73
TAYLOR, Mrs. (2)
1791–92
TAYLOR, Mrs. (3) S. T. [formerly Miss HERBERT,
q.v. Married Charles TAYLOR, q.v.]
1796–97, 1797–98, 1798–99, 1799–1800,
1800–01, 1801–02, 1802–03, 1803–04
TAYLOR, Miss
1799–1800
TEBAY, Master (later Mr. J.)
1795–96, 1796–97, 1797–98, 1798–99,

TEBAY, Master (later *Mr.* J.) (*cont.*)
1799–1800, 1800–01, 1801–02, 1802–03, 1803–04, 1804–05

TEBAY, Mrs.
1803–04

TEBAY, Master I.
1796–97, 1797–98

TEBAY, Master S.
1799–1800

TEBAY, Master T.
1796–97, 1797–98, 1798–99, 1801–02, 1802–03

TEBAY, Miss
1795–96, 1796–97, 1797–98, 1798–99, 1799–1800, 1800–01, 1801–02, 1802–03, 1803–04, 1804–05

TEBAY, Miss S.
1798–99, 1799–1800, 1800–01, 1801–02, 1802–03, 1803–04, 1804–05

THOMPSON, Mr.
1803–04, 1804–05

TITTORE, Miss [later Mrs. COLLS, *q.v.*]
1788–89

TOWNSEND, Miss
1770–71, 1771–72, 1772–73

TURNER, Mr. (1)
1763–64, 1765–66

TURNER, Mr. (2)
1799–1800, 1800–01

TWIST, Miss
1781–82, 1782–83, 1783–84, 1784–85, 1785–86, 1786–87

TWISTLETON, Mrs.
1794–95

VERNON, Mr.
1781–82*

VOLANGE, Mme.
1803–04*

WAKER, Mr.
1755–56, 1756–57, 1757–58, 1758–59

WAKER, Mrs.
1756–57, 1757–58, 1758–59

WALKER, Mr. (Box Book Keeper, Bristol)
1779–80, 1781–82, 1782–83, 1783–84, 1784–85, 1785–86, 1787–88, 1790–91, 1791–92, 1792–93, 1793–94, 1794–95

WALLIS, Miss Tryphosa Jane
1789–90, 1790–91, 1791–92, 1792–93, 1793–94, 1795–96,* 1796–97,* 1797–98*

WARD, Mr.
1787–88, 1788–89, 1789–90

WARD, Mrs.
1772–73, 1773–74, 1774–75, 1775–76, 1776–77, 1777–78, 1778–79, 1779–80

WARRELL, Mrs.
1787–88, 1788–89

WARRELL, Master
1788–89

WARRELL, Miss Eliza [later Mrs. ATKINS, *q.v.*]
1787–88, 1788–89, 1795–96

WATERHOUSE, Mr.
1786–87, 1787–88, 1788–89

WATSON, Mr. (Jnr.)
1803–04

WATTS, Mr.
1759–60, 1760–61, 1762–63, 1763–64, 1764–65, 1765–66, 1766–67, 1767–68, 1768–69, 1769–70, 1770–71, 1771–72, 1772–73, 1773–74, 1774–75

WAYTE, Mr.
1767–68

WEBB, Miss [later Mrs. MARSHALL, *q.v.*]
1792–3

WEBBER, Mr.
1802–03, 1803–04, 1804–05

WEST, Mr. (1)
1775–76

WEST, Mr. (2)
1791–92

WEST, Master and Miss
1773–74

WEWITZER, Miss
1781–82, 1782–83, 1783–84

WHEELER, Mrs.
1774–75, 1776–77

WHEELER, Miss Frances
1773–74, 1774–75, 1775–76, 1776–77, 1777–78, 1778–79, 1779–80, 1780–81, 1781–82, 1783–84*

WHITE, Mr.
1759–60, 1760–61, 1761–62

WILKINSON, Mr. Tate
1757–58, 1760–61

WILKINSON, Miss
1755–56

WILLIAMS, Mr. (1)
1759–60

WILLIAMS, Mrs.
1759–60

WILLIAMS, Mr. (2)
1800–01, 1801–02, 1802–03

WILLIAMS, Miss
1786–87

WILLIAMSON, Mr. (1)
1753–54

WILLIAMSON, Mr. (2)
1783–84, 1784–85

WILLIAMSON, Mr. (3) David
1794–95, 1795–96, 1796–97, 1797–98, 1798–99, 1801–02 (as prompter)

WILLOUGHBY, Miss
1768–69

WILSON, Mrs.
1796–97

WINDSOR, Mrs. [formerly Mrs COOKE and Miss
DANIELS, *q.v.*]
1804–05
WINSTONE, Mr. Richard (Treasurer, Bristol)
1779–80, 1780–81, 1781–82, 1782–83,
1783–84, 1784–85
WOOD, Mr.
1767–68, 1768–69
WOOD, Mrs.
1767–68, 1768–69
WOOD, Miss
1767–68, 1768–69, 1783–84, 1784–85
WOODLEY, Mr. (Prompter)
1803–04, 1804–05
WOOLLEY, Mr. (Painter)
1760–61

WORDSWORTH, Mr.
1784–85, 1785–86, 1786–87, 1787–88,
1788–89, 1789–90, 1790–91
WORKMAN, Mrs.
1762–63
WORTLEY, Mrs.
1767–68
WRENCH, Mr. Benjamin
1804–05
WRIGHT, Miss Charlotte [later Mrs. BLANCHARD,
q.v.]
1783–84, 1784–85, 1785–86, 1786–87
YATES, Mrs. [?Sarah]
1795–96
YOUNGER, Mrs.
1779–80

Index of Plays

Note

Sub-titles are recorded (and cross-referenced) only where they are sometimes used alone in the source material, or to distinguish between two pieces with similar main titles.

Author's names are indicated where known. Two names linked by 'and' indicates a collaboration. Links by '/' indicate later adaptation. The most radical Shakespearian adaptations in use are indicated, but not all the possible modifying hands.

The occasional fugitive piece listed may possibly be a recitation or olio rather than a dramatic piece proper. In cases of doubt it has seemed better to record than to omit.

BRITONS TRIUMPHANT
1797, 1798

BROTHERS, The (E. Young)
1753

BROTHERS, The (R. Cumberland)
1770, 1796, 1797, 1798

BRYSTOWE (Floor and R. Meyler)
1788, 1789, 1790, 1791, 1792, 1794

BUSYBODY, The (Mrs. S. Centlivre)
1753, 1754, 1755, 1756, 1757, 1758, 1760,
1763, 1767, 1768, 1769, 1770, 1771, 1772,
1777, 1778, 1780, 1781, 1783, 1787, 1788,
1789, 1791, 1795, 1796, 1803

BUXOM JOAN (T. Willett)
1780, 1781

CABINET, The (T. J. Dibdin)
1802, 1803, 1804

CAERNARVON CASTLE (J. Rose)
1794, 1795

CAMP, The (R. B. Sheridan)
1779, 1780, 1781, 1803

CAPRICIOUS LOVERS, The (R. Lloyd)
1771, 1772, 1773, 1774, 1775, 1776, 1777,
1778, 1780, 1781, 1783, 1784, 1792

CARACTACUS (W. Mason)
1781, 1782

CARELESS HUSBAND, The (C. Cibber)
1756, 1758, 1775, 1776, 1780, 1781

CASINO, The
1780

CASTLE OF ANDALUSIA, The (J. O'Keeffe)
1784, 1785, 1787, 1788, 1789, 1790, 1797,
1798, 1801, 1805

CASTLE OF SORRENTO, The (H. Heartwell and G.
Colman the Younger)
1799, 1800, 1801

CASTLE SPECTRE, The (M. G. Lewis)
1798, 1799, 1800, 1801, 1802, 1803, 1804,
1805

CATHERINE & PETRUCHIO (W. Shakespeare/D.
Garrick)
1756, 1757, 1758, 1764, 1765, 1766, 1767,
1769, 1770, 1774, 1775, 1781, 1782, 1788,
1789, 1791, 1792, 1793, 1794, 1795, 1797,
1798, 1800, 1801, 1802, 1803, 1804

CATO (J. Addison)
1751, 1763

CAVE OF HECATE, The
1797, 1798

CHANCES, The (F. Beaumont and J. Fletcher/D.
Garrick
1754, 1755, 1773, 1774, 1775, 1776, 1777,
1778, 1780, 1782, 1787, 1798

CHAPLET, The (M. Mendez)
1754, 1755, 1756, 1757, 1763, 1765, 1766,
1767, 1769, 1770, 1771, 1773, 1775, 1776,
1779, 1780, 1786

CHAPTER OF ACCIDENTS, The (Mrs. S. Lee)
1780, 1781, 1782, 1783, 1784, 1785, 1786,
1787, 1788, 1789, 1791, 1792, 1793, 1794,
1795, 1796, 1798, 1800, 1801, 1803

CHEAP LIVING (F. Reynolds)
1801

CHEATS OF SCAPIN, The (?T. Otway or J. Ozell)
1755, 1791

CHILD OF NATURE, The (Mrs. E. Inchbald)
1790, 1791, 1792, 1793, 1794, 1795, 1796,
1797, 1798, 1799, 1802, 1803, 1804, 1805

CHILDREN IN THE WOOD, The (T. Morton)
1794, 1795, 1796, 1797, 1799, 1800, 1801,
1802, 1803, 1804, 1805

CHIMNEY CORNER, The (W. Porter)
1798, 1800

CHIT CHAT (B. Walwyn)
1782

CHOLERIC MAN, The (R. Cumberland)
1775

CHRONONHOTONTHOLOGOS (H. Carey)
1755, 1771, 1776, 1788

CITIZEN, The (A. Murphy)
1763, 1765, 1766, 1767, 1768, 1769, 1770,
1772, 1773, 1774, 1775, 1777, 1779, 1781,
1782, 1783, 1784, 1785, 1786, 1787, 1788,
1789, 1791, 1792, 1793, 1798, 1800, 1801,
1802, 1804

CLANDESTINE MARRIAGE, The (G. Colman the
Elder and D. Garrick)
1767, 1768, 1769, 1770, 1771, 1772, 1773,
1774, 1775, 1776, 1777, 1778, 1779, 1780,
1781, 1782, 1783, 1784, 1786, 1788, 1789,
1791, 1792, 1795, 1796, 1797, 1798, 1799,
1804

CLEONE (R. Dodsley)
1759, 1782

COAT AND BADGE [v. THE WATERMAN]
1805

COBBLER OF PRESTON, The (C. Bullock and
C. Johnson)
1750

COLUMBUS (T. Morton)
1793, 1794, 1795, 1796

COMEDY OF ERRORS (W. Shakespeare/?T. Hull
or W. Woods)
1792, 1793, 1796

COMMISSARY, The (S. Foote)
1771, 1772, 1773, 1774, 1775, 1776, 1778,
1799

COMMITTEE, The (Sir R. Howard)
1754, 1759, 1764, 1766

COMUS (J. Milton/G. Colman the Elder)
1754, 1755, 1756, 1757, 1758, 1759, 1760,
1761, 1763, 1773, 1774, 1775, 1776, 1777,
1778, 1779, 1780, 1789, 1797, 1798, 1799,
1800, 1801, 1802, 1803

CONFEDERACY, The   (J. Vanbrugh)
1751, 1752, 1754, 1756, 1758, 1761
CONQUEST OF ST. EUSTACIA, The
1781
CONSCIOUS LOVERS, The   (R. Steele)
1750, 1751, 1753, 1754, 1755, 1756, 1757,
1758, 1759, 1760, 1762, 1763, 1765, 1767,
1768, 1770, 1771, 1772, 1774, 1775, 1776,
1779, 1780, 1781, 1782, 1783, 1784, 1785,
1786, 1787, 1788, 1789, 1790, 1791, 1794,
1796
CONSTANT COUPLE, The   (G. Farquhar)
1754, 1755, 1756, 1759, 1765, 1766, 1769,
1770, 1774, 1779
CONTRIVANCES, The   (H. Carey)
1750, 1757, 1758, 1759, 1760, 1762, 1767,
1769, 1772, 1773, 1780, 1781, 1785, 1786
COOPER, The   (T. A. Arne)
1776, 1777, 1795, 1796, 1797, 1798, 1799,
1800, 1801, 1802
COUNTERPLOT, The   (T. Goodall)
1788
COUNTESS OF SALISBURY, The   (H. Hartson)
1771, 1777, 1778, 1779, 1780, 1781, 1782,
1783, 1788, 1789, 1791, 1794
COUNT OF NARBONNE, The   (R. Jephson)
1782, 1783, 1798, 1799
COUNTRY GIRL, The   (W. Wycherley/D. Garrick)
1788, 1789, 1790, 1791, 1792, 1793, 1795,
1800, 1802, 1804
COUNTRY LASSES, The   (C. Johnson)
1752, 1753, 1755, 1760, 1765, 1766, 1767,
1771
COUNTRY WIFE, The   (W. Wycherley/J. Lee)
1775, 1783
COZENERS, The   (S. Foote)
1778, 1780, 1782
CRITIC, The   (R. B. Sheridan)
1780, 1781, 1782, 1783, 1785, 1786, 1787
CROSS PURPOSES   (W. O'Brien)
1772, 1773, 1774, 1775, 1776, 1777, 1779,
1781, 1785, 1787, 1788, 1789, 1790, 1791,
1792, 1793, 1794, 1795
CROTCHET LODGE   (T. Hurlstone)
1795
CUPID TURNED POSTILLION   [v. A TRIP TO
SCOTLAND]
1793
CURE FOR THE HEARTACHE, A   (T. Morton)
1797, 1798, 1799, 1800, 1801, 1802, 1804,
1805
CYMBELINE   (W. Shakespeare/D. Garrick)
1772, 1774, 1775, 1776, 1777, 1778, 1779,
1780, 1781, 1783, 1784, 1786, 1787, 1788,
1789, 1790, 1791, 1792, 1793, 1794, 1795,
1797, 1798, 1799, 1800, 1801, 1802, 1803,
1804

CYMON   (D. Garrick)
1774, 1775, 1776, 1777, 1778, 1779, 1781,
1783, 1784, 1787, 1788, 1789, 1790, 1791,
1793, 1796, 1797, 1798, 1801
CYRUS   (J. Hoole)
1772, 1773, 1801, 1802

DAMON AND PHILLIDA   (C. Cibber/C. Dibdin)
1751, 1752, 1753, 1754, 1756, 1757, 1759,
1760, 1761, 1762, 1766, 1767, 1780, 1781,
1782, 1796
DAPHNE AND AMINTOR   (I. Bickerstaffe)
1764, 1770, 1771, 1772, 1773, 1774, 1775,
1776, 1781, 1800
DEAD ALIVE, The   (J. O'Keeffe)
1785, 1787, 1789, 1793, 1805
DEAF AND DUMB   (T. Holcroft)
1801, 1802, 1803
DEAF LOVER, The   (F. Pilon)
1780, 1783, 1784, 1785, 1787, 1788, 1789,
1790, 1791, 1792, 1801, 1802, 1803, 1805
DEATH OF HARLEQUIN, The   [v. THE FORTUNE
TELLER and HARLEQUIN SKELETON]
1781
DELAYS AND BLUNDERS   (F. Reynolds)
1802, 1803
DESERTED DAUGHTER, The   (T. Holcroft)
1796, 1797, 1798, 1799, 1805
DESERTER, The   (C. Dibdin)
1774, 1775, 1776, 1777, 1778, 1780, 1782,
1783, 1784, 1785, 1786, 1787, 1788, 1790,
1791, 1792, 1793, 1794, 1795, 1796, 1798,
1799, 1801, 1802, 1803, 1804
DESERTER OF NAPLES, The   [?Dibdin's THE
DESERTER, q.v.]
1803
DESERT ISLAND   (A. Murphy)
1800
DEUCE IS IN HIM, The   (G. Colman the Elder)
1764, 1765, 1766, 1767, 1768, 1769, 1770,
1771, 1773, 1777, 1782, 1783, 1785, 1787,
1788, 1791, 1795, 1797
DEVIL TO PAY   (C. Coffey and J. Mottley)
1753, 1755, 1756, 1758, 1761, 1762, 1763,
1764, 1765, 1766, 1767, 1768, 1769, 1772,
1773, 1774, 1775, 1776, 1777, 1778, 1779,
1780, 1781, 1782, 1783, 1784, 1787, 1788,
1789, 1790, 1792, 1793, 1794, 1796, 1797,
1800, 1801, 1802, 1803, 1804, 1805
DEVIL UPON TWO STICKS, The   (S. Foote)
1778, 1779, 1780, 1781, 1782, 1790, 1792
DIGNITY OF THE STAGE, The
1760
DISBANDED OFFICER, The   (J. Johnstone)
1789
DISCOVERY   (Mrs. F. Sheridan)
1773

DISH OF MR. FOOTE'S TEA
1752, 1753, 1760
DISSIPATION   (M. P. Andrews)
1781
DISTREST MOTHER, The   (A. Philips)
1751, 1764, 1766, 1776, 1780, 1782, 1784,
1786, 1790, 1799, 1801, 1803
DIVORCE, The   (I. Jackman)
1793
DOCTOR & APOTHECARY, The   (J. Cobb)
1797, 1798, 1799, 1800, 1801, 1802, 1804,
1805
DOLDRUMS, The   (J. O'Keeffe)
1800
DON JUAN   (C. Delpini)
1795, 1796, 1797, 1798, 1805
DON QUIXOTE IN ENGLAND   (H. Fielding)
1756, 1789, 1790
DOUBLE DISGUISE, The   (Mrs. J. Hook)
1792, 1793, 1796, 1799
DOUBLE FALSEHOOD, The   (L. Theobald)
1780, 1781, 1784, 1793
DOUBLE GALLANT, The   (C. Cibber)
1762, 1763, 1765, 1766, 1767
DOUBLE MISTAKE   (Mrs. E. Griffith)
1766
DOUGLAS   (J. Home)
1757, 1758, 1759, 1760, 1770, 1772, 1775,
1776, 1779, 1780, 1781, 1782, 1785, 1786,
1792, 1794, 1796, 1798, 1799, 1800, 1801,
1805
DRAGON OF WANTLEY, The   (H. Carey)
1775, 1776, 1777, 1778, 1782
DRAMATIST, The   (F. Reynolds)
1790, 1791, 1792, 1793, 1795, 1796, 1798,
1801, 1802, 1804
DREAMER AWAKE, The   (E. J. Eyre)
1795
DRUIDS, The
1790
DRUMMER, The   (J. Addison)
1757, 1759, 1776, 1790, 1791, 1792, 1794,
1797, 1803
DUENNA, The   (R. B. Sheridan)
1778, 1779, 1780, 1781, 1782, 1783, 1784,
1785, 1788, 1789, 1791, 1793, 1794, 1795,
1797, 1798, 1800, 1801, 1802, 1803, 1804,
1805
DUKE AND NO DUKE, A   (N. Tate/J. Thurmond)
1757, 1758, 1759, 1760, 1770
DUPLICITY   (T. Holcroft)
1781, 1782, 1792, 1794, 1795, 1797

EARL GOODWIN   (Mrs. A. Yearsley)
1789

EARL OF ESSEX, The   (H. Brooke or H. Jones) [v.
also THE UNHAPPY FAVOURITE]
1753, 1754, 1755, 1756, 1758, 1765, 1772,
1773, 1783, 1784, 1790, 1791, 1792, 1793,
1804
EARL OF WARWICK, The   (T. Francklin)
1767, 1771, 1773, 1778, 1795, 1796, 1797,
1800, 1801
EDGAR AND EMMELINE   (J. Hawkesworth)
1778, 1779, 1780, 1783, 1792, 1794, 1795,
1796, 1797, 1798, 1799, 1800, 1801, 1803,
1805
EDWARD AND ELEANORA   (J. Thomson/T. Hull)
1775, 1776, 1779, 1780, 1782, 1790
EDWARD THE BLACK PRINCE   (W. Shirley)
1751, 1754
ELECTION, The   (M. P. Andrews)
1774
ELFRIDA   (W. Mason)
1780, 1781, 1782
ELOISA   (F. Reynolds)
1787
ENCHANTED WOOD, The
1783, 1784
ENGLISHMAN IN PARIS, The   (S. Foote)
1760, 1763, 1766, 1774, 1792
ENGLISH MERCHANT, The   (G. Colman the Elder)
1767, 1770, 1771, 1772, 1773, 1775, 1782,
1783, 1787, 1789, 1790, 1791, 1792
EPHESIAN MATRON, The   (I. Bickerstaffe)
1777, 1781
ERROR OF THE MOMENT, The
1803
EURYDICE   (H. Fielding or D. Mallet)
1754
EVERY MAN IN HIS HUMOUR   (B. Jonson/D.
Garrick)
1753, 1756, 1772, 1773, 1774, 1776, 1778,
1796
EVERY ONE HAS HIS FAULT   (Mrs. E. Inchbald)
1793, 1794, 1795, 1796, 1797, 1798, 1799,
1800, 1801, 1802, 1805

FAIR CIRCASSIAN, The   (S. J. Pratt)
1782
FAIR PENITANT, The   (N. Rowe)
1750, 1751, 1754, 1756, 1764, 1772, 1775,
1776, 1777, 1780, 1781, 1783, 1784, 1785,
1788, 1789, 1790, 1792, 1795, 1796, 1798,
1799
FAIR QUAKER OF DEAL, The   (C. Shadwell/E.
Thompson)
1752, 1758, 1760, 1766, 1768, 1770
FALSE AND TRUE   (Moultrie)
1799, 1800, 1801, 1802, 1805
FALSE APPEARANCES   (H. S. Conway)
1790

FALSE DELICACY   (H. Kelly & D. Garrick)
1768, 1771, 1772, 1783

FAMILY PARTY, The   (ascribed to G. Colman the Younger)
1792

FANCY'S BOWER
1784

FARMER, The   (J. O'Keeffe)
1788, 1789, 1790, 1791, 1792, 1793, 1794, 1795, 1796, 1797, 1798, 1800, 1801, 1802, 1803, 1804, 1805

FARMHOUSE, The   (J. P. Kemble)
1789, 1790, 1791, 1792, 1793, 1794, 1798, 1800, 1801, 1802, 1804

FASHIONABLE LEVITIES   (L. MacNally)
1798

FASHIONABLE LOVER, The   (R. Cumberland)
1772, 1773, 1774, 1775, 1776, 1777, 1779, 1780, 1783, 1784, 1785, 1787, 1788, 1789, 1790, 1791, 1792, 1793, 1794, 1795, 1798

FATAL FALSEHOOD   (Mrs. H. More)
1779, 1780, 1781

FATHERS, The   (H. Fielding)
1779

FEMALE CURIOSITY or THE CLOCK-CASE
1780

FEMALE FORTUNE TELLER, The   (C. Johnson)
1766

FIRST FLOOR, The   (J. Cobb)
1787, 1788, 1790, 1791, 1793

FIRST LOVE   (R. Cumberland)
1796, 1797

FIVE THOUSAND A YEAR   (T. J. Dibdin)
1799

FLITCH OF BACON, The   (H. Bate)
1778, 1779, 1780, 1781, 1782, 1783, 1785, 1786, 1787, 1788, 1789, 1790, 1791, 1792, 1793, 1794, 1795, 1796, 1798, 1799, 1800, 1801

FLORA or HOB IN THE WELL   (C. Cibber/J. Hippisley)
1753, 1755, 1759, 1760, 1761, 1769, 1774, 1775, 1777, 1781, 1782, 1783, 1784, 1785, 1786, 1787, 1788, 1793, 1794, 1795, 1805

FLORIST FEAST, The   [? = THE AURICULA FEAST, q.v.]
1765

FLORIZEL AND PERDITA or THE SHEEP SHEARING   (W. Shakespeare/D. Garrick) [from THE WINTER'S TALE, q.v.]
1760, 1763, 1765, 1766, 1767, 1769, 1770, 1780, 1781, 1794, 1796, 1798, 1800

FOLLIES OF A DAY, The   (T. Holcroft)
1785, 1786, 1787, 1789, 1790, 1792, 1794, 1795, 1796, 1797, 1798, 1799, 1800, 1801, 1802, 1803, 1805

FULLY AS IT FLIES   (F. Reynolds)
1801, 1802, 1803

FONTAINBLEAU   (J. O'Keeffe)
1785, 1786, 1790, 1791, 1795

FONTAINVILLE FOREST   (J. Boaden)
1795, 1796, 1797

FOP'S FORTUNE, The   [v. LOVE MAKES A MAN]

FORTUNE'S FOOL   (F. Reynolds)
1797

FORTUNE'S FROLIC   (J. T. Allingham)
1799, 1802

FORTUNE TELLER, The   [v. DEATH OF HARLEQUIN and HARLEQUIN SKELETON]
1781

FOUNDLING, The   (E. Moore)
1752, 1753, 1755, 1759, 1760, 1764, 1766, 1767, 1768, 1769, 1771, 1776, 1777, 1782, 1783, 1784, 1787, 1789, 1791, 1794

FRANCE AS IT WAS   [from FONTAINBLEAU, q.v.]
1795

FUGITIVE, The   (J. Richardson)
1792, 1793, 1794, 1795, 1798, 1801

FUNERAL, The   (Sir R. Steele)
1765, 1766, 1767, 1769, 1770, 1772, 1777, 1778, 1779, 1781, 1784, 1788, 1789, 1791, 1794

GALLICK GRATITUDE
1790

GAMESTER, The   (E. Moore and D. Garrick)
1752, 1753, 1754, 1755, 1756, 1781, 1782, 1783, 1784, 1786, 1787, 1788, 1791, 1793, 1794, 1796, 1798, 1799, 1800, 1801

GENEROUS IMPOSTER, The   (T. L. O'Beirne)
1781

GENEROUS TARS   [from THE POSITIVE MAN, q.v.]
1798

GENTLE LAIRD, The
1783

GENTLE SHEPHERD, The   (A. Ramsay/R. Tickell/?C. Vanderstop, Mrs. M. Turner)
1782, 1783, 1784, 1785, 1786, 1787, 1788, 1789, 1790, 1791, 1792, 1793, 1794, 1796, 1803

GEORGE BARNWELL or THE LONDON MERCHANT   (G. Lillo)
1751, 1753, 1755, 1757, 1759, 1764, 1768, 1769, 1770, 1771, 1772, 1773, 1774, 1775, 1778, 1780, 1782, 1783, 1784, 1785, 1786, 1787, 1788, 1789, 1791, 1792, 1794, 1796, 1797, 1798, 1799, 1800, 1801, 1802, 1803, 1804, 1805

GERMAN HOTEL, The   (T. Holcroft)
1791

GHOST, The   (Mrs. S. Centlivre/Anon.)
1771, 1772, 1773, 1774, 1775, 1776, 1777, 1778, 1780, 1781, 1782, 1784, 1786, 1793, 1794, 1795, 1798, 1799, 1803, 1804, 1814

GIL BLAS OF SANTILLANE   (R. Bates)
1789, 1790

GOLDEN PIPPIN, The (K. O'Hara)
1774, 1775, 1777, 1778, 1779, 1780, 1781, 1789, 1793

GOODNATUR'D MAN, The (O. Goldsmith)
1769, 1770, 1771, 1776, 1805

GRECIAN DAUGHTER, The (A. Murphy)
1772, 1773, 1774, 1775, 1776, 1778, 1779, 1780, 1781, 1782, 1783, 1785, 1786, 1788, 1789, 1791, 1792, 1794, 1795, 1796, 1797, 1799, 1800

GRETNA BLACKSMITH, The
1804, 1805

GRETNA GREEN (C. Stuart)
1787

GUARDIAN, The (D. Garrick)
1759, 1760, 1762, 1763, 1765, 1766, 1770, 1771, 1772, 1779, 1780, 1781, 1787, 1789, 1792, 1793, 1794, 1796, 1798, 1803

GYPSY PRINCE (T. Moore)
1801

HAMLET (W. Shakespeare)
1750, 1751, 1752, 1753, 1754, 1755, 1756, 1757, 1759, 1760, 1761, 1762, 1765, 1766, 1767, 1768, 1769, 1770, 1772, 1773, 1774, 1775, 1776, 1777, 1778, 1779, 1780, 1781, 1782, 1783, 1784, 1785, 1786, 1788, 1789, 1790, 1791, 1792, 1794, 1795, 1796, 1797, 1798, 1799, 1800, 1802, 1803, 1804

HAMPTON COURT FROLICKS
1799

HARLEQUIN
1772, 1773

HARLEQUIN AND COLUMBINE
1774

HARLEQUIN AT STOCKWELL
1772, 1773

HARLEQUIN'S EULOGIUM
1797

HARLEQUIN FLORIST
1764

HARLEQUIN'S FROLICKS
1796

HARLEQUIN'S INVASION OF THE REALMS OF SHAKESPEARE (D. Garrick)
1779

HARLEQUIN'S METAMORPHOSES
1772, 1773, 1775

HARLEQUIN NECROMANCER [v. THE NECROMANCER]

HARLEQUIN RANGER
1753

HARLEQUIN'S REVELS
1757, 1758

HARLEQUIN SKELETON [v. THE DEATH OF HARLEQUIN]
1781

HARLEQUIN TOUCHSTONE
1779, 1780, 1781, 1782

HARMONIC MEETING, The
1782, 1783

HARTFORD BRIDGE (W. Pearce)
1793, 1794, 1795, 1796, 1797, 1799

HARVEST HOME
1782, 1783

THE HAUNTED HOUSE or THE DRUMMING GHOST [v. THE DRUMMER]
1790

HAUNTED TOWER, The (J. Cobb)
1791, 1792, 1793, 1794, 1795, 1796, 1797, 1798, 1799, 1800, 1802, 1803, 1805

HEIR AT LAW, The (G. Colman the Younger)
1797, 1798, 1799, 1800, 1801, 1802, 1803, 1804, 1805

HEIRESS, The (J. Burgoyne)
1786, 1787, 1788, 1789, 1790, 1791, 1793, 1794, 1795, 1803

HENRY II (T. Hull)
1774, 1775, 1776, 1777, 1778, 1779, 1780, 1781, 1782, 1783, 1788, 1790, 1793, 1794

HENRY IV (W. Shakespeare)
1750, 1751, 1752, 1756, 1757, 1760, 1763, 1770, 1772, 1773, 1775, 1776, 1777, 1778, 1785, 1786, 1787, 1789, 1790, 1794, 1795, 1796, 1797, 1798, 1802, 1803, 1804, 1805

HENRY V (W. Shakespeare)
1777, 1778, 1780, 1781, 1793, 1794, 1798, 1801, 1803, 1804

HENRY VIII (W. Shakespeare)
1757, 1762, 1779, 1780, 1795, 1796, 1804

HENRY AND EMMA
1777

HERO OF THE NORTH (W. Dimond)
1804

HE WOU'D BE A SOLDIER (F. Pilon)
1787, 1788, 1789, 1790, 1791, 1792, 1797

HIGHLAND REEL (J. O'Keeffe)
1790, 1791, 1792, 1793, 1794, 1795, 1796, 1797, 1798, 1799, 1801, 1803, 1804

HIGH LIFE BELOW STAIRS (J. Townley and D. Garrick)
1759, 1760, 1762, 1763, 1764, 1765, 1767, 1769, 1772, 1773, 1775, 1776, 1777, 1778, 1780, 1781, 1784, 1786, 1787, 1788, 1790, 1795, 1797, 1803

HOBB IN THE WELL [v. FLORA]

HOBBY HORSES
1790

HONEST THIEVES (T. Knight)
1799

HONEST WELCHMAN, The (J. Hippisley)
1783

HONEST YORKSHIREMAN, The (H. Carey)
1750, 1751, 1752, 1755, 1756, 1757, 1758,

HONEST YORKSHIREMAN, The (*cont.*)
1759, 1762, 1763, 1764, 1767, 1768, 1773, 1774, 1776, 1777, 1778, 1780, 1786, 1788
HONEY MOON, The (J. Tobin)
1805
HORSE AND THE WIDOW, The (T. J. Dibdin)
1799
HOTEL, The (T. Vaughan)
1776, 1777
HOTTENTOTS, The (E. J. Eyre)
1802
HOUSE TO BE SOLD, A (J. Cobb *or* J. Baylis)
1805
HOW TO GROW RICH (F. Reynolds)
1793
HUMOURIST, The (J. Cobb)
1786, 1787, 1788, 1789, 1790, 1791, 1792, 1793
HUMOURS OF AN ELECTION, The (F. Pilon)
1781
HUNTER OF THE ALPS, The (W. Dimond)
1804, 1805
HUNT THE SLIPPER (H. Knapp)
1787, 1795
HYPOCRITE, The (I. Bickerstaffe)
1773, 1774, 1775, 1778, 1780, 1782, 1786, 1787, 1788, 1789, 1792

I'LL TELL YOU WHAT (Mrs. E. Inchbald)
1786, 1787, 1788, 1789, 1792
INCONSTANT, The (G. Farquhar)
1758, 1759, 1760, 1763, 1769, 1770, 1780, 1781, 1782, 1786, 1791, 1800, 1801, 1805
INFLEXIBLE CAPTIVE (Mrs. H. More)
1775
INGENIOUS VALET, The
1787
INKLE AND YARICO (G. Colman the Younger)
1788, 1789, 1790, 1791, 1792, 1793, 1794, 1796, 1797, 1798, 1799, 1801, 1803, 1804, 1805
INTRIGUING CHAMBERMAID, The (H. Fielding)
1752, 1755, 1756, 1763, 1768, 1769, 1770, 1785
INVASION, The (F. Pilon)
1778, 1794
IRISHMAN IN LONDON, The (W. M'Cready)
1793, 1794, 1796, 1797, 1798, 1805
IRISHMAN'S VAGARIES, The (W. C. Oulton)
1800
IRISH MIMIC, The (J. O'Keeffe)
1795, 1796, 1798, 1802
IRISH WIDOW (D. Garrick)
1772, 1773, 1774, 1775, 1776, 1777, 1780, 1781, 1782, 1784, 1785, 1786, 1787, 1792, 1794, 1795, 1796, 1798, 1799

IRON CHEST, The (G. Colman the Younger)
1800
ISABELLA (T. Southerne/D. Garrick)
1780, 1781, 1787, 1791, 1794, 1795, 1799, 1800, 1801, 1802
ITALIAN MONK, The (J. Boaden)
1800
IT'S ALL A FARCE (J. T. Allingham)
1805

JABAL'S TRAVELS
1798
JACOB GAWKEY'S RAMBLE
1792
JANE SHORE (N. Rowe)
1751, 1752, 1754, 1757, 1765, 1766, 1767, 1772, 1773, 1774, 1775, 1776, 1777, 1779, 1780, 1781, 1782, 1783, 1786, 1787, 1789, 1790, 1791, 1792, 1793, 1794, 1795, 1796, 1798, 1799, 1801, 1804
JEALOUS WIFE, The (G. Colman the Elder)
1762, 1763, 1764, 1765, 1766, 1767, 1768, 1770, 1771, 1772, 1773, 1774, 1776, 1777, 1779, 1782, 1783, 1785, 1786, 1787, 1788, 1789, 1790, 1791, 1792, 1796, 1798, 1802, 1803, 1804, 1805
JEW, The (R. Cumberland)
1794, 1795, 1796, 1797, 1798, 1799, 1801, 1802, 1803, 1805
JEW AND THE DOCTOR, The (T. J. Dibdin)
1798, 1799, 1800, 1801, 1802, 1803, 1804
JOHN BULL (G. Colman the Younger)
1803, 1804, 1805
JOVIAL CREW, The (M. Concanen, E. Rooke and W. Yonge)
1763
JUBILEE, The (D. Garrick)
1770, 1772, 1773, 1797, 1798
JULIA DE ROUBIGNE (C. Metcalfe)
1790, 1791

KIND IMPOSTER, The [*v.* SHE WOU'D AND SHE WOU'D NOT]
1763, 1767
KING AND THE MILLER OF MANSFIELD, The (R. Dodsley)
1753, 1754, 1755, 1756, 1757, 1759, 1760, 1767, 1768, 1780, 1781, 1782, 1783, 1788, 1789, 1790, 1793, 1800
KING CHARLES I (W. Havard)
1783
KING JOHN (W. Shakespeare)
1776, 1777, 1782, 1789, 1793, 1801, 1804
KING LEAR (W. Shakespeare/N. Tate)
1752, 1753, 1756, 1758, 1759, 1767, 1770, 1771, 1773, 1774, 1776, 1783, 1784, 1785, 1787, 1788, 1791, 1792, 1793, 1794, 1795, 1798, 1801, 1803

KNOW YOUR OWN MIND   (A. Murphy)
1777, 1778, 1779, 1780, 1781, 1782, 1783,
1784, 1785, 1786, 1787, 1788, 1789, 1790,
1791, 1794, 1795, 1796, 1797, 1798, 1799,
1800, 1801, 1802, 1803, 1804, 1805

LADIES' CATCH CLUB, The
1798

LADIES' FROLICK   (J. Love)
1772, 1773, 1774, 1776, 1778

LADY OF THE MANOR   (W. Kenrick)
1779, 1780

LADY'S LAST STAKE, The   (C. Cibber)
1755, 1756, 1765, 1766, 1769

LAUGH WHEN YOU CAN   (F. Reynolds)
1799, 1805

LAW OF LOMBARDY, The   (R. Jephson)
1779, 1780, 1781, 1782, 1783, 1794

LETHE   (D. Garrick)
1750, 1751, 1752, 1753, 1755, 1756, 1757,
1758, 1759, 1760, 1762, 1763, 1767, 1768,
1770, 1774, 1775, 1776, 1780, 1781, 1785,
1786, 1790, 1796, 1799

LIE OF THE DAY, The   (J. O'Keeffe)
1798

LIFE   (F. Reynolds)
1801, 1802, 1803, 1804

LIFE OF THE DAY, The
1797, 1798, 1805

LIFE'S VAGARIES   (J. O'Keefffe)
1795

LIKE MASTER LIKE MAN   (T. Ryder)
1772, 1773, 1779, 1780, 1785

LILLIPUT   (D. Garrick)
1776, 1777, 1778, 1779, 1795

LINCO'S TRAVELS   (D. Garrick)
1778, 1781, 1783, 1785

LIONEL AND CLARISSA   (I. Bickerstaffe)
1769, 1771, 1772, 1773, 1774, 1775, 1777,
1778, 1779, 1780, 1781, 1783, 1784, 1785,
1788, 1789, 1790, 1791, 1792, 1793, 1794,
1795, 1796, 1798, 1799, 1800, 1801, 1803,
1804, 1805

LITTLE HUNCHBACK, The   (J. O'Keeffe)
1792, 1795, 1796

LIVERPOOL PRIZE, The   (F. Pilon)   [v. THE
BRISTOL PRIZE]
1779

LOCK KEY   (P. Hoare)
1796, 1797, 1798, 1799, 1800, 1801, 1802,
1803, 1804, 1805

LONDON HERMIT, The   (J. O'Keeffe)
1793, 1800

LONDON MERCHANT, The   [v. GEORGE
BARNWELL]

LOOK BEFORE YOU LEAP   (H. Robson)
1803

LORD OF THE MANOR, The   (J. Burgoyne)
1781, 1783, 1793

LOTTERY, The   (H. Fielding)
1751, 1752, 1753, 1755, 1756, 1757, 1759,
1760, 1767, 1773

LOUISA
1786

LOVE A LA MODE   (C. Macklin)
1792, 1793, 1801, 1802

LOVE AND MONEY   (Benson)
1796

LOVE AT A VENTURE   (Mrs. S. Centlivre)
1755

LOVE AT FIRST SIGHT   (D. Crauford or J. Yarrow
or T. King)
1763, 1765, 1782

LOVE FOR LOVE   (W. Congreve)
1753, 1755, 1756, 1763, 1770, 1775, 1777,
1782, 1783

LOVE IN A CAMP   [v. PATRICK IN PRUSSIA]

LOVE IN A VILLAGE   (I. Bickerstaffe)
1766, 1767, 1768, 1769, 1770, 1771, 1772,
1773, 1774, 1775, 1776, 1777, 1778, 1779,
1780, 1782, 1783, 1784, 1786, 1787, 1788,
1789, 1790, 1792, 1793, 1794, 1795, 1798,
1799, 1800, 1801, 1803, 1804, 1805

LOVE LAUGHS AT LOCKSMITHS   (G. Colman the
Younger)
1803, 1804, 1805

LOVE OF FAME, The
1795

LOVE MAKES A MAN or THE FOP'S FORTUNE   (C.
Cibber)
1751, 1752, 1753, 1755, 1756, 1758, 1760,
1763, 1764, 1767, 1769, 1770, 1776, 1777,
1778, 1786, 1787, 1788, 1789, 1790, 1793,
1796, 1797, 1798

LOVER'S OPERA, The   (W. Chetwood)
1750, 1753

LOVER'S QUARRELS   (J. Vanbrugh/T. King)   [v.
THE MISTAKE]
1799, 1800, 1805

LOVER'S VOWS   (Mrs. E. Inchbald)
1798, 1799, 1800, 1801, 1802, 1803, 1804,
1805

LOVE'S FRAILTIES   (T. Holcroft)
1794

LOVE'S LAST SHIFT   (C. Cibber)
1765, 1766

LOVEWELL AND FANNY   [from THE
CLANDESTINE MARRIAGE, q.v.]
1781

LUBIN AND ANNETTE   (C. Dibdin)
1797

LYAR, The   (S. Foote)
1768, 1769, 1770, 1771, 1772, 1773, 1774,

1776, 1778, 1786, 1787, 1789, 1790, 1791, 1792, 1794, 1795, 1796, 1797, 1799, 1801, 1804

LYING VALET, The (D. Garrick)
1751, 1752, 1753, 1755, 1756, 1759, 1762, 1763, 1766, 1767, 1769, 1770, 1771, 1772, 1773, 1778, 1781, 1783, 1784, 1785, 1787, 1788, 1789, 1791, 1792, 1795, 1797, 1798, 1800

MACBETH (W. Shakespeare/W. Davenant, *et. al.*)
1751, 1753, 1754, 1756, 1757, 1759, 1760, 1763, 1767, 1769, 1770, 1772, 1773, 1774, 1775, 1776, 1777, 1778, 1779, 1780, 1783, 1784, 1786, 1787, 1789, 1790, 1791, 1792, 1793, 1794, 1795, 1796, 1797, 1798, 1799, 1800, 1801, 1802, 1803, 1804

MAGIC OF HOPE, The
1804, 1805

MAHOMET (J. Miller/J. Hoadly)
1783, 1784, 1785, 1790, 1791

MAID OF BRISTOL, The (J. Boaden)
1803, 1804

MAID OF THE MILL, The (I. Bickerstaffe)
1767, 1768, 1769, 1770, 1771, 1772, 1773, 1774, 1775, 1776, 1778, 1779, 1780, 1781, 1782, 1783, 1784, 1786, 1787, 1788, 1789, 1791, 1792, 1793, 1796, 1797, 1799, 1801, 1802, 1803, 1805

MAID OF THE OAKS, The (J. Burgoyne)
1782, 1783, 1784, 1786, 1787, 1788, 1789, 1791, 1792, 1793, 1801

MALE COQUETTE (D. Garrick)
1762, 1763, 1765

MANAGEMENT (F. Reynolds)
1800

MAN OF BUSINESS, The (G. Colman the Elder)
1774

MAN OF QUALITY, The (J. Lee)
1776, 1783, 1784, 1788, 1789, 1790

MAN OF THE WORLD, The (C. Macklin)
1802, 1805

MAN'S BEWITCHED, The (Mrs. S. Centlivre)
1763

MAN'S THE MASTER, The (W. Davenant/H. Woodward)
1775, 1776, 1780

MARIAN (F. Brooke)
1789, 1794

MARINERS, The (S. Birch)
1796, 1797

MARRIAGE PROMISE, The (J. T. Allingham)
1803, 1804

MARRIED MAN, The (R. Jenkins)
1786

MASK'D FRIEND, The (T. Holcroft)
1797

MATILDA (T. Francklin)
1775, 1776, 1779, 1789

MATRIMONY (J. Kenney)
1805

MAYOR OF GARRET, The (S. Foote)
1765, 1766, 1767, 1770, 1773, 1777, 1778, 1780, 1781, 1783, 1784, 1792, 1798

MEASURE FOR MEASURE (W. Shakespeare)
1750, 1751, 1754, 1755, 1756, 1763, 1779, 1780, 1782, 1792

MEDLEY, The
1776

MERCHANT OF VENICE, The (W. Shakespeare)
1753, 1754, 1755, 1756, 1757, 1759, 1761, 1762, 1766, 1767, 1771, 1772, 1774, 1775, 1776, 1777, 1778, 1779, 1780, 1781, 1782, 1783, 1784, 1786, 1789, 1791, 1792, 1793, 1794, 1795, 1796, 1798, 1799, 1801, 1802, 1803, 1804

MEROPE (A. Hill)
1757, 1776, 1777, 1785, 1786

MERRY WIVES OF WINDSOR, The (W. Shakespeare)
1750, 1753, 1755, 1756, 1757, 1760, 1762, 1763, 1767, 1769, 1770, 1774, 1775, 1776, 1777, 1778, 1787, 1788, 1789, 1793, 1794, 1795, 1796, 1802, 1804

METAMORPHOSES OF HARLEQUIN, The
1763, 1765, 1766, 1767, 1768

MIDAS (K. O'Hara)
1767, 1770, 1771, 1772, 1773, 1774, 1775, 1776, 1777, 1778, 1779, 1781, 1782, 1783, 1784, 1785, 1786, 1787, 1788, 1789, 1793, 1794, 1795, 1796, 1797, 1798, 1802, 1803

MIDNIGHT HOUR, The (Mrs. E. Inchbald)
1788, 1789, 1790, 1791, 1792, 1793, 1796, 1797, 1798, 1799, 1800, 1801, 1802, 1803, 1804, 1805

MIDSUMMER NIGHT'S DREAM, A (W. Shakespeare)
1794, 1795

MILESIAN, The (I. Jackman)
1778, 1779, 1780, 1790, 1791

MILLERS, The (Joubert)
1803

MINOR, The (S. Foote)
1761, 1805

MISER, The (H. Fielding)
1753, 1755, 1756, 1763, 1767, 1769, 1770, 1773, 1775, 1777, 1784, 1785, 1786, 1787, 1795, 1797, 1798

MISS IN HER TEENS (D. Garrick)
1750, 1751, 1752, 1753, 1754, 1756, 1757, 1766, 1767, 1768, 1773, 1774, 1782, 1783, 1784, 1789, 1793, 1794, 1797, 1805

MISTAKE, The (J. Vanbrugh) [*v.* LOVER'S QUARRELS]
1757, 1758, 1798, 1799, 1800, 1805

MOCK DOCTOR, The (H. Fielding)
1751, 1752, 1753, 1754, 1755, 1756, 1757, 1759, 1762, 1766, 1768, 1770, 1772, 1773, 1786

MODERN ANTIQUES (J. O'Keeffe)
1790, 1791, 1792, 1797, 1798

MOGUL TALE, A (Mrs. E. Inchbald)
1787

MORE WAYS THAN ONE (Mrs. H. Cowley)
1784, 1785, 1792, 1796, 1797

MOUNTAINEERS, The (G. Colman the Younger)
1794, 1795, 1796, 1797, 1798, 1799, 1800, 1802, 1803, 1804, 1805

MOURNING BRIDE, The (W. Congreve)
1750, 1752, 1755, 1776, 1778, 1781, 1782, 1788, 1789, 1799, 1801

MOUTH OF THE NILE, The (T. J. Dibdin)
1798, 1799

MUCH ADO ABOUT NOTHING (W. Shakespeare)
1755, 1756, 1757, 1758, 1759, 1760, 1763, 1765, 1769, 1772, 1773, 1774, 1775, 1776, 1778, 1779, 1780, 1781, 1782, 1783, 1785, 1786, 1787, 1788, 1789, 1790, 1791, 1792, 1793, 1794, 1795, 1796, 1797, 1798, 1800, 1802, 1803, 1804

MUSICAL LADY, The (G. Colman the Elder)
1762, 1768, 1769, 1770, 1771, 1772, 1773

MY GRANDMOTHER (P. Hoare)
1794, 1795, 1796, 1797, 1798, 1799, 1800, 1801, 1802, 1803, 1804

MYSTERIOUS HUSBAND, The (R. Cumberland)
1783, 1784, 1785, 1786

NABOB, The (S. Foote)
1778

NATURAL SON, The (R. Cumberland)
1785, 1786, 1787, 1793, 1794, 1796

NAVAL PILLAR, The (T. J. Dibdin)
1800

NAVAL REVELS
1799

NECK OR NOTHING (D. Garrick)
1772, 1773, 1780

NECROMANCER, The (? after J. Rich)
1782, 1783, 1784, 1785, 1786

NEGRO, The
1795

NETLEY ABBEY (W. Pearce)
1795

NEW PEERAGE, The (H. Lee)
1787, 1788

NEW-RAIS'D RECRUITS, The
1756

NEW WAY TO PAY OLD DEBTS (P. Massinger)
1784, 1785, 1786

NEXT DOOR NEIGHBOUR, The (Mrs. E. Inchbald)
1791, 1792, 1793

NOSEGAY, The
1782

NO SONG NO SUPPER (P. Hoare)
1790, 1791, 1792, 1793, 1794, 1795, 1796, 1797, 1798, 1799, 1800, 1801, 1802, 1803, 1804, 1805

NOTE OF HAND, The (R. Cumberland)
1774, 1785

NOTORIETY (F. Reynolds)
1792, 1793

OBI (J. Fawcett)
1800, 1801

OF AGE TOMORROW (T. Dibdin)
1802, 1803, 1804, 1805

OLD FAIRY OF THE WOODS, The
1755, 1756, 1757, 1759

OLD MAID, The (A. Murphy)
1762, 1763, 1764, 1765, 1766, 1767, 1768, 1771, 1772, 1773, 1776, 1785, 1786, 1787, 1788, 1795, 1796, 1797, 1798, 1800, 1801, 1802, 1804, 1805

OLD ROBIN GRAY
1784, 1785, 1786

ONE RAKE IN A THOUSAND (R. Jenkins)
1783, 1784

ONLY TWO LEFT, The
1760

ORACLE, The (Mrs. S. M. Cibber)
1755, 1756, 1758, 1759, 1783

ORDER OF THE GARTER, The (D. Garrick)
1783

OROONOKO (T. Southern/J. Hawkesworth)
1754, 1763, 1768, 1771, 1772, 1773, 1776, 1779, 1785, 1786, 1802

ORPHAN, The (T. Otway)
1750, 1752, 1757, 1767, 1776, 1777, 1780, 1781, 1786, 1791, 1793

ORPHAN OF CHINA, The (T. Francklin or A. Murphy)
1770

OTHELLO (W. Shakespeare)
1750, 1751, 1752, 1754, 1755, 1756, 1757, 1758, 1760, 1765, 1766, 1773, 1774, 1775, 1777, 1780, 1781, 1782, 1784, 1785, 1786, 1788, 1790, 1795, 1796, 1797, 1798, 1801, 1802, 1803, 1804, 1805

OUT OF THE FRYING PAN
1763

OXONIAN IN TOWN (G. Colman the Elder)
1774

PADLOCK, The   (I. Bickerstaffe)
 1769, 1770, 1771, 1772, 1773, 1774, 1775,
 1776, 1777, 1778, 1779, 1780, 1781, 1782,
 1783, 1784, 1785, 1786, 1787, 1788, 1789,
 1790, 1791, 1792, 1793, 1794, 1795, 1797,
 1798, 1799, 1800, 1801, 1802, 1803, 1804
PANNEL, The   (J. P. Kemble)
 1790, 1800, 1801
PANTOMIME GALIMAUFRY, A
 1799
PARAGRAPH, The   (P. Hoare)
 1804, 1805
PATRICK IN PRUSSIA or LOVE IN A CAMP   (J.
 O'Keeffe)
 1786, 1787, 1791
PAUL & VIRGINIA   (J. Cobb)
 1800, 1801, 1802, 1803, 1804, 1805
PEEP BEHIND THE CURTAIN, A   (D. Garrick)
 1800
PEEPING TOM OF COVENTRY   (J. O'Keeffe)
 1786, 1787, 1789, 1793, 1798, 1801, 1804
PERCY   (Mrs. H. More)
 1778, 1779, 1780, 1781, 1782, 1783, 1785,
 1786, 1790, 1791, 1793, 1795, 1797, 1800,
 1801, 1802
PHAEDRA & HIPPOLITUS   (E. Smith)
 1754
PHILASTER   (F. Beaumont and J. Fletcher/G.
 Colman the Elder)
 1777, 1778, 1779, 1796
PHOEBE or THE BEGGAR'S WEDDING   (C.
 Coffey/T. Cibber)
 1751, 1752, 1753, 1757, 1763, 1769
PHYSIC
 1783
PIGMIES, The
 1783
PILGRIM, The   (J. Vanbrugh)
 1751, 1752, 1753, 1755, 1760, 1761, 1763,
 1767, 1783, 1784, 1785, 1789, 1791, 1795,
 1796, 1797, 1801
PIZARRO   (R. B. Sheridan)
 1799, 1800, 1801, 1802, 1803, 1804, 1805
PLAIN DEALER, The   (W. Wycherley/I.
 Bickerstaffe)
 1776, 1777
PLYMOUTH IN AN UPROAR   (E. Neville)
 1779, 1780
POINT OF HONOUR, The   (C. Kemble)
 1800, 1801, 1802, 1803, 1804, 1805
POLLY   (J. Gay)
 1777
POLLY HONEYCOMBE   (G. Colman)
 1760, 1761, 1762, 1763, 1765, 1767, 1768,
 1769, 1775, 1776
POOR GENTLEMAN, The   (G. Colman the
 Younger)
 1801, 1802, 1803, 1804

POOR SAILOR, The   (J. Bernard)
 1796, 1797
POOR SOLDIER, The   (J. O'Keeffe)
 1784, 1785, 1786, 1787, 1788, 1789, 1790,
 1791, 1792, 1793, 1794, 1795, 1796, 1797,
 1798, 1799, 1800, 1801, 1802, 1803, 1804,
 1805
POOR VULCAN   (C. Dibdin or K. O'Hara)
 1783, 1784, 1785, 1786, 1789, 1791, 1795,
 1796, 1797, 1798, 1803
PORTRAIT, The   (G. Colman the Younger)
 1774, 1775, 1777, 1778, 1781
POSITIVE MAN, The   (J. O'Keeffe)
 1782, 1787, 1793, 1794, 1795, 1796, 1798 [as
 THE GENEROUS TARS]
PRESS GANG, The   [v. TRUE BLUE]
 1780
PRISONER AT LARGE, The   (J. O'Keeffe)
 1792, 1793, 1795, 1796, 1803, 1805
PRIZE, The   (P. Hoare)
 1793, 1794, 1795, 1796, 1797, 1798, 1799,
 1800, 1801, 1802, 1803, 1804, 1805
PRODIGAL, The   (F. G. Waldron)
 1794
PROVOK'D HUSBAND, The   (C. Cibber and Sir J.
 Vanbrugh)
 1752, 1755, 1756, 1757, 1758, 1759, 1760,
 1761, 1762, 1763, 1765, 1766, 1767, 1768,
 1769, 1771, 1772, 1774, 1775, 1776, 1777,
 1778, 1779, 1780, 1781, 1782, 1783, 1784,
 1785, 1786, 1787, 1788, 1789, 1790, 1791,
 1792, 1793, 1794, 1795, 1796, 1797, 1798,
 1799, 1800, 1801, 1803, 1804, 1805
PROVOK'D WIFE, The   (J. Vanbrugh)
 1752, 1753, 1756, 1757, 1758, 1759, 1760,
 1764, 1769, 1774, 1775, 1780
PUPPET SHOW, The
 1763, 1773, 1774
PURSE, The   (J. C. Cross)
 1794, 1795, 1796, 1798, 1799, 1800, 1801,
 1802, 1805

QUAKER, The   (C. Dibdin)
 1777, 1778, 1779, 1780, 1781, 1782, 1783,
 1784, 1785, 1786, 1787, 1788, 1789, 1791,
 1792, 1793, 1794, 1795, 1796, 1797, 1798,
 1799, 1800, 1801, 1802, 1803, 1804, 1805
QUARTER OF AN HOUR BEFORE DINNER, A   (J.
 Rose)
 1795, 1796
QUEEN MAB   (H. Woodward)
 1751, 1752, 1753, 1754, 1755, 1756, 1757,
 1759

RAGE, The   (F. Reynolds)
 1794, 1795, 1796, 1797, 1798
RAISING THE WIND   (J. Kenney)
 1803, 1804, 1805

RAYMOND AND AGNES   (C. Farley)
1797, 1798, 1799, 1800

RECEIPT-TAX, The   (J. Dent)
1783

RECRUITING OFFICER, The   (G. Farquhar)
1752, 1753, 1755, 1759, 1760, 1768, 1769,
1775, 1779, 1783, 1790

RECRUITING SERJEANT, The   (I. Bickerstaffe)
1772, 1773, 1775, 1776, 1777, 1778, 1780,
1781, 1782, 1783, 1794, 1795, 1796, 1797,
1798, 1800, 1801, 1802, 1803

RED CROSS KNIGHTS, The   (J. G. Holman)
1800, 1802

REFUSAL, The   (C. Cibber)
1762, 1763, 1764, 1765, 1766, 1767

REGATTA, The
1779

REGENT, The   (B. Greatheed)
1788, 1789

REGISTER OFFICE   (E. Morton or J. Reed)
1774, 1775, 1779, 1780, 1783, 1787, 1788,
1790, 1791, 1801, 1805

REHEARSAL, The   (G. Villiers/R. Wilson or C.
Clive)
1755, 1756, 1757, 1758, 1759, 1767, 1768,
1769, 1772, 1773, 1774, 1775, 1776, 1781,
1782

REPARATION, The   (M. P. Andrews)
1784

REPRISAL, The   (T. G. Smollett)
1757, 1758, 1760, 1778, 1787, 1788

RETALIATION   (L. MacNally)
1782, 1794

REVENGE, The   (E. Young)
1750, 1774, 1775, 1776, 1784, 1786, 1787,
1794

REVIEW, The   (G. Colman the Younger)
1801, 1802, 1804, 1805

RICHARD COEUR DE LION   (J. Burgoyne or L.
MacNally)
1801, 1802, 1803

RICHARD II (W. Shakespeare)
1754, 1755, 1768

RICHARD III (W. Shakespeare/C. Cibber)
1751, 1752, 1753, 1754, 1755, 1757, 1759,
1761, 1762, 1765, 1766, 1767, 1768, 1769,
1772, 1773, 1774, 1775, 1776, 1778, 1779,
1780, 1781, 1783, 1784, 1785, 1786, 1787,
1788, 1791, 1792, 1793, 1794, 1795, 1796,
1797, 1799, 1801, 1802, 1803, 1804

RIVAL CANDIDATES, The   (H. Bate)
1775, 1776, 1777, 1778, 1779, 1780, 1781,
1783, 1784, 1785, 1786, 1787, 1788, 1789,
1790, 1792

RIVAL QUEENS, The   (N. Lee)
1761

RIVALS, The   (R. B. Sheridan)
1775, 1776, 1777, 1778, 1779, 1780, 1781,

1782, 1783, 1784, 1785, 1786, 1787, 1788,
1789, 1790, 1791, 1794, 1795, 1797, 1798,
1799, 1800, 1801, 1802, 1803, 1804, 1805

RIVAL SOLDIERS, The   (J. O'Keeffe)
1797, 1798, 1799, 1801, 1803, 1804, 1805

ROAD TO RUIN   (T. Holcroft)
1792, 1793, 1794, 1795, 1796, 1797, 1801,
1803, 1804

ROBIN HOOD   (L. MacNally)
1785, 1786, 1787, 1788, 1789, 1790, 1791,
1792, 1793, 1794, 1795, 1796, 1798, 1799,
1800, 1801, 1802, 1803, 1804, 1805

ROBINSON CRUSOE (attributed to R. B. Sheridan)
1781, 1782, 1783, 1784, 1785, 1786, 1787,
1788, 1789, 1791, 1792

ROMANCE OF AN HOUR   (H. Kelly)
1775, 1785, 1787, 1800, 1811

ROMAN FATHER   (W. Whitehead)
1754, 1785, 1791, 1792, 1794, 1797

ROMAN REVENGE   (A. Hill)
1753

ROMANTIC Lady
1795

ROMEO & JULIET   (W. Shakespeare/D. Garrick)
1751, 1753, 1754, 1756, 1757, 1758, 1759,
1760, 1761, 1762, 1764, 1767, 1771, 1772,
1774, 1775, 1777, 1779, 1782, 1783, 1784,
1786, 1788, 1789, 1790, 1792, 1793, 1794,
1795, 1796, 1797, 1799, 1800, 1802, 1804

ROMP, The   (Lloyd)
1788, 1789, 1790, 1791, 1792, 1793, 1794,
1795, 1796, 1797, 1800, 1801, 1802, 1803,
1804, 1805

ROSE & COLIN   (C. Dibdin)
1796, 1797, 1798, 1803

ROSE WREATH   (J. Palmer)
1781, 1782

ROSINA   (F. Brooke)
1783, 1784, 1785, 1786, 1787, 1789, 1790,
1791, 1792, 1793, 1794, 1795, 1796, 1797,
1798, 1799, 1800, 1801, 1802, 1803, 1804,
1805

ROYAL MERCHANT, The   (H. Norris)
1752, 1762

ROYAL SUPPLIANTS, The   (J. Delap)
1781

RULE A WIFE AND HAVE A WIFE   (F. Beaumont
and J. Fletcher/J. Love)
1754, 1755, 1756, 1757, 1758, 1759, 1763,
1771, 1772, 1773, 1775, 1776, 1777, 1778,
1779, 1781, 1784, 1785, 1786, 1787, 1788,
1789, 1792, 1793, 1794, 1795, 1798, 1800,
1801, 1803

RUNAWAY, The   (Mrs. H. Cowley)
1776, 1777, 1779, 1784

SADAK AND KALASRADE   (T. J. Dibdin)
1802, 1803, 1804

STUDENT'S FROLIC
1786, 1787

SUCH THINGS ARE (Mrs. E. Inchbald)
1787, 1788, 1789, 1790, 1791, 1792, 1794,
1795, 1797, 1803

SUCH THINGS WERE (P. Hoare)
1788, 1789, 1790

SULTAN, The (I. Bickerstaffe)
1783, 1787, 1790, 1791, 1793, 1794, 1795,
1796, 1797, 1798, 1799, 1800, 1801, 1804,
1805

SURRENDER OF CALAIS (G. Colman the
Younger)
1792, 1793, 1794, 1796, 1797, 1798, 1799,
1800, 1801, 1802, 1803, 1805

SUSPICIOUS HUSBAND, The (B. Hoadly)
1751, 1753, 1756, 1757, 1758, 1759, 1760,
1764, 1765, 1767, 1769, 1770, 1771, 1773,
1774, 1775, 1777, 1778, 1780, 1782, 1784,
1785, 1786, 1787, 1788, 1790, 1791, 1793,
1795, 1796, 1797, 1799, 1801, 1802, 1803,
1804

SYLVESTER DAGGERWOOD (G. Colman the
Younger)
1797, 1798, 1799, 1800, 1801, 1802, 1803,
1804, 1805

TALE OF MYSTERY, A (T. Holcroft)
1803, 1804, 1805

TALE OF TERROR (H. Siddons)
1804

TAMERLANE (N. Rowe)
1754, 1755, 1796, 1797, 1798, 1801

TANCRED AND SIGISMUNDA (J. Thomson)
1757, 1759, 1760, 1779, 1780, 1782, 1784,
1788, 1789, 1790, 1791, 1793

TANNER OF YORK, The (J. Arthur)
1750

TELEGRAPH, The (J. Dent)
1795

TEMPEST, The (W. Shakespeare/? W. Davenant
and J. Dryden)
1751, 1752

TENDER HUSBAND (Sir R. Steele)
1752, 1756

THOMAS AND SALLY (I. Bickerstaffe)
1763, 1764, 1765, 1766, 1767, 1768, 1769,
1770, 1772, 1773, 1779, 1781, 1782, 1783,
1784, 1785, 1787, 1788, 1789, 1790, 1793,
1794, 1796

THREE OLD WOMEN WEATHERWISE (G. S.
Carey)
1774, 1783

THREE AND THE DEUCE, The (P. Hoare)
1803

THREE WEEKS AFTER MARRIAGE (A. Murphy)
1781, 1784, 1785, 1786, 1787, 1788, 1797,
1805

THREE WEEKS BEFORE MARRIAGE
1797

TIMANTHES (J. Hoole)
1780

TIMES, The (Mrs. E. Griffith)
1780, 1781, 1782, 1786

TIT FOR TAT (G. Colman the Elder)
1796

TO MARRY OR NOT TO MARRY (Mrs. E.
Inchbald)
1805

TOM THUMB THE GREAT (H. Fielding/K. O'Hara
or Mrs. E. Haywood and W. Hatchett)
1754, 1755, 1758, 1781, 1782, 1783, 1784,
1785, 1786, 1787, 1788

TONY LUMPKIN IN TOWN (J. O'Keeffe)
1780

TOUCHSTONE, The (C. Dibdin)
1779, 1780, 1781

TOYSHOP, The (R. Dodsley)
1780, 1781, 1782, 1783

TRANSFORMATION
1789

TRICK UPON TRICK (J. Yarrow)
1769, 1770, 1771, 1772

TRIP TO NEWMARKET (R. Cumberland)
1774, 1775

TRIP TO SCARBOROUGH, A (R. B. Sheridan)
1777

TRIP TO SCOTLAND, A (W. Whitehead)
1770, 1771, 1774, 1775, 1776, 1781, 1783,
1784, 1788, 1789 [and 1793 as CUPID TURN'D
POSTILLION]

TRISTRAM SHANDY (L. MacNally)
1801

TRUDGE AND WOWSKI (T. Knight) [from INKLE
AND YARICO, q.v.]
1790, 1791, 1792

TRUE BLUE (from H. Carey, NANCY) [v. THE
PRESS GANG]
1781, 1782, 1783, 1796

TRUE-BORN IRISHMAN, The (C. Macklin)
1801

TRUE-BORN SCOTCHMAN, The (C. Macklin)
1783

TRY AGAIN (or THE SUSPICIOUS BROTHER)
1793

TURNPIKE GATE, The (T. Knight)
1800, 1801, 1804

TWELFTH NIGHT (W. Shakespeare)
1757, 1758, 1772, 1776, 1789, 1790

TWIN RIVALS, The (G. Farquhar)
1763, 1770

TWINS, The (T. Hull or W. Woods)
1793

TWO MISERS, The (K. O'Hara)
1775, 1776, 1777, 1778, 1780, 1781, 1784,

TWO MISERS, The (*cont.*)
1785, 1787, 1788, 1791, 1792, 1794, 1797,
1798, 1802
TWO STRINGS TO YOUR BOW (R. Jephson)
1791, 1792, 1795, 1798, 1799, 1800, 1802,
1803

UNEQUAL MATCH, The
1773
UNHAPPY FAVOURITE, The (J. Banks) [or alternative title for THE EARL OF ESSEX, *q.v.*]
1789, 1790
UPHOLSTERER, The (A. Murphy)
1759, 1761, 1762, 1769, 1783, 1784, 1785,
1788

VALENTINE AND ORSON (J. O'Keeffe)
1796, 1797
VARIETY (R. Griffith)
1782
VENETIAN OUTLAW (R. W. Elliston or J. Powell)
1805
VENICE PRESERV'D (T. Otway)
1750, 1766, 1767, 1772, 1773, 1774, 1775,
1776, 1777, 1778, 1779, 1780, 1781, 1782,
1783, 1784, 1785, 1786, 1787, 1788, 1789,
1790, 1791, 1792, 1795, 1803, 1804, 1805
VETERAN TAR, The (S. J. Arnold)
1801
VILLAGE LAWYER, The (W. M'Cready)
1792, 1805
VIRGIN UMASKED, The (H. Fielding)
1750, 1751, 1753, 1754, 1755, 1756, 1757,
1758, 1760, 1761, 1762, 1767, 1768, 1769,
1782, 1783, 1788, 1789, 1790, 1791, 1792,
1795, 1798, 1800, 1802
VOICE OF NATURE, The (J. Boaden)
1803, 1804
VOLUNTARY CONTRIBUTIONS (W. Porter)
1798
VOLUNTEERS, The
1803

WALKING STATUE, The
1760
WANDERING JEW, The (A. Franklin)
1798, 1799
WATERMAN, The (C. Dibdin)
1774, 1775, 1776, 1777, 1778, 1779, 1780,
1781, 1783, 1784, 1785, 1786, 1787, 1788,
1789, 1790, 1791, 1793, 1794, 1795, 1798,
1799, 1801, 1802, 1803, 1804, 1805
WAY OF THE WORLD, The (W. Congreve)
1751, 1753, 1756
WAYS AND MEANS (G. Colman the Younger)
1791, 1792, 1793, 1794, 1795, 1796, 1798,
1799, 1800, 1802, 1803, 1804, 1805

WAY TO GET MARRIED, The (T. Morton)
1796, 1797, 1798, 1799, 1800, 1801, 1802,
1803
WAY TO GET UNMARRIED, The (J. C. Cross)
1796, 1797
WAY TO KEEP HIM, The (A. Murphy)
1760, 1763, 1769, 1770, 1771, 1772, 1773,
1776, 1777, 1778, 1779, 1780, 1781, 1782,
1784, 1785, 1786, 1787, 1791, 1792, 1794,
1798, 1799, 1803, 1804
WAY TO WIN HIM, The [*v.* THE INCONSTANT]
WEDDING DAY, The (Mrs. E. Inchbald)
1797, 1798, 1799, 1801, 1804
WEDDING RING, The (C. Dibdin)
1773, 1774, 1775
WERTER (F. Reynolds)
1785, 1786, 1787, 1789, 1792
WEST INDIAN, The (R. Cumberland)
1771, 1772, 1773, 1774, 1775, 1776, 1777,
1779, 1781, 1782, 1783, 1784, 1785, 1786,
1787, 1788, 1789, 1790, 1792, 1793, 1794,
1795, 1796, 1798, 1799, 1800, 1802, 1803,
1804
WHAT D'YE CALL IT, The (J. Gray)
1755, 1756, 1757, 1763, 1767, 1776, 1789
WHAT NEWS [*v.* THE UPHOLSTERER]
1783
WHAT WE MUST ALL COME TO (A. Murphy)
1765
WHEEL OF FORTUNE, The (R. Cumberland)
1795, 1796, 1797, 1798, 1799, 1800, 1802,
1803, 1804
WHICH IS THE MAN? (Mrs. H. Cowley)
1783, 1784, 1785, 1786, 1788, 1789, 1790,
1792, 1793, 1794, 1796, 1802, 1803, 1805
WHIM, The or THE MAGICIAN'S TRIUMPH
1786, 1788, 1789
WHO'D HAVE THOUGHT IT!
1763
WHO'S THE DUPE (Mrs. H. Cowley)
1779, 1780, 1781, 1782, 1783, 1784, 1785,
1787, 1788, 1789, 1790, 1791, 1792, 1795,
1798, 1799, 1802, 1804, 1805
WHO WANTS A GUINEA? (G. Colman the
Younger)
1805
WIDOW'D WIFE, The (W. Kenrick)
1770
WIDOW'S VOW, The (Mrs. E. Inchbald)
1786, 1787, 1795
WIFE OF TWO HUSBANDS, The (J. Cobb)
1804
WIFE'S RELIEF, The (C. Johnson)
1763
WILD OATS (J. O'Keeffe)
1791, 1792, 1793, 1794, 1795, 1796, 1797,
1799, 1801, 1802, 1803, 1804, 1805

WILL, The   (F. Reynolds)
  1797, 1798, 1799, 1800, 1801, 1802, 1803,
  1804, 1805
WILL FOR THE DEED, The   (T. J. Dibdin)
  1804, 1805
WILLIAM TELL   (H. Siddons)
  1795, 1796
WINTER'S TALE, The   (W. Shakespeare) [v.
  FLORIZEL AND PERDITA]
  1789, 1790
WISE MAN OF THE EAST, The   (Mrs. E. Inchbald)
  1800
WIT AT A PINCH
  1760
WIVES AS THEY WERE   (Mrs. E. Inchbald)
  1798, 1799, 1802
WONDER, The   (Mrs. S. Centlivre)
  1752, 1756, 1757, 1758, 1760, 1762, 1765,
  1769, 1771, 1772, 1774, 1777, 1778, 1783,
  1785, 1786, 1787, 1788, 1789, 1790, 1791,
  1792, 1793, 1794, 1795, 1796, 1797, 1798,
  1799, 1800, 1802, 1803, 1804

WOODMAN, The   (H. Bate)
  1802, 1803
WORD TO THE WISE   (H. Kelly)
  1772, 1773, 1778, 1782, 1783, 1786, 1789,
  1790, 1796, 1797, 1801, 1802

YOUNG ACTRESS, The
  1801, 1802
YOUNG QUAKER, The   (J. O'Keeffe)
  1787, 1788, 1789, 1790, 1791, 1794, 1795,
  1796, 1799, 1800, 1802, 1805

ZAPHIRA   (F. Gentleman)
  1755
ZARA, TRAGEDY OF   (A. Hill)
  1754, 1755, 1756, 1781, 1782, 1796
ZORAIDA   (W. Hodson)
  1780
ZORINSKI   (T. Morton)
  1797, 1798, 1799, 1800, 1801

List of Subscribers

John Adrian, London
Alberta University, Dept. of English, Edmonton, Canada
J. Askew, Preston
Bath City Libraries
George Benson, London N6 6EJ
Birkbeck College, University of London
Mrs. G. M. F. Bissett, Reading, Berkshire
B. H. Blackwell Ltd., Booksellers, Oxford
Ted Bottle, Coalville, Leicester
Bristol University, Dept. of Drama
Bristol University, Dept. of Extra Mural Studies
British Broadcasting Company, London
British Drama League
V. J. Bulman, Wolverhampton
Joseph A. Byrnes, Elizabeth, New Jersey, U.S.A.
Calgary University, Alberta, Canada
Case Western Reserve University, Cleveland, Ohio, U.S.A.
P. M. L. de Grouchy, Southampton
Detroit Public Library, Michigan, U.S.A.
Drama Board, Oxford
Exeter University, Drama Dept.
Linda Fitzsimmons, Newcastle upon Tyne
Folkestone Library
Wm. George's Sons Ltd., Bristol
George Gregory, Bookseller, Bath
George Harding's Bookshop, London
George Washington University, Washington, D.C., U.S.A.
W. J. Herbert, London
C. B. Hogan, Woodbridge, Connecticut, U.S.A.
Jardine's Bookshop, Manchester
Anna Kelly, The Circus, Bath
Lancaster University
Leeds City Libraries
Leicester College of Education
Liverpool City Libraries
Liverpool University Library

London University Library
Macaulay Book Co. Ltd., Rushington, Sussex
Dr. Arthur W. McDonald, St. Andrews College, Lourinburg, North Carolina, U.S.A.
Angus Mackay, London
J. W. McKenzie, Ewell, Surrey
Richard Macnutt Ltd., Booksellers, Tunbridge Wells, Kent
Manchester City Education Committee
Manchester City Libraries
Metropolitan Toronto Central Library, Ontario, Canada
J. A. Mitchley, Harlow, Essex
Motley Books Limited, Mottisfont Abbey, Romsey
Mount Holyoke College, Dept. of English, South Hadley, U.S.A.
Christopher Murray, Killiney, Co. Dublin, Ireland
Nagoya University, Nagoya, Japan
North Wales University College Library
The Philbrick Library, California, U.S.A.
R. J. Rhymes, London
Miss Sybil Rosenfeld, Queensway, London
Rowman and Littlefield, Totowa, New Jersey, U.S.A.
Royal Library, Copenhagen K, Denmark
Royal School, Bath
Basil Savage, London
Searights Bookshop, Bath
K. G. Smith, Cedric Road, Bath
Society for the Propogation of the Gospel, University Bookshop, Durham
Swansea University College Library
Universitets Biblioteket, Oslo
University of Western Ontario, Ontario, Canada
Victoria and Albert Museum, London
Peter Wood, Gt. Shelford, Cambridge